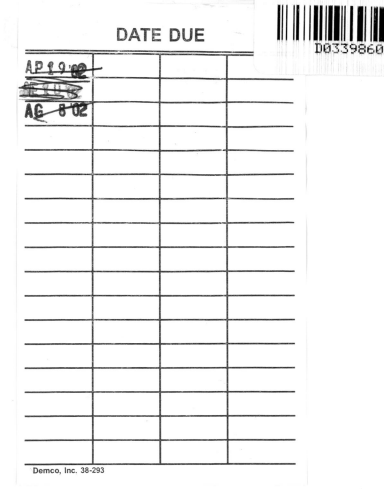

...ed by Oxfam GB in association with Oxfam International in 2000

© Oxfam GB 2000

ISBN 0 85598 428 7

A catalogue record for this publication is available from the British Library.

Available from Bournemouth English Book Centre, PO Box 1496, Parkstone, Dorset, BH12 3YD, UK
tel: +44 (0)1202 712 933; fax: +44 (0)1202 712 930; email: oxfam@bebc.co.uk

and from the following agents:

USA: Stylus Publishing LLC, PO Box 605, Herndon, VA 20172-0605, USA
tel: +1 (0)703 661 1581; fax: + 1 (0)703 661 1547; email: styluspub@aol.com

Southern Africa: David Philip Publishers, PO Box 23408, Claremont 7735, South Africa
tel: +27 (0)21 674 4136; fax: +27 (0)21 674 3358; email: orders@dpp.co.za

For details of local agents and representatives in other countries, consult our website:
http://www.oxfam.org.uk/publications.html, or contact Oxfam Publishing, 274 Banbury Road, Oxford OX2 7DZ, UK
tel: +44 (0)1865 311 311; fax: +44 (0)1865 312 600; email publish@oxfam.org.uk

Printed by Redwood Books, Bath, England

Oxfam GB is a registered charity, no. 202 918, and is a member of Oxfam International.

Front cover: Studying in the shade at Bidibidi school, Ikafe, Uganda. *Photo*: Jenny Matthews/Oxfam.

Contents

Tables

Figures

Acknowledgements

This book started out as a report prepared for the 1998 launch of *Education Now* – an Oxfam campaign on the right to education. It was revised and updated in mid-2000. Both the original report and the subsequent revisions benefited from the comments, support, and advice of many people.

Special mention should be made of Dianna Melrose and Justin Forsyth, respectively past and present Policy Directors in Oxfam (Great Britain). Both of them made detailed comments on the draft chapters, and equally detailed suggestions for improving them. Patrick Watt worked as a researcher on the original report. His contribution was invaluable, as was his good humour throughout a frantic period of research and writing. Oliver Brown also provided research support, especially in the collection and analysis of data. We all struggled with technical problems in developing the Education Performance Index in Chapter 3, until Caterina Ruggeri-Laderchi, of Queen Elizabeth House, Oxford University, put us out of our misery. She takes the credit for developing the formula used in constructing the Index, though not the blame for any of the shortcomings with the concept.

The preparation of this book would not have been possible without the support and contributions of a large number of colleagues in Oxfam. They include Seth Amgott, Marta Arias, Tony Burdon, Carolyn Culey, Siddo Deva, Paloma Escudero, Andrew Hewett, Kate Horne, Jan Klugkist (now working with the Dutch Foreign Ministry), Veena Siddharth (now working with the World Bank), Mohga Smith, Ines Smyth, Quynh Tran, Phil Twyford, Lydia Williams (now working with the US Treasury), Heather Grady, and Lot Felizco.

The analysis presented in this report draws on a series of Background Papers commissioned in 1997. A full list of contributors is included in an appendix. But special mention should be made of Michael Kelly (University of Lusaka), Taimur Hyat (University of Oxford), Tilleke Kiewied (Novib), Kate Dyer (MAARIFA), and Sergio Haddad (Acao Educativa, Brazil). They each provided insights and perspectives that influenced the overall analysis in the report.

Since the launch of original report, Oxfam has participated in the development of the Global Campaign on Education – an alliance of trades unions and non-government organisations from over forty countries. Many members of the Global Campaign have influenced this book, either in discussion or through comments on draft chapters. They include Charles Abugre (ISODEC, Ghana), David Archer (ActionAid), Tom Bediako (Education International), Rasheda Choudhury (Campaign for Popular Education, Bangladesh), Anne Jellema (ActionAid), Eli Jouen (Education International), Botlhale Nong (South Africa Non-Government Organisation Coalition), David Norman (Save the Children), Khailash Satyarthi (Global March Against Child Labour), and Camila Croso Silva (Acao Educativa, Brazil).

Several international institutions and individuals have generously shared their experience and research materials with the author. Oxfam owes a great debt of gratitude to the following staff members of the United Nations Children's Fund (UNICEF), all of whom have generously contributed their time to inform our work on education: Mary Piggozi, Elaine Furness, Sheldon Shaeffer, Andre Roberfroid, Eva Jespersen, and Jan Vandemoortele. Some of the ideas presented in the book draw unashamedly on perspectives developed in the United Nations Development Programme's Human Development Reports, and on discussions with Richard Jolly and Sakiko Fukada Parr, respectively the Principal Co-ordinator and Director of the Reports. The book has benefited also from discussions with staff in the United Nations Education, Scientific and Cultural Organisation (UNESCO), and in particular with Svein Osttveit, Anne Muller, and Dieter Berstecher. The author has also benefited from discussions with Cecilia Ugaz (World Institute for Development Economics Research), Sanjay Reddy (Harvard University), Gavin Williams (Oxford University), and Christopher Colclough (Institute for Development Studies, Sussex University). Victoria Brittain of the *Guardian* has provided support and encouragement throughout, and along with her colleagues Charlotte Denny, Larry Elliott, and Madeline Bunting has played an important role in informing public debate on the scale of the challenge that faces poor countries as they strive to provide adequate basic education for all of their citizens. Michael Holman of the *Financial Times* has long been a source of inspiration for researchers and policy advisers working on Africa, and Oxfam has benefited on countless occasions from his advice (and occasional strictures). In their own ways, each of the journalists mentioned above has shown that the highest journalistic standards can be combined with a sense of political commitment and passion to make the world a better place.

The campaign for universal education launched by the initial report on which the book is based has brought Oxfam into contact with many policy makers from developing countries, as well as bilateral aid donors, the World Bank, the International Monetary Fund (IMF), and other agencies. While these exchanges have often been robust, the author has benefited enormously from the insights and perspectives they have provided. I would like to express particular thanks to Axel van Trotsenberg, Jeff Katz, Maris O'Rourke, and Adrian Verspoor of the World Bank. Neither Antony Boote nor Hugh Bredenkamp of the IMF will agree with the parts of this book that deal with their organisation, but they have helped to inform Oxfam's understanding of problems associated with debt and structural adjustment. The book has also benefited from discussions with representatives of the donor community, among them Steve Packer, Eamon Cassidy, and David Mepham (of the British Government's Department for International Development), Ronald Siebes (Ministry of Foreign Affairs, the Netherlands), Marilyn Blaeser (Canadian International Development Agency), and Kaviray Appadu (Swedish International Development Agency).

Special mention should be made of the work of Jean Drèze and Amartya Sen, the President of Oxfam GB. Their work on India has helped to change our understanding of the relationship between education and human development. In a world where globalisation is increasing the benefits of education, along with the costs of educational deprivation, it remains as relevant today as ever.

The schedule for the production of this book placed several of my Oxfam colleagues under extreme pressure. Anni Long and Helen Walsh helped with the typing and the preparation of graphics, and Catherine Robinson, the editor, has been enormously supportive throughout.

Last but far from least, the biggest vote of thanks goes to my daughter, Rosa. At first, she had the natural suspicion that any twelve-year-old might harbour about a parent writing a book in favour of children spending more time in school. But children understand injustice better than most of us, especially when it involves other children. Anyway, she tolerated a preoccupied and absent father for longer than it was reasonable to expect of her.

Kevin Watkins
Oxford, August 2000

Introduction

The broken promise

'I go to school because I want to learn. People with education have a better life. But our school has many problems. The classes are very crowded, and there are no blackboards or chalk. Some children have textbooks, but the parents of the poor children cannot afford books, notepads, or pencils. It is hard for my parents to pay school fees. Many children in my village do not go to school, because their parents are too poor. My brother and sister have both dropped out of primary school, because my parents had no money.'

'I feel bad that my schooling was ended. I was a good and regular student. I always answered the questions asked in class ... I want to go back to school, so I can make something of my life.'[1]

Two voices from two different continents. The first is that of a twelve-year-old Tanzanian girl in the third grade of primary school; the second that of a teenage Indian girl who was withdrawn from school during Grade 6. Their words summarise more powerfully than any statistics the reality behind the education crisis in poor countries.

The education crisis does not count as news in the rich world. The human faces of the victims – like the two children cited above – are invisible. More media attention is lavished on the fluctuations of financial markets, civil conflicts, and natural disasters than on the human costs of deprivation in education. Yet the destructive impact of the education crisis is more powerful than any earthquake or civil war. It is consigning millions of the world's most vulnerable citizens – its children – to a future of poverty and insecurity. It is widening already scandalous income gaps between rich and poor countries, and rich and poor people. And it is undermining efforts to improve child health and nutrition.

More than half a century has now passed since the Universal Declaration of Human Rights made education a fundamental right. It decreed that all governments have a responsibility to provide free and compulsory basic education. Ten years ago, at the 1990 World Conference on Education for All, held in Jomtien, Thailand, more than 150 governments promised to act on this commitment. They promised that by the year 2000 adult illiteracy rates would be halved, and that all children would enjoy the right to a good primary education.

Ten years on, that promise has been comprehensively broken. No human right is more systematically or extensively violated by governments than the right of their citizens to a basic education. When governments met at the World Education Forum in Dakar, Senegal, in 2000, they reaffirmed the commitments made at Jomtien, promising to achieve universal primary education by 2015. There is little evidence to suggest that they will be any more successful this time around.

The facts of the education crisis tell their own story. As the global economy is transformed by information technology, an estimated 855 million people – one in six of the world's population – are functionally illiterate, and the number is rising. The next generation of illiterates is already being recruited from the ranks of the poor. More than 125 million children of primary-school age – one in five of the total number in developing countries – will not see the inside of a classroom this year. Another 150 million will drop out of primary school, most of them before they have had an opportunity to acquire basic literacy and numeracy skills. Like their parents, these children will be denied the opportunities that an education can provide.

In the industrialised countries, parents complain about the state of school buildings, or the lack of computers. Their concerns are legitimate; but the problems facing parents and children in poor countries are of a different order. In much of the developing world, education is of an abysmal quality. 'School' is often a set of crumbling mud walls, often lacking even the most basic sanitation facilities. Classes of eighty children or more are common. Textbooks, notepads, and pencils are luxury items, available only to those with wealthy parents, and classrooms often lack blackboards and chalk.

Thomas Hobbes, the seventeenth-century English philosopher, feared that life without a strong government would be 'nasty, brutish, and short'. His words could equally be used to describe the reality of education for millions of children in poor countries. But the costs of the education crisis in developing countries are not shared equally across all members of society. It selects its victims on the basis of wealth and gender.

Poor children are less likely to enrol in school, and more likely to drop out early, than children of well-off families. Moreover, poverty intensifies gender-determined inequalities. Girls from poor households are far less likely to have access to an education than those from wealthier households. Inequalities in education ensure that poverty is transmitted across generations. In India, the richest fifth of the population has achieved universal primary-school enrolment. Yet fewer than half of the children of the poorest fifth of households progress beyond the first grade. In principle, education is a right enshrined in the Indian constitution. In practice, it is a privilege from which the poor are excluded.

In most countries young girls are bearing the brunt of the crisis. There is at the very heart of education a system of 'gender apartheid', under which opportunity is distributed on the basis of inherited chromosomes, rather than universal entitlement. Two-thirds of the children not in school – and a similar proportion of adults who are illiterate – are female.

The human costs of the education crisis

Education matters because it is a fundamental human right, and because it is intrinsically important in its own right. It opens new horizons and raises the quality of life. But education is also a means to achieving wider human-development ends, including higher living standards, improved public health, and democratisation. It is one of the most powerful catalysts for poverty reduction. Viewed from a different perspective, educational deprivation is an equally powerful cause of poverty.

In Ghana, children of educated mothers are twice as likely to survive to their fifth birthday as are children of uneducated mothers.

The human costs of the crisis in education are beyond estimation. There is an unmistakable correlation between child deaths and the education status of parents, especially mothers. In Ghana, children of educated mothers are twice as likely to survive to their fifth birthday as are children of uneducated mothers. In Pakistan, it has been estimated that providing 1000 girls with an extra year of schooling would have the effect of preventing around 60 infant deaths: it is not just the millions of Pakistani girls denied an education today who will suffer the consequences of their government's negligence.

In a world where 12 million children die each year, no cause merits more urgent action than girls' education. Yet the gender gap in educational opportunity is closing far too slowly, especially in the two regions – sub-Saharan Africa and South Asia – that account for the overwhelming majority of child deaths. Five years ago, the world's governments set themselves the target of reducing child death rates by two-thirds before 2015. That target will be missed without a concerted effort to close the gender gap in education.

The same applies to the 2015 target of halving the number of people living in extreme poverty. Educational deprivation acts as a powerful brake on progress in this area for two reasons: it undermines economic growth and it excludes the poor from participating in the benefits of growth. Education is good for growth, because it enables people to develop the skills needed to innovate and raise productivity. Each additional year in school is estimated to raise the output of an African farmer by around 8 per cent a year. For households living on the poverty line, this can mean the difference between being able to afford essential drugs and adequate food and not being able to afford them. Improving access to education would do more than boost growth. Exclusion from educational opportunity excludes the poor from market opportunities. Progress towards universal education would enhance the quality of growth, increasing the rate at which it is converted into poverty reduction by increasing the share of national wealth captured by the poor.

Each additional year in school is estimated to raise the output of an African farmer by around 8 per cent a year.

The current costs of educational deprivation pale into insignificance against the future costs. We live in an increasingly knowledge-driven global economy. New technologies are transforming the way in which wealth is produced and distributed. In the past, the comparative advantage of countries rested on their stock of capital and natural resources. In future, national prosperity will depend increasingly on education. All other factors are dropping out of the equation. The income-distribution patterns of tomorrow will increasingly reflect the distribution of educational opportunity. This distribution is already enormously unequal. On average, a five-year-old child entering the school system of an industrialised country today can expect to receive 15-17 years of full-time education. In much of Africa and South Asia, a child of five can expect less than five years of full-time education. Only 3 per cent of Africa's and 8 per cent of South Asia's children proceed beyond secondary school. In Latin America, despite the region's relative prosperity, almost one-third of all children fail to complete their primary schooling. These enormous gulfs in educational opportunity will intensify the inequalities that separate rich and poor countries. They will also exacerbate national inequalities in income, undermining efforts to achieve equitable growth and reduce poverty.

Prospects for sub-Saharan Africa are particularly dire. The region accounts for about one-tenth of the world's children of primary-school age, but for one-third of all such children who are not in school. This is now the only region in the world in which numbers out of school are going up. By 2015, it will account for more than three-quarters of children not in school. This has profound implications for Africa's place in the world economy. Educational deprivation will translate into slow economic growth, a diminishing share of world trade and investment, and – ultimately – rising poverty. Failure to tackle this crisis will leave Africa as an enclave of despair in an increasingly prosperous global economy, with attendant implications for conflict and stability.

Digital divides and global inequality

Inequalities in education are intimately linked to inequalities in access to information technology. The UN Secretary General has warned of the dangers of a 'digital divide', as new telecommunication technologies by-pass the poorest countries.[2] The divide is already a reality. Over 90 per cent of world telecommunications traffic takes place within and between Europe, North America, and countries of the Pacific Rim. Meanwhile, half of the world's population has never used a telephone, let alone logged on to the Internet. In Nelson Mandela's words: 'Eliminating the distinction between information-rich and information-poor countries is critical to eliminating other inequalities between North and South.'[3]

So far, efforts to address the 'digital divide' have focused on the development of grandiose, multi-billion dollar schemes for technology transfer. Governments in the Group of Seven industrialised countries have developed ambitious partnerships with private-sector firms, aimed at providing poor countries with better access to the technologies on which future wealth creation depends. At one level, the intent is highly laudable. At another, it is profoundly irrelevant. In countries where fewer than one in two children progress through the primary-school system, where most leave the system without basic numeracy and literacy skills, and where mass illiteracy prevails, no amount of technology will have the desired effect. Attempting to close the wealth gap through technology transfer is like decorating the top layer of apartments in a skyscraper without taking action to deal with the rotten foundations. It is at the base of the education system, where children have the opportunity to acquire the skills that will equip them for flexible life-long learning, that action is needed. And it is here that the international community should be concentrating its political and financial resources.

A decade of failure

The 1990 World Conference on Education for All created renewed hope. It set bold targets for the future and promised new forms of partnership. Southern governments pledged to support their commitments with

5

policy reforms that would accord a higher priority to education. Northern governments promised to back these reforms with decisive action in the form of increased aid, debt relief, and the reform of structural adjustment programmes. When they met at the World Education Forum in Dakar in 2000, governments made many of the same commitments and promises. Yet the same governments have comprehensively failed to honour the commitments made ten years ago, thus casting doubt on their most recent promises.

Both sides of the deal struck at the World Conference on Education for All have renounced their obligations. Developing countries have failed to translate government rhetoric on the importance of education into real budget provisions. And the industrialised countries have failed to provide the increased aid, debt relief, and wider reforms needed to turn the right to education into a reality for the world's poor.

Governments in sub-Saharan Africa, the region facing the greatest challenge, devote some $7bn a year to military expenditure, which is more than double what they spend on primary education.

Poverty is a major constraint on the financing capacity of Southern governments. Even so, few of them have given basic education sufficient priority in national budgets. Many attach far more weight to military expenditure. Take the case of India, where there are more than 30 million children not in school – more than in any other country. The national education infrastructure is in a state of chronic disrepair. Yet India spends far more on military hardware than on the education of its children. In fact, it allocates less than 1 per cent of GDP to primary education, one of the lowest levels of investment in the developing world – and less than half of the national investment in Uganda, which is a far poorer country.

Unfortunately, the case of India is not untypical. Governments in sub-Saharan Africa, the region facing the greatest challenge, devote some $7bn a year to military expenditure, which is more than double what they spend on primary education.

Inadequate public investment translates into classrooms without books, schools without sanitation facilities, demoralised and underpaid teachers, and high costs to parents. When public spending declines, the costs of financing education are transferred to households. In much of Africa it costs more than one-fifth of average household income to send a single child to primary school – and the poorest are often unable to pay. The Universal Declaration of Human Rights may stipulate that basic education should be free; but for the poor it is an unaffordable commodity.

Cost is only one of the barriers excluding children from school – albeit one of the highest. Distance is another. In Zambia, it is not uncommon for rural children to have to walk more than five miles to school, exposed to risks that cause great anxiety to their parents. In Pakistan, parents cite distance from school as the single most important reason for keeping girls at home. The quality of education is another problem. Poor households make enormous efforts to provide their children with educational opportunities. But where costs are high and the perceived benefits are low, there is little incentive to allocate the household's meagre resources to education. In cultures where a lower value is ascribed to girls' education, financial pressures on families are likely to mean that female children will be the last into school and the first out in the event of hardship.

Northern governments are justifiably critical of Southern governments that fail to prioritise basic education in their national budgets. Yet they too have reneged on their commitments. In the decade that has passed since the World Conference on Education for All, they have cut their international aid budgets to the lowest-ever level. Sub-Saharan Africa alone has lost some $4bn. And it is not just the overall aid effort that has been found wanting. Collectively, the industrialised countries invest less than 2 per cent of their aid budgets in primary education – less than 20 per cent of total aid for the education sector. Any African government that divided its education budget between primary schools and higher levels of education in a similar proportion could expect to be roundly condemned by the donor community.

The failure extends beyond aid budgets. At the 1990 Jomtien conference, Northern governments promised 'innovative and equitable formulae' to resolve the debt problems of poor countries. These failed to materialise, leaving sub-Saharan Africa paying some $12bn in annual debt servicing during the 1990s – around three times the level of government spending on primary education.

The Heavily Indebted Poor Countries (HIPC) Initiative, announced at the end of 1996, raised hopes of reform. But only eight countries have so far received debt relief – on a scale that is so far inadequate. With 2 million children out of school and one textbook shared among thirty children in rural areas, Tanzania will be spending almost twice as much on debt servicing as on primary education *after* debt relief under the terms of the HIPC Initiative. Zambia will be spending more on debt than on health and education services *combined*. This is in a country where child malnutrition is on the increase, and primary-school enrolment rates are lower than in 1980. Creditor policies on debt relief continue to attach too much weight to the ability of debtor governments to finance debt repayments, and not enough to human-development needs.

As the major shareholders in the International Monetary Fund, Northern governments must also accept responsibility for the damage inflicted by its policies. Much has been made of the Fund's conversion to a poverty-focused mission. Yet its programmes have been associated with deep cuts in education spending. In sub-Saharan Africa, at least 14 countries have reduced *per capita* spending on education, acting under the auspices of the IMF.[4] In East Asia, the Fund's programmes prolonged and deepened a recession that has had devastating consequences for education. The education budget in Indonesia has fallen by one-third, and the dropout rate for children from poor households has quadrupled in the space of two years.

Rhetorical flourishes at international conferences come free of charge. Providing children with decent education requires real investment.

But perhaps the greatest failing in the decade since the World Conference on Education for All has been the failure to develop a coherent plan for achieving the targets adopted. This is a problem that goes beyond education. During the 1990s, a succession of UN summits set goals for social development without defining the strategies through which the necessary financial and political resources could be mobilised.

Concern over the financial implications of the targets themselves no doubt accounts for part of this failing. Rhetorical flourishes at international conferences come free of charge. Providing children with decent education requires real investment. But the goal of achieving universal primary education within a decade, as envisaged at the 1990 Jomtien conference, is easily and eminently affordable.

Indicative estimates by the UN and the World Bank suggest that it would cost an additional $8bn per annum to achieve universal primary education within a ten-year period. This figure represents about 0.02 per cent of global GDP – or around four days' worth of global military spending. Measured against the potential gains in human welfare – improved public health, more rapid economic growth, and reduced poverty reduction – that universal primary education would bring, this would be a small investment with a high rate of return.

International action to honour the commitment to universal primary education would also help to restore the credibility of multilateralism and international co-operation. In 1947 the US Secretary of State,

George Marshall, launched an international plan 'against hunger, poverty, desperation and chaos'. The Marshall Plan restored economic growth in the collapsed economies of Europe, helping to create the broader foundations for post-war recovery. At one stage, it was absorbing more than 2 per cent of the USA's gross domestic product – ten times what aid donors collectively provide to poor countries today, and one hundred times the amount of global income required to finance universal primary education. When it was launched, the Marshall Plan provoked intense opposition, on the grounds that it was unaffordable and unworkable; but it succeeded, because it was driven by a genuinely internationalist vision, and guided by leadership of a high quality.

That quality has been conspicuous by its absence in relation to the great social challenges facing us today – and nowhere more so than in education. Instead of plans of action backed by resources, we have vague wish-lists of targets drawn up at endless rounds of high-level summits that have so far delivered nothing.

From Jomtien to Dakar: towards a global initiative

The first decade of the new millennium started in the same fashion as the final decade of the last one, with a major international summit on education. In the time-honoured fashion of UN summits, old principles were reaffirmed, vague declarations were made, and a new *Framework for Action* was adopted. But the World Forum on education in Dakar may have marked the start of a new era in international co-operation on education.

The Framework marks a step forward in four important respects. First, it re-affirms the right of all children to a free education: a commitment that was missing from the 1990 Jomtien declaration. Second, it calls on every developing-country government to prepare, by 2002, a national action plan, setting out how it will achieve the international development target of universal primary education by 2015. Third, it recognises that many of the poorest countries lack the financing capacity to achieve this goal within a reasonable time-frame. The Framework establishes the important principle that 'no countries seriously committed to education for all will be thwarted in their achievement of this goal by a lack of resources'. Fourth, the Framework includes an unequivocal commitment to supporting national education reforms with an international initiative: 'The international community will deliver on (its) collective commitment by developing with immediate effect a global initiative aimed at developing the strategies and mobilising the resources needed to provide effective support to national efforts.'[5]

It is too early to tell whether these encouraging words will mean anything in practice. As an editorial in the *Financial Times* commented immediately after the World Forum on education: 'How soon the initiative is delivered, how it will be implemented and how it will be funded, will together prove the acid test of whether a broken promise has been followed by empty words.'[6] But the Framework has provided a very clear yardstick against which to measure government actions.

From national planning to international action

Accelerated progress towards education for all will depend critically upon what happens at the national level. Governments need to mobilise the resources required for achieving universal education, and they need strategies for overcoming the huge equity gaps whose parameters are determined by income, gender, region, and ethnicity.

No child should be excluded from education because of the poverty of his or her family. Governments should establish timetables for eliminating direct and indirect fees.

Under the Dakar Framework, governments are expected to establish clear budget priorities for education. There are no blueprints for public investment. However, in countries where a large proportion of the primary-school population does not complete primary education, the aim should be to invest at least 3 per cent of GDP on basic education – a level that few countries currently achieve. The Dakar Framework also calls on governments to identify strategies for reducing inequalities in education, especially those related to gender. Once again, there are no blueprints. National strategies need to take into account local realities and to build on partnerships between governments, non-government organisations, and local communities. However, there are some broad principles that should guide the national plans:

- **End charges for basic education.** No child should be excluded from education because of the poverty of his or her family. Governments should establish timetables for eliminating direct and indirect fees.

- **Integrate education into national poverty-reduction strategies.** Poverty remains the main obstacle to achieving education for all. It is therefore important that education reforms are integrated into anti-poverty strategies that are in turn institutionalised in macro-economic reform programmes. Equally important is the participation of civil society in the development of national education strategies.

- **Build on existing education-sector strategies.** National plans should define clear targets for accelerating progress towards universal primary education, along with the funding gaps to be filled through increased aid under the global initiative. The objective should be to shorten the time-frame for achieving education for all, with an immediate focus on universal primary education.

- **Reduce gender-linked disparities.** Unequal opportunities for girls could be redressed by recruiting and training local female teachers, eliminating the male bias in curricula and related materials, providing bursaries for girls' education, and locating schools closer to the communities they serve.

- **Improve the quality of education.** Adapting the curriculum to local needs, adjusting the school calendar to local circumstances (such as seasonal labour demands), teaching in local languages, and improving training and support for teachers are among the most important requirements.

- **Involve parents and local communities.** The real experts in understanding why poor children do not go to school, or why they drop out, are the poor themselves. National education planning should include a far stronger commitment to involving the poor in education, both in assessing problems and in identifying solutions.

National education action plans must not become an exercise in tokenism, merely geared towards meeting donors' reporting requirements. There are also dangers of duplication. Many countries are already developing strategies for the education sector – strategies that already define target dates and financing requirements for achieving universal primary education. The purpose of the national action plans should be to identify the financial and wider policy requirements for accelerating progress.

Northern governments' recognition of the fact that, without additional financial support, many countries will be unable to achieve universal primary education within a realistic time-frame is encouraging. So, too, is their commitment in principle to ensuring that no credible national plan fails for want of financial support. The next step is to identify a mechanism for translating principle into practice. How will Northern governments ensure that good policies in poor countries are backed with the resources that they need to succeed?

The funding of the initiative ought to be the least problematic part of the equation. Northern governments could mobilise an additional $4bn a year – half the estimated costs of achieving universal primary education

– through increased aid and deeper debt relief. Given the scale of the crisis in sub-Saharan Africa, and the large gap between financing capacity and the resource requirements for achieving the 2015 targets, the global initiative should include a special plan of action for the region.

Stated in absolute terms, the level of finance necessary to achieve education for all appears very great. But it is equivalent to less than one-fifth of the reduction in aid since 1992. Expressed differently, it represents 0.01 per cent of the combined wealth of the industrialised countries. Deeper debt relief could be an important source of new financing for education, especially in sub-Saharan Africa. Instead of defining debt sustainability on the basis of what heavily indebted countries are able to pay their creditors, far more weight should be attached to what poor countries can afford to pay in the light of their human-development needs. An upper limit of around 10 per cent should be set on the proportion of government revenue directed to debt servicing. If the savings from debt relief could be channelled through dedicated poverty-reduction funds for investment in education, they would provide real and tangible benefits for the poor.

An upper limit of around 10 per cent should be set on the proportion of government revenue directed to debt servicing.

Mechanisms are needed to ensure that governments in developing countries are able to access, on a guaranteed basis, additional resources from the global initiative. Above all, this means establishing clear criteria for eligibility. Once a government has developed a strong national policy framework and established a proven track-record in reform, it should automatically be entitled to financing from the global initiative. This does not mean creating another layer of bureaucracy and donor conditionality; but it does mean identifying well-defined benchmarks against which to assess performance.

Ultimately, the success – or failure – of the global initiative adopted at Dakar will depend on political will. Failure to act on the commitments made at Dakar will carry a high price. If current trends continue, the 2015 target of universal primary education will be missed by a wide margin. This matters, not just because education is an intrinsically important aspect of development in its own right, but also because slow progress in education will undermine efforts to achieve the wider human-development targets set for 2015. These include the halving of extreme poverty, and a two-thirds reduction in child mortality.

Civil society has a crucial role to play in generating the political will needed to achieve the 2015 targets, at both global and national levels. In the space of a few years, the international campaign for debt relief, led by Jubilee 2000, has transformed the international agenda. Similar alliances are developing in education. In 1998, the Global Campaign for Education was launched as part of an international effort by non-government organisations to influence the agenda for the World Forum on education. This campaign is now operating in more than 40 countries. It brings together representatives of the world-wide movement to end child labour, non-government organisations working with landless people in Brazil, disabled people in India, and rural communities in Ghana. It includes the world's largest confederation of teachers' unions – Education International – and international development agencies. Many of the provisions in the Dakar Framework reflect demands made by the Global Campaign. And members of the campaign are now working at both a national level and an international level to hold governments accountable for the commitments they have made. The unifying theme is a recognition that change in education requires political mobilisation and action to change attitudes.

Summary of the book

This book is about some of the central challenges facing the international community in the effort to ensure good basic education for all. Chapter 1 examines the critical role of education in human development and poverty reduction. That role is becoming more important as globalisation and technological change increase the potential benefits of education, and the costs of educational deprivation.

Chapter 2 looks at the progress that has been achieved during the decade since the 1990 World Conference on Education for All. It uses as a yardstick the various targets that have been set at UN summits. In each case, achievement has fallen far short of aspiration. This chapter shows that, if current trends continue, none of the education targets set for 2015 will be achieved. Although the analysis concentrates on quantitative indicators, the chapter also reviews the quality of education across different developing regions. Although trends are difficult to establish, it is clear that there is a huge qualitative deficit.

Chapter 3 addresses the theme of inequality in education. There are huge gaps in educational opportunity between rich and poor countries. These gaps are increasingly shaping the distribution of global wealth. But the education gaps *within* countries are also large. The most important sources of national inequality are wealth, gender, rural–urban divisions, and ethnicity. This chapter develops a new analytical tool – the Education Performance Index (EPI) – to rank developing countries.

The EPI provides a snapshot of the average situation in a particular country. These averages conceal intra-country differences. Using the EPI to measure the performance of different regions and social groups within a country reveals the true extent of national inequalities.

Chapter 4 examines some of the main barriers to achieving education for all. At a household level these include the financial cost and also the opportunity cost of sending children to school, the distance from home to school, gender-related constraints, and demands for child labour. Public spending plays a critical role in defining education opportunities for the poor, since poverty often precludes recourse to private providers. However, patterns of government spending seldom reflect a commitment to achieving good-quality, universal basic education. Part of the problem is under-investment – but inequity in the distribution of public spending further erodes educational opportunities for the poor. This chapter reviews public-spending patterns. It also looks at two dominant trends in education policy: decentralisation and privatisation. The first of these trends has the potential to generate benefits in terms of accountability and service provision, but it has also been associated with widening inequalities based on wealth. The second trend – towards reliance on private education – reflects the under-performance of public education, and offers little real hope in terms of meeting the 2015 targets of universal primary education.

Chapter 5 critically examines the failure of international co-operation over the past decade. It shows that, contrary to the letter and the spirit of the 1990 Jomtien conference, aid budgets have been cut, debt relief has been inadequate, and IMF programmes have eroded the provision of education services.

Chapter 6 reviews the respective roles of the State and non-State actors in education. It argues that effective State action holds the key to sustained progress, and that the efficiency of the State can be enhanced by building on community-based initiatives. In some countries such initiatives have been successfully 'scaled up' into district and national education planning.

Chapter 7 provides a brief overview of what was agreed at the Dakar World Forum on education and it sets out an agenda for reform.

1

Education and human development: the 2015 targets and the challenge of globalisation

Writing two and a half thousand years ago, the Greek philosopher Aristotle declared the central purpose of education to be the attainment of 'the good life', or the enrichment of the quality of life.[1] Since Aristotle believed that States existed only for the sake of promoting 'the good life', it went without saying that they should educate all of their citizens. Society and the individual alike would suffer from the absence of education. In fact, few States have provided universal education on the basis of its intrinsic value. For much of human history, education has been viewed as a means to other ends, rather than as an end in itself. Nation-building, national security, political imperatives, economic growth, and the socialisation of children have all been advanced as justifications for the provision of education, sometimes to the frustration of reformers. Writing during the course of a debate on primary education in Britain during the 1870s, T.H Huxley famously lamented the failure of the various protagonists to consider the intrinsic value of education:

The politicians tell us, 'you must educate the masses because they are going to be masters'. The clergy join in the cry, for they affirm that the people are drifting away from the church ...The manufacturers and capitalists swell the chorus. They declare that ignorance makes bad workmen; that England will soon be unable to turn out cotton goods or steam engines cheaper than other people ... And a few voices are lifted up in favour of the doctrine that the masses should be educated because they are men and women with unlimited capacities. [2]

Until quite recently, much the same might have been said about debates on human development. It is true that education was 'rediscovered' as a development theme in the 1970s; but this owed less to the view that education was intrinsically important than to a recognition that it was essential for economic growth, which was seen as the real measure of development. In the terminology adopted and popularised by the World Bank, education was a form of 'human capital' capable of generating high returns for economic growth.[3]

It was not until the early 1990s that the idea of education being an end in itself became part of mainstream thinking about development. The catalyst for change was the work of the Indian economist Amartya Sen, which was communicated to a wider audience through the United Nations' *Human Development Report*. At a time when development thinking was dominated by economic indicators of welfare, Sen shifted the debate to define poverty in terms of 'capabilities' – a term denoting the potential of poor people to do the things that contribute to their welfare. He wrote that low income was one aspect of poverty, but deprivation was about something more than material wealth: it was also about the absence of what Sen called 'fundamental freedoms', which included the attributes associated with good health and education, and the ability to influence institutions affecting one's life.[4] Education is for Sen as important as income, because it is needed to realise human potential in a broader sense. The new approach did not deny the broader benefits of education; but it powerfully reasserted the view, first elaborated by Aristotle, that education did not have to be justified in terms of its instrumental value. In Sen's words: 'Something that is of intrinsic importance can, in addition, be instrumentally momentous without compromising its intrinsic value.'[5]

The intrinsic importance of education – and the importance of Sen's work – is today reflected in its inclusion in the international development targets agreed by governments. These were adopted at a series of UN meetings in the 1990s, and later by the Development Assistance Committee of the Organisation for Economic Cooperation and Development (OECD).[6] These targets marry income-based indicators of human development with wider capability indicators. They include the following goals:

- **Income-poverty reduction:** The proportion of people living in extreme poverty, defined as less than $1 per day, should be reduced by at least half by 2015.
- **Child health**: By 2015, the death rate for infants and children under the age of five should be reduced by two-thirds of the 1990 level in all countries.
- **Maternal health**: Maternal mortality rates should fall by three-quarters of their 1990 level by 2015.
- **Education**: There should be universal primary education by 2015, with the disparity between girls and boys in primary and secondary schools eliminated by 2005.

Chapter 2 of this book examines in detail progress towards the goal of universal primary education. In this chapter we examine the potential benefits of education for advances in other areas of human welfare, principally health and poverty reduction. As suggested by Amartya Sen, progress in education does have 'instrumentally momentous' consequences in relation to the wider 2015 targets. Women's education in particular is among the most powerful determinants of trends in public health and child mortality. Income-poverty reduction is a function of two factors: the rate of growth and the distribution of income. Education generates important benefits in both areas. It is positively associated with the rising productivity and innovation upon which economic growth depends. Equally importantly, improved access to education can help the poor to participate in markets on more equitable terms, improving the distribution of income in the process. Globalisation, and the associated emergence of increasingly knowledge-based systems of production, is strengthening the links between education and poverty reduction, both nationally and internationally.

The human-development gains generated through education are the product of acquired skills and attitudes. At another level, they reflect a less tangible but more powerful set of advantages conferred through education. These relate to empowerment, or the capacity of poor people to influence institutions, processes, and policies that affect their lives. Educated women and their children enjoy better health than their uneducated counterparts, partly because they have better access to information; but also because they are more confident and assertive in demanding services. What is true for individuals is also true for society. Education does not provide a guarantee of formal democracy, let alone of genuinely participatory democracy. But popular education is a necessary condition for democracy to take root. That is why the struggle for education has always been a central theme in the struggle for democracy.

One way of capturing the human-development benefits associated with education is to consider how progress towards the 2015 target of universal primary education might influence progress in other areas. The first part of this chapter sets the scene by providing a progress report on the (highly unsatisfactory) rate of progress towards the goals of improved health and reduced income-poverty. Improved access to education would reverse this trend. The second part examines evidence on the relationship between education and health on the one hand and income-poverty and economic growth on the other. This evidence is unequivocal. Education for girls and women is not just a basic right: it is a precondition for achieving the 2015 goals for reducing child-mortality rates. The third part of this chapter explores the links between education, economic growth, income distribution, and poverty reduction. It shows that exclusion from education acts as a brake on growth and a source of extreme income inequality, slowing the rate of poverty reduction. The fourth section shows how globalisation is increasing the benefits associated with education, and raising the costs of exclusion from education. The final section provides an overview of the relationship between education and democracy.

The 2015 targets: a progress report

International development targets (IDTs) figure prominently in the dialogue between aid donors and developing countries. The IDTs are regularly reaffirmed at high-level summits, endorsed by governments, and included in the policy statements of donors and international financial institutions. Unfortunately, reaffirmation has not been accompanied by progress on anything like the scale required. While there are large variations in performance within and between regions, the IDTs will be missed by a wide margin if current trends continue.

The record on child mortality

The 2015 target of reducing child-mortality rates (CMRs, or deaths below the age of five years) by two-thirds provides a yardstick against which to measure wider developments in public health. Mortality rates among children are a highly sensitive indicator of health and nutritional status, and of access to basic services.

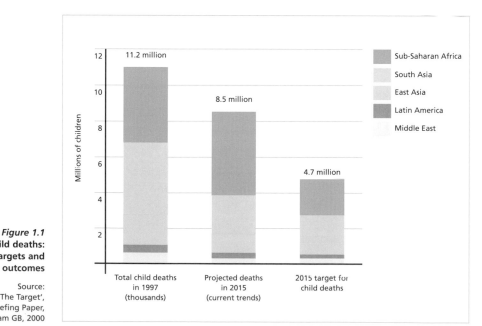

Figure 1.1
Child deaths:
2015 targets and
projected outcomes

Source:
'Missing The Target',
Oxfam Briefing Paper,
Oxfam GB, 2000

There are serious problems in attempting to measure trends, since survey data are irregular and of variable quality. The data that are available suggest that CMRs are declining too slowly for the 2015 targets to be met on current trends, as illustrated in Figure 1.1. For developing countries as a group, CMRs have been falling at around 1.2 per cent a year, or less than half of the required rate.[7] One way of measuring the human cost of this shortfall is to consider how many more deaths are occurring as a result of it. For the year 2000, the gap between the target child-mortality rate and the actual rate translates into approximately 1.7 million child deaths, graphically illustrating the enormous human costs associated with failure to achieve the 2015 goals.[8] Projecting 1990–1997 trends forwards to 2015, and taking into account demographic changes, the gap between the target child-mortality rate and the actual rate will be equivalent to more than four million deaths per annum.

Problems are especially acute in sub-Saharan Africa, which has the highest average child-mortality levels (147 per 1000 births). Child deaths are declining at less than one-quarter of the required rate needed, and on current trends the region will account for 70 per cent of the shortfall in relation to the 2015 target.[9] This has important implications for the distribution of premature child deaths. With approximately 10 per cent of the global population under the age of five years, sub-Saharan Africa currently accounts for more than one-third of child deaths. If current trends continue, it will account for 57 per cent of child deaths by 2015 (Figure 1.2). South Asia currently accounts for another one-third of child

Figure 1.2
Trends in child deaths in sub-Saharan Africa

Source:
'Missing The Target',
Oxfam Briefing Paper,
Oxfam GB, 2000

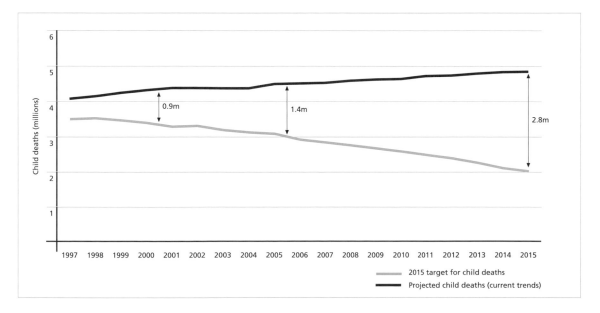

deaths. It too is off target, with child mortality falling at around half the target rate. East Asia has achieved relatively low rates of child mortality, but regional indicators are heavily distorted by the good performance of China (with an under-five mortality rate of 47 per 1000 births).

Data on maternal mortality rates, another of the 2015 targets, are of insufficient quality and consistency to capture broad trends. What evidence there is suggests little cause for optimism. There are 18 countries in which the maternal mortality rate (MMR) exceeds 1000 deaths for each 100,000 live births.[10] Several countries with large populations that have achieved significant progress in other areas – such as Indonesia and Bolivia – have failed to reduce MMRs that are exceptionally high in relation to average incomes and other poverty indicators.

Child-mortality rates in Brazil are ten times higher for the poorest 20 per cent than for the richest 20 per cent.

Developments in child and maternal mortality reflect a wide range of old and new problems. The oldest of all is persistent poverty. Thirty per cent of children in South Asia and 15 per cent in sub-Saharan Africa suffer from low birth-weight as a result of inadequate nutrition. More than one billion people lack access to basic health facilities, many of which in turn lack even the most basic essential drugs. Inadequate public investment reinforces vulnerability to illness, both because it limits access to services, and because it results in the cost of service provision being transferred to poor households in the form of user-charges. Almost two-thirds of health expenditure in low-income countries is now accounted for by households – double the proportion for high-income countries.[11] The higher susceptibility of poor households to illness, coupled with their inability to afford treatment, partly accounts for differences in health outcomes. In countries such as Ghana and Peru, higher-income groups are almost twice as likely to receive treatment during an episode of sickness as the poorest 20 per cent. Child-mortality rates in Brazil are ten times higher for the poorest 20 per cent than for the richest 20 per cent.[12]

Among the new problems that have emerged, HIV/AIDS poses especially serious threats. Two-thirds of the 33 million HIV-infected individuals are sub-Saharan African, and the figure is rising. The HIV/AIDS epidemic is an important cause of child mortality, both because of mother–child transmission, and because of indirect effects that reinforce household poverty. As a direct consequence of the epidemic, several countries in eastern and southern Africa have suffered either an increase in child-mortality rates – as in Kenya, Zambia, and Zimbabwe – or a slowdown in the decline of child mortality.[13] Rich countries are attempting to control the impact of HIV/AIDS on their citizens through novel drug treatments that are too expensive for poor countries; and vaccine research is focused on viral strains prevalent in Europe and North America. Failure to develop more effective strategies for addressing the problems of developing countries, where 95 per cent of HIV victims live, will put the 2015 targets out of reach for many countries.[14]

Income-poverty targets

Improved access to education, especially for girls, has the potential to accelerate progress towards the targets set for reducing the rates of child deaths and maternal mortality. Evidence presented in this chapter suggests that education may be the single most powerful force for achieving the 2015 goals.

As in the case of health, the international development targets for income-poverty reduction are ambitious – and progress has been equally disappointing. The 2015 goals now look increasingly unattainable.

In stark contrast to the hyperbole that accompanied UN summit commitments on poverty, the achievements of the 1990s were limited. The decade began with 1.2 billion people living on less than $1 a day – and it ended with a similar number in the same position. While the incidence of poverty declined, so that the percentage of people living in poverty fell from 29 per cent to 24 per cent, this was insufficient to counteract the effects of population growth.[15]

There were marked regional variations in income-poverty performance during the 1990s (see Figures 1.3 and 1.4). These can be briefly summarised as follows:

- **Sub-Saharan Africa**: As with other development indicators, there is a widening gap between sub-Saharan Africa and other developing regions. The incidence of poverty did not change during the 1990s, leaving almost half of the population – 291 million people – living on less than $1 a day. Both the incidence of poverty and the poverty gap, or the average distance of the poor from the poverty line, are wider in Africa than in any other region.

- **South Asia**: Economic growth rates for South Asia have been stronger than for Africa, but the decline in the incidence of poverty has been insufficient to offset an increase in the number of poor people, by around 27 million.

- **East Asia**: East Asia continued its rapid progress in poverty reduction during the first half of the 1990s, with 174 million people being lifted above the poverty line, and the incidence of poverty falling from 27 per cent to 15 per cent. However, the financial crisis in 1997 represented a huge setback, with the incidence of poverty rising by almost 50 per cent in Indonesia alone. Economic recovery from the crisis has been stronger in some countries (such as Korea) than others (like Indonesia), raising questions about the capacity of the region to remain on track to meet the 2015 targets.

- **Latin America**: Like South Asia, the Latin American region achieved relatively strong growth in the 1990s, but poverty incidence has remained constant, with another five million people being added to the ranks of the poor.

- **Middle East**: Income-poverty incidence, using the $1 a day indicator, is lower in the Middle East than for any other region, and it continued to decline in the 1990s. However, the absolute number of poor people fell only slightly, to 5.5 million.

Growth and distribution

Future trends in income poverty will be determined by the overall rate of economic growth and the extent to which poor people participate in growth. For any given level of average income, the extent of poverty will depend on how income is distributed. The larger the share of any increment to growth captured by the poor, the stronger the linkage between economic growth and poverty reduction.[16] Conversely, the greater the initial level of inequality, the lower the rate at which income

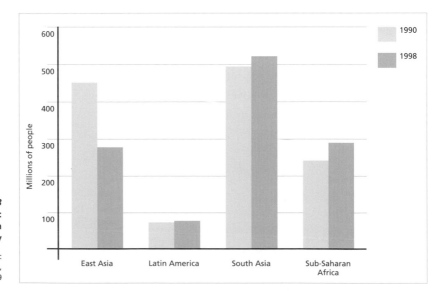

Figure 1.3
Poverty-reduction trends: numbers living on less than $1 per day

Source:
Global Development Finance, World Bank, Washington, 1999

22

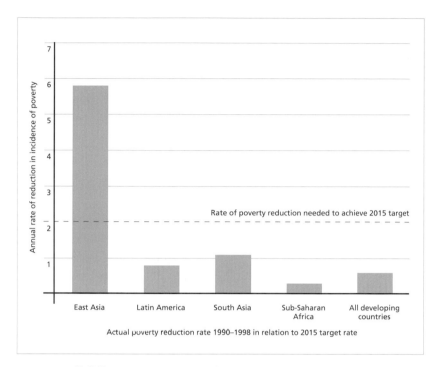

Figure 1.4
Annual poverty-reduction trends, 1990-1998

Source:
Global Development Finance,
World Bank, Washington, 1999

poverty will fall at any given growth rate. Crudely stated, more unequal societies are less efficient at converting growth into poverty reduction. This has important implications for poverty reduction.

Distributional factors have had an important bearing on income-poverty reduction trends. One survey, based on changes in household-income data from 44 countries, found that similar rates of growth had produced rates of poverty reduction that varied by a factor of five, depending on patterns of income distribution.[17] Some regions have been far more successful than others at converting economic growth into poverty reduction. For instance, each percentage point of economic growth in East Asia reduced the incidence of poverty at around three times the rate achieved in Latin America. The abysmal rate of poverty reduction achieved by Latin America during this period, and the rise in the absolute number of poor people, owes as much to distributional factors as to slow growth.

In situations where initial income inequalities are high, and where the poor fail to capture a bigger share of any increment in growth than the non-poor, wealth creation is unlikely to translate into rapid poverty reduction. As illustrated in Figure 1.5, there are large variations in the share of national income captured by the poorest income groups. In Brazil, the poorest 20 per cent capture on average 2 cents out of every $1 generated through growth. For Vietnam, the equivalent figure is 8 cents out of every $1. In other words, Brazil has to grow at four times the rate of Vietnam to achieve the same average income gain among the poorest 20 per cent of its population.[18] Clearly, any move towards more equitable income distribution would strengthen the relationship between growth and poverty reduction in Brazil, as it would in other countries.[19]

The problem from a poverty-reduction perspective is that current patterns of growth are shifting distributional patterns in the wrong direction. Evidence from a large number of countries suggests that income distribution is becoming increasingly unequal. This is true of countries previously characterised by relatively flat income distribution (Thailand, China, and Vietnam), highly unequal countries (such as Mexico), very poor countries (such as Ethiopia), and higher-income countries (much of the Former Soviet Union).[20] This trend is acting as a brake on poverty reduction. In India, which is home to half of those living on less than $1 a day, the rate of poverty reduction slowed during

Figure 1.5
**Percentage share of income:
poorest 20 per cent and
richest 20 per cent**

Source:
World Development Indicators,
World Bank, Washington, 1998

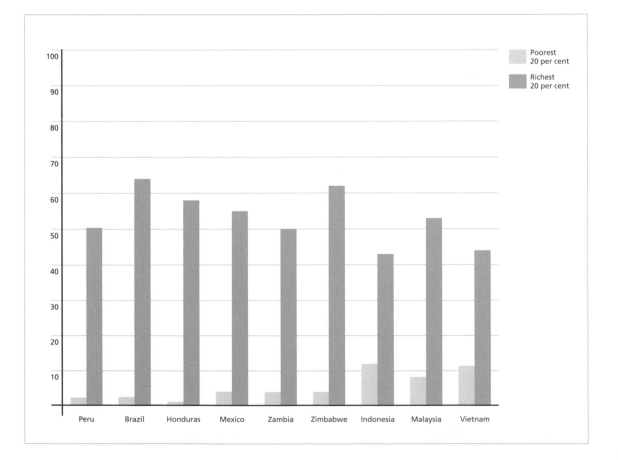

the second half of the 1990s, despite strong growth, especially in rural areas.[21] Increasing differences in income between coastal and inland areas in China have weakened the link between growth and poverty reduction, with survey data pointing to a slight increase in the number of poor since 1996.[22] These are not isolated cases. According to one of the most detailed and systematic data surveys of inequality so far conducted, the trend towards inequality appears to be global in character. The survey in question covers 77 countries over the period since 1960, with inequality rising in more than 45 cases. In the majority of cases, the trend towards increased inequality began during the 1980s and continued into the 1990s, raising questions about the pattern of growth achieved during this period.[23]

The relentless drift towards increasing inequality raises fundamental questions about the attainability of the 2015 targets. One scenario developed by the World Bank based on past growth trends and existing distribution patterns projects an *increase* in both the head-count index of poverty and the number of poor people over the next decade. Particularly steep increases are projected for sub-Saharan Africa and Latin America, with the number of poor increasing by 115 million and 52 million respectively. [24] This is consistent with findings from other research. In order for sub-Saharan Africa to meet the 2015 targets on the basis of existing patterns of income distribution, the region would have to achieve minimum per capita growth rates in excess of 3.5 per cent a year. This is exceptionally high by the standards of the past decade, during which real per capita growth has averaged less than 1 per cent. Clearly, any anti-poor bias in the pattern of growth would worsen an already dire prognosis.[25]

Extreme income inequality not only weakens the link between growth and poverty reduction, but also undermines economic growth. It was once assumed that any attempt at redistribution would act as a brake on growth by creating disincentives to investment. More recently, a large body of evidence has emerged to suggest that high levels of inequality are bad for growth, as well as for poverty reduction.[26] There are various explanations. Large land-holdings tend to produce less efficiently than small and medium-sized holdings. Meanwhile, poverty and inadequate access to productive assets and marketing infrastructure create obvious barriers to risk-taking, while low incomes restrict both the size of local markets and domestic savings and investment. Whatever the underlying causes, economic efficiency and equity are inextricably linked. This suggests that improved income distribution has the potential to produce a double benefit for poverty reduction, in the form of more dynamic and more widely dispersed economic growth.

There is a counter view to the argument that redistributive growth is the most effective mechanism for poverty reduction. Researchers in the World Bank have claimed that economic growth is the primary motor for poverty reduction, and that distributional issues are, at best, of secondary importance.[27] Their claim rests on empirical data purporting to show that, *on average*, growth benefits the poor and rich alike on a one-to-one basis, because the benefits of growth are distributed in accordance with the existing pattern of income distribution. The argument has had an important influence on the debate on growth and poverty reduction, shifting the emphasis away from policies for achieving redistribution and towards a more narrowly 'growth-oriented' perspective.

Few people would deny either that economic growth is a necessary condition for poverty reduction, or that the poor generally benefit from growth. But averages obscure large variations. As noted above, some countries are far more efficient than others at converting growth into poverty reduction. The real policy goal in any poverty-reduction strategy, especially in any highly unequal society, should be that of increasing the share of income captured by the poor, since this will increase the rate of poverty reduction. Even if it is true that rich and poor benefit from growth in proportion to their existing share of national income, in highly unequal societies this means that growth will simply reproduce inequality. Failure to change distribution patterns, with the poor capturing a bigger share of growth than their existing shared national income, will slow the rate of poverty reduction, rather than simply reproducing inequality.

There are three broader problems with the World Bank's perspective. First, it is based on data up to the early 1990s, and has therefore failed to capture the increasingly unequal income-distribution patterns associated with more recent growth periods. Second, it ignores some of the lessons of recent history. In Latin America, the number of people living in poverty increased by more than 50 million during the 1980s. Research by the Inter-American Development Bank attributed over half of this increase to changes in income distribution favouring the wealthy against the poor.[28] Third, whatever the broad relationship between growth and distribution, it is increasingly clear that, with existing patterns of income distribution, the 2015 targets will not be met through growth alone.

Global income distribution and poverty

National income distribution determines the rate at which particular countries translate growth into poverty reduction. But international income distribution also influences the scope for poverty reduction, since it determines the average income levels in different countries. The size of that average income, and how wealth is distributed among different groups, will determine the incidence of poverty at the national level. Other things being equal, the bigger the share of global wealth captured by the poorest countries, the higher their average incomes and – subject to domestic income-distribution factors – the lower the incidence of poverty.

Global distribution trends are as disturbing from a poverty-reduction perspective as national income trends. International income inequality has been increasing at a rate that is probably without precedent, widening the gap between the average incomes of the rich and the poor in the process. The ratio of the average GNP per capita of the richest countries with one-fifth of the world's population and countries accounting for the poorest fifth has increased from 30:1 in 1960 to 60:1 in 1990, and around 74:1 today.[29] Extreme as national income inequalities may be, even in Latin America, the world's most unequal region, they are less extreme than international inequalities. One way of measuring inequality is through the Gini coefficient, measuring the extent of departure from a situation of complete income equality. As shown in Figure 1.6, income is shared among rich and poor countries even more unequally than it is shared among rich and poor Brazilians.

Global income-distribution trends reflect the way in which global wealth, and any increment to it, is shared between rich and poor countries. At present, high-income countries accounting for about 20 per cent of the world's population account for 80 per cent of global GDP. Sub-Saharan Africa, with 10 per cent of world population, accounts for 0.6 per cent. Because economic growth has stagnated in many developing countries, the wealth gap is widening. The average annual growth in income per capita was negative in 50 countries during 1990–1998, only one of them an OECD country.

Changes in global income distribution are needed if the poorest countries are to achieve the 2015 targets. Capturing a larger share of global GDP will require a dramatically improved growth performance on the part of these countries, but it will also mean that they have to capture a larger share of world trade. This is because international trade has been expanding faster than global GDP, with the result that it is an increasingly important engine of growth. Among developing regions, only East Asia has succeeded in capturing a significantly larger share of world trade (although even now it accounts for only 10 per cent of the total). South Asia has been increasing its share, but still accounts for less than 1 per cent of the total, while Latin America's share has remained static (at less than 4 per cent), and sub-Saharan Africa's share is diminishing from already marginal levels (of less than 1 per cent). As we show in the fourth section of this chapter, globalisation is making it increasingly difficult to change this pattern, because international trade is becoming increasingly knowledge-intensive, with the most dynamic growth happening in sectors requiring highly educated populations.

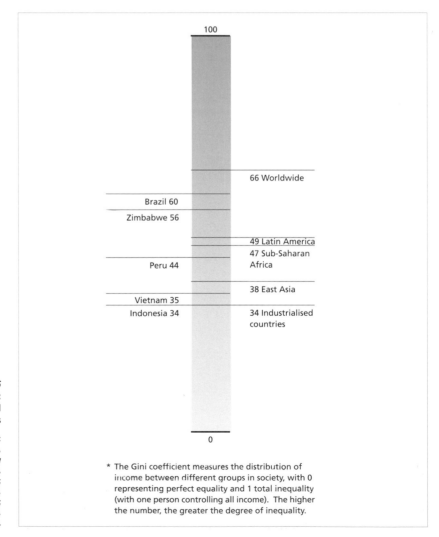

Figure 1.6
Measuring inequality:
global, regional, and national
Gini coefficients

Sources:
K. Deninger and L. Squire,
*A New Data Set Measuring
Income Inequality*,
Washington: World Bank, 1996;
Human Development Report 2000,
New York: UNDP, 2000;
World Development Indicators1998,
Washington: World Bank, 1998.

* The Gini coefficient measures the distribution of income between different groups in society, with 0 representing perfect equality and 1 total inequality (with one person controlling all income). The higher the number, the greater the degree of inequality.

Education and health: the potential benefits

As in the case of health services, improved access to education would enhance prospects for the attainment of the 2015 targets. The potential benefits of education for poverty reduction would flow partly from more rapid economic growth; and partly from improved income distribution, both at a national level and at a global level.

Accelerated progress towards the 2015 goals for reducing child-mortality rates will require action across a wide range of policy areas. Improved provision of public services is one such area. But developments in health will be shaped by progress in other areas, including income-poverty reduction and education. A 'virtuous circle' operates here, because better health is one of the requirements for raising the incomes and educational status of the poor.

Education influences health outcomes through a variety of channels. Increased access to information, changing attitudes, and increased confidence are among the most important. In terms of improving prospects for reaching the targets set for reducing child deaths, improved access to good-quality education is among the most important requirements.

Maternal education and child health

Nowhere are the human-development costs associated with mass exclusion from education more apparent than in relation to women's education. While the educational status of men makes an important difference to child health, it is a far less important variable than the education of women. Mothers typically assume responsibility for the welfare of children, including their nutritional status and their contacts with health-service providers. Education can empower women to make more informed choices, to demand better services, and to influence family decisions in a direction conducive to child welfare.[30]

The correlation between parental education and child mortality has been extensively documented. In almost all countries, child-death rates are inversely related to the level of maternal education. The more educated the mother, the healthier she and her child are likely to be. Comparative research focused on 33 countries during the 1980s found that each additional year of maternal education reduced childhood mortality by about 8 per cent.[31] For mothers completing five years of primary education, the risk of childhood mortality decreased by around 45/1000 births. In countries where one child in every four dies before reaching the age of five, as in much of sub-Saharan Africa, the mass exclusion of girls from basic education has clear implications: it is costing millions of lives. Mortality rates for the children of Ghanaian mothers with some education are twice as high as for children born to mothers with no education.[32] Figure 1.7 illustrates the relationship between maternal education and child mortality for a group of seven countries.

It is difficult to isolate the effects of education on child mortality from other factors, such as the level of income poverty. Even so, in many countries the effects of education appear to outweigh those associated with income. In Pakistan, the infant-mortality rate is 34 per cent higher among the poorest 20 per cent of households than among the richest 20 per cent. But in households where the mother has no education, the infant-mortality rate is 60 per cent higher than in households where the mother has some education (Figure 1.8).[33] Education, in this case, is almost twice as significant as income in determining survival prospects. Cross-country comparisons underline the central role of education in explaining differences in child-mortality rates. After controlling for socio-economic differences, one survey of 28 countries showed that mothers' education was the single most important influence on child mortality, especially after the first year of life.[34]

The benefits of women's education for child health are especially marked in countries with deeply entrenched patterns of gender inequity. In most countries, there are slightly more females in the total population than males. However, there are marked deviations from this pattern. In India,

Figure 1.7
Child-mortality rates by maternal education levels: selected countries (1995)

Source:
G. Bicego and A. Ahmad,
Infant and Child Mortality,
Demographic and Health Survey
No. 20, Macro International, 1996

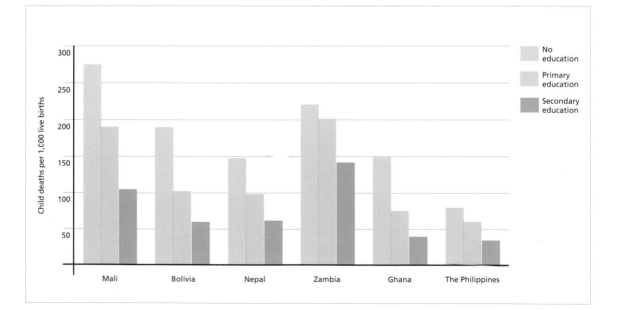

for example, there are more males than females. One of the reasons for this is that child-mortality rates have historically been higher for girls than boys. Female education appears to have a strong influence in correcting gender-determined bias in survival rates. Statistical surveys from northern India have found that the children of mothers who have completed primary school are significantly less likely to die in early childhood than children whose mothers have failed to complete primary education, regardless of their sex. However, the benefits are greater for girls. The average education-effect reduces child deaths for girls by 10 per cent, compared with 7 per cent for boys.[35] Education status had a far greater effect than rural–urban differences, or income status. Daughters in wealthy families with uneducated mothers were often at greater risk of dying than their counterparts in poor households with educated mothers. The overall effect of women's education in this context is that it saves children's lives and gives daughters a more equal chance of survival.

The causal factors responsible for such outcomes are difficult to establish. One reason why survival rates for children of educated women are higher is that they are less likely to be malnourished. In Zimbabwe, almost one-quarter of children with uneducated mothers suffer from malnutrition – three times the proportion for children with mothers who

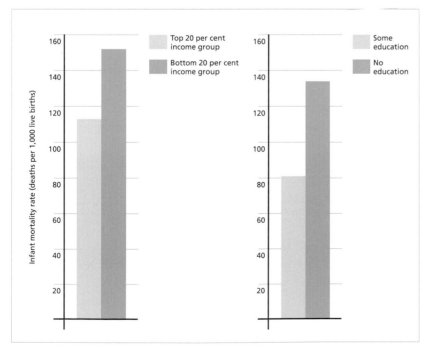

Figure 1.8
Infant mortality in Pakistan (deaths per 1000 live births: link to maternal education and household income)

Source:
Pakistan Integrated Household Survey 1995-1997,
Government of Pakistan

have had some secondary education. This difference is associated with income, but education confers benefits that can at least partially compensate for the disadvantage of low income. The ability to make use of information, openness to new ideas that challenge conventional assumptions about gender, and improved understanding of nutrition all play a role. So does increased confidence in dealing with service-providers. Educated mothers are not only better able to gain information about health matters and nutrition: they are also far more likely to make use of preventative health-care services and to demand timely treatment.[36]

The timeliness of referrals, uptake of immunisation, and use of ante-natal services and clinics are all positively associated with education. Each of these factors reduces the risks associated with many potentially life-threatening illnesses. For example, swift responses to acute respiratory infections and early treatment of diarrhoea through the use of simple rehydration therapies could save many lives. Evidence from Zambia (Figure 1.9) shows that educated women are more likely both to identify the need for treatment at an earlier stage and to demand treatment. Women with a secondary education are some 30 per cent more likely to take their children to a clinic for treatment than women with no education.[37] This is consistent with evidence from a large number of countries. In rural south India, the participants in an adult education programme demonstrated a far better understanding of common illnesses and their causes, as well as of potentially life-saving remedies, than did non-participants. They were also far more likely to use modern health services. Primary education is similarly correlated with service uptake.[38] In Mozambique, a government survey in 1998 found that mothers who had completed grades 1–5 were almost twice as likely to vaccinate their children as illiterate mothers. The same mothers were 22 per cent more likely to possess a health card, indicating a higher level of contact with health clinics.[39] Research in India found that mothers with four years of education were twice as likely to register for ante-natal care as mothers with no education, and three times as likely to immunise their children.[40] Both ante-natal care and immunisation were significant determinants of mortality.

Increased confidence is the least tangible but probably most powerful source of improved health outcomes. Non-economic factors are important in explaining the health behaviour of poor people. Women in particular frequently cite staff rudeness, uncertainty over their rights, and a lack of confidence as reasons for not seeking treatment for illnesses.[41] Education can empower women in their interactions with service providers. It makes it more likely that they will have read information about health problems, and that they will be more confident in explaining these problems and demanding treatment. In the Ibadan region of Nigeria, detailed research at health facilities found that literate women bring in sick children for treatment at an earlier stage, and that they are more likely to demand – and get – a specific diagnosis.[42]

There is an unfortunate tendency in some quarters to view education as little more than a tool for achieving lower birth rates. Education does have this effect. In South Asia, the fertility rate for women with seven or more years of education is 35 per cent lower than for women with no education.[43] But changes in fertility reflect a more important change in the ability of women to exercise greater control over their lives. Better-educated women marry later and space births over longer periods, with benefits for maternal and child health. One-third of Bangladeshi women

Figure 1.9:
Zambia: relationship between mother's education and maternal and child health

Source:
M. Kelly, 'Primary Education in a Highly Indebted Country: The Case of Zambia', unpublished background paper, Oxfam GB, 1998

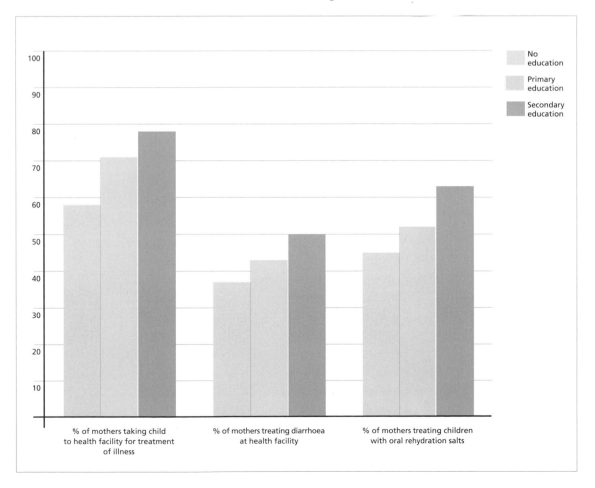

with a primary education report using contraceptives, compared with one-quarter of women with no education.[44] Once again, the causal links are complex and variable. Better education creates opportunities for employment and income generation, which in turn create incentives for later marriage. Improved access to information and increased self-confidence raise the demand for contraception, and enable women to express that demand. Whatever the precise mechanisms at play, maternal education is one of the keys to achieving the 2015 targets for reducing maternal mortality rates.

Important as education is to improved public health, it is not the sole factor. Income-poverty is the primary driver of child malnutrition – and education does not override the structural disadvantages associated with poverty. Moreover, it is difficult in practice to separate the influence of education from that of income in explaining household behaviour. Better-educated households are less likely to be poor, and the poorest households are more likely to suffer educational disadvantage. The benefits of education are conditioned by local social, economic, and cultural conditions. In some cases, the benefits may be weaker among the extreme poor than among less disadvantaged social groups.[45] But even within low-income groups, maternal education is positively associated with better nutrition, partially compensating for other aspects of deprivation. Given that some 160 million children worldwide suffer from malnutrition, which is the main cause of premature death, this underlines the scale of the potential benefits of achieving universal education.

Education and HIV/AIDS

Progress towards the international development targets is compromised by a range of new threats to health, the most serious of which is HIV/AIDS. The HIV/AIDS epidemic represents a global threat which will slow down, or even reverse, improvements in health indicators in many countries. Apart from its direct impact on health, the epidemic is impoverishing families and overwhelming already under-financed health services. The most recent of the international development targets, adopted in 1990, envisages a 25 per cent reduction in HIV infection among 15–24 year olds by 2005.[46] Education has a vital role to play in meeting this target.

Drawing on responses to household surveys from 32 countries, recent research has shown that knowledge and awareness of HIV/AIDS-related problems is strongly linked to education, especially among women and girls. For instance, the proportion of women who do not know that HIV infection can be transmitted to children is three times higher for uneducated women than for educated women, while the proportion believing that there is no way of avoiding HIV/AIDS is four times higher.[47] In Zambia, infection rates among educated women started to decline in the mid-1990s, while the infection rate among women without any formal education has remained constant. There is similar evidence from Uganda, where infection rates among women with a secondary education have fallen, relative to those for illiterate women. Disaggregating child-mortality data for Kenya to take into account the education of mothers also illustrates the potential for reducing vulnerability. While the national CMR began to increase at the end of the 1980s, it continued to decline for the children of mothers who had attained post-primary education.[48]

It would be wrong to overstate the potential role of education in combating the HIV/AIDS epidemic. Yet it is clear that improved access to education could make a difference. Attendance at school provides children with an opportunity to gain access to relevant information and to transform this information into behavioural changes. At the same time, education can empower women to exercise greater control. Given that teenage girls in Africa are five times more likely to be infected by HIV than boys, girls' education is an obvious priority.

Female education and human development:
breaking the transmission of poverty

Women's education does not merely create one-off benefits for child health. Apart from being an important objective in its own right, it helps to overcome wider gender-determined inequalities and to create virtuous circles of human development and poverty reduction. The critical role of female literacy and education in furthering human development emerges forcefully from comparisons between different countries, and between different regions of the same country.

Differences in education have played an important role in the social development of India's States, as contrasts between Kerala and northern States such as Uttar Pradesh and Bihar clearly demonstrate.[49] One of the distinguishing features of Kerala's development was the early promotion of female literacy. This provided a basis for advances in public health and other areas. Unlike Kerala, female literacy rates and enrolment rates for girls in other States are much lower than for boys. Figure 1.10 shows how gender-linked disadvantage in education interacts with other aspects of gender-based disadvantage in Uttar Pradesh and Bihar; and how Kerala's achievements in education are reflected in other areas of social

In Zambia, infection rates among educated women started to decline in the mid-1990s, while the infection rate among women without any formal education has remained constant.

development, such as child health and life expectancy. Women in Kerala live 24 years longer on average than women in Bihar. Meanwhile, fewer than one-quarter of women in Bihar and Uttar Pradesh are literate, compared with 86 per cent of women in Kerala. These differences in education are of direct relevance to the 2015 targets for child mortality, as witnessed by the fact that a child born in Uttar Pradesh is seven times more likely to die before his or her first birthday than a child born in Kerala.

Evidence from India confirms that female literacy has a far stronger effect on child welfare than a general increase in living standards among the poor, or a rise in male literacy. While Kerala has a slightly higher average income than Uttar Pradesh, its social indicators are far better than other States – such as Andhra Pradesh and Punjab – which have far higher levels of income. Male literacy rates are also higher in Kerala than in other States, but the effects of male literacy appear to be far weaker in relation to child mortality than is female literacy. Keeping other factors constant, an increase in the female literacy rate from 22 per cent to 75 per cent was found to reduce the child-mortality rate by 30 per cent – almost double the reduction achieved by a comparable increase in male literacy. Halving income poverty had the effect of reducing the child-mortality rate by 2 per cent.[50]

Comparisons between countries reinforce the picture that emerges from inter-State differences in India. While low income is inevitably associated with deprivation in other areas of human welfare, some countries have

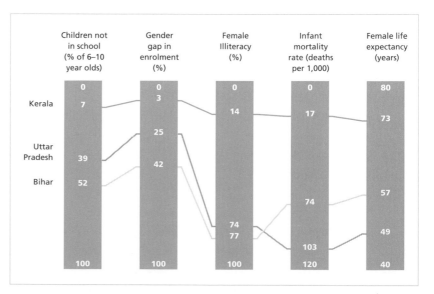

Figure 1.10
Women's education and social-development indicators: Kerala, Uttar Pradesh, and Bihar

Sources:
Primary Education in India,
Washington: World Bank, 1997;
T. Krishnan, 'The route to social development in Kerala', in
S. Mehrotra and R. Jolly:
Development with a Human Face,
Oxford: Clarendon Press, 1998;
J. Dreze and H. Gazder,
'Uttar Pradesh: the burden of inertia', in J. Dreze and A. Sen:
Indian Development,
Oxford: Clarendon Press, 1997.

achieved far better levels of human development than others that have higher average incomes. Figure 1.11 contrasts the performance of Pakistan with that of Vietnam, a country with lower average incomes and higher income-poverty levels.[51] More than half of Vietnam's population lives below the poverty line. What is striking is that, despite this intense deprivation, Vietnam has achieved far higher levels of female literacy, which have in turn contributed to social advances in other areas. Child-mortality rates in Pakistan are three times higher than in Vietnam, and maternal mortality rates are twice as high. As in India, the distribution of educational opportunity appears to be one of the most important factors. Vietnamese women aged between 20 and 24 are three times as likely to have finished primary school than their counterparts in Pakistan. Moreover, they are as likely to complete primary school as males in the same age group, whereas Pakistani women are half as likely to complete school as men.

The examples of Kerala and Vietnam demonstrate beyond reasonable doubt that education can help to overcome the constraints on human development imposed by income poverty. By contrast, States such as Uttar Pradesh in India and countries like Pakistan demonstrate the wasted potential and suffering associated with under-attainment in education. According to World Bank estimates, educating 1000 girls in Pakistan would cost the State approximately $40,000 a year.[52] This investment would prevent about 60 infant deaths. Leaving aside for a moment the fundamental human right of Pakistani girls to enjoy a basic education, this points to a low-cost route to improved human welfare.

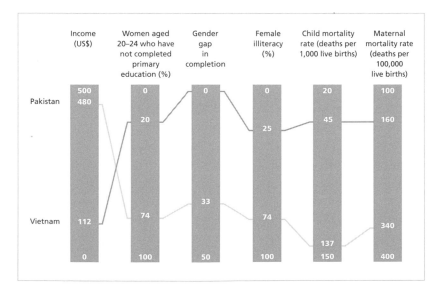

Figure 1.11
Income, education, and social-development indicators: Vietnam and Pakistan

Sources:
Integrated Household Survey, 1995-1999, Government of Pakistan; *Education in Vietnam*, Government of Vietnam, Hanoi, 1996

The multiple benefits of female education are cumulative, in that they become mutually reinforcing over time, with the advantages transmitted across generations. It is not just that educated children are likely to be more productive and healthier, with attendant benefits for poverty reduction. They are also more likely to educate their own children. Here too the benefits of maternal education are particularly strong, with educated mothers far more likely than uneducated mothers to send their daughters to school. In Tanzania, the daughters of mothers who have had a primary education are 11 per cent more likely to enrol in primary school than are the daughters of uneducated mothers.[53] To the extent that education enhances the ability of women to control their fertility, lower population growth will also generate advantages for education. Slower growth in the school-age population will reduce pressure on the education system, and enable the government to increase spending per pupil and provide a better-quality education. It follows that investing in girls' education today is one of the most effective strategies for progressing towards universal primary education in the future.

The multiple benefits of female education are cumulative, in that they become mutually reinforcing over time, with the advantages transmitted across generations.

Education, poverty, and health

Recognising the potential of education as a catalyst for development does not mean that education policy can be treated in isolation. Schools are not islands that are somehow separated from the wider social and economic environment; nor are they immune from the effects of poverty, malnutrition, and ill health. Educational deprivation contributes to poverty, helping to transmit it across generations. But poverty also limits the ability of poor households to take advantage of educational opportunities. In the absence of integrated strategies for addressing these problems, many of the potential benefits of education will be lost.

Despite the enormous shortfalls that remain, governments have significantly increased access to primary education. Four out of every five children of primary-school age now attend school, a greater proportion than ever before. However, the widening coverage of education systems has exposed the problem of poverty-related illness. Millions of children are attending school in a state of poor health or poor nutrition – or both. In the early 1990s, the World Bank estimated that children in the age range 5–14 accounted for 11 per cent of the total global burden of disease, with infectious and parasitic diseases the largest contributor.[54] More than 95 per cent of this disease burden was concentrated in developing countries. Poor health before and during school years can have devastating consequences in terms of impaired cognitive development, under-performance, and withdrawal from school.

While education generates health benefits, health problems can undermine progress in education. Nutritional status is among the most important determinants of educational attainment, yet the diets of almost 226 million children in the developing world – 40 per cent of the total – are poor in either proteins or vitamins.[55] One of the largest studies ever undertaken of the anthropometric status of rural school-children in five countries – Ghana, Tanzania, Indonesia, Vietnam, and India – found stunting (low height-for-age) rates ranging from 48 to 56 per cent, and underweight (low weight-for-age) rates ranging from 34 to 62 per cent.[56] Such findings have important implications for educational attainment, because stunting in the first two years of life has been shown to reduce test scores in children aged 8–11, and to contribute to late enrolment. One study conducted in Cebu, the second-largest city in the Philippines, found that children whose growth was stunted in their childhood scored up to 30 per cent lower in IQ tests in primary school than children who had not been stunted.[57] Achieving education for all in the midst of mass hunger is not a sustainable goal.

Achieving education for all in the midst of mass hunger is not a sustainable goal.

Like malnutrition, micro-nutrient deficiencies in children can negatively affect their learning ability and increase their susceptibility to infection.[58]

- **Iron-deficiency anaemia (IDA)**. It is estimated that 210 million schoolchildren suffer from IDA, which is related to insufficient intake of iron-rich foods and can also be caused by parasitic infections. One recent survey, of 13,000 rural children in six African countries, found 40 per cent suffering from IDA, rising to 75 per cent in Tanzania. IDA afflicts more than half of pre-school-age children in India.

- **Iodine deficiency**. This affects an estimated 60 million children. The consequences include severe mental retardation and mild forms of motor and cognitive deficits.

- **Vitamin A deficiency**. This affects 85 million schoolchildren. It is an important cause of blindness and impaired immune functions, increasing the risk of illness from infectious disease.

Malnutrition and micro-nutrient deficiencies are closely associated with poverty-related health problems, and they undermine the learning potential of children from poor households. Poor sanitation renders the poor more vulnerable to the water-borne diseases and infection that hamper education and often threaten life. Roundworms and the intestinal parasitic infection trichuriasis both affect approximately one billion people, with schoolchildren the most heavily infected group.

Malaria claims the lives of one in twenty children under the age of five in sub-Saharan Africa alone, subjecting millions more to protracted bouts of illness. In some countries it accounts for up to half of school days missed for medical reasons.[59] Diarrhoea, which claims the lives of 3.3 million children annually, has highly adverse consequences for school attendance and performance.

As the evidence presented earlier suggests, education can help to address problems of health and nutrition; but getting sick and under-nourished children into a classroom is not a helpful starting point for maximising the benefits associated with education. Too often, the education strategies developed by governments, and supported by donors, place an emphasis on building classrooms and training teachers, with insufficient attention paid to the underlying causes of ill health in the communities served by schools.

There are high costs associated with failure to develop education and health policies in an integrated fashion. During 1997/98, Oxfam International and the Child Health Development Centre of Makerere University in Uganda carried out household-level research, examining the health status of four communities.[60] The study was undertaken at a time when school enrolments were rising, following the withdrawal of school fees for primary education. It showed that some of the potential benefits of increased access to education were being lost as a result of widespread health problems. In each of the communities covered, at least one-quarter of the households interviewed reported an episode of sickness among children during the month preceding the interview. In one urban settlement in Kampala, more than 60 per cent of households interviewed gave the same answer. In Apac, a poor rural district in the north of the country, two-thirds of households had a child suffering illness. The most common illnesses identified were diarrhoea, malaria, and respiratory infections.

The research revealed wider education problems linked to health. Parents and teachers reported that children – especially young girls – were frequently withdrawn from school to tend sick relatives, missing valuable learning time a result. The cost of treating health problems was another important factor. In extreme cases, unaffordability resulted in poor households simply being excluded from health provision. More commonly, it leads to delayed treatment, with attendant implications for child health. This strongly suggests that the policy of introducing free primary education should have been linked to initiatives aimed at reducing – or eliminating – the costs of basic health care. The lack of adequate water and sanitation provision, identified by poor communities as the major cause of ill health among children, is another priority.

Education systems can provide a useful mechanism for addressing health problems. Early-childhood development programmes can help to counteract the educational disadvantages associated with poverty. These programmes provide primary-care interventions, including pre-natal care, immunisation, oral rehydration therapies, control of respiratory infections, and vitamin supplementation. Apart from the immediate health benefits, they can contribute to improvements in educational attainment later in life. Schools can provide a focal point for community health efforts. For instance, the Partnership for Child Development, an international collaboration between UN agencies, non-government organisations, drugs companies, and academic institutions, has pioneered low-cost systems for delivering de-worming drugs to children through schools.[61] Pilot programmes in Ghana and Tanzania have trained teachers to administer simple tests for identifying infection and administering low-cost treatments. The need for intervention by medical personnel in determining individual dosage for treatment has also been reduced.

Studies in Benin, Burkina Faso, and Togo have all found that school meals have the effect of raising children's test scores.

Well-designed in-school nutrition programmes can help to alleviate the nutritional problems of school-age children.[62] In the Indian State of Gujarat, more than three million children receive free school meals, with vitamin A and iron supplements. Studies in Benin, Burkina Faso, and Togo have all found that school meals have the effect of raising children's test scores. In Peru, a school-breakfast programme, which included an iron-fortified ration, was shown to increase dietary intakes of energy by 25 per cent and iron by 46 per cent. Other positive outcomes reported include reduced vulnerability to seasonal hunger, improved immunity to infectious disease through reduced micronutrient deficiency, and increased motivation for parents to send their children to school and have them attend regularly. Programmes can be targeted to reduce inequalities between boys and girls. In Pakistan, an intervention supported by the World Food Programme provided two tins of oil to families whose girls attended school for a minimum of 20 days a month. Attendance in the schools participating in the programmes increased from 76 per cent to 93 per cent.

The design of such programmes is not unproblematic. Poorly targeted school-meal programmes can result in relatively wealthy households capturing a disproportionately large share of food subsidies, especially where large numbers of poor children are not in school; or where, as is often the case, programmes are concentrated on urban areas. This has been a continuing problem in Peru, where an urban bias in food transfers has produced modest benefits for the rural poor.[63] Similarly, many poor countries lack the administrative capacity to deliver effective programmes, opening the door to corruption and the misappropriation of food stocks by officials. While the costs of the food provided may be modest, there are often high costs associated with transportation, warehousing, and distribution. These costs need to be considered in the light of alternative forms of transfer.

Education and income-poverty

Education is critical to the achievement of the 2015 target of reducing the incidence of extreme poverty by half. At a household level, educational status is one of the strongest influences on income and poverty. The lower the level of educational attainment, the greater the vulnerability to income-poverty. What is true for households is true also for national economies, with average income levels reflecting levels of access to education. As we saw earlier, the rate of poverty reduction is dictated by the rate of economic growth and the share of national wealth captured by the poor. Improvements in both areas depend critically on advances in education.

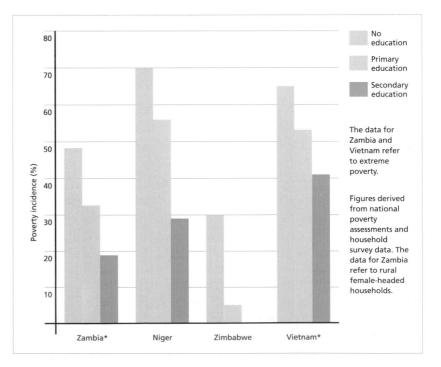

Figure 1.12:
Poverty incidence and education status: selected countries

Education and household poverty

The causal relationship between education and poverty is much debated. Does lack of education cause poverty; or does poverty lead to a lack of education? As in health-related studies, causal connections are difficult to establish. Income levels typically reflect educational attainment, but poverty – and its associated problems of illness and poor nutrition – is a powerful barrier to educational attainment. The precise patterns of association between income poverty and deprivation vary from country to country. What does not vary is the disproportionate representation of the under-educated in the ranks of the poor.

For households, as for national economies, educational deprivation is a passport to low income, vulnerability, and poverty (see Figure 1.12). In Vietnam, two out of three households headed by somebody with no education live below the poverty line. The share declines to one half for those with primary education, and to 41 per cent for those with secondary education. In Zambia, rural women with no education are twice as likely to be living in poverty as counterparts who have attended secondary school. About two-thirds of the most extremely poor households are headed by someone with no education, compared with fewer than one-third of non-poor households.[64]

Does lack of education cause poverty; or does poverty lead to a lack of education?

Economists have attempted to capture the benefits of education by estimating the rates of return on investment, both for individuals and for societies.[65] The 'private' rate of return, or the benefit to individuals, is generally calculated by comparing the financial costs of education with the benefits, usually measured in terms of future income flows. The 'social' rate of return takes into account what society has to pay in order to educate the individual in question. Using data from the 1960s and 1970s, the World Bank built a strong case for investment in primary education on the basis of rates of return estimated at over 20 per cent for sub-Saharan Africa.[66] The problem is that wages in the region have fallen sharply since then, so that the marginal returns to investment in education are lower than average returns.[67] If education policy were framed in accordance with standard market rules for investment, it would be the marginal rate of return that influenced public-spending decisions.

These are good reasons why policy makers should look beyond rates of return. One problem with the World's Bank approach is that labour markets can artificially depress rates of return (for instance, through gender-linked discrimination, leading to lower wages for women), or inflate rates of return (for example, through politically motivated interventions to increase wages for civil servants), making it impossible to establish any real link between education and productivity. From a poverty-reduction perspective, what matters more than estimated rates of return are the real effects of education in terms of increasing the value of the main assets of the poor: namely, their output and their labour.

The benefits of education are especially strong in agriculture. Evidence from many countries shows a positive association between productivity and the number of years spent in school. Higher productivity in turn leads to increased output and income flows, reducing the vulnerability of poor households. Cross-country research based on data covering 13 developing countries suggests that, after taking into account differences in land, labour, and capital, each year of additional education raises farm output by 2 per cent.[68] Here too the potential benefits of education are cumulative, because growth in the incomes of the rural poor generates demand for small-scale enterprises and manufacturing. In Indonesia, the multiplier effect of rural growth on manufacturing during the 1970s was large, with each percentage-point increase in farming matched by a 1.5 per cent increase in non-agricultural output.[69]

One study in India found that four years of basic education increased economic returns to innovation by about one-third – considerably more than the returns to spending on agricultural extension.

The precise causal links between education and productivity are difficult to establish, but an enhanced capacity to innovate appears to be one of the most important. More educated households are more likely to adopt new technologies, and to generate higher returns from those technologies. One study in India found that four years of basic education increased economic returns to innovation by about one-third – considerably more than the returns to spending on agricultural extension.[70] Such studies clearly indicate the economic potential inherent in education, but realisation of that potential depends on access to productive assets and marketing infrastructure. In the Indian case, returns were highest in areas where the availability of infrastructure and producers' access to marketing facilities were most developed, underlining the fact that public investment in education can increase the efficiency of public investment in economic infrastructure.

Does the relationship between education and output apply in sub-Saharan Africa? Given that past improvements in education in the region have been weakly associated with economic growth, such questions are legitimate.[71] The combination of weak macro-economic policies and external problems that has conspired to produce economic stagnation has clearly limited the potential benefits of education at a national level. However, at a household level the benefits of education appear to be as robust as in other developing regions. In Uganda, four years of primary education were found to raise farm output by about 7 per cent, when other factors were accounted for. For households living on the margins of subsistence, these are significant gains.[72] To a Ugandan coffee farmer, they can mean the difference between being able to afford urgently needed medicines, new tools, seeds, and food and having to manage without them.

The benefits of education are equally pronounced in labour markets. One of the reasons why education offers an escape route from poverty is that it creates opportunities to earn higher incomes, whether in the form of wages, or through trading activity. Education cannot compensate for disadvantages associated with working in low-wage environments in which the poor are often discriminated against, but it can increase relative earning power. In Latin America, workers who have completed primary school will earn on average 50 per cent more in their first job than workers who have not attended school. In Brazil and Mexico, they earn twice as much. The gap widens to 120 per cent for a worker with twelve years of education.[73] There is a positive correlation between income and education even in the informal sector, where school qualifications are of limited relevance. Evidence from Honduras, Guatemala, and El Salvador indicates that each additional year of education is linked to a 5–10 per cent increase in informal-sector earnings. Returns to female education in the informal sector are even higher: more than twice the average returns for males, in the case of Thailand.[74]

Evidence from Honduras, Guatemala, and El Salvador indicates that each additional year of education is linked to a 5–10 per cent increase in informal-sector earnings.

The association between education and income is not automatic. Precise outcomes are shaped by power relations in local markets, culture, and political decisions. Gender is one of the key determinants of the distribution of benefits from education.[75] Where women face unequal access to productive resources and services, the scope for realising the potential gains of education is restricted. The same is true where women earn less than men for doing similar work, as they do in most countries; or where men capture a disproportionately large share of higher-paid jobs. Such forms of labour-market discrimination are important, not least because they can act as a disincentive for parents to invest in schooling for girls. Even where education does generate increased earning power, intra-household arrangements may result in the benefits being transferred to men. All of these factors have a significant bearing on female poverty. Even so, women's earning capacity is strongly linked to education. In Bangladesh, the average earnings of a woman with secondary-school education are seven times those of a woman with no education.[76] Similarly, the average earnings of urban women with a completed primary education in Bolivia are 38 per cent higher than for women with only an incomplete primary education. Women with a secondary education earn 130 per cent more than women with no education.[77] In each of these cases, the exclusion of girls from educational opportunities produces a higher incidence of poverty among adult females.

Economists have extensively researched the benefits of education in terms of the productivity and income gains for poor households. For the most part they have 'discovered' outcomes that are manifestly obvious to the vast majority of poor people. Participatory poverty-assessments consistently carry the message that the poor see education as a mechanism for escaping the poverty trap, and for stopping the transmission of income-poverty across generations. One of the main reasons why poor people value education is that it enables them to produce their way out of poverty, which in turn acts as a stimulus for economic growth and reduces dependence on social-welfare transfers.

'Knowledge is our most powerful engine of production ...The most valuable of all capital is that invested in human beings.'

Education and economic growth

Economic growth is a necessary requirement for progress towards poverty reduction. While there are many countries that could be far more efficient in converting growth into poverty reduction, no country in history has sustained an attack on poverty in the midst of economic decline. Economic growth matters because it determines the size of the economic cake to be shared out among members of a society, and hence the average level of income; and education matters to economic growth because it provides the skills and abilities on which the latter depends.

The strong links between education and economic growth are not a recent discovery. Towards the end of the nineteenth century, the British economist Alfred Marshall wrote: 'Knowledge is our most powerful engine of production ...The most valuable of all capital is that invested in human beings.'[78] By this stage, British governments were uncomfortably aware of the accuracy of his observation. The neglect of basic education had left the country far behind its rivals, with devastating consequences for national prosperity (see the box on page 54).

Almost one hundred years were to pass before Marshall's insight was integrated into mainstream economics. In the 1950s, economists such as Robert Solow were puzzled by data showing that factors of production such as capital, land, and labour could not fully explain changes in productivity.[79] They attributed the unexplained part of the equation to education. In the 1980s, Theodore Schultz and Gary Becker, winners of the Nobel Prize for economics, worked this finding into what became known as the 'human capital growth theory'. Human capital was defined as the stock of useful knowledge acquired in the process of education.[80] Investment in this stock, so the argument ran, generated the skills needed to increase productivity and raise wages. Later research on growth rates across a large number of countries found that the accumulation of physical capital typically accounted for fewer than one-third of variations, with human capital playing a far more important role.

Investment in basic education is now widely accepted as a powerful engine for accelerating economic growth, especially in developing countries. Some of the most powerful evidence comes from East Asia, where research by the World Bank found that primary-school enrolment rates in 1960 were almost twice as important as investment levels in explaining the subsequent growth performances of South Korea, Indonesia, and Malaysia.[81] Cross-regional comparisons are even more telling. They suggest that initial investment levels are less important than primary-school enrolment rates in explaining growth differences between East Asia and other developing regions after 1960. In the case of sub-Saharan Africa, where education was four times more important than investment in influencing growth differences in comparison with East Asia, such findings need to be treated with caution. Huge aggregations and broad averages inevitably obscure other important factors, such as institutional capacity; and it is difficult to isolate the influence of education. Even so, there is overwhelming evidence that East Asia's economic success could not have been built on the educational levels that characterise other developing regions today. The critical point is not that education indicators for East Asia are better now than in sub-Saharan Africa or much of Latin America and South Asia. It is that economic growth itself was built on far higher levels of educational attainment than might have been expected on the basis of average incomes. Like Germany in the nineteenth century, South Korea was a nation of schools before it was a nation of thriving manufacture. Increased levels of education meant that people could utilise increasingly sophisticated technologies, with rising levels of productivity supporting sustained increases in real wages and a decline in poverty. Economic analysis suggests that, had South Korea's performance at the primary-school level remained equivalent to that of Pakistan, by 1985 the country's per capita GDP would have been about 40 per cent lower than that actually achieved.[82]

Like Germany in the nineteenth century, South Korea was a nation of schools before it was a nation of thriving manufacture.

Comparisons between East Asia and other developing regions graphically illustrate the scale of the education challenge that lies ahead. Adult literacy rates in sub-Saharan Africa and India today are lower than they were in Thailand and South Korea in 1960. Comparisons between East Asia and Latin America are equally striking, in that they demonstrate how growth and educational improvement can become mutually reinforcing. In the early 1970s, the average extent of education in the 'Asian miracle' economies was 3.5 years, roughly the same as in Latin America. By the early 1990s, this period had increased to six years, compared with less than five years in Latin America.[83] The lost potential for growth in Latin America is enormous.

Comparisons between East Asia and other developing regions graphically illustrate the scale of the education challenge that lies ahead. Adult literacy rates in sub-Saharan Africa and India today are lower than they were in Thailand and South Korea in 1960.

Some of the literature on 'human capital' creates the impression that improved education levels provide an immediate route to more rapid growth. This impression is wrong in one crucial respect. Education may be a necessary condition for achieving more rapid economic growth, but it is not a sufficient condition. It cannot be assumed that increasing educational attainment automatically generates higher growth. Improved access to good-quality education has the effect of increasing the supply of skilled labour. But the growth generated as a result will be determined by the ability of the economy to absorb that labour at rising levels of productivity. It is perfectly possible to combine outstanding progress in education with an abysmal economic performance, as witnessed by the experience of countries such as Cuba, Zimbabwe, and Russia. Where weak macro-economic management is restricting employment opportunities or depressing productivity, increase in the supply of skilled labour may not be matched by increased demand for that labour. This in turn will have the effect of limiting productivity and wage gains, leading to skilled labour replacing unskilled labour and declining wages for the latter.

The Zimbabwean experience is instructive.[84] During the 1980s, the country invested a higher proportion of its national income in education than almost any other country, achieving near-universal primary education in the space of a few years after Independence. Secondary-school enrolment also rose sharply. However, slow economic growth meant that by the end of the decade only 30,000 formal-sector jobs were being created for every 200,000 school-leavers. Weak macro-economic policies geared towards capital-intensive, rather than labour-intensive, growth undermined the benefits of investment in education. While education unquestionably contributed to the impressive improvements in social indicators achieved by Zimbabwe in the decade after

Independence, average wages and incomes stagnated. By the end of the decade, a vicious circle had developed, with slow economic growth and the resulting pressure on government revenues making it increasingly difficult to sustain public investment in education, which was dramatically cut in the early 1990s.

Education and income distribution

The distribution of educational opportunity has an important bearing on the distribution of income. Illiteracy and the absence of skills provided through education prevent poor people from participating in markets on equitable terms, and from responding to the opportunities created by economic reform. In countries where rapid growth is increasing the demand for, and returns to, skilled labour relative to unskilled labour, income inequalities will widen, slowing the rate of poverty reduction.

Creating growth on the foundations of highly unequal education systems results in benefits biased in favour of the wealthy. Empirical research has found that the effect of educational inequality in producing income inequalities rises until the average time in school reaches 6.3 years, after which it declines.[85] In much of sub-Saharan Africa, the average time in school is three–four years, and it is less than six years in Latin America. The time-honoured comparison between East Asia and Latin America illustrates the consequences of educational inequality.[86] In Korea, the proportion of workers with high-school and post-secondary qualifications increased rapidly after the early 1970s, while the proportion of workers with elementary-school qualifications or less fell to only 8 per cent of the total. The wage premium for skilled labour consequently fell. Over the two decades up to the mid-1980s, the average income of those who had completed higher education declined from 97 per cent above the average wage to 66 per cent above it. By 1986, the income gap between workers with high-school qualifications and those with only primary-school qualifications had fallen by one-third. In Brazil, by contrast, the wage premium earned by workers with higher education, already much larger than in Korea, remained unchanged. The earnings of those with the benefit of higher education had reached 156 per cent of the average wage – more than double the gap in Korea.

One reason is to be found in Brazil's failure to combine economic growth with greater equity in the distribution of educational opportunity. In the 1950s, Brazil had higher primary-school completion rates – 60 per cent, compared with 36 per cent in South Korea – but by the mid-1980s South Korea's primary-completion rates were four times higher than those of Brazil. Today, fewer than half of all Brazilian children complete primary school, a level that South Korea had surpassed by the mid-1950s.[87] Those who have not attained this level are effectively excluded from climbing the wage ladder. The associated income inequalities help to account for the weak links between growth and poverty reduction in Brazil.

Just as many of the benefits associated with globalisation are cumulative and mutually reinforcing, so too are the costs of educational disadvantage. Gaps in educational opportunity are ultimately reflected in income gaps between rich and poor. So any attempt to achieve greater equity in income distribution needs to start by closing gaps in educational attainment. These are very large in many developing countries. The difference between median grades completed by 15–19 year olds from the poorest 40 per cent and richest 20 per cent is three years in Indonesia, four years in Mali and Brazil, and ten years in India. Using the same criteria, attainment gaps between boys and girls range from two–three years for countries such as Benin and Côte d'Ivoire to six years in Pakistan.[88]

The vicious circle of educational deprivation and poverty is not restricted to developing countries. In the industrialised world too, educational attainment has a significant impact on future life chances. Childhood disadvantage frequently leads to low educational attainment; low educational attainment leads to low pay and limited employment prospects, which in turn lead to low income and the denial of opportunities for the next generation. The children of those on low incomes carry the disadvantages associated with poverty into the school system. The case of Britain illustrates the cycle of deprivation.[89] One indicator of the extent of child poverty in Britain is the number of children qualifying for free school meals. Average pass rates in secondary schools are around 50 per cent higher in schools where fewer than 5 per cent qualify than in schools where 20 per cent or more qualify. Failure at school provides a passport to other forms of deprivation. The rate of unemployment among adults who left school before the age of sixteen is twice as high as for those who completed secondary school, and their average earnings are 60 per cent lower. These income differences are transmitted to the next generation. Even at the age of 22 months, children from the richest 40 per cent of households score higher in aptitude tests than children whose parents are in the poorest 40 per cent, and these differences widen over time.

Education systems have an important role to play in breaking the cycle of poverty and increasing opportunity. For three decades after the Second World War, education acted as a 'great leveller' in the United States.

Education and poverty in the USA

The USA was one of the first countries to develop a publicly financed education system. After the Second World War, the extension of that system helped to reduce income inequalities and extend opportunity. Today, it acts to reinforce the disadvantages associated with poverty.

Some of the problems are rooted on the supply side, in the high schools that serve poor communities. In 1997 the Department of Education's Report on the Condition of Education found that schools with the highest proportion of poor children were under-financed, while the nation's richest schools were spending one-third more per pupil than its poorest schools. Schools serving the poor were also provided with the least-trained teachers, with pupils in poor schools twice as likely to be taught by a mathematics teacher without a specialised knowledge of the subject. Schools in poor neighbourhoods were also under-equipped: more than 70 per cent of teachers in poor schools reported the absence of essential teaching materials.

Because secondary schools serving the poorest communities are unable to provide students with a good-quality basic education, the influence of household poverty within the education system is becoming increasingly marked. Rising levels of poverty among children, as a result of low pay and changes in the welfare system, have intensified the problem. More than 14 million American children – about one in five – now live below the poverty line. These children are more exposed to illness, family stress, inadequate parental support, and nutritional problems – and they are far more likely to fail at school.

The impact of rising poverty is reflected in disturbing signs that progress towards equity in education has been halted. Racial, social, and ethnic gaps are widening again. Moreover, at a time when a college education is becoming increasingly important to escape low pay and vulnerability in the labour market, the gap between children from wealthy and poor households is widening.

- Youths from poor families score lower on national tests of reading, mathematics, and vocabulary. They are twice as likely as other pupils to have to repeat a grade, and three times more likely to be expelled from school.

- The children of poor households are more likely to drop out of high school. In 1996, young adults living in the poorest 20 per cent of households were 11 times more likely than their peers from the richest 20 per cent to drop out of high school. One-third of Hispanic children drop out before the 9th grade – three times the rate for the rest of the population.

- The children of rich households are far more likely to go to college. More than 80 per cent of children from the wealthiest households who graduate from high school proceed to college, compared with only 34 per cent for children from the poorest households. Meanwhile, white high-school graduates are four times more likely to complete college than their African-American or Hispanic counterparts.

The disparity in educational opportunities is continued into adult life. Approximately half of all food-stamp recipients in 1997 had not graduated from high school, underlining the link between educational deprivation in childhood and adult poverty. More than one-third of adults who received public assistance had the lowest level of literacy skills in a National Adult Literacy Survey commissioned by the US Congress. Perhaps more than in any other industrial society, the distribution of income and opportunity in the USA reflects the institutionalised disadvantages facing poor children from birth.

The unequal distribution of opportunities for education has had a profound and growing impact on the trend towards increasing income inequality. The underlying reasons for this trend are disputed: some accounts stress the role of technological change, others the impact of cheap imports, and still others failures in manufacturing policy. What is not in dispute is the fact that differences in education and skill levels are increasingly linked to income inequalities. Income disparity has widened fastest between people who graduated from college and those who graduated from high school, or dropped out before graduation. Average wages for those who graduated only from high school have fallen by 15 per cent over the past two decades.

(Sources: Children's Defence Fund, *The State of America's Children,* CDF, 1998; D. McMurrer and I. Sawhill, *Getting Ahead: Economic and Social Mobility in America,* Washington: Urban Institute Press, 1998; National Centre for Education Statistics, 'Drop-out Rates in the US', 1996, US Department of Education, December 1997.)

But, as more recent evidence from the USA and Britain confirms, schools can magnify the effects of poverty and social polarisation (see the box on page 51). This is why education policy needs to be developed as part of a wider strategy for overcoming poverty and social disadvantage.

Education and globalisation

Differences in education provide an important part of the explanation for existing inequalities in the distribution of wealth between countries and within countries. However, important as education is today, it will play an even more important role in determining future patterns of income distribution. This is because knowledge, and the ability to process it, is increasingly shaping the production of wealth, and the distribution of wealth between countries and between households.

As education grows in importance, income distribution within countries will increasingly reflect the distribution of educational opportunity. At an international level, the distribution of global wealth will follow similar patterns. The existing income gap between 'education-rich' and 'education-poor' countries has the potential to turn into a chasm, with devastating implications for global poverty-reduction prospects. As Nelson Mandela has written: 'Eliminating the distinction between information rich and information poor countries is critical to eliminating other inequalities between North and South.'[90] Technology transfer has a role to play in the elimination of this division; but without rapid progress towards universal primary education, the foundations needed to close the 'digital divide' between rich and poor nations will not be in place.

Globalisation and the 'knowledge economy'

International economic life is being transformed by a revolution that began approximately two decades ago. Globalisation, or the surge in flows of trade and finance, is part of that revolution – but only a minor part. The more fundamental shift has been in the way that wealth is produced. Two hundred and fifty years ago, the first Industrial Revolution was driven by steam power, physical labour, and money. Comparative advantage was defined by endowments of these resources. The textile mills of Lancashire were able to produce cloth because they had access to water-power and capital. Technological innovation was important, but the technologies that drove the Industrial Revolution wererelatively simple. This began to change during the second industrial revolution at the end of the nineteenth century, when industries were transformed by innovations in organic chemistry and electromagnetism.

Physical resources remained central to wealth creation, but the capacity to develop and adapt scientific innovations became critical. Countries lacking in this area – such as Britain – were left behind (see the box on page 54). Today, new technologies are further weakening the relationship between physical resources and wealth production. In future, economic wealth and prosperity will be derived largely from an intangible resource widely referred to as 'knowledge capital'.[91]

The transformation from a world dominated by physical factors of production to one dominated by knowledge implies a shift in the locus of economic power as profound as that which took place after the first Industrial Revolution. It is a shift which has important implications for the role of education. As production processes and trade become more knowledge-intensive, patterns of wealth distribution will increasingly reflect the distribution of educational opportunity, both within countries and between countries. Failure to close the education divide now separating rich and poor will undermine efforts to achieve the more equitable patterns of economic growth essential for the reduction of poverty. Countries that fail to develop education systems capable of responding to the challenge will fall further behind, with attendant costs to their citizens. In the nineteenth century, Britain failed to manage the transition from the first to the second industrial revolution partly because of the chronic neglect of basic education – a salutary lesson for governments at the start of the twenty-first century.

In the nineteenth century, Britain failed to manage the transition from the first to the second industrial revolution partly because of the chronic neglect of basic education – a salutary lesson for governments at the start of the twenty-first century.

Information technologies are at the heart of the new processes driving wealth creation. Productivity and competitiveness are, to an increasing extent, determined by knowledge generation and information processing.[92] New information and communications technologies, based on micro-electronics and telecommunications, provide the infrastructure for the new economy. The background to the development of this infrastructure is complex, but the key point is that telecommunications and information technology are converging, since both depend on the digital transmission of 'bits', or data written in the binary language understood by computers. The resulting technological advances have been dramatic. The capacity of computers, communications networks, and information storage and retrieval systems has grown faster than any technology in history.[93] Over the past decade, the processing power of computers using the same-sized micro-chip has increased one hundredfold, while the speed with which they operate has multiplied a thousandfold. At the same time, the cost of digital transmission and computer equipment has fallen dramatically, and the range and

Education and national prosperity – Britain as a bad example

The intimate relationship between education and national prosperity is not a recent discovery. At the start of the twentieth century, the British Prime Minister, Arthur Balfour, lamented the fact that his country was 'behind all continental rivals in education'. He was not understating the problem. By 1870, when Britain was embarking on the timid reforms that would ultimately lead to the principle of State financing for compulsory universal primary education, one child in every 1000 attended secondary school – one-quarter of the ratio achieved in France. But it was not until the turn of the century that British policy makers finally acknowledged that the country's under-financed, poor-quality and class-ridden education system had helped to erode the competitiveness of the national economy.

Some historians have challenged the view that education, or a generalised lack of it, contributed to Britain's industrial decline. They point out that the enormous expansion of national wealth produced in the century after the Industrial Revolution was achieved without a huge investment in education. But the technological triumphs of the first phase of industrialisation were relatively simple inventions, based as they were on 'learning by doing'.

During the second half of the nineteenth century, the pattern of innovation changed, with the marriage of science and technology opening a new era. The major technological advances required knowledge of scientific subjects such as organic chemistry (in the field of dyes and textiles, and pharmaceuticals) and electromagnetism (in dynamos and generators), and their application required increasingly skilled workforces. In iron and steel, Britain continued to lead in innovation, but it was the industries of Germany and the USA that applied the new technologies. Britain pioneered the chemical industry, but by 1910 it was producing only one-third of the output achieved by German industries. In machine-tools it was the USA that led the way in applying new technologies to mass-production industries. And by 1910, US companies were providing the finance and technology to electrify the London Underground system. In the space of less than half a century, Britain had been transformed from the leading and most dynamic industrial economy into the most sluggish and conservative industrial economy.

The contrast with its industrial rivals is striking. Most had seen the economic potential inherent in the development of mass education systems and had invested heavily in this area. In France, technical colleges, industrial schools, and a local schools system was established in the first half of the nineteenth century. German governments invested heavily in developing a network of trade and technical schools during the same period. It was these schools that provided the chemists who developed the corporations such as Hoescht, BASF, Bayer, and Agfa, that swept Britain out of international markets. In the United States, the textile magnates of New England laid the foundations of a mass public education system in the 1840s. Their motives were not even remotely altruistic. They wanted better-educated workers to raise productivity and scientists to innovate, all in the interests of enlarging profit margins and overtaking Britain. The increasing reliance on formal mass education for the diffusion of scientific knowledge had momentous consequences, both in opening up new branches of knowledge and in linking education systems to economic activity.

Yet in the midst of this explosion of educational activity, British governments agonised over the merits of using taxes to pay for education, and over the political threats of educating the working classes. By 1850, when countries such as the Netherlands, Switzerland, France, and Germany had achieved virtually universal primary education, Britain had fewer than half of its children in school, and was spending far less per pupil. It was not until the 1880s that primary education became compulsory and free; there was no public system of secondary education until 1902; and it was not until 1914 that the school-leaving age was raised to 14. The main purpose of mass public education was to provide working-class children with the rudiments of instruction as cheaply as possible, and with a premium on values stressing obedience. State support was linked to pupils passing tests in basic literacy and numeracy and to 'payment by results' – a system which encouraged rote-learning and was condemned by a contemporary Chief Inspector of schools as 'an ingenious instrument for arresting the mental growth of the child'.

(Sources for box opposite: W. Carr and A. Harnett, *Education and the Struggle for Democracy,* Buckingham: Open University Press, 1997; A. Green, *Education and State Formation: the Rise of Education Systems in England, France and the USA,* Basingstoke: Macmillan, 1990; D. Landes, *The Wealth and Poverty of Nations,* London: Little, Brown and Company, 1998; E. Hobsbawm, *Industry and Empire*, London: Penguin, 1968.)

sophistication of services provided (from faxes to virtual private networks) is constantly increasing. One service in particular – the Internet – has transformed the flow and accessibility of information. The World Wide Web has created some 60 million documents since 1992 (it took the US Library of Congress 195 years to collect 14 million books). The Internet is one of the fastest-growing sites of international commercial activity.

According to some accounts, the increased volume of trade and investment activity in international economic relations is what is driving globalisation. This is at best a partial truth. While economic transactions between countries are intensifying, this aspect of globalisation is not new. The changes are more quantitative than qualitative. What is new is the technological infrastructure underpinning globalisation. The convergence of computers and telecommunications has created a global community in which time-zones are more important than geographical borders.[94] Information technology has removed time and distance from the competitive equation. It has also produced a new source of wealth: knowledge applied to create value. For firms and national economies alike, wealth generation is now largely based on the application of ideas and information to production and marketing. This change is reflected in efforts in the World Trade Organisation and elsewhere by transnational companies to increase the returns to knowledge through patents. Since knowledge is the key input in the production of profit, there is a powerful corporate self-interest in maximising returns through patents that raise the cost of knowledge transfer.

Some aspects of the Information Revolution are immediately visible, especially to populations living in rich countries. Others are less visible, but no less important in the way that they are reshaping social and economic life. The rise of service industries, the development of global financial markets, the increasing mobility of capital, the globalisation of production under the auspices of transnational companies, and the expansion of an English-language, USA-dominated, homogenised 'world culture' and 'world media' are all manifestation of the Information Revolution. Changes in economic life have been equally dramatic. The average weight of one dollar's worth of US exports has halved since 1970. The reason: an increase in the knowledge component

55

of final value.[95] Whether in washing machines, pharmaceuticals, or cars, the value generated by knowledge-based inputs is increasing. Some 70 per cent of the average value in US cars can now be traced to this source, according to one estimate – and more North Americans are now employed in making computers than in the car industry. For the industrialised countries as a whole, the World Bank estimates that more than half of GDP is accounted for by the production and distribution of intangible knowledge.[96]

For the industrialised countries as a whole, the World Bank estimates that more than half of GDP is accounted for by the production and distribution of intangible knowledge.

The growing importance of information to the generation of wealth is most clearly apparent in the US economy. By one calculation, the value of the USA's stock of intangible investment (research and development, education and training) overtook the value of the stock of physical capital (buildings and machinery) in the 1980s. In terms of market capitalisation, Microsoft long ago overtook companies such as Ford and General Motors, which have traditionally dominated the industrial landscape. Capital-intensive, knowledge-based industries are the new growth centres in the US economy. At the beginning of 1999, the Internet company America On Line was valued at $66bn, compared with a market value of $52bn for General Motors – but it employed 10,000 people, compared with 600,000 for General Motors.[97] Even allowing for stock-market over-valuation, something fundamental has changed. The surge in productivity growth in the USA was twice as high in the second half of the 1990s as in the 1980s, and was in large part the product of heavy investment in new information technologies in the first half of the decade. While the USA has led the way, all other OECD countries are following a similar path.

It is not just the national economic life of OECD countries that is being transformed. The knowledge revolution has also left its mark on international trade. The share of high-technology goods in international trade has doubled over the past two decades. It now represents about one-fifth of the total value of international trade – and the trend is unmistakably upwards. Since 1980, the share of value added to exports by high-technology goods has risen by over 50 per cent in the USA, and by over 100 per cent in Britain.[98] Over the same period, the share of non-mineral primary commodities in international trade has fallen by half, to 13 per cent, and terms of trade for labour-intensive manufactured goods are now deteriorating almost as rapidly as those for primary commodities.[99] Meanwhile, payments to holders of patents are increasing by 20 per cent per annum, again reflecting the growing importance – and value – of knowledge in technology transfer. The clear implication is that countries unable to add value to production through the application of knowledge-based production processes will occupy an increasingly marginal role in international trade.

Implications for developing countries and poverty reduction

Like any process of historical change, globalisation is changing the distribution of economic wealth and power. It is creating winners and losers, both at an international level and within countries. The winners are those with the skills and assets that they need to participate in the new knowledge-based global economy: the losers are those without. For poor people in poor countries, there are major opportunities; the creation of jobs linked to software industries in India is one example. But the threats are immense. Globalisation and new technologies are rapidly increasing the returns to education at a time when there are massive inequalities in educational opportunity. For the millions of poor households denied the chance of even the most rudimentary education, and for countries where average education levels are low, globalisation points clearly in the direction of rapid marginalisation. As wealth becomes more concentrated in rich countries and among higher-income households, the prospects for reaching the 2015 target of halving income poverty will recede.

Most countries in sub-Saharan Africa do not have even one computer for every 1000 people.

Part of the problem can be traced to 'the digital divide', or inequality in access to new technologies. The changes in communications and information technology underpinning the new economic order have been concentrated overwhelmingly in North America, Europe, and the Pacific Rim, regions with high per capita incomes and almost universal access to telephones. More than 90 per cent of telecommunications traffic takes place between countries in these regions. Almost all people in these countries depend on telephones, to a greater or lesser degree, in their daily lives. But more than half of the world's population, living in poor countries, has never used a telephone.[100] Almost one-third of the world's population lives in countries that, taken together, have fewer than 19 million telephone lines between them – fewer than in Italy. Whereas developed countries have 37 telephone lines for every 100 people, developing countries have only 2.3 lines, and there are more telephone lines in Tokyo than in the whole of sub-Saharan Africa.[101]

Access to information technology is equally distorted. Most high-income industrialised countries have more than 315 computers for every 1000 people. Most countries in sub-Saharan Africa do not have even one computer for every 1000 people. This is hardly surprising, given that computers are expensive and need a reliable source of power, which is lacking in much of Africa.[102] But inadequate access to computers is one of the forces that threatens to exclude many poor countries from participating in the global economy on more equitable terms.

The consequences of rapid technological change are already being felt. Much of the economic analysis of new technology has focused on the hi-tech end of the market. Increasingly, though, success in adding value to exports and capturing a larger share of the final market price of agricultural and mineral exports depends on the processing of market information on prices, storage, and demand. Inability to operate in the information market is already costing desperately poor countries foreign exchange and government revenue. Over the past decade, the share of the 42 Least Developed Countries in world exports has fallen from 1 per cent to 0.5 per cent. Given that exports account on average for 25 per cent of GDP, this has grave implications for poverty reduction. But any attempt to reverse this decline will require a marked increase in the value added to exports through local knowledge, implying a prior improvement in average education performance. Much the same is true for other developing countries. Over the past three decades, only East Asia has significantly increased its share of world trade. Developing countries as a group still account for only about one-fifth of global trade flows. Once again, changing this picture will require a stronger performance in the knowledge-intensive sectors of international trade that are growing most rapidly.

Making access available and affordable to poor countries and poor people should be viewed as a central part of the development process.

Closing the digital divide

What can be done to bridge the digital divide separating rich and poor countries? Efforts to address this question have tended to focus on support for technology transfer – and there is no doubt that much more could be done in this area. Ultimately, however, no amount of technology transfer will be able to compensate for the huge inequalities in education that divide rich from poor.

This is not to understate the potential benefits of the new technologies for poverty reduction. As with any technology, the impact of information technologies on inequality and poverty will depend on how they are deployed and who has access to them. Making access available and affordable to poor countries and poor people should be viewed as a central part of the development process. In Bangladesh, the Grameen Bank, which provides micro-credit to small producers, has built on its experience to extend access to cellular technology.[103] Its telecommunications business uses micro-credit to enable members, mainly women, to obtain global telecommunications lines and cellphones, on the condition that they in turn sell access to their lines at controlled prices to other village members. So far, 65,000 villages have been targeted for the next six years. Recent evaluations by the Canadian government's development ministry point to important benefits for women who are enabled to reduce transport costs, achieve higher prices, and reduce middleman costs.

Education is another area that can benefit. Communications technologies can provide access to resources, and facilitate teacher support and curriculum development. The African Virtual University, based in Nairobi, is aiming to increase university enrolments and improve the quality and relevance of instruction throughout the region. To date it has installed 27 satellite receiver terminals, and it has developed a digital library to compensate for the chronic shortage of scientific journals.[104] In the industrialised countries, governments, schools, and industry have pioneered new approaches to facilitate interactive distance learning. There is scope for adapting these initiatives for use in developing countries.

Technology transfer dominates much of the debate on how best to close the 'digital divide'. Some of the Group of Seven industrialised countries are developing major initiatives in this area, including the United States, Japan, and Britain. This is in keeping with the broader received wisdom of the day. The World Bank in particular has made much of the potential for developing countries to leap over the digital divide by importing new technologies. It points out that while the start-up costs for ICT industries are enormous, import costs for computers and telecommunication equipment are relatively cheap, and getting cheaper. Technological innovation can be imported, so the argument runs, and installed in the local economy.

Even at a superficial technical level, this approach understates some of the more complex problems related to technology transfer. The process of technological 'catching-up' will impose a huge burden on the balance of payments of many countries. Unsustainable debt, deteriorating terms of trade, and, in many of the poorest countries, chronic trade deficits are major barriers to the importation of high-technology goods. Another problem is rooted in international trade rules. These are designed to raise the cost of technology transfer through intellectual-property protection. Under World Trade Organisation rules, patent protection is provided for twenty years, giving 'owners' of technology exclusive rights – including the right to extract royalty payments from importing countries. Reducing the scope and duration of patent protection would help to reduce import costs, but this is an area in which the rhetoric of Western governments on poverty reduction is at odds with their commercial self-interest. There are powerful corporate interests at stake, and Northern economies stand to benefit most from strong patent rules. In 1995, licensing and royalty payments exceeded $60bn, with the USA running a trade surplus in intellectual-property payments to $20bn.[105] Stronger rules on intellectual property thus have the effect of increasing the costs of technology transfer and stifling innovation in poor countries, widening the knowledge gap in the process. They will also reinforce the domination of richer countries in world trade, with adverse distributional effects. Direct foreign investment can, to some degree, overcome financial constraints in technology transfer by installing cutting-edge technologies in developing countries. As globalisation increases the mobility of capital and creates international production systems, this is already happening to some degree. The problem is that investment flows are highly concentrated in a small group of developing countries, and foreign investors seldom prioritise the transfer of cutting-edge technology.

What and how children are taught in primary school, and the numbers of children entering and completing secondary school are crucial determinants of the quality of higher education.

Recognition of such problems has prompted some governments in developing countries to place a premium on the development of local technological capacity, with investment in higher levels of education made the central priority. At one level this is justified. In the new global economy, the production of knowledge, as well as its adaptation to the context of a particular country, is associated with university teaching and research. But high and fast-rising university enrolments must be built on solid foundations if they are to contribute to sustained growth. What and how children are taught in primary school, and the numbers of children entering and completing secondary school are crucial determinants of the quality of higher education.

Therein lies the real problem. In much of sub-Saharan Africa, more than half of the primary-school age group is denied the opportunity of even the most rudimentary primary education, and fewer than one-third of children make the transition to secondary school. In Latin America it is not uncommon for more than one-quarter of children to drop out of primary school. Failure at the primary-school level restricts the flow of students into higher levels of education. Poor-quality teaching at this level also hampers efforts to develop the flexible learning skills needed in the new economy. Perhaps more importantly, the failure of primary-education systems produces the mass illiteracy that excludes people from the opportunities created by new technologies. Low average levels of educational attainment restrict the capacity of poor countries to integrate new technologies into the economy in a manner that generates a wide dispersion of benefits. Brazil can import the latest computer hardware; but, with only half of its children completing secondary school, it is ill-equipped to develop the productive system needed to accommodate it – let alone to ensure that the poor will benefit. Similarly, even if foreign investors do transfer state-of-the-art information technologies to Africa, with university enrolment rates of around 7 per cent and half of the population illiterate, high-technology sectors are bound to remain isolated enclaves producing high-value-added goods in low-value-added economies.

It is, of course, true that basic education alone is insufficient to equip countries and people with the flexible learning skills essential for success in the new economy. Ultimately, a far higher proportion of children will need to enter higher education, where the skills associated with new technologies can be learned and developed. But effective higher-education systems cannot be built on the foundations of grossly inadequate basic education systems, especially when a significant proportion of the population does not even have access to these systems. That is why achievement of basic education for all is a precondition for more equitable patterns of globalisation and closure of the digital divide.

The knowledge economy and income distribution

It is not just the digital divide between rich and poor countries that will influence future patterns of income distribution. The growing division between 'education-rich' and 'education-poor' countries is reflected at the household level within countries. There is strong evidence that technological progress has increased the wages of skilled, educated workers relative to those of unskilled workers lacking education, with those excluded from educational opportunity being left further behind.

Rising inequality between skilled and unskilled people is not a distant threat. It is already happening. In the industrialised world, the penalties faced by those without knowledge and skills are growing at an unprecedented rate. The lowest 10 per cent of wage earners in the USA have seen their income fall by 20 per cent since 1980 in real terms; the top 10 per cent are earning approximately 10 per cent more. Income disparities have widened fastest between adults with a college degree and those who do not progress beyond high school.[106] In several other OECD countries, inequality has increased more dramatically than at any time in the past hundred years. In Britain, income levels for the poorest 10 per cent fell during the 1980s, even as overall incomes were rising. It is estimated that education differences accounted for about one-third of the increase in inequality. The generalised shift of the economy towards more knowledge-intensive industries was a contributory factor. The wage gap between degree holders and adults with no formal qualifications increased from 61 per cent to 89 per cent over the period 1978–92.[107]

Social fault-lines between the skilled and the unskilled are also emerging in many developing countries. As in the industrialised world, there are winners and loser in the new knowledge-based economy, but all too often it is the wealthy who dominate the ranks of the winners, and the poor who account for the overwhelming majority of the losers. While trends in income distribution reflect a diverse array of influences associated with domestic policies, liberalisation, global economic integration, and technological change, differences in access to education are critical. In Latin America, the ratio of the income of the bottom 20 per cent to the top 20 per cent is the lowest in the world, roughly 1:16 – and divisions rooted in education are perpetuating the problem. During the 1990s, the wage gap between the skilled and the unskilled increased by 30 per cent in Peru, by 20 per cent in Colombia, and by 25 per cent in Mexico.[108]

Foreign investment in China is concentrated in the high-growth coastal areas, which have the highest levels of educational attainment.

Latin America is an extreme case of income inequality, but it is not alone in experiencing widening social divisions. Thailand has the fastest-growing rate of income inequality in the world, in part because the demand for educated labour employed in export industries has exacerbated a widening gap between urban and rural incomes. In China and Vietnam, liberalisation programmes have spurred growth, yet large sections of the population have not benefited. In each case, it is the regions, districts, and households with the most limited access to education – interior China, highland Vietnam, rural Mexico – that are being left behind. Foreign investment in China is concentrated in the high-growth coastal areas, which have the highest levels of educational attainment. In Vietnam, rapid growth has been concentrated in lowland delta areas, which have benefited from rice-market liberalisation, and in Ho Chi Minh City, which has experienced a surge of foreign investment. The poorest provinces – such as the Central Highlands and Northern Uplands – with the weakest education base have suffered the slowest growth. In Mexico, the poverty-belt states in the south where educational deprivation is most intense are being left further and further behind a more prosperous north, which is linked to the US economy through trade and investment.

Set against these problems, globalisation has created some spectacular success stories. One example is Bangalore, India's 'Silicon Plateau' and the centre of a thriving software industry. Skill levels here are exceptionally high, and employment opportunities have grown dramatically. The value of its exports, mainly to the USA, exceeds $1bn per annum.[109] One of the fastest-growing parts of the industry is the 'remote maintenance' sector, which carries out computerised repairs for companies in other parts of the world. Yet for all the success achieved by Bangalore and a few other centres in India, the benefits in terms of poverty reduction have been limited. Poor people excluded from the new economy by illiteracy and poverty derive few benefits. This is one of the reasons why the link between economic growth and poverty reduction in India is weakening. As economist Amartya Sen has written:

New centres of excellence such as Bangalore can prosper and flourish. Yet even 100 Bangalores would not solve India's poverty and deep-seated inequality. For this to happen, many more people must participate in growth. This will be difficult to achieve across the barriers of illiteracy, ill health and inequalities in social and economic opportunities.[110]

Education, democracy, and empowerment

There is a paradox at the heart of current debates on education. As suggested in this chapter, there is overwhelming evidence that education generates important benefits for human development. It is associated with more rapid and more equitable growth, it contributes to reductions in child mortality, and it enhances public health. Many of the gains result from the fact that education empowers people, enabling them to exercise greater choice and to exert more control over the events that shape their lives. There is, however, a dark side to education. The broad purpose of national education systems is to prepare children to participate in the economic, political, and social activities of the country, and to accept its values.[111] Education is also used to transmit culture, to reinforce the status quo and, in some cases, to project attitudes that promote ideas of superiority and inferiority. Moreover, for all its liberating qualities, many children experience formal education as a system of learning that restricts initiative and creativity, rather than nurturing them.

The relationship between education, democracy and empowerment, is complex. Education is clearly not a sufficient condition for democracy. At the same time, mass exclusion from education is as bad for democracy as it is for poverty reduction. There is also a sense in which education can create an impetus towards democracy, even if this is not what governments have in mind. As J.K Galbraith has written, 'Education not only makes democracy possible; it also makes it essential.'[112] Mass education creates the skills needed to assess and monitor government actions. It also creates the demand to be heard. Constitutions, legislation, and international treaties may provide the judicial backing for civil and political rights, but it is education that creates the 'voice' through which rights can be claimed and protected.

Education and democracy: old themes in a current debate

Debates about the relationship between education and governance are not of recent origin. They were thriving in fourth century BC in Athens, where Aristotle castigated law-makers for leaving the provision of education to private households. '*It is*', he wrote, '*a lawgiver's duty to arrange for the education of the young. In States where this is not done, the quality of the constitution suffers.*'[113]

Throughout history, reformers have seen education as a source of liberation – and as a driving force for democratisation. Tom Paine, whose views inspired the architects of the American constitution, saw education as an inherent right of citizenship and a precondition for good governance. As he put it in *The Rights of Man* in 1791: '*A nation under a well-regulated government should permit none to remain uninstructed. It is monarchical and aristocratic government only that requires ignorance for its support.*'[114] He went on to propose a tax on the wealthy to finance the education of the poor – an option that most governments in Latin America still refuse to contemplate, more than 200 years later. In nineteenth-century Britain, the Chartist movement and radical reformers like Mary Wollstonecraft and William Lovett took up this theme. They saw education not just as a right in itself, but as a tool of emancipation and the key to achieving wider political and social rights, including more representative government, the eradication of child labour, and basic trade union rights.[115]

It was not only radical social reformers who saw popular education as part of a wider strategy for achieving democracy. Economists today frequently justify investment in education on the grounds that it is essential to economic success. Classical economists had a different view. They were interested in education more as a right of citizenship than as a means to increased productivity.[116] Adam Smith was a strong advocate of universal basic education, arguing that it would enhance the dignity of work and improve social cohesion. Because the invisible hand of the market would, in Smith's view, invariably fail to finance the education of the poor, he advocated public financing almost one hundred years before it became a reality.[117] In similar vein, John Stuart Mill argued that there could be no real political rights if people lacked the educational skills to understand and use them. This perspective led him to the unfortunate conclusion that the uneducated should not have the right to vote. But it also prompted him to depart from his broader philosophy, which was premised on the conviction that States should play a minimal role. He dismissed out of hand the dominant view of Britain's upper classes that State taxation to finance free education would be an infringement of their liberty. *'Is it not,'* he wrote, *'a self-evident axiom that the state should require and compel the education ... of every human being who is born its citizen?* [118]

In nineteenth-century Britain, the notion of economic reform meant very different things to different protagonists in the debate. For much of the upper class, the demand for popular education presented two serious problems: it was politically threatening and potentially costly. In an effort to dispel such fears, part of the reform camp emphasised the value of education as a low-cost option for servicing the needs of industry, while at the same time reinforcing social control. 'It is not proposed,' wrote a prominent advocate of reform, 'that the children of the poor should be educated in a manner to elevate their minds above the rank they are destined to fill in society.'[119] Mass education was to be designed primarily to create a supply of not particularly skilled but well-disciplined workers to operate in large-scale industrial units. Repetitive mass instruction was seen as a useful preparation for a system of low-wage employment, and it was inextricably bound up with the maintenance of social order and protection of vested interest. The corollary of the limited aim of mass education was a curriculum designed to promote rote-learning, mastery of basic literacy and numeracy, and respect for authority.[120] William Lovett criticised the pedagogy of his day, condemning it as *'a rote-learning, memory-loading system dignified by the name of education'*. Along with other reformers, he argued for education to be geared towards personal development. But rote-learning remained the order of the day until well into the twentieth century.[121]

Nowhere was State action in education less oriented towards realising human potential than in the colonies of European powers. It is sometimes forgotten that, in much of the developing world, education systems were developed under colonial authorities whose motivations owed less to considerations of personal development and democracy than to those of cost and self-interest. Their guiding theme was that any education provision should be cheap, financed out of local revenue, and geared to the labour needs of the colonial administration. Where education was provided, it typically involved the export of Western-style education, aimed at preparing a small (predominantly male) population for service in the administrative system. European powers exported their languages, their curricula, and their teaching methods, systematically eroding local cultures in the process.[122] African children were taught about European geography, European 'discoveries' of African rivers and mountains, and European history. In the 1920s, the African Education Commission condemned what it described as a wholesale failure to adapt school work to African conditions, to respect native languages, to invest in teacher training, and to extend coverage of basic education systems.[123] Its report fell on deaf ears. As the African historian Walter Rodney later wrote, 'Colonial schooling was education for subordination.'[124]

At Independence in the early 1960s, fewer than 3 per cent of Africa's young people attended secondary school, and adult illiteracy rates stood at over 80 per cent.

Colonised countries suffered not just from an excess of Europeanised education, but from a deficiency in provision. When Dutch rule ended in Indonesia, fewer than 10 per cent of adults were literate. At Independence in the early 1960s, fewer than 3 per cent of Africa's young people attended secondary school, and adult illiteracy rates stood at over 80 per cent. Little of the fantastic wealth generated by colonialism found its way back into the education of local populations. As late as 1958, the British Colonial Office decreed that full primary education was unaffordable in Northern Rhodesia (modern Zambia), despite the huge transfer of finances that was taking place in favour of Britain.[125]

Resentment at the failure to extend educational opportunity fuelled the rise of nationalist movements. In Africa, the first generation of post-Independence leaders such as Julius Nyerere, Jomo Kenyatta, and Kwame Nkrumah made universal primary education a central theme in wider strategies to develop national self-reliance.[126] Yet some aspects of the colonial legacy survive down to this day in the shape of top–down education planning, irrelevant curricula, inappropriate languages of instruction, and an undue emphasis on rote-learning.

The potential for empowerment

Efforts to establish a causal relationship between education, democracy, and the rule of law have been far from convincing. Many countries that have performed very strongly in education (such as China) have, by most standards, achieved levels of democracy that compare unfavourably with far weaker performers (such as India). Other countries have combined high levels of educational attainment with highly authoritarian governance – Malaysia and Singapore being two obvious examples.

Few governments have prioritised democracy and empowerment in developing their education systems. Economic modernisation and 'nation-building' have figured far more prominently. In South Korea, the extension of public education in the 1950s was driven by a concern to increase skill levels in the interests of rapid growth. In Indonesia, the development of mass education at the start of the 1960s was motivated by a concern to promulgate an authoritarian political ideology, and to instil an unquestioning acceptance of authority. Almost all countries have seen education as an element of 'nation-building', which is often a euphemism for the suppression of minority cultures. In Latin American countries such as Peru and Guatemala, schools have been seen as vehicles for promoting the use of the Spanish language and a dominant view of nationhood, in which indigenous peoples figure only to the extent that they are expected to accept both.[127]

But whatever the intention of governments, the rapid expansion of educational opportunity has the potential to produce unplanned outcomes, including an increased 'voice' for the poor. Even where education systems are designed with oppressive intent, they frequently produce political protest. In South Africa, the Bantu Education Act of 1953, which placed the stamp of *apartheid* firmly on the country's education system, prompted a campaign of protest which lasted, with a varying degree of intensity, until the end of the *apartheid* era. Initially, the protest was led by Africans educated under the previous regime, among them Nelson Mandela.[128] In similar fashion, the leaders of the anti-colonial movements that led Africa to independence were products of missionary-school systems. Student protests in countries such as China, Indonesia, and South Korea provide further evidence of the potential for education to produce dissent.

Even where education systems are designed with oppressive intent, they frequently produce political protest.

The impact of education on democracy may be more powerful at a local level. Within communities, education can give individuals the self-confidence needed to engage in discussions and to influence decisions. One study in Nepal found that almost half of rural women who had completed a nine-month basic literacy course said that they would be confident about expressing their views to the community, compared with only 4 per cent of non-literate women.[129] Responses during a World Bank poverty assessment in Bangladesh pointed to similar outcomes. Women with a secondary education were three times more likely to attend a political meeting than women with no education. Although less tangible than improved health or higher incomes, such outcomes clearly reflect the importance of education for political participation.[130] Education imparts the skills and confidence needed to participate in political processes, from which the uneducated are often excluded. Almost half the population of Kerala, India's most literate State, read a newspaper on a regular basis; one-quarter of rural labourers are regular readers. This compares with a national average of one in five people, and 2 per cent of rural labourers, reading newspapers.[131] While literacy is only one element required for real democracy, the near universal literacy attained in Kerala means that people can make informed judgements and access the information needed to assess the performance of public bodies.

Social movements in some countries have made education reform an integral part of a broader agenda for political democratisation. In Brazil, education indicators for landless rural communities compare unfavourably with those for much poorer countries in sub-Saharan Africa. Poverty, under-investment by government, and a curriculum widely perceived as being irrelevant to local needs are among the causes. The Movimento Sem Terra (SMT), the landless people's movement, has responded by placing education at the centre of its activities.[132] Because the landless are highly mobile, 'moving schools' have been developed, to follow the communities they serve. Wherever land occupations take place, the MST establishes schools and provides teachers. School curricula have been adjusted to meet local needs – and to assert the importance of claiming basic rights. The environment, agriculture, and the history of social movements in Brazil all figure prominently. Teacher-training programmes emphasise the participation of children and the development of an active learning environment. Adult literacy classes attached to the schools use materials directly relevant to local needs, including literature on health and basic rights. Above all, education is seen both as a source of individual advancement, and as a mechanism for achieving community empowerment and real democracy at a local level.

In other contexts, local non-government organisations are using similar techniques to protect rights through basic education. In Cambodia, Oxfam is working with tribal people in remote upland areas on the north-eastern border with Laos and Vietnam. These people have been hunting, gathering, and cultivating in the area for generations, but their land rights are being eroded by concessions granted to foreign timber companies. Many of the concessions are negotiated through political and legal processes from which tribal communities are excluded, in part as a result of their illiteracy. While ancestral rights are recognised in law, the relationship between these rights and private property rights is complex, and powerful vested interests have been able to use the judicial process to pursue their claims. One local NGO has developed course materials for adult education, designed simultaneously to improve

Almost half the population of Kerala, India's most literate State, read a newspaper on a regular basis; one-quarter of rural labourers are regular readers.

literacy skills and to increase local knowledge of how to use the legal system in defence of ancestral land rights.

Several NGOs have developed an expertise in the development of teaching and literacy materials that relate to local conditions. The REFLECT programme, pioneered by the British NGO ActionAid, is perhaps the best-known example. It has developed highly participative methods of instruction, with a premium placed on the acquisition of literacy skills through materials that reflect locally useful knowledge. Such approaches have the potential to reinforce democracy at a local level, because literacy is an important asset for communities seeking greater accountability from local authorities. In Mali, the government introduced a radical decentralisation strategy in the mid-1990s, aimed at transferring authority over a wide range of public services to district and regional bodies. However, it provided little public information about how the new system would operate. The information that was provided came in the form of written notices – of limited value to illiterate rural populations. One community-based organisation, supported by Oxfam, responded by developing a radio broadcasting service – Radio Douentza – linked to a distance-learning programme. The programme mobilised a network of literacy facilitators who used radio programme to run classes and communicate information about decentralised service provision. These examples could be multiplied many times over. They demonstrate the critical importance attached to education on the part of communities seeking to claim their basic rights, while at the same time working for political change.

Much has been made of the tension between education as a source of empowerment and democratisation, and education as a source of subordination, the transmission of power relations, and the preparation of individuals for narrow economic roles. Some have argued that education provided through formal State systems is inherently oppressive, placing an emphasis on the development of 'alternative' structures. Such approaches are of limited relevance for the vast majority of poor people. The real challenge is to reform attitudes to education and school practices. Evidently, getting girls into schools designed to reinforce their limited role as providers and carers is not a strategy for empowerment. Similarly, the application of rote-learning technologies to equip children with minimal levels of numeracy is not a viable education strategy for the twenty-first century, any more than it was for the nineteenth. Some of the presumed tensions in education reform may be more apparent than real. Education is a national investment, and it needs to transmit, among other things, economically useful knowledge. For poor people themselves, education is valuable because it is perceived as a route to success in hostile markets, and as a source of higher income. But education also has to equip individuals with the skills that they need to make informed judgements about their lives, and about the political processes in which they participate.

2

Education for all: promises and progress

Education has featured prominently in the targets set at international summits. At the 1990 World Conference on Education for All, held in Jomtien, Thailand, under the auspices of UN agencies and the World Bank, more than 155 governments adopted an ambitious set of goals, including universal primary education by the year 2000 and an 'expanded vision' of high-quality education for all. An amended version of these goals was adopted at the 1995 World Summit on Social Development, which shifted the target date for achieving universal primary education to 2015, and introduced the transitional target of gender equity by 2005. The World Education Forum, meeting in Dakar in 2000, brought the target-setting exercise full circle, marking the tenth anniversary of the Jomtien conference. It brought together more than 180 governments, whose representatives collectively reaffirmed their commitment to the vision of that conference.

Progress has been achieved since the first targets were set in 1990. Primary-school enrolment has increased, and the gender gap has narrowed. However, the rate of progress has been far too slow to achieve the targets set, especially in relation to gender equity. This has damaging implications not just for the state of education, but also for the wider 2015 human-development targets. In the words of the final communiqué adopted at the World Forum on education: 'Without accelerated progress towards education for all, national and internationally agreed targets for poverty reduction will be missed.'[1]

The first part of this Chapter briefly summarises the background to the international development targets for education. The second part examines the progress achieved in education since the Jomtien conference, and the prospects for 2015. The picture that emerges is uniformly bleak. All of the major quantitative targets have been missed by a wide margin, raising serious questions about the attainability of the 2015 goals. Qualitative progress is as important as quantitative progress, for the obvious reason that there is little point in extending the coverage of poor-quality education systems that fail to equip children with the skills they need in life. The second half of the chapter considers the quality of education, highlighting the scale of the deficit across all developing regions.

The education targets

The practice of setting international development targets during the 1990s reflected a resurgence of approaches to social development based on human rights. This marked a distinctive shift from the 1980s, when the notion that human-rights criteria could be extended to the social and economic responsibilities of States came under attack from doctrines stressing the primacy of market forces. The role of government, in the view of these doctrines, was not to protect inalienable social and economic rights, but to facilitate the expansion of markets, and to accept the social consequences of market outcomes.[2]

By the end of the decade, growing unease over the inequalities associated with radical free-market prescriptions had shifted the balance. The 1989 Convention on the Rights of the Child applied a human-rights framework to child rights, with education figuring prominently. Recalling the Universal Declaration of Human Rights, it confirmed the commitment of all signatories (in Article 29) to make primary education compulsory and available free to all, and to work towards a wide range of qualitative goals.[3] In similar vein, the World Conference on Education for All in Jomtien reaffirmed the basic human right to education.[4] It also set out a bold and ambitious vision for translating the commitment to human rights into concrete strategies for action. Delivering on the right to education was, in the words of the Jomtien *Declaration* adopted by governments, 'a common and universal human responsibility'. The *Declaration* went on to outline an 'expanded vision' for education, with a focus on quality, child development, and the needs of the poorest countries. New partnerships, the mobilisation of additional resources, and more equitable relations between the developing and the developed worlds were central to the new vision. Six core goals were identified, combining a range of quantitative and qualitative targets in what was described as 'an expanded vision' of education for all. These were as follows:

- The expansion of early childhood care and development, especially for the poor and disadvantaged.
- Universal access to (and universal completion of) primary education by the year 2000.
- The reduction of adult illiteracy rates to one half of the 1990s levels by 2000, with an emphasis on female literacy.
- Improved learning achievement, based on the attainment of defined levels of performance with 'the focus of basic education ... on actual

learning acquisition and outcome, rather than exclusively upon enrolment ... and completion of certificate requirements'.

- Expansion of basic education and training for adults and youths.

- Improved dissemination of the knowledge, skills, and values required for sustainable development.[5]

The Jomtien conference

None of the basic ideas adopted at Jomtien was new; but at a time when progress towards education for all had stalled in many regions, when North–South co-operation was at a low ebb, and when the education systems of developing countries were collapsing under the burden of debt, economic stagnation, and rapid population growth, the conference appeared to set a new course.[6] Strong commitments were made on all sides. It was recognised that ultimate responsibility for achieving the targets set rested with Southern governments, who pledged to develop national education strategies and accord more weight to education in national budget priorities. Northern governments implicitly acknowledged that insufficient aid, unsustainable debt, and badly designed structural adjustment programmes had contributed to the education crisis in many countries, and promised action in each of these areas (see Chapter 6). The targets set were acknowledged to be highly ambitious. But the scale of the problem demanded decisive action. The *Declaration and Framework for Action* adopted by governments captured the sense of urgency that pervaded the World Conference on Education for All. Educational deprivation was identified as a cause as well as a consequence of widening income disparities within and between nations, of civil strife, and of poverty.

Educational deprivation was identified as a cause as well as a consequence of widening income disparities within and between nations, of civil strife, and of poverty.

Perhaps more than any other international summit in the 1990s, the World Conference on Education for All succeeded in conveying a sense that targets could be translated into meaningful action at regional, national, and international levels. The *Framework for Action* set out strategies at each of these levels and conveyed the clear message that the goal of education for all was attainable. Targets had a dual role, serving both to signal a political commitment and to provide a yardstick for measuring progress. As the *Framework* put it: 'Time-bound targets convey a sense of urgency and serve as a reference point against which indices of implementation and accomplishment can be compared ... Observable and measurable targets assist in the objective evaluation of progress.'[7]

The impetus created by Jomtien was reflected in a succession of international conferences sponsored by the UN during the first half of the 1990s.[8] The World Summit for Children (1990), the World Summit for Social Development (1995), and the Fourth World Conference on Women (1995) each produced declarations which integrated targets for basic education into wider strategies for human development. The declarations adopted at these subsequent summits envisaged a more moderate pace of reform, with the target date for universal primary education shifted from 2000 to 2015. But the use of targets to indicate progress towards what were established as basic human rights remained intact. The World Conference on Women deepened the commitments made on gender in education, setting the target date of 2005 for gender equality in primary-school enrolment and completion.

All of these education goals have been adopted by the Development Assistance Committee (DAC) of the OECD and are enshrined in the aid policies of many of its member states. Along with the UN and the World Bank, the DAC has also defined two key indicators for gender equity in education. At a school level, gender equity is defined as the enrolment rate for girls, expressed as a percentage of the enrolment rate for boys. A target for adult literacy has also been developed. This is expressed as the adult female literacy rate as a percentage of the male literacy rate, with the target being 100 per cent by 2015. Like the World Conference on education, the DAC sees the education targets as a mechanism for defining policy priorities and measuring outcomes. In the words of the 1996 report that adopted the UN targets: 'A few specific goals will help to clarify the vision of a higher quality of life for all people, and will provide guideposts against which progress towards that vision can be measured'.[9] By the same token, they provide a yardstick against which the extent of failure to achieve progress can be assessed.

The quantitative targets

Using the targets initially adopted by the World Conference on Education for All and subsequently adopted by the DAC, it is possible to assess progress in four areas where clear quantitative targets have been set:

- primary-school enrolment
- completion rates
- gender equity
- literacy.

It is important to stress at the outset that data on education are highly unsatisfactory. The most widely available indicator is the gross enrolment rate, which measures the total number of children enrolled in school as a percentage of the primary-school age cohort. However, enrolment is only a weak proxy for progress towards universal primary education. It does not capture levels of attendance or completion, nor does it provide an insight into the quality of education received by children in school. Another problem is that an increase in repetition has the effect of raising the gross enrolment rate. More useful as an indicator of progress is the net enrolment rate, which shows the ratio of children enrolled within the primary-school age cohort (usually 6–11 years of age). Unfortunately, net enrolment-rate data are notoriously unreliable. In the assessment and projections summarised below, we have used the most comprehensive recent data set for net enrolment rates, prepared for the mid-term review of the World Conference on Education for All, but the findings should be treated as indicative. Problems with enrolment data require that estimates for gender equity should be treated with similar caution. In the case of literacy, few developing countries conduct reliable surveys on a systematic basis, and divergent definitions of illiteracy restrict the scope for comparison across countries.

If all children of primary-school age were to receive a good-quality basic education lasting for at least four years, the problem of illiteracy could be resolved for the next generation.

Primary-school enrolment

If all children of primary-school age were to receive a good-quality basic education lasting for at least four years, the problem of illiteracy could be resolved for the next generation. Of course, this would not address the enormous backlog of adult illiteracy. Nor would it address the problems of over-age children who have dropped out of school. Both these problems require flexible responses in the State system, allied to support for non-formal education and adult-literacy schemes. But the rate of enrolment for children aged 6–11 into primary school – the net enrolment rate – is an important indicator of progress towards the goal of universal primary education.

Even within countries, there are often wide variations in estimates of the number of children not in school, depending on whether household-survey data or Education Ministry figures are used. Such considerations make estimating the total number of children out of school worldwide a hazardous affair, with international agencies producing divergent estimates (see the box on the next page). Our estimate is that 125 million children aged between 6 and 11 were not in school in 1995 – around one in five of all children in this age group. This is somewhat higher than the figure produced by UNESCO in its mid-term review of Jomtien (110 million), but broadly in line with estimates from the World Bank and UNICEF.

The problem with education statistics

How many children are not in school? The question is an important one, since it has implications for the financing and targeting of efforts to achieve universal basic education. Unfortunately, it is impossible to answer with any certainty.

According to UNESCO's mid-term review of the plan of action adopted at Jomtien, there were 110 million children out of school in 1995. The same organisation's World Education Report puts the figure at 145 million, while UNICEF estimated the 1995 figure at 135 million. Global estimates such as these are as good as the national reporting systems on which they are based – and these systems are exceptionally weak.

The Education Minister in Bangladesh has publicly complained that national estimates of the size of the population of primary-school age vary by about 2 million children. In Pakistan, subtle changes in enrolment and population data have had dramatic consequences. In 1997, an official estimate put the number of children out of school at 11 million. One year later, using different enrolment and age-cohort statistics, the numbers had fallen by half – a notional achievement which, on current trends, it will take the Pakistan Government several decades to emulate in reality.

International data-gathering in education is in a chaotic state. One reason for this is that the official definition of 'primary-school age' varies between countries (it is 5–9 in Pakistan and 7–13 in Zambia, for example). This problem is compounded by the fact that the internationally used range of 6 to 11 often does not conform to national ranges. Inevitable problems in data collection follow. They are compounded by the dubious use of data. For example, UNESCO uses the official government of India net enrolment ratio of 87 per cent. National household surveys, which many observers think are more accurate, suggest that the real NER is between 75 per cent (the World Bank figure) and 70 per cent (the figure used by UNICEF). Depending on which of the latter figures is used, the number of Indian children out of school rises by between 8 and 11 million, which is between 9 and 11 per cent of UNESCO's estimates of the global total of children not attending school in 1995.

Education-financing arrangements often exacerbate data-collection problems. In India, transfers of finance from the federal government to States, and from States to districts, are linked to the numbers of children enrolled – hence the incentive to over-report. Under-reporting is also common. An extensive survey of 200 school registers in Uganda for the period 1990–1996 revealed a 60 per cent increase in enrolment. Yet official national figures suggested that enrolments had stagnated over the same period. One likely explanation is that schools were required to send tuition fees that they levied on children to district education authorities. The smaller the number of children reported, the smaller the transfer. District bodies colluded in the under-reporting, since this reduced the per capita transfer of funds that they were required to make, thus releasing funds for spending in other areas.

Good statistics can help to identify social groups facing extreme problems in enrolment and completion. They can also help to identify financing requirements for achieving progress towards education for all. In most countries, however, the least information is available from the poorest areas, making it difficult to establish the scale of need. One of Oxfam's partners in Bangladesh is addressing the lack of data. The Campaign for People's Education (CAMPE) is a coalition of 450 NGOs working across the country, with a concentration in its poorest districts. Recognising the need to increase the awareness of the government and of donors about the education problems facing poor communities, CAMPE carries out an annual 'Education Watch' exercise, collecting data on a wide range of education indicators relevant to policy-makers. The exercise is a participative one, carried out with the involvement of local communities. Thus, their voice is heard in the identification of education problems, and they are involved in the formulation of responses.

Improved data-collection is a vital part of the education-reform process. At a national level, policy makers need to base their strategies on more accurate and regular flows of information. Collecting that information in a participative way can help to identify local solutions to local problems, as in Bangladesh. One of the most positive outcomes of the Education for All process has been the development of a dedicated statistical institute that will support the development of national capacity and help to consolidate the reporting systems of UNESCO, UNICEF, and the World Bank.

Measured against the original Jomtien target of universal primary education by 2000, there has been a huge shortfall in achievement. It is hard to quantify the extent of this shortfall. But if net enrolment had increased on an annualised basis at the rate required to achieve the 2000 goal, there would have been 61 million fewer children out of school in 1995.

Figure 2.1 shows the geographical and gender distribution of children of primary-school age who are not in school. It illustrates the scale of gender discrimination. Girls account for two out of every three children who are not enrolled – and there has been no decline in this ratio. On a regional basis, South Asia and sub-Saharan Africa account for the vast majority of out-of-school children: 56 million and 45 million respectively. These two regions have the lowest net enrolment rates, with more than 40 per cent of sub-Saharan African children and 20 per cent of South Asian children not registering at school (see Figure 2.2).

Behind this static picture are some widely divergent regional trends. In South Asia, a slowdown in population growth and a sustained increase in net enrolment, amounting to over 5 per cent during the period 1990–95, reduced the numbers out of school by 22 million. In East Asia, Latin America, and the Middle East, primary enrolment rates are relatively high. Each of these regions is within reach of achieving universal enrolment. That said, regional averages obscure national variations. In sub-Saharan Africa, some countries – such as Uganda and Malawi – have achieved rapid increases in enrolment. Conversely, some countries in Latin America – including Haiti and Guatemala – have enrolment rates of less than 70 per cent, as does Pakistan. But in broad terms, the

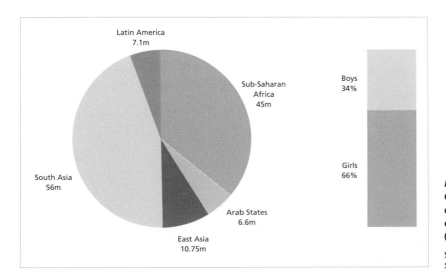

Figure 2.1
Geographical and gender distribution of the 125 million children out of school, 1995 (aged 6-11)

Source: Derived from UNESCO, *Statistical Yearbook*, Paris, 1997

77

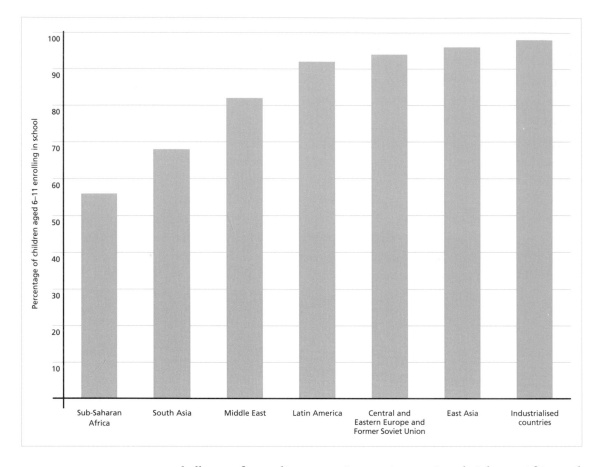

Figure 2.2
Primary net enrolment rates

Source: UNICEF,
The State of the World's Children,
New York, 1998

challenge of extending access is most intense in sub-Saharan Africa and South Asia.

In terms of enrolment levels, sub-Saharan Africa faces the most severe problems. Enrolment rates have increased, but only by just over 2 per cent a year, which is less than half of the rate of increase in the size of the primary-school population.[10] The gap between population-growth rate and enrolment-growth rate left 2 million more African children out of school in 1995 than in 1990. The region now has the highest ratio of children between the ages of 6 and 11 to the total population in the developing world, adding to the already formidable problems that it faces in progressing towards universal primary enrolment. As in other areas of human development, high population growth has undermined sub-Saharan Africa's ability to meet targets in basic education.

The overall picture in sub-Saharan Africa obscures the full extent of the problems facing the region. A group of 16 countries, accounting for more than half of the total population of African children aged 6–11, suffered a decline in net enrolment during the first half of the 1990s. This group includes Mozambique and Ethiopia, which have some of the world's lowest enrolment rates, as well as Nigeria, Tanzania, and Zambia. Several countries affected by conflict, including Sudan, Somalia, Liberia, and Rwanda, experienced either negligible growth in enrolments, or reversals.

Projections towards 2015: Africa's looming crisis

If current trends continue, what will be the global total of children out of school in 2015 – the target date for universal primary education? The question is hard to answer. Future outcomes are never a simple continuation of past trends. Moreover, any projection is highly sensitive to the choice of reference years selected. Notwithstanding these caveats, simple projections can help to identify broad patterns of change and some of the major problems that will emerge in the absence of public action.

We have developed one such projection for this report. It uses two simple variables to estimate numbers out of school in 2005 and 2015.[11] These variables are the trend rate for net enrolments over the period 1990–1995 and the trend rate in population increase for the 6–11 year-old age group over the same period. For countries that experienced a decline in enrolment over the trend period, we froze the net enrolment rate at its 1995 level, making the admittedly artificial assumption that the situation in these countries will neither deteriorate nor improve.

The picture that emerges from our projection is presented in Figure 2.3. There are two central findings. First, the current rate of progress in enrolment is too slow to reach the target of universal primary education by 2015. The number of children out of school will continue to decline, but far too slowly. About 96 million children will be out of school in 2005. In 2015, a quarter of a century after the World Conference on Education for All, 75 million will still be out of school. This suggests that, without a renewed commitment to the attainment of education for all, the international development target will be missed by a wide margin.

The second finding points unmistakably to a deepening crisis in sub-Saharan Africa, with failure in education reinforcing poverty-deepening marginalisation in international trade. Alone among developing regions, sub-Saharan Africa will see an increase in the number of children out of school between 1995 and 2015, with the number rising by 9 million. On present trends, South Asia's share in the total of children not in school will fall by half to 28 per cent in 2005, declining to less than 10 per cent over the period to 2015.

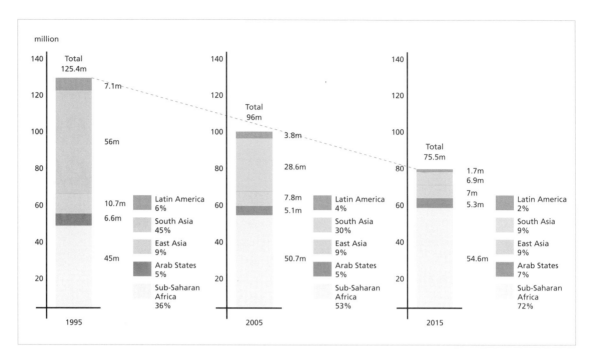

Figure 2.3
**Numbers and regional
distribution of children
out of school:
1995 and projection to 2015**

Source:
Derived from UNESCO *Statistical
Yearbook*, Paris, 1997

The implication of these projections is that sub-Saharan Africa will account for a fast-growing proportion of the total worldwide number of children not in school. At present, about 12 per cent of all children aged between the ages of 6 and 11 live in Africa. These children account for just over one-third of all children out of school. By 2005, their share in the total number out of school will have risen to just under a half, and by 2015 three out of every four children of primary-school age not in school will live in Africa. All developing regions will continue to face acute challenges in meeting the goal of good-quality education for all; but sub-Saharan Africa is the only region in which a large section of the population will be denied the opportunity to take even the first step on the education ladder by entering primary school. The face of a child not attending school over the next decade is increasingly likely to be that of an African child.

The full extent of the challenge facing sub-Saharan Africa becomes apparent where enrolment trends are disaggregated. There are 29 countries in the region where net enrolment rates are growing at less than half the level required to achieve universal enrolment by 2015. Sixteen of these countries, accounting for almost half of all children aged between 6 and 11 in the region, registered declining enrolment rates (see Figure 2.4).

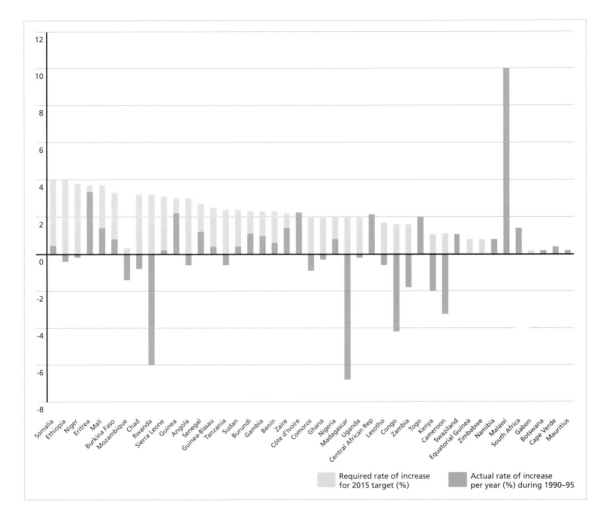

Required rate of increase for 2015 target (%)

Actual rate of increase per year (%) during 1990–95

Figure 2.5 summarises what the net enrolment profile in sub-Saharan African countries will look like in 2015, if 1990–95 trends are projected forwards on a country-by-country basis (freezing at 1995 levels the rates for the 16 countries where enrolment levels are falling). Twenty-two countries in the region will have enrolment rates of less than 70 per cent, with another nine countries achieving enrolment rates of less than 50 per cent.

Allowing for the fact that any projection can capture only the broad parameters of change, the implications for human development remain a cause for great concern. Investment in education opportunity should be creating a framework for recovery in Africa. Instead, the educational gulf already separating the region from the rest of the world is widening. This is happening at a time when, for reasons outlined in the previous

Figure 2.4
Sub-Saharan Africa: annual % rate of increase required for universal enrolment by 2015 and actual rate of increase, 1990-1995

Sources:
Derived from UNESCO
Statistical Yearbook, Paris, 1997; and UNESCO
World Education Report 1998, Paris 1998

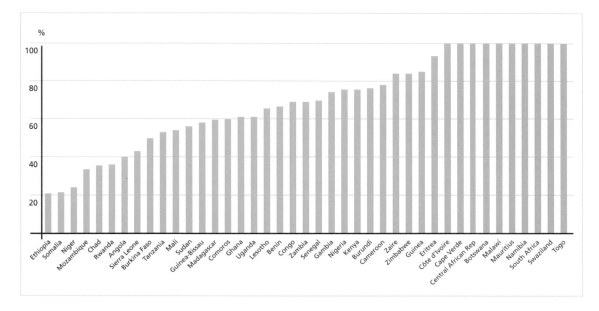

Figure 2.5
**Sub-Saharan Africa: projected
net enrolment rates in 2015**

Sources:
Derived from UNESCO
Statistical Yearbook, Paris, 1997;
and UNESCO
World Education Report 1998,
Paris 1998

chapter, success in the global economy demands increased levels of knowledge and skills. The stark reality is that unless determined action is taken to alter the trends outlined in our projection, the human resources needed to drive sub-Saharan Africa's recovery in the twenty-first century will not exist, with attendant consequences in terms of poverty, illiteracy, disease, and mortality, and social breakdown.

Achieving the mid-term targets

What would be required to get sub-Saharan Africa 'on track' for the 2015 target of universal primary education? A helpful way of addressing this question is to set a mid-point transitional date. To establish such a target, we calculated, country by country, the average annual rate of growth in net enrolment required to achieve universal enrolment by 2015. We did this by taking actual enrolment rates for 1995 and establishing the annual rate of increase needed to achieve universal enrolment by 2015, identifying the transitional target for 2005 in the process. We compared this target with the net enrolment rate projected for 2005 for each country, taking into account the 1990 net enrolment rate and the 1990–95 rate of increase in enrolment. Once again, we froze the net enrolment rates for countries that had experienced a decline. In order to quantify the gap between target and achievement, we factored into the equation the number of additional children who would have to be enrolled to meet the 2005 target.

Figure 2.6 summarises the results. It shows that only ten countries in sub-Saharan Africa are 'on track', while a large group of countries –

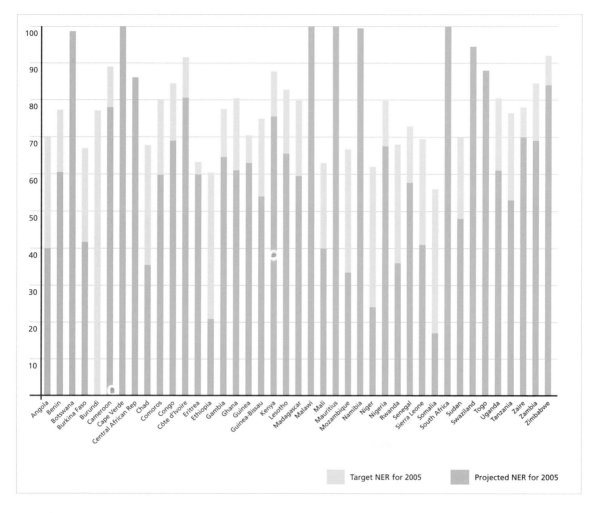

including Chad, Ethiopia, Somalia, and Niger – will fail to get further than half-way to the 2005 enrolment target. In quantitative terms, the scale of the deficit is enormous. Figure 2.7 shows that in order to achieve the 2005 target, sub-Saharan Africa must enrol an additional 22 million children by 2005, over and above existing trend enrolments. This is the minimum requirement for making the 2015 goal of universal primary education a practical possibility. To put the figure into context, it represents fully 14 per cent of the total population of primary-school age.

Even this figure understates the full extent of the challenge facing many of the poorest countries. In order to meet the 2005 transitional target, large numbers of children currently not in school must be enrolled, as exemplified below:

- Ethiopia: 5.3 million (three times the present net enrolment ratio)

Figure 2.6
The 'mid-term' deficit: projected net enrolment rates for sub-Saharan Africa

Sources:
Derived from UNESCO
Statistical Yearbook, Paris, 1997; and UNESCO
World Education Report 1998, Paris 1998

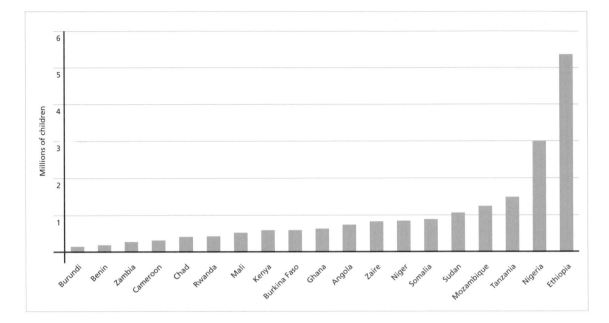

Figure 2.7
**Enrolment deficit for 2005:
selected countries in
sub-Saharan Africa**

Sources:
Derived from UNESCO
Statistical Yearbook, Paris, 1997;
and UNESCO
World Education Report 1998,
Paris 1998

- Tanzania: 1.7 million

- Mozambique 1.2 million children (double the current net enrolment rate)

- Sudan: 1 million

- Rwanda: half a million

- Zambia, Burkina Faso, Ghana, and Mali: just under half a million each.

The point of this exercise is not to suggest that the challenge is impossible. Several countries in the region have achieved dramatic progress since 1995. In Malawi and Uganda, the withdrawal of school fees and increased public investment in education have given a powerful impetus towards the achievement of universal primary enrolment. But in many countries the increase in enrolment rates required over the coming years is comparable with those achieved, in considerably more favourable circumstances, after independence. Today, unsustainable debt and slow economic growth mean that governments lack the financing capacity to sustain progress on the scale required.

HIV/AIDS and education

The HIV/AIDS crisis adds to the scale of the challenge facing sub-Saharan Africa. The region has been hit harder than any other by the pandemic, with more than thirty countries suffering prevalence rates in excess of 10 per cent. Nine out of every ten of the world's children carrying the virus are African.[12] In the most severely affected countries in eastern and central Africa, HIV/AIDS is undermining public investment in education, creating shortages of trained teachers, and stretching already limited education budgets.

Some of the most serious consequences of HIV/AIDS for education are being experienced at the household level. As HIV/AIDS takes its toll of human health and life, poor families are being subjected to twin pressures: they are losing income at a time when the costs of health treatment are rising. Spending on the education of children is often a casualty in the tough budget choices that have to be made. Millions of school-aged children are being forced to leave school in order to care for sick relatives or to work in order to supplement family incomes. As the principal carers, young girls are especially badly affected. In the worst-affected countries, such as Malawi and Zambia, it is estimated that almost one-third of children have lost one or both parents. Many of these children are being cared for by impoverished relatives, themselves lacking the resources needed to send a child to school. Providing the child victims of HIV/AIDS with educational opportunities that are affordable and responsive to their special needs will deepen Africa's education crisis.

In 1999, AIDS-related illnesses were estimated to have claimed the lives of more than 1000 teachers in Zambia – double the number three years earlier.

One of the most serious problems facing education planners in responding to the HIV/AIDS crisis concerns the teaching profession, which has been devastated by the pandemic. Infection rates of up to 40 per cent are reported from Zambia and Malawi. In 1999, AIDS-related illnesses were estimated to have claimed the lives of more than 1000 teachers in Zambia – double the number three years earlier. These deaths outstrip the number of graduates emerging from the country's teacher-training colleges. While Zambia represents a bad case, governments across the region will have to make the medium-term investments needed to maintain the supply of trained teachers, while at the same time taking the immediate measures needed to cover for teachers absent because of AIDS-related illness.

Regional variations

While sub-Saharan Africa will account for a growing share of children out of school, the extent of the education problem in other regions should not be understated. The Middle East and Latin America are closest to achieving universal enrolment, and there has also been rapid progress in South Asia and East Asia. But within each region, major pockets of deprivation remain.

South Asia. On current trends, the proportion of the total number of children out of school accounted for by South Asia will fall by half between 1995 and 2005, and decline to one-tenth by 2015. An increase in net enrolment rates in India and Bangladesh accounts for most of this change. On current trends, Bangladesh could achieve universal primary enrolment early in the next decade, while India could achieve it before 2015. Progress towards universal completion (see below) has been slower in both countries. Within South Asia, Pakistan will account for a growing share of children not in school. By 2005 it will account for 40 per cent of the region's children out of school, compared with 27 per cent in 1995. The country needs to increase the number of children in school by 2 million in order to meet the 2005 transitional target for universal enrolment in 2015. Enrolment rates for Afghanistan are among the lowest in the world, at less than 30 per cent, leaving almost 3 million children out of school. In Nepal, enrolment rates are increasing, but far too slowly to achieve the 2015 target. The country needs to increase enrolments by about 600,000 over current trend levels by 2005, in order to get back on track for the 2015 target.

East Asia. Even before the financial crisis, the rate of growth in primary-school enrolment had begun to slow in Thailand and Indonesia. There is evidence (Chapter 6) that it may now be negative, although the biggest impact of the financial crisis appears to have been in the transition from primary to junior-secondary school. Net enrolment rates for Cambodia and Laos are comparable to those found in sub-Saharan Africa.

Middle East. Several countries in the Middle East are off track for the 2015 target. They include the poorest country in the region as well as the richest. On present trends, approximately 2.6 million Yemeni children will not be in school in 2015. The 2005 target for closing this deficit is one million additional enrolments. Enrolment levels have also fallen in Saudi Arabia and Iraq.

Latin America. Latin America's most serious enrolment deficits are in Haiti and Guatemala, where the enrolment rates are respectively 35 per cent and 68 per cent. Other low-income countries – such as Nicaragua, Honduras, and El Salvador – have been moving slowly towards universal enrolment, although there will be negative effects as a result of Hurricane Mitch, which inflicted great damage on much of the region in 1998. Chile and Colombia also suffered major reversals in enrolment rates during the first half of the 1990s, albeit from relatively high levels.

Completion rates

School enrolment represents only the first step towards a basic education. The broad international consensus is that at least four years of good-quality education are needed for children to acquire literacy and numeracy skills on a sustainable basis, although this represents at best a minimal requirement. Unfortunately, millions drop out of school before this requirement has been met, many of them before completing even the first two grades. High drop-out rates undermine the potential benefits of high enrolment rates, especially where drop-outs occur during the early school years. They also result in the waste of scarce public investment resources.

More than 150 million children in developing countries, almost one-third of the total, start school but do not complete Grade 5.[13] These children are denied the opportunity to acquire the literacy, numeracy, and broader life-skills needed to escape the poverty trap. As might be expected, drop-out rates are highest in regions with the lowest average incomes and lowest enrolment rates (see Figure 2.8). In South Asia, 40 per cent of children – 67 million in total – drop out before completing primary school. In Africa, one in every three children – 22 million in total – drops out.

High enrolment rates are no guarantee of high completion rates. Latin America has achieved near universal enrolment, but one in every four children drops out before completing primary education. Several countries in Latin America, among them Peru, Colombia, Brazil, Bolivia, and the Dominican Republic, have completion rates that compare unfavourably with the regional average for sub-Saharan Africa (Figure 2.9). High rates of drop-out also blemish the performance of countries in East Asia that have achieved very high levels of enrolment.

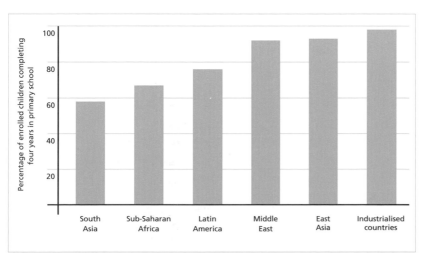

Figure 2.8
Regional completion rates (%)

Source:
UNICEF, *The State of the World's Children 1998*, New York, 1998

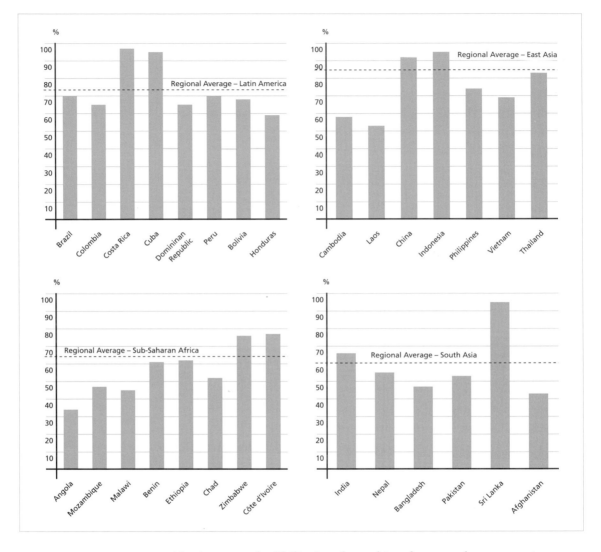

Figure 2.9
**Regional completion rates:
percentage of enrolled
children completing four years
of primary school,
selected countries, 1995**

Sources:
UNESCO: *Achieving Education For
All: Statistical Document,*
Paris, 1996;
UNICEF, *The State of the World's
Children 1998,* New York, 1998

For instance, the Philippines has achieved net enrolment rates in excess of 90 per cent, but three-quarters of children drop out before reaching Grade 5.

Low completion rates cast a different light on enrolment data and the rate of progress towards universal primary education. For example, Ethiopia has one of the lowest rates of enrolment in the world and one of the largest gender gaps. Fewer than one-third of boys and one-tenth of girls aged 6–11 start school, and one quarter of those who do start school drop out during the first two grades.[14] Girls are more likely than boys to drop out in the early stages. The average time spent in education for those who drop out is 2.7 years. In Mozambique, fewer than half of the children who enter Grade 1 reach Grade 5.

As such facts suggest, low enrolment rates do not reveal the full extent of the problem facing many countries in Africa. Conversely, progress in increasing enrolment rates overstates the achievement of many countries in South Asia, because it has not been accompanied by improvements in completion rates. In India, about 20 million children of primary-school age who enter primary school – one-third of the total number enrolled – leave without having acquired basic skills of literacy and numeracy. On average, each of these children will complete only 2.4 years of education.[15] Similarly, Bangladesh has made rapid strides towards universal enrolment; but for every 100 children entering Grade 1, 65 will drop out before reaching Grade 5.

Where school drop-outs are concentrated in the early years, the benefits associated with enrolment are extremely limited. It is not uncommon to find extremely high drop-out rates in the first two grades, even in countries where fewer than half of all children enrol. In Pakistan, nearly half of the children who enrol drop out before completing their schooling, the vast majority in Grades 1 and 2.[16] The situation in Nepal is even worse. Two out of every three children drop out of school before reaching Grade 5, more than 80 per cent of them before the end of the second year.[17]

Low primary-school completion rates are the result of a wide variety of factors. On the demand side, families may withdraw children from school because they are needed to work, because they cannot afford four years of schooling, or because of gender barriers. On the supply side, low completion rates may reflect problems with the quality of instruction, especially where this leads to high rates of repetition. These issues are discussed more extensively in Chapter 4.

Low completion rates have an important bearing on poverty, equity, and human development for an obvious reason: namely, the poor account for the vast majority of those who drop out. The equity and efficiency of public investment in education also suffer as a consequence of low completion. Where large numbers of children leave the system without having acquired basic literacy and numeracy skills, much of the public investment made in their education is wasted. Moreover, low completion rates lead to a low rate of progression into secondary and higher levels of education, with damaging implications for the development of the national human-resource base.

Repetition: the prelude to dropping out
Low completion rates are intimately linked to the problem of grade repetition, which results when teaching is of insufficient quality for

children to meet the standards for progressing to the next level. By prolonging the primary-school cycle, repetition increases the per capita costs of education, enlarges class sizes, and creates pedagogical problems associated with teaching over-age children. Apart from discouraging children, repetition also increases the direct and indirect costs of education to households. For poor households in particular, this is likely to result in children dropping out of school.[18] In the case of young girls, many of whom start primary school late and drop out with the onset of puberty, repeating grades diminishes the prospects for acquiring basic literacy and numeracy skills.

Under optimal conditions, each primary-school child would spend one year in each grade, completing a five-grade cycle in five years. When pupils repeat grades or drop out, the average number of pupil years required to progress through the cycle increases. Taking into account both repetition and drop-out rates, the average number of years taken to complete Grade 5 varies between five in China, Cuba, and Botswana, seven in Colombia, Brazil, Ethiopia and Mali, and more than 11 years in Mozambique and Chad (see Figure 2.10).[19]

Figure 2.10
Average number of years taken to complete Grade 5 in selected countries

Source:
UNESCO, *Wasted Opportunities: When Schools Fail*, Paris, 1998

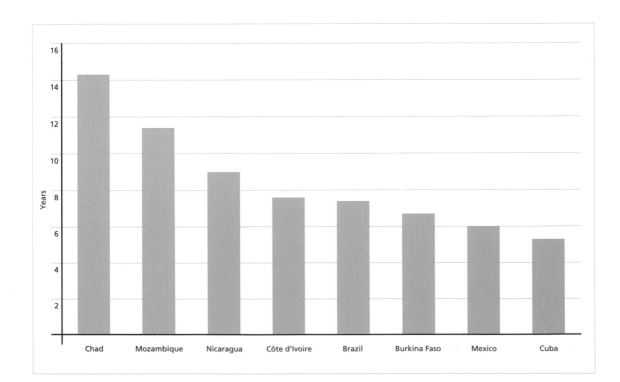

All developing regions experience relatively high rates of repetition. The poor performance of Latin America is particularly striking, because it is comparable with far poorer regions. Almost one-third of children in primary school in Latin America are repeating a grade. The additional cost to the region's education systems has been estimated at $4 billion.[20] Because much of the repetition takes place in early grades, it reduces the resources available for each child in these grades, while adding to problems of overcrowding. In countries such as Brazil, Honduras, and Peru, more than one in five children in Grade 1 are repeating, a fact that suggests an appalling qualitative deficit in teaching and the learning environment.[21] In the case of Peru, it takes eight years on average for a child to progress through the primary-school system – 40 per cent longer than would be the case if repetition were not necessary.[22] Completing the first two grades takes an average of three years, although the rate of repetition is far higher in poorer highland areas.

For poor households using limited financial resources to get their children through school, the consequences of high rates of repetition can be devastating. These costs rise as children reach the age at which they would normally start contributing their labour to the household. In Nepal, more than 60 per cent of children in Grades 1 and 2 are repeating, a fact that helps to explain the high drop-out rates noted above.[23] Repetition can have the effect of reinforcing gender inequality in access to primary schools. Since poor households depend heavily on the labour of young girls, there is an implicit cost in terms of lost labour-time when girls go to school. This cost is one of the biggest barriers to more rapid progress towards primary education (see Chapter 4), and repetition has the effect of increasing it. In Ethiopia, higher repetition rates for girls mean that the average time it takes them to complete primary school is extended by one year, compared with six months for boys.[24] The resulting costs to households reinforce the deep gender-based disparities in school enrolment and completion.

Some countries have tried to reduce repetition rates through a policy of automatic promotion. The problem is that, in the absence of a supportive teaching environment, automatic promotion amounts to a policy of problem-displacement. Burkina Faso has introduced virtually automatic promotion for the first three grades. This has produced a marked decline in repetition rates for the first two grades, but very high rates of repetition – amounting to about 40 per cent – in Grade 6, where children prove unable to pass the test for transfer to lower-secondary school.

Gender equity

Gender-based discrimination in education has many dimensions. It is not just that girls are less likely to be in school and more likely to drop out of school. All too often the attitudes of teachers and parents serve to lower the expectations and ambitions of girls, with the education system serving to reinforce conventional assumptions. The international development target of equality in primary and secondary school enrolment by 2005 does not fully capture the range of gender discrimination, but it does provide a useful indicator of one dimension.

At the global level, the gender gap in primary and secondary-school enrolment is narrowing. However, the rate at which it is narrowing is far too slow – and the 2005 goal is now almost certainly beyond reach. As in other areas, the overall picture obscures significant national variations. It also obscures what might be considered as a perverse narrowing of the gender gap in Africa, where part of the reason for the modest improvement in gender equity can be traced to a decline in male enrolment rates.

The human consequences of the slow rate of progress towards gender equity in education are sometimes buried beneath statistical data. One way of illustrating these consequences is to ask a simple question: how many more girls would have been in school in 1995, if governments had achieved the rate of progress towards gender equity that they promised at Jomtien? On a regional basis, the answers are that an additional 12 million girls would be in school in South Asia; an extra 3 million girls in Africa; and 4 million more girls in East Asia.

Figure 2.11 shows the major trends in gender equity, as defined by the 2005 international development target (i.e. the ratio of girls' enrolment to boys'). At the primary-school level, the gender-equity gap was smaller in 1995 than in 1985, though the gap has been closing at a very slow rate from an extremely wide starting point. In South Asia and sub-Saharan Africa, girls' enrolment represented respectively only 74 and 83 per cent of boys' enrolment – a marginal increase over the position a decade earlier. The gender gap is closing slowest in the two regions where it is largest.

Using school attendance as an indicator of gender equity points to an even less encouraging picture. In South Asia, the percentage share of girls in school attendance increased by 0.2 per cent in the first half of the 1990s – a rate of growth which places the region on track for gender equity about two centuries hence. Over the same period, the proportion of girls in sub-Saharan Africa's primary schools increased by 0.5 per cent, putting the region on a trajectory for gender equity in 50 years' time.

In several respects, this disconcerting picture understates the problem. At least part of the improvement in gender equity achieved in sub-Saharan Africa has been a consequence of falling enrolment rates, with the position of boys deteriorating slightly faster than that of girls in many countries. One study charting gender-equity trends between 1980 and 1995 found that the ratio of girls to boys in school had increased in 28 of the 39 countries for which time-series data were available.[25] In almost half of these cases, the reduction occurred because the proportion of boys in school fell faster than the proportion of girls. This perverse outcome is hardly to be regarded as a positive source of gender equity. Since 1990, the net enrolment rate for girls has fallen in 18 countries. This is in a region where girls' net enrolment rate is less than 50 per cent in 19 countries. In several countries with particularly large gender gaps in enrolment – including Nigeria, Niger, Angola, and Burundi – the gap between boys and girls widened.

While the gender gap is narrowing slightly in South Asia, the aggregate picture conceals divergent performances. In Afghanistan, which has one of the widest gender gaps in the world, the share of girls in primary school fell by 8 per cent between 1990 and 1995, with the net enrolment rate for girls falling to 14 per cent, or one-third of that for boys. Similarly, the proportion of girls in school in Pakistan fell by about 10 per cent during the first half of the 1990s, with enrolment-rate increases for girls lagging behind those of boys. Had the gender ratio in primary education for Pakistan been the same in 1995 as it was in 1990, an additional 1.5 million girls would have been in school. On a more positive note, some countries in the region have achieved significant improvements in

Figure 2.11
Girls' enrolment as a percentage of boys' enrolment: selected years for all developing regions*

Source:
UNESCO, *Statistical Yearbook 1997,* Paris, 1997

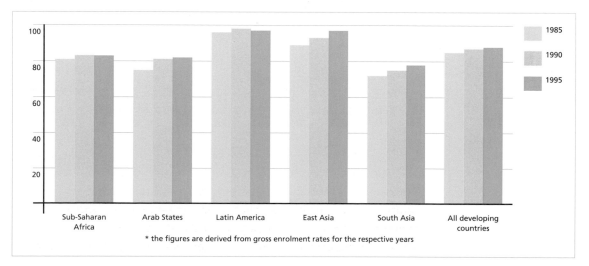

* the figures are derived from gross enrolment rates for the respective years

gender equity, showing what can be achieved in the right policy environment. Twenty years ago, the proportion of girls to boys attending primary school in Bangladesh was about 40:60. Today, the ratio is 49:51. The improvement has been a consequence of a 'catching-up' process in which enrolment rates for girls have been increasing at twice the rate for boys for the past ten years.

Dispelling the myth that there is an automatically negative correlation between Islam and gender representation in schools, Arab States increased the share of girls in school by about 2 per cent in the first half of the 1990s, four times the overall rate for developing countries. In much of Latin America and the Caribbean there is an inverse gender gap, with fewer boys attending school than girls. However, several countries in the region figure prominently at the wrong end of the world league table for gender equity, with girls' enrolment rates at least 30 per cent lower than male enrolment rates in Colombia, Haiti, and Guatemala.

Failure to achieve the targets for gender equity set at international summits raises fundamental questions about the commitment of governments to some of the most basic human rights. If the right to education is an entitlement based on citizenship, then the failure to accord equal treatment to girls and boys represents a serious and systematic violation of fundamental human rights, including those enshrined in the Convention on the Rights of the Child and the Convention on Elimination of Discrimination Against Women. Given the powerful links between maternal education and other dimensions of human development, including child and maternal health, the shortfall against the gender-equity targets also has profound implications for poverty reduction. As suggested in Chapter 1, the human-development losses are cumulative and persist across generations. This is because girls who have not been given educational opportunities are less likely to educate their own children, especially their daughters.

Literacy

The Jomtien Conference envisaged adult illiteracy rates falling to half of their 1990 level by the year 2000. Subsequent conferences abandoned targets for literacy, except in one important respect. The goal of gender equity in literacy by 2015 is now a core part of the OECD strategy.

Trends in adult literacy reflect progress in primary education, for the obvious reason that most adults acquire their literacy skills in school. Not surprisingly, the slow and uneven rate of progress towards universal primary education has undermined progress towards improved adult literacy. At a global level, literacy levels have improved at less than one-quarter of the rate required to halve illiteracy between 1990 and 2000. Best estimates suggest that one in five of the developing world's population will still be illiterate in 2010.[26]

In the mid-1990s, there were 872 million adult illiterates in the developing world, two-thirds of them women. The distribution of illiteracy is highly concentrated in certain regions and countries. More than 60 per cent of illiterate adults live in South Asia, and almost 75 per cent live in nine countries (see Figure 2.12). It should be emphasised that these estimates almost certainly understate the full extent of the literacy problem. In many cases, attendance at school is used as a measure of determining literacy, although the relationship is often weaker than might be expected. Many children leave school with limited literacy skills, which they lose by adulthood. The case of Bolivia illustrates this. On the basis of school-attendance data, official figures suggest that about 20 per cent of the adult population is illiterate. National surveys to test

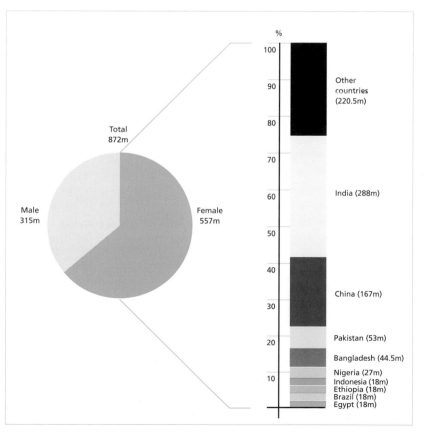

Figure 2.12
Distribution of adult illiteracy by gender and country (1995)

Source:
UNESCO, *Adult Education in a Polarising World*, Paris, 1997

functional literacy – people's ability to write, and read simple letters or newspaper stories – put the illiteracy rate at between 35 and 50 per cent.[27]

Illiteracy is not the sole preserve of the developing world. Large numbers of people in the industrialised countries also suffer disadvantages associated with weak literacy skills. One recent survey of young adults in the USA found that fewer than 5 per cent of those aged 20–25 could not read or write at all, but that almost 25 per cent had problems in reading texts that required more than simple decoding.[28] The International Adult Literacy Survey showed that low literacy levels were a problem across the OECD countries. In the USA, Britain, and Ireland, close to one-quarter of the adult population scored on the lowest level of the literacy and numeracy scales, more than double the proportion for the Netherlands, Sweden, and Germany.[29] While these scales reflect a measurement of relative rather than absolute illiteracy (in that they measure the distribution of skills, rather than success or failure in a specific test), poor performance is strongly correlated with low income.

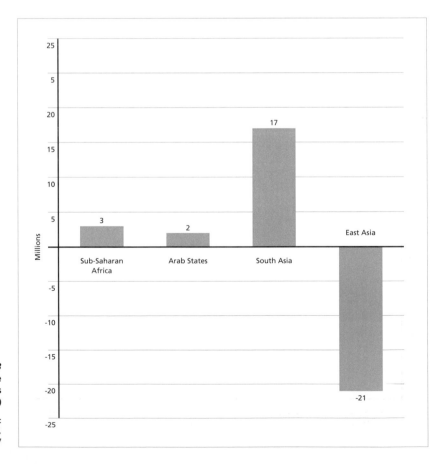

Figure 2.13
Change in number of illiterate people: developing regions (1990-1995)

Source:
UNESCO, *Statistical Yearbook 1997*, Paris, 1997

Slow progress

Progress towards the eradication of illiteracy in the developing world has been consistent, but consistently slow: too slow to prevent an increase in the overall numbers of adult illiterates. Since 1980, illiteracy rates have fallen by about 15 per cent. However, this has been insufficient to counter the combination of population growth and the failure of school systems to accelerate progress towards universal primary education. As a result, there are 24 million more illiterate adults in the developing world today than in 1980 – and 4 million more than when the World Conference on Education for All was held in 1990 (see Figure 2.13). The progress report for the period since the Jomtien conference makes particularly sombre reading. Almost the entire reduction in illiteracy achieved since 1990 has taken place in East Asia. The number of illiterate people has increased by 17 million in South Asia and 3 million in sub-Saharan Africa. The number of illiterates was expected to reach 881 million by the year 2000.

As in the case of gender equity, the wide gap between the rate of progress envisaged under the international development targets and actual outcomes implies large losses measured in terms of human development. Had illiteracy rates been halved, in line with these targets, there would have been 80 million fewer adult illiterates in the world in 2000. The strong correlation found in almost all developing countries between illiteracy and income-poverty suggests that slow progress in literacy has contributed to the slow rate of progress towards the 2015 targets.

Gender inequalities in adult literacy remain persistent and deep. Although female literacy rates have increased relative to male literacy

Figure 2.14
Female literacy as a percentage of male literacy, 1980-1995

Source:
Derived from UNESCO,
Statistical Yearbook 1997, Paris, 1997

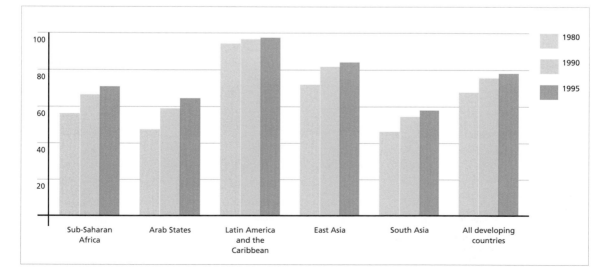

rates in all developing regions, the rate of progress towards equity has been painfully slow (see Figure 2.14). There are important regional variations. Gender differences persist in East Asia, but at far higher levels of overall literacy than in other developing regions. Here, three-quarters of women are literate, compared with 90 per cent of men. However, female literacy rates are increasing at twice the rate of male literacy rates, so that the gap is closing. The slowest progress has been made in South Asia, sub-Saharan Africa, and the Middle East, the three regions with the widest gender gaps.

- In **South Asia,** only one-third of women are literate, compared with two-thirds of men. The number of illiterate women in the region increased by 15 million between 1990 and 1995 — more than twice the increase in numbers of male illiterates. Although literacy rates are rising, they remain desperately low in most countries. In Pakistan, only 25 per cent of women are literate, compared with 50 per cent of men, and in two countries, Nepal and Afghanistan, fewer than 15 per cent of women are literate.

- In **sub-Saharan Africa**, fewer than half of all adult women are literate, compared with two-thirds of adult men. The gender gap in literacy has closed by only 3 per cent over 25 years, and the number of illiterate females increased from 84 million to 87 million between 1990 and 1995, while the number of male illiterates remained static. Women's literacy rates are still below 30 per cent in 15 countries, among them Ethiopia, Mozambique, Niger, Burkina Faso, Senegal, and Mali.

- The female literacy rate in **Arab countries** is only 44 per cent, compared with 68 per cent for males. Because Arab countries have succeeded in reducing gender gaps in enrolment and completion rates far more successfully than South Asia or sub-Saharan Africa, they are projected to achieve gender equity in literacy, with a literacy rate of 70 per cent, in about 2010.

Future prospects

There is a pressing need to accelerate the rate of progress towards gender equity in literacy. In global terms, overall trends will be heavily influenced by developments in South Asia, which accounts for the bulk of world illiteracy. The slow rate of progress achieved in this region is captured in Figure 2.15, which projects the current rate of closure for the gender gap into the future. It indicates that India will achieve gender equity in literacy in about 2060; and Pakistan will achieve gender equity in literacy in the last quarter of the next century.

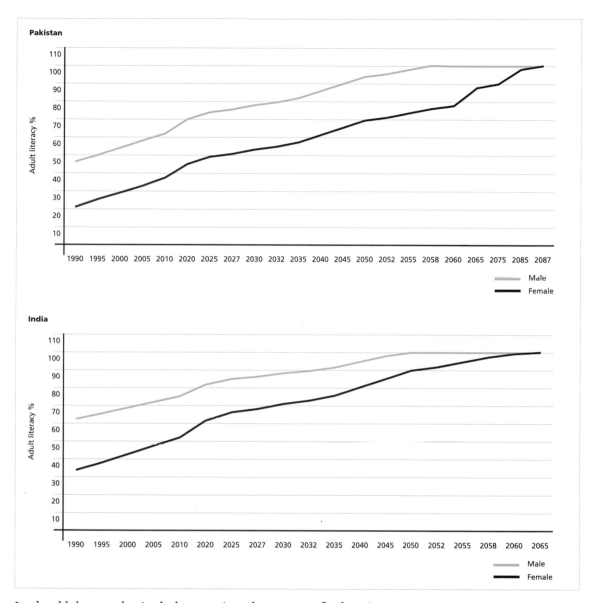

Pakistan

India

Figure 2.15
Gender literacy gap: rate of closure in India and Pakistan

Source:
Derived from data in UNESCO
Statistical Yearbook 1997,
Paris, 1997

It should be emphasised that, as in other areas of education, past performance and current trends do not necessarily dictate future outcome. Rapid improvements are possible in adult literacy. In China, the incidence of illiteracy has fallen dramatically during the lifetime of a single generation. An adult born in 1960 is four times as likely to be illiterate as a Chinese teenager today (see Figure 2.16). Contrast this with the experience of Pakistan. Here too illiteracy rates have declined over time, but at less than one-tenth of the rate achieved in China. As a result, a Pakistani child aged between 10 and 14 is only 30 per cent less likely to be literate than an adult born in 1960. What matters in this comparison

Figure 2.16
**Comparison of literacy and
schooling across age cohorts:
Pakistan and China**

Sources:
World Bank, *China 2020*,
Washington, 1997;
Government of Pakistan,
*Pakistan Integrated Household
Survey: Round One, 1995-1996*,
Islamabad, 1997;
UNESCO, *Statistical Yearbook 1997*,
Paris, 1997

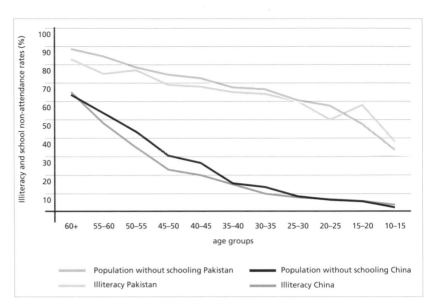

is not just the absolute differences between the two countries, but the differences in their rate of progress. Over the past 50 years, Pakistan has halved the rate of illiteracy, while China has reduced it by a factor of 12.[30]

What are the requirements for reducing adult literacy? For the next generation, the most vital ingredients are progress towards universal enrolment, universal completion, and high-quality education. One of the reasons why Pakistan's illiteracy rate has fallen so slowly is that progress towards universal enrolment in school has been slow, while drop-out rates have been high. China, by contrast, has been highly successful in extending coverage of the school system.

While formal education systems hold the key to reducing illiteracy, schools alone cannot resolve the problem. For one thing, the huge backlog of adult illiteracy associated with the past failure of education systems needs to be addressed. In this context adult education has a crucial role to play, although experience in this area has been mixed.[31] In China, adult-literacy programmes have mobilised children to teach basic literacy and numeracy. These programmes stretch back over three decades and continue today in more than 200,000 'parent schools'. More recently, Namibia's National Literacy Programme has achieved some success in reducing adult illiteracy levels. In contrast, the Indian government's Total Literacy campaign, launched in the mid-1980s, has been less successful. It has achieved highly uneven outcomes across the country, because a lack of political will in some States obstructed its effective implementation. Community-based adult-literacy programmes, such as the REFLECT programme developed by ActionAid (see Chapter 6), have contributed to national literacy efforts by developing highly participative approaches to learning. Prospects for success in future efforts at a national level will depend partly on the success of governments in integrating such programmes into their national strategies.

The quality of education

Whether expanded access to education translates into meaningful benefits for individuals and society depends on whether children acquire the knowledge, reasoning abilities, skills, and values that they need. High rates of enrolment and completion are imperfect indicators of progress in these areas. As the World Declaration on Education observed in 1990, participation in schooling is not an end in itself, but a means to the end of a good-quality education.

Part of the problem with assessing trends in education quality is that it is an inherently elusive concept, difficult to define and measure even in one country. Cross-country comparisons are even more hazardous. There are no internationally agreed standards for measuring progress – or setbacks – over time.[32] Nor is there a precise consensus on what should be measured. Literacy and numeracy are obvious indicators of school performance, but the 'education geared towards tapping each person's talents and potential (...) so that they can improve their lives and transform their societies', advocated at the World Education Forum in Dakar, is harder to assess.[33]

In the industrialised countries, debate on education quality has been dominated by two schools of thought. The 'Effective Schools' approach has relied on quantitative analytical techniques to determine how much of a student's academic achievement can be explained by different school inputs, taking into account the social environment in which the school operates.[34] The 'Schools Improvement' approach has focused more on processes within the school, especially the relationships between teachers and children. Research methods have tended to be more qualitative than quantitative, concentrating on the attitudes and interactions that define the learning environment.[35] Issues such as motivation, parental involvement, and team spirit among teachers have been seen as more relevant to learning outcomes than physical inputs, such as the state of school building and equipment.

Until recently, debate in developing countries has been dominated by the Effective School tradition. At its worst, this embodied a production-line approach to education, in which schools were seen as factories that operated by using inputs (teachers and books), to transform raw material (children) into a desired end-product (children capable of passing exams). Over the past decade, however, the debate about quality has moved on. It is increasingly recognised that the purpose of education is not simply to convey a body of knowledge, but to teach children how to learn, solve problems, make judgements, and apply knowledge in a flexible and creative way.[36] This broader approach is reflected in the Convention on the Rights of the Child, Article 29, which calls for 'the development of the child's personality, talents and mental and physical abilities to their fullest potential'. It was given a powerful impetus by the World Conference on Education for All, which popularised the notion of 'learning for life'.[37] In this framework, the acquisition of literacy and numeracy skills is seen as one element of basic education. The process of learning and the learning environment are seen as equally important. Emphasis is placed on the extent to which children are able to express their views and their self-esteem – and the extent to which learning systems are geared towards local needs.

The World Conference on Education for All called for the development of education systems that – in addition to transmitting information – transmitted 'life-skills', broadly defined as the skills needed to prepare children for the problems they will face in terms of health, nutrition, and conditions in local markets. But 'life-skills' refers also to the development of the learning potential needed to respond to the challenges posed by global integration, including an ability to adapt to fast-changing situations through continued education and absorption of relevant knowledge. Education policy is gradually moving beyond its dominant concern with initial schooling, towards emphasising the need for lifelong learning.

If the success of education is to be gauged by what – and how – children learn, existing measurement systems are severely inadequate. Most of the mechanisms currently in place are administered as part of a selection procedure. The Monitoring Learning Achievement programme being developed by UNESCO and UNICEF is an attempt to break this mould, transcending the traditional focus on exam results to cover a wider range of factors relating to attitudes, values, and self-esteem.[38] However, the programme is still in an early stage of development.

Notwithstanding the immense difficulties associated with quality assessment, there is a broad consensus on the elements associated with good-quality education. These may be broadly summarised as follows.

Motivated teachers. Learning opportunities are reduced when teachers are poorly motivated, poorly trained, and unable to foster a child-centred learning environment. High rates of teacher absenteeism reduce rates of attendance and undermine parental confidence in school systems. Teachers play a crucial role in determining the expectations of children and how they relate to the school environment.

An appropriate curriculum and good teaching materials. In many countries, the school curriculum is widely perceived as being of limited relevance for local needs. The availability of teaching material – especially textbooks – is one of the most powerful determinants of learning outcomes. The curricula and textbooks used in many countries contain a strong gender bias, which restricts opportunities for girls.

Appropriate language teaching. Acquisition of literacy skills in a familiar language is of great importance in determining education performance. Appropriate language policies can dramatically improve the educational achievements of children from poor communities.

The school environment. The physical environment has an important bearing on education outcomes and on parental perceptions of child safety (and hence on enrolment rates).

Promoting community participation. Parental engagement with schools and participation in school management and decision making have an important bearing on school performance.

Measured by these criteria, many developing countries fail to meet minimal standards. Children are frequently taught in overcrowded classrooms by unqualified and unmotivated teachers, who are poorly paid and lack support. Teacher absenteeism is widespread, eroding public confidence in the value of education. Learning is further constrained by dilapidated schools, inadequate facilities, limited supply of learning materials, weak curricula, disregard for minority cultures and languages, gender bias, and instructional methods which inhibit, rather than nourish, the potential of children. The following excerpts from reports of field visits to schools illustrate the experience of primary education suffered by millions of school children.

- 'There are ten classes for over 1000 children, leading to chronic over-crowding. Most classrooms are bereft of teaching materials and furniture, except for a table used by the teacher. The blackboards have disintegrated. Many teachers report that they cannot get hold of chalk. Books and writing materials are a rarity, with six children in Grade 3 sharing one mathematics book. Children sit on stones or on the floor. The vast majority of teachers have had minimal training. In many cases, lessons take place under trees. Few of the schools have access to a reliable source of water, and the latrine facilities are inadequate.' *(Oxfam field visit to Shinyanga, an area in the central-southern region of Tanzania)*

- 'There are around 60 children from the Hmung ethnic community in a classroom which should accommodate fewer than half this number. Their ages range from 6 to 15. Three grades share the same room, with three teachers conducting lessons simultaneously. The language of instruction is Kinh, which most of the younger children are unable to follow. There is a strong emphasis on discipline and rote-learning, with no visible participation from the children themselves in the learning process.' *(Oxfam field-visit report on a school in Lao Cai district in the Northern Upland region of Vietnam)*

- 'In effect, the primary schools we visited were little more than child-minding centres. In most cases, even if more than one teacher was present, we found that all children had been gathered together in one place, irrespective of age or grade, and were only expected to maintain a semblance of order. ... Supervision took one of the following forms: watching the children from a desk or chair; asking one senior child to maintain order; letting the children look after themselves. In many schools the ambience was nothing short of chaotic.' *(PROBE survey of primary schools in Uttar Pradesh)*[39]

Such accounts could be reproduced many times over. Below we examine the learning outcomes associated with inadequate education environments and identify some of the underlying problems.

Learning outcomes

While education is about the acquisition of 'life-skills' in a broad sense, failure to gain basic literacy and numeracy increases the probability that poverty will be transmitted across generations. It also reduces the possibility of lifelong learning, widening the gap between those who take advantage of such opportunities and those who cannot.

There have been several attempts to compare reading and mathematical skills across countries. However, the limited coverage of the studies and the fact that most have provided a simple snapshot picture, rather than a linear trend analysis, make it difficult to assess progress. Even so, the evidence points to widespread problems. Many of the children who pass through the school system come out lacking even the most basic skills.

Three grades share the same room, with three teachers conducting lessons simultaneously. The language of instruction is Kinh, which most of the younger children are unable to follow.

The following findings testify to the scale of the problem.

- In a nationwide sample of 11–12 year olds in Pakistan, only 34 per cent of those who completed primary school could read with comprehension; and more than 80 per cent could not write a simple letter. Another study found that fewer than 10 per cent were competent in basic reading.[40]

- In a study covering 22 States in India, the average Grade 4 achievement level was 32 per cent in mathematics and science, compared with a pass mark of 35 per cent.[41]

- In Zambia, a major national survey tested the reading ability of Grade 6 pupils, designating minimum and desirable performance standards. Only 25 per cent of pupils reached the minimum-performance benchmark, and 2 per cent of pupils gained the desirable performance level. In other words, three-quarters of Grade 6 pupils were judged to leave primary education in a state of illiteracy.[42]

- In Tanzania, a standard test is applied in Grade 4, with the pass rate set at 25 per cent. One survey covering 45 schools in 1993 discovered a mean score of 15 per cent, with 10 per cent of students scoring zero in mathematics. Scores for the Primary School Leaving Certificate exam are also extremely low, ranging from 18 to 38 per cent across worse- and better-performing districts.[43]

In some cases, the learning skills of children who have completed primary school are only marginally better than for children who have not completed school.

Such outcomes help to explain why so many children emerge from school systems either in a state of illiteracy, or likely to return to illiteracy in a short space of time. Measured in terms of educational outcomes, the return to investment in school systems in many countries is often abysmally low. In some cases, the learning skills of children who have completed primary school are only marginally better than for children who have not completed school.

In Bangladesh, a national test called the Assessment of Basic Competency (ABC) has been used to test the knowledge of children in reading, writing, and arithmetic. Because the test is independent of the school curriculum, it can be used to compare the ability of school children to use the skills they have acquired with that of children who have not attended school. In a national survey conducted in 1998, 42 per cent of 11–12 year-olds were able to pass the test. More striking was the finding that only 57 per cent of children who had passed through Grade 5 were able to pass. The survey concluded: 'The ABC is a very preliminary test and one would expect that any child passing through the primary cycle should easily qualify ... The results ... call for a critical look at the whole system of primary education in the country.'[44] The ABC findings confirm earlier World Bank assessments. These found that only 64 per cent of boys and 57 per cent of girls completing primary school achieved literacy. Problems of quality become apparent in Grade 2, where only 5 per cent of children tested meet basic competency levels.[45]

Although regular assessments of learning achievement in Africa are rare, those that have been carried out have produced results that show the region both lagging far behind other developing regions, and performing very badly in terms of absolute outcomes. Recent national assessments for Ghana illustrate the scale of the problem. In the mid-1990s, a survey covering children in Grade 6 of primary school found that only 3 per cent were able to pass a basic literacy test, with only 1.5 per cent passing a similar numeracy test.[46] Pass rates in rural schools were no better than one per cent. This low level of educational attainment at the primary level has undermined wider efforts to reform the education system. Fully one-third of the children coming out of primary school are unable to proceed to secondary school because they cannot achieve the grades required. The case of Ghana is not untypical. In parts of sub-Saharan Africa, education scores based on multiple-choice tests are so low that they are almost random, indicating that there is little or no value in attending school.[47] Under these circumstances, it is not difficult to see why many poor households regard spending on education as a bad use of scarce resources.

In parts of sub-Saharan Africa, education scores based on multiple-choice tests are so low that they are almost random, indicating that there is little or no value in attending school.

Poverty makes an important contribution to low educational attainment. Inadequate nutrition and susceptibility to poor health limit learning potential, as do low levels of public spending in education. However, higher average incomes are not automatically correlated with good-quality outcomes. This is illustrated by international comparisons of academic performance. In Latin America, elite private schools in the region, accounting for perhaps 15 per cent of enrolled children, perform on a par with private schools in the USA and countries in East Asia. But public schools perform far worse. In 1992, two Brazilian cities took part in the International Assessment of Educational Progress, which tested the science and mathematics abilities of 13-year-olds; they were ranked next to last, just above Mozambique.[48] There is little evidence of progress since then. In 1997, almost 500,000 Brazilian children in lower-secondary schools were included in a basic language and mathematics test. The average scores were 15 per cent and 25 per cent respectively below the benchmark for satisfactory performance.[49]

While East Asia is often seen as a model for high standards in primary schooling, there are wide variations in the region. South Korea and Singapore consistently score near the top in international comparisons, but the Philippines scored close to the bottom in the international curriculum-based maths and science achievement test (TIMMS). Moreover, elementary-school students' performance in achievement tests administered by the Department of Education in the Philippines has been deteriorating. As in Latin America, this illustrates the weak link between high levels of enrolment on the one side and school performance on the other. The Philippines has a primary-school enrolment rate to compare with that of the industrialised world, allied to educational outcomes similar to some of the worst-performing regions in the developing world.[50]

The inclusion of 'life-skills' in test exercises has produced some interesting results. In China, the UNESCO–UNICEF Monitoring Learning Achievement project has been used to assess school performance. While schools were shown to be producing strong results in literacy and numeracy, the project found that the use of rote-learning techniques, with children acting as passive recipients of knowledge, was limiting their potential to utilise the knowledge gained. It concluded: 'The teaching–learning process in China needs to emphasise more problem-solving skills and the ability to apply knowledge in dealing with real-life problems.'[51]

For life-skills as for other aspects of learning, there are often wide variations within the school system. In Bangladesh, the inclusion of life-skills in the literacy and numeracy components of the ABC test showed that attendance at school generated more benefits. Around 29 per cent of all children and 46 per cent of those with five years of schooling satisfied the basic education criteria – still a distressingly poor outcome in terms of school performance. But in the primary-school sector there was a wide range of achievement. Children attending non-formal primary schools in the NGO sector consistently outperformed their counterparts in government schools, both in the standard numeracy and literacy exercises and in the life-skills component. Almost twice as many children in non-formal primary education – 66 per cent of the total – succeed in passing the basic test, which indicates the potential benefits associated with the teaching methods and curriculum design in these schools.[52]

The school environment
Anyone assessing the adequacy of school facilities would check the state of buildings, the availability of desks, chairs, and basic instructional

materials, and the state of water and sanitation facilities. While there are no internationally agreed standards in many of these areas, there are minimal requirements for the creation of an environment conducive to learning. For millions of children, these requirements are not being met, as a consequence of years of under-funding and inefficiency.

Learning in many countries is constrained by the limited availability of teaching materials. In 1995 a joint UNICEF/UNESCO study of the state of education in 14 least-developed countries revealed that school is often little more than a child-care facility, and an unsafe one at that. In ten of the 14 countries, one-third or more of pupils were being taught in classrooms without usable blackboards. A similar proportion attended schools in urgent need of repair. More than 30 per cent of pupils did not have desks or chairs. Almost one-third of pupils were attending schools that could not provide safe drinking water. In eight of the eleven countries in Africa covered, more than half of the students in the top grade of primary school did not have access to a mathematics textbook.[53]

In some cases, the term 'school' creates a misleading impression: 15 per cent of 'schools' have no building.

As such facts indicate, many countries are unable to provide even the most basic requirements for protecting the health of children in school, let alone an education of acceptable quality. The absence or inadequacy of latrines and access to safe water have obvious health implications, and can be a deterrent to girls' enrolment. All too often, school is a high-risk environment for contracting disease, and a low-achievement environment for learning:

- In Pakistan, only half of government schools have safe water, and 70 per cent have no latrines. In some cases, the term 'school' creates a misleading impression: 15 per cent of 'schools' have no building.[54]

- In Tanzania, schools officially have on average one toilet for every 89 children, four times less than the recommended number – representing a national deficit of 20,000 latrines for primary schools. The true situation is almost certainly worse. The deficit in basic teaching materials is equally marked. Textbook availability ranges from one book to every four children in better-served districts, to one book for every 40 in some of the poorer rural areas. An additional 34,223 classrooms would be needed to reduce the average class size from the current level of over 75 to a maximum of 40 per class.[55]

- In Yemen, one half of schools lack access to safe water, and more than 80 per cent of children do not have a chair or a desk. A field survey carried out in 1997 revealed that at least half of the country's schools were in urgent need of repair.[56]

- In Peru, fewer than 5 per cent of schools in highland areas have adequate water, drains, and electricity. Few primary students have textbooks, and schools have little or no teaching material to support teachers' activities.[57]

Shortages of pedagogical equipment are particularly damaging, because teaching tools, such as textbooks and blackboards, are significant determinants of achievement in low-income countries.[58] Not surprisingly, children who have textbooks and other reading material perform far better than those who do not. The impact of textbooks, paper, pencil, and chalk is especially strong in countries suffering the greatest scarcity. Research in India found that children in schools where a full set of basic instructional material was available scored two to three times higher in tests than children in schools where such materials were not available.[59] Such findings graphically illustrate the high educational costs associated with shortages of low-cost inputs. In Zambia, more than one-quarter of children are being taught in classrooms that have no chalk; fewer than half have a notebook, and fewer than 10 per cent have a pencil.[60] These shortfalls in basic provision severely diminish the potential benefits associated with public investment in the education infrastructure.

It is not uncommon, especially in urban areas, for teachers to be instructing classes of more than 100 children.

Official statistics frequently obscure the full extent of the deficit in teaching materials. For instance, field surveys conducted in Uganda during 1999 found an average pupil/textbook ratio of 1:30, compared with a government figure of 1:7.[61] Across sub-Saharan Africa there are marked differences in textbook availability between urban and rural areas – and books become scarcer the farther the school is located from the distribution centre. In many cases, State monopolies in the supply of textbooks result in poor quality, erratic supply, and high cost.

Large class sizes are a major factor that inhibits educational performance. It is not uncommon, especially in urban areas, for teachers to be instructing classes of more than 100 children. Although evidence on the relationship between class size and performance is mixed, it is relatively rare, except in remote rural areas, for class sizes to fall below 40 – widely regarded as the ceiling for effective teaching. The scale of work required to achieve the Jomtien vision of 'education for all' is vast. For instance, in East Asia alone, it would be necessary to train an additional 2 million teachers to achieve a 40:1 ratio.[62]

The role of teachers
The quality of education depends on more than the state of school buildings and equipment. Equally important are curricula (which define what is

to be taught), pedagogical inputs, and class size. But perhaps the most fundamental requirement for good-quality education is the presence of well-motivated and skilled teachers. Teachers are at the heart of the education system. Yet while the importance of education has been increasingly widely recognised, the status of teachers has deteriorated. Low salaries, poor accommodation, inadequate professional support, and reduced social status have all combined to lower the level of teacher morale, and – in many cases – diminish the quality of teaching.

Teacher morale and deployment

Teachers were among the professional groups worst affected by the economic crisis that swept many developing countries in the 1980s. When governments cut public spending under the auspices of IMF–World Bank adjustment programmes, education budgets went into steep decline, along with the teachers' salaries that typically accounted for more than 90 per cent of recurrent spending. The erosion of salaries in Africa has left teachers in many countries with official salaries that represent half of the national income-poverty line. Many of the better teachers have reacted by leaving the profession. Those who have remained in the system have been forced to supplement their incomes by a variety of extra-curricular activities; inevitably, the resulting absenteeism damages children's education.[63] One consequence of the erosion of official salaries has been the institutionalisation of parental contributions to teacher-funds, often in the form of unrecorded, unofficial transfers. This is an example of pressure on education budgets fostering the unofficial privatisation of education financing, by transferring responsibility to household budgets.

In some cases, living standards for teachers have deteriorated at an astonishing rate. In 1980, the starting salary of a Zambian teacher was about $310 per month (at current prices). By 1997 a newly qualified teacher could expect to earn less than $65 a month – just above the national poverty line. In real terms, taking into account inflation, the average income for a teacher in 1998 was 75 per cent lower than it was two decades earlier.[64] In such circumstances it is remarkable that teachers continue to teach, despite being so poorly paid, and despite lacking the resources needed for their work.

Inadequate salaries are compounded in many countries by insufficient professional support. Good-quality teaching requires investment not just in training but also in in-service support. In many countries such support is either non-existent, or provided for only a few days every year. There are exceptions to this rule. Several countries have developed training and support programmes for teachers that place more emphasis on class-room practice and continuous in-service support. For example, in Guangzhou province of China, schools have responded to shortages of fully qualified teachers by developing shorter qualification courses, but then providing intensive in-service support and continuing training through short-term release courses.[65] Teacher development is institutionalised within the school system, with teaching hours managed to reflect the development needs of teachers.

In many countries the problem of teacher deployment is as serious as that of teacher recruitment. Burkina Faso gradually increased the number of trained teachers during the 1990s. Of the 2600 teachers recruited each year since 1994, some 700 receive the official two-year training provided by the Ecoles Nationales des Enseignants du Primaire (one year in college and one in the classroom). Thus two-thirds of teachers remain untrained. But the more serious problem is an imbalance between supply and demand. There are chronic shortages of teachers in the Sahelian areas of the north-east and in much of the south-west, where education indicators are the poorest in the country. In the national capital of Ouagadougou, by contrast, there are enough teachers to accommodate an additional 10,000 children.[66] The failure of governments to develop the recruitment strategies and incentives needed to meet the demand for teachers to work in more remote areas is a recurrent problem in the developing world.

In some places, effective strategies have been developed to address problems associated with teacher deployment. In the early 1980s, Zimbabwe was faced with chronic shortages of teachers as school enrolment increased. It responded by introducing double-shift teaching to reduce overcrowding in classrooms, so that one group would be taught in the mornings and another in the afternoon. Low-cost teacher-training methods were developed to minimise the time that teachers spent in training colleges, and to maximise the time they spent in classrooms.[67] Extensive use was made of teacher assistants and untrained staff working under supervision.

Since 1990, governments have followed this example in an effort to improve efficiency in school systems flawed by chronic shortage of funds. Countries have attempted to circumvent problems such as a shortage of teachers in various ways, including standardising class sizes, introducing multi-grade teaching, and developing multi-shift systems.[68] The Ghanaian government has reallocated staff from administrative tasks to teaching; and in Senegal unit costs have been lowered through a combination of redeployment and multi-grade teaching. Namibia and Côte d'Ivoire have also introduced multi-grade teaching in remote rural areas.

However, such reforms cannot succeed without appropriate institutional support. Multi-grade teaching requires specific skills, but it is often introduced without investing in training for teachers already in service. Similarly, untrained teachers can be very useful, provided that they are working with trained teachers, in a supportive role. But shortages of trained teachers place unrealistic demands on untrained, or insufficiently trained, assistants. This has happened in Burkina Faso, where more than one-third of rural schools operate multi-grade classes. Teaching quality has suffered because of the extensive use of assistants who have not been trained effectively in multi-grade teaching.

Effective teaching time

Adequate teaching time is a vital ingredient for good-quality education. Effective instruction demands that 800–1000 hours of teaching are provided each year.[69] Unfortunately, most school systems fall short of this mark, with the result that children do not spend enough time in school to complete a basic curriculum. Teacher absenteeism, often linked to economic pressures, is a major contributory factor.

There are wide national discrepancies in primary-school calendars. The primary-school year lasts for 180 days in Pakistan and Nepal, 190 days in Zambia, 200 days in Bangladesh, and 220 days in India.[70] But whatever the formal school year, there is a large gap between intended and actual instruction time. In theory, schools in Nepal operate on average for six hours a day. In practice, teaching time averages less than three hours per day, reducing the actual time spent by children in lessons from more than 1000 hours (similar to Indonesia's level) to just 540 hours.[71] Teacher absenteeism accounts for an estimated 60 per cent of the shortfall. Child sickness, weather conditions, household labour demand, and time spent on manual labour in schools further reduce the amount of time spent in the classroom. In turn, limited learning time sets the stage for low levels of achievement, the repetition of grades, and disincentives for parents to send their children to school.

In some cases, the real teaching time available to children from poor households is even more restricted. In India, the Public Report on Basic Education (PROBE) team found that the effective teaching time in school averaged two hours per day for 150 days – around one-third of the official figure. Teacher absenteeism was a major contributory factor. Unannounced visits to 15 schools in the Indian State of Uttar Pradesh found that two-thirds of teachers were absent on the day of the visit, while only two out of 15 schools had a full complement of teachers. It was rare for school to start on time in the morning, or to continue beyond mid-day.[72]

The case is not untypical. When interviewed in household surveys, parents often cite the limited amount of time spent by their children in school on learning activities as a major source of frustration. That frustration intensifies when attendance at school entails costs for the household budget. In Pakistan, a survey of government schools in Baluchistan found that one-fifth of teachers were not attending. Such findings help to explain why parents are often reluctant to invest scarce resources in education, and why the quality of education provided through public school systems is so poor. More than 90 per cent of parents covered in one survey in Baluchistan identified the persistent absence of teachers as a major factor hindering their child's education.[73]

While teacher absenteeism is in part a symptom of low pay, the problem is exacerbated by unaccountable school systems and top–down education planning which allows parents very limited influence. Community management and ownership of schools is one of the most effective ways of reducing teacher absenteeism, as the experience of the Shiksha Karmi schools in India and of the Bangladesh Rural Advancement Committee (BRAC) schools in Bangladesh demonstrates (see Chapter 6). However, parents frequently perceive teachers as being hostile and insensitive to the needs and interests of their children. In rural India, government teachers are mainly drawn from the ranks of higher classes and castes, and their salaries and job security place them in the more affluent sections of society. The PROBE survey found high levels of tension between teachers and local communities in many of the villages surveyed, especially in those with sharp divisions based on class or caste. Co-operation in formal institutions such as the Village Education Committee was minimal, and parents of poor children felt excluded from the school.[74]

In the North West Frontier Province of Pakistan, 60 per cent of teachers in primary school had failed the basic Grade 5 mathematics test.

Poor qualifications

Even when teachers attend school regularly, many are too poorly trained or provided with insufficient support to deliver an adequate service. Many teachers, especially those serving poor communities, do not have sufficient mastery over their subjects to meet basic learning goals. In the North West Frontier Province of Pakistan, 60 per cent of teachers in primary school had failed the basic Grade 5 mathematics test.[75] In Tamil Nadu State in India, only half of Grade 4 teachers could correctly answer

80 per cent of questions in a mathematics test for children at that level.[76] One of the factors behind these trends is the decline in living standards experienced by teachers. Many countries have witnessed an increase in the number of unqualified teachers, because those who are qualified seek out better-paid jobs. In Peru, the proportion of unqualified primary teachers has doubled over the past decade, and now represents more than half of the total.[77]

Better teacher-training is crucial. It is, not, however, a substitute for the recruitment of well-educated teachers; and it cannot fully compensate for low levels of educational attainment. Although the evidence is inconsistent, teachers with less than a secondary education appear to achieve worse results than their counterparts who graduated from secondary school. In Pakistan, for instance, students of teachers who had completed secondary school consistently outscored those students whose teachers had not progressed beyond primary.[78] Yet more than half of primary-school teachers have only completed primary school themselves before undergoing four years of residential training.

In Brazil, teachers' salaries are now less than half their 1980 level in real terms, with the result that few qualified people wish to enter the profession.

In educational systems with a low rate of progression from the primary to the secondary system, it is difficult to recruit teachers who have been through secondary school, illustrating how an inadequate primary-education system can create self-reinforcing problems. Once again, low remuneration can act as a further impediment. In Brazil, teachers' salaries are now less than half their 1980 level in real terms, with the result that few qualified people wish to enter the profession. About one in ten primary-school teachers in the country has had only an elementary education.[79]

The problem is not confined to the fact that many teachers lack knowledge about the subjects they are teaching; it is also true that the vast majority are trained to place a premium on rote-learning, rather than active participation. There is now a substantial body of classroom-based evidence pointing to the critical role of a positive environment in educational achievement. Students' achievements are enhanced by interactive teaching methods and active group work, and by pupils recounting what they have read. The development of numeracy skills through problem solving rather than rote-learning also improves achievement levels. Unfortunately, even where standards of formal qualification are higher, teacher training often perpetuates mechanistic and teacher-centred methods which are ill equipped to bring out the best in children. To cite one assessment: 'Teaching methodology is very poor. Owing to firmly entrenched traditions of status and hierarchy, education is seen as a one-way transfer of information from teacher to pupil, in which the latter plays a passive role. The emphasis is on the ability to retain facts, and the capacity to recite is seen as evidence of comprehension. The attitude toward education is that one size fits all.'[80]

The country in question is Cambodia, but the description would apply with equal force to many others. Pre-service training is often carried out by people with limited experience of working in classrooms, and almost no experience of child-centred teaching methods. Teacher-training programmes frequently place a premium on discipline, often producing unfortunate outcomes in the classroom. Fear of beatings and humiliation emerges as a recurrent theme in the accounts given by children of their experience in school – and that fear often contributes to decisions to stay away.

Female teachers

One of the most significant determinants of education quality for girls is the presence of a female teacher. A higher number of female teachers is desirable for many reasons, not least because women in positions of authority represent role models.[81] Female teachers are also far better placed than their male counterparts to respond to problems faced by girls at school, especially when they reach puberty. By contrast, the gender bias of male teachers in the classroom often results in a lack of self-confidence among girls. In socio-cultural settings where contact between females and males is limited, evidence suggests that the recruitment of female teachers can enhance girls' enrolment and attainment in school. Unfortunately, South Asia and sub-Saharan Africa, the developing regions with the largest gender gap in educational outcomes, are also the regions with the lowest ratios of female to male teachers. In South Asia, only one-third of all teachers are women.[82]

Limited recruitment of female teachers undermines the potential benefits of public investment in education by reducing qualitative outcomes. Household surveys in Ethiopia show that the presence of female teachers is likely to encourage parents to send their children to school, both because it gives them an increased sense of security, and because it improves learning among girl students.[83] This assessment is backed by evidence from a number of countries. In competency tests conducted in Pakistan, young girls educated by female teachers score 25 per cent higher than those taught by males.[84]

It is not just the qualitative aspects of education performance that suffer from the under-representation of female teachers. The presence of female teachers also exercises a positive influence on enrolment rates for girls: gender gaps are narrower in schools with a higher proportion of female teachers. Sri Lanka has the highest rate of female-teacher recruitment in South Asia, and the lowest gender gap in enrolment. In India, the proportions of female teachers vary from 20 per cent in Bihar, which has some of the country's widest gender disparities, to 67 per cent in Kerala, with India's lowest gender disparity. The PROBE survey found that only 21 per cent of teachers were female, with an even lower representation of women in senior posts. Almost two-thirds of the schools surveyed did not have a single female teacher.[85]

There are no simple solutions to the problem of insufficient female recruitment. The same cultural constraints that require girls to be taught by women often make it difficult to attract women into teaching posts, especially in the rural areas, where shortages of female teachers are most pronounced. High-profile campaigns to change attitudes and attract women to a career in teaching have an important role to play. Beyond this, innovative strategies are needed at various levels. As a first step, recruitment policies for women teachers may need to be modified, especially in countries where few girls proceed beyond lower-secondary grades. Allowing young women to enter teacher training with lower levels of educational attainments and then providing support could help to remove one barrier to entry. The provision of grants to support girls through teacher-training colleges would also help, as would salary incentives and travel expenses for working in rural areas. However, even with these incentives, many female teachers may be unwilling to work in remote areas away from their homes. Many of the more successful non-government interventions have addressed this problem by focusing on local recruitment, with local women trained to teach in their communities.

The curriculum and language of instruction

The school curriculum has an important bearing on educational outcomes. It defines what is to be taught and gives general direction as to the duration of instruction. Weak curriculum design can prevent children from realising their full educational potential. Problems in this respect range from inappropriate content to inadequate consideration for the needs of children who speak minority languages.[86]

In most developing countries, the primary curriculum is geared towards preparing students for secondary school and higher levels of education. Curricula, textbooks, and teacher training are often based on assumptions and objectives that do not reflect local realities, or the learning needs of most students.[87] There is an undue emphasis on learning facts and preparing for examinations that determine access to the next level of education, regardless of the fact that many children will not make the transition. In sub-Saharan Africa, vocational subjects such as agriculture and trade typically account for less than 5 per cent of the curriculum, although these subjects are likely to represent better vehicles for transmitting literacy and numeracy skills than rote-learning does. Topics such as health, water and sanitation, and protection of the environment are dealt with only as marginal subjects, despite their obvious relevance to the lives of children from poor households. A further problem is that official primary curricula often cover too wide a range of subjects, with insufficient priority given to core learning skills in basic literacy and numeracy.[88]

Another major obstacle to learning in many countries is the language of instruction. Pupils learn to read and acquire other skills more quickly if they are at first taught in their mother tongue.[89] Moreover, if the language of instruction is not the one spoken at home, parents are more likely to be excluded from the education process, with damaging implications for the child's development. In many cases, second-language teaching increases the likelihood of children having to repeat grades, thereby exacerbating the risk of drop-out.

Curricula, textbooks, and teacher training are often based on assumptions and objectives that do not reflect local realities, or the learning needs of most students.

Despite this, second-language teaching remains a pervasive problem. In many developing countries, the language of instruction is that of the former colonial power. The first public school system in Burkina Faso was developed at the end of the last century by the French government, as a means of consolidating the colonial system. Today, the system is less elitist at the primary level in terms of access, but the educational content still bears a strong French influence, and most schools continue to use French as a medium of instruction. In Bolivia, 60 per cent of the population do not speak Spanish as a mother tongue; yet educational materials in the nine major languages spoken by indigenous peoples are often unavailable in highland areas, and Spanish is the medium of instruction from Grade 1.[90] Mother-tongue teaching is also inadequately developed across much of East Asia. In Vietnam, ethnic-minority languages are spoken by 13 per cent of the population, yet Kinh, the language spoken by the majority of Vietnamese, is the only language used in schools.[91] This helps to explain why the children of ethnic minorities reach far lower levels of education, especially when they have had not pre-school training in the dominant Kinh language.

Reforming policy
There are practical solutions to each of these problems. Community involvement in developing curricula and textbooks can increase the relevance and quality of education. The experiences (discussed in

Chapter 6) of the Escuela Nueva programme in Colombia, the Bangladesh Rural Advancement Committee, and the *pedagogie convergente* in Mali have helped to identify some of the key elements for successful alternative strategies. These models have modified school calendars to match agricultural calendars and labour demands, and they have developed teaching methods that promote more active and co-operative learning.[92] The curriculum is designed to reflect local needs, and children are able to proceed at their own pace through the system, which reduces repetition rates.

The question of language is more complex. Parents themselves are often ambivalent. On the one hand, they often see instruction in the dominant language as a vital requirement for enhancing employment prospects, negotiating with traders, and dealing with local officials. On the other hand, parents recognise that second-language teaching leads to under-performance. Clearly, proper consideration needs to be given to the demand for education in languages seen by parents as opening doors to more remunerative employment. It also needs to be recognised that language issues are politically and culturally contentious. There are, however, constructive solutions to the language problem.

Evidence from a large number of countries suggests that school performance improves where the first two to three years of instruction are in the child's mother tongue, with the dominant language introduced first as a subject for study and later as the medium of instruction. Under a model developed by UNICEF in Peru, basic reading and writing skills are taught in the mother tongue in Grade 1, with Spanish introduced as a second language. Instruction progressively shifts towards Spanish, which becomes the sole teaching language only in Grade 6.[93] This model has been adapted in other countries. For example, the government of Burkina Faso has introduced pilot projects through 'satellite schools' which introduce French during the second year. However, the Education Ministry has been slow to integrate the lessons of this project into the national system.

Teaching minority-language groups requires special skills, a fact that is seldom recognised. In Vietnam, teacher-training programmes do not provide much instruction in teaching Kinh as a second language. Few specialised teaching materials are available, and limited use is made of bilingual teaching assistants. Oxfam is working with local education authorities in ethnic-minority areas to address these problems.[94] There are, however, acute shortages of teachers who speak ethnic-minority languages, one of the most basic requirements for achieving a sustained improvement. The problem is self-reinforcing: poor-quality language teaching reduces the flow of ethnic-minority children through the school system, thereby limiting the scope for increased recruitment.

Unlike many countries, Vietnam has recognised the special needs of ethnic-minority groups. However, the policies implemented to address these problems have frequently produced perverse outcomes. One such policy is that of reducing the curriculum in ethnic minority areas from the standard 180 weeks to 120 weeks. The ethnic-minority curriculum was prompted by a concern that low enrolment and high drop-out rates in minority areas were the product of higher levels of household demand for child labour in agricultural production. But while there are clearly advantages in adapting the curriculum to the realities of seasonal labour calendars, the ethnic-minority system is designed to achieve lower levels of cognitive skills, and will result in poorer education outcomes. The dual-curriculum system reinforces through official policy the informal disadvantages that minorities such as the Hmung already face. The danger is that this will reinforce the poverty and marginalisation of ethnic-minority communities, by creating a two-tier system. As it is, children in ethnic-minority areas are often taught for far fewer hours than the official minimum. Oxfam research among the Hmung community in Vietnam's Northern Upland region showed that children often spent no more than 1.5 hours in school, many of them having to walk for longer than this to get there.

Oxfam research among the Hmung community in Vietnam's Northern Upland region showed that children often spent no more than 1.5 hours in school, many of them having to walk for longer than this to get there.

It is not only developing-country governments that have failed to address language problems. In some cases, the governments of developed countries have displayed a flagrant disregard for local languages. Over the past 25 years, Australia's Northern Territory has successfully introduced bilingual education programmes for Aboriginal children. These programmes have attracted Aboriginal children into school and helped to address major inequalities in the provision of education. Much remains to be done, because Aboriginal children in remote areas are far behind the average level of literacy. Yet in 1998, the Northern Territory government cancelled the bilingual teaching programmes in their entirety. No explanation has so far been given, despite representations from aboriginal groups, supported by Community Aid Abroad (Oxfam in Australia). Apart from posing obvious threats to the Aboriginal community, the Northern Territory's action represents a clear breach of the government's obligations, set out in the Convention on the Rights of the Child, to protect and respect the rights of indigenous people.[95]

119

Children with disabilities

Good-quality education is available to only a small proportion of children with special needs. Children with disabilities, especially girls, are far less likely to attend primary school. Many of those who do go to school receive an education that is entirely inappropriate. Educational disadvantage prevents children with special needs from gaining the skills and confidence that they need to avoid extreme poverty in adulthood. Begging is the most common form of livelihood for people with disabilities in developing countries.

As in other areas of education, data on disability are notoriously poor. The World Health Organisation (WHO) estimates that about one in ten children in developing countries has special needs in education. If this is broadly correct, there are some 62 million children of primary-school age coping with disability. Taking into account older children who have not completed primary education would multiply this figure by a factor of three. Probably fewer than 2 per cent of children with disabilities in developing countries are in school. It follows that the disabled are disproportionately represented among those out of school — and that reaching the disabled should be a central theme in strategies for achieving education for all.

Limited coverage through special schools
Efforts to educate disabled children have focused in the past on private voluntary effort and the provision of separate special-needs schools. These schools provide children with access to specialised teaching skills, but their coverage is limited.

- In Zambia, more than half of all disabled adults have received no education, which is almost double the proportion for the population at large. There are 120 special schools in the country, reaching out to about 25,000 children among a disabled population of primary-school age in excess of 175,000.
- China invested heavily in the expansion of special-needs schools in the 1980s. Today, however, these schools cater for only about 130,000 students out of an estimated disabled-child population in excess of 8 million. Fewer than 2 per cent of the country's blind children and 0.3 per cent of those with learning difficulties are in school.

- In the early 1990s it was estimated that India had some 3 million children in need of special education, but specialised institutions – almost all of them voluntary – were catering for fewer than one per cent of those with learning difficulties.

Limited coverage has not been the only problem associated with specialised education. Placing disabled children in separate educational establishments can have the effect of reinforcing their sense of isolation and separation from the wider community. It can also reinforce negative social attitudes that are at the heart of the problems confronting disabled members of the community. Children with disabilities are often viewed by their parents as a source of shame, and by wider society as 'problems' in need of separate treatment. The sense of separateness that this engenders adds to the exclusion and emotional distress experienced by disabled people.

Towards inclusive education
Recognition of the limitations of specialised schools, allied to campaigning by disabled people's organisations, has started to change approaches to provision for those with special needs. The principle of inclusive education is now widely accepted. In 1994, at the World Conference on Special Needs Education, governments adopted the principle that 'those with special educational needs must have access to regular schools which should accommodate them within a child-centered pedagogy capable of meeting these needs'.

The new consensus is that children and young people with special needs should be included in the educational arrangements made for the majority of children. Special schools, or units within normal schools, are seen as having a role to play in providing for children with disabilities who cannot be catered for elsewhere. But investment in these schools is now seen as having the primary purpose of providing professional support to regular schools in the form of specialised teacher training and curricula development.

Translating inclusive principles into practice is difficult, even in industrialised countries. Spain exemplifies the philosophy of developing inclusive education within the regular school system, and it has invested heavily in making the transition. Class sizes have been reduced, all schools are guaranteed access to a special-needs support team, specialised textbooks have been developed and made available, and teachers have been trained to respond to the special needs of disabled children.

Unlike Spain, many developing countries are attempting to make the transition to inclusive special-needs provision without making the necessary investments. Education ministries now use 'inclusive' rhetoric as a matter of course when describing their policies on disability. The reality is that chronic under-investment in education is preventing this rhetoric from being translated into reality. Ordinary classroom teachers receive limited guidance on how to teach children with disabilities; appropriate teaching materials – such as large-print books for visually impaired children – are not available; and furnishings and facilities are not adapted to the needs of disabled pupils. Many of these problems have been addressed in the context of specific projects and programmes. For instance, the UK charity, Save the Children, has worked with the government of Ghana in developing curricula and teacher-training modules in twenty poor districts. In China, the government has piloted an integrated education project that is bringing disabled children into the mainstream kindergarten system.

And India has introduced inclusive education into its mainstream national teacher-training programmes. The problem is that progress has been limited and piecemeal.

Integrating disabled children into over-crowded classes that lack basic textbooks and well-motivated teachers is a policy for exclusion, not inclusion. What is needed is the integration of provision for disabled children into mainstream national education plans designed to improve the overall quality and accessibility of the education system. Within these plans, far greater investment is required in the development of specialised teaching skills and staff support, and in the provision of special teaching materials.

(Sources: M. Kelly, 'Primary Education in a Heavily Indebted Country: the Case of Zambia', Oxford: Oxfam Policy Department, 1998; P. Mittler, 'Special needs education: an international perspective', *British Journal of Special Education*, Vol 22 (3), 1995; J. Lynch, *Provision for Children with Special Educational Needs in the Asia Region,* World Bank Technical Paper 261, Washington, 1994; Save the Children, *Inclusive Education*, London, 1998; UNESCO, *The Salamanca Statement and Framework for Action on Special Needs Education,* Paris, 1994.)

Inequalities in education

Economists typically think about poverty and inequality in terms of income. Countries are divided into low-income and high-income groupings, and people into low-income and high-income households. Differences in wealth matter, because they define opportunities for reducing poverty. But differences in wealth reflect deeper inequalities in life-chances, including inequalities in education. As economic activity becomes increasingly knowledge-based, disparities in educational opportunity will play a more important role in determining the distribution of income and poverty.

This chapter is about inequality in education. The first section explores the widest of all divides: that separating the citizens of rich countries from those of poor countries. Left intact, this divide will cause global income-distribution to become even more distorted in favour of the wealthy. But global inequalities of educational opportunity are not just a matter of crude differences between North and South. Disparities between developing countries are also marked, with important implications for the distribution of income between developing regions. The second part of this chapter examines South–South disparities. It does so by using a new analytical tool – the Education Performance Index (EPI) – to rank countries on the basis of their achievements at the primary-school level.

Comparisons between regions and countries provide an insight into average performance. But in education, as in other areas, averages conceal differences based on wealth, gender, region, ethnicity, and other factors. The third section of the chapter examines the distribution of opportunities for education within developing countries. National inequalities in education are often greater than North–South inequalities. Just as the latter reinforce highly unequal patterns of income distribution in the global economy, inequality in the distribution of national opportunities for education enables the wealthy to capture a disproportionately large share of national wealth. These national inequalities cast the global education crisis in a new light. The crisis is fundamentally a crisis for the poor, since there are only a few countries in which the rich have not achieved universal basic education. The final section uses a disaggregated version of the EPI to capture the extent of inequality across a wide range of dimensions by ranking different regions of the same country.

North–South inequalities

Contrasts between a typical primary school in Europe or the United States and a similar facility in rural sub-Saharan Africa or South Asia capture some of the dimensions of global inequality in education. In much of the developing world, 'school' is often a dilapidated mud building with crumbling walls. More than 80 children, many of them under-nourished, might be crammed into a classroom, sitting on the floor with scarcely a book, pencil, or notepad to share. Their teachers, most of them untrained, may have second jobs to make ends meet. Rote-learning will be the order of the day. Water and sanitation facilities are likely to be grossly inadequate. Primary schools in industrialised countries face problems of their own – but they are problems of a different order. Teachers are well trained, class sizes are smaller, paper and pencils will be in plentiful supply. The school will have a library, and probably computers. The walls will be decorated with the work of the children, maps, and other visual aids. Each child will have access to a set of core textbooks. While the national media and parents' associations may take the view that schools are in a state of perpetual crisis, it is a crisis of a different order than that which prevails in the developing world.

Financing gaps

The material contrasts between the education systems of rich and poor countries reflect huge disparities in financing capacity. The problem is not that poor countries spend a smaller share of their national wealth on education than rich countries. In fact, sub-Saharan Africa spends a larger share of its GDP – around 5.6 per cent – on education than the OECD countries spend, though many countries in the region spend far less than the average. Measured in terms of public effort, Africa has been investing more in primary education than other regions, and also increasing that effort over time. The problem is that disparities in wealth translate into huge disparities in spending, which in turn produce highly unequal outcomes in terms of public provision for basic education. This is especially true when, as in Africa's case, economic decline reduces the absolute value of any given proportion of GDP invested in education.

Some indication of the financial divide separating education systems in the developed and developing worlds can be provided by a simple profile of expenditure (see Figure 3.1). With one-fifth of the world's population, the industrialised countries account for more than four-fifths of total public spending on education.[1] At the other extreme, South Asia accounts for almost 25 per cent of the world's population, but for only

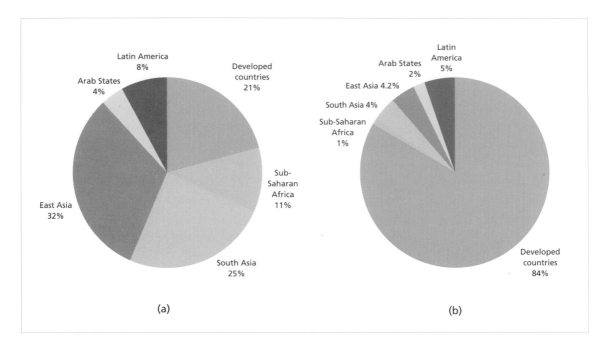

(a)

(b)

Figure 3.1
**(a) Distribution of world
population (1995)
(b) Spending on education**

Source:
UNESCO, *Statistical Yearbook 1997,*
Paris, 1997

4 per cent of spending on education. Sub-Saharan Africa, with 10 per cent of the world's population, accounts for only 1 per cent of public investment in education. The absolute differences in overall spending levels are enormous. On average, the OECD countries spend $4636 per student through public finance for primary and secondary education, compared with $165 per student in developing countries and $49 in sub-Saharan Africa (see Figure 3.2).

Part of the problem of achieving greater equity in educational opportunity is that disparities in financing are large and continue to grow. To take relative spending in 1980 as the point of comparison, per capita public spending on education in sub-Saharan Africa and South Asia is now 60 per cent lower than average spending in the industrialised world. In Latin America, it is one-third lower (see Figure 3.3). Only East Asia has closed the financing gap in education, although this picture has almost certainly changed in the wake of the financial crisis. While inefficiencies in public spending contribute to the education gap separating rich and poor countries, differences in national wealth, related in turn to the distribution of global income, are the main determinant of the financing gap.

Demographic factors are reinforcing the effects of differential growth rates and initial income inequalities. In the industrialised countries, the size of the population aged under 15 has contracted by about 6 per cent

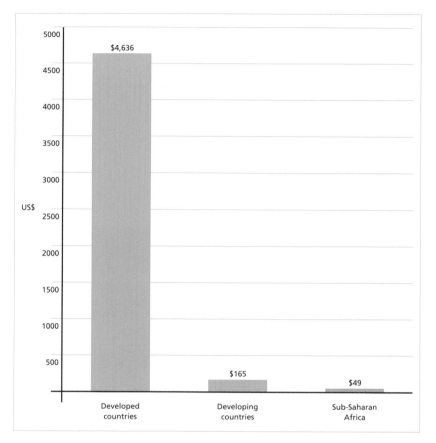

Figure 3.2
Public spending per student on primary and secondary education (1995)

Source:
UNESCO, *Statistical Yearbook 1997*, Paris, 1997

since 1970, while per capita incomes have grown at more than 2 per cent a year. Spending per pupil has risen significantly as a result, even though the share of GDP allocated to education has been static. In developing countries, the population aged under 15 has grown by one-third over the same period, while problems of economic stagnation and debt have, in many cases, reduced financing capacity. The importance of demographic trends can hardly be overstated. At any given level of average income and unit cost of schooling, countries with higher rates of population growth will face relatively higher per capita costs in progressing towards education for all. In the developed countries, children aged 6–11 typically comprise 5–8 per cent of total population, and population growth is now zero. In sub-Saharan Africa, the 6–11 age group typically represents more than 15 per cent of the population, rising to 20 per cent for countries such as Tanzania, Zambia, and Uganda.[2] It is not just that the education budgets of these countries are infinitesimally smaller than those of developed countries, but that these smaller budgets must cover a primary-school population that is three times larger in relative terms.

Figure 3.3
**Public expenditure on
education: percentage change
in developing regions in
relation to developed countries
(1980-94)***

Source:
UNESCO, *Statistical Yearbook 1997*

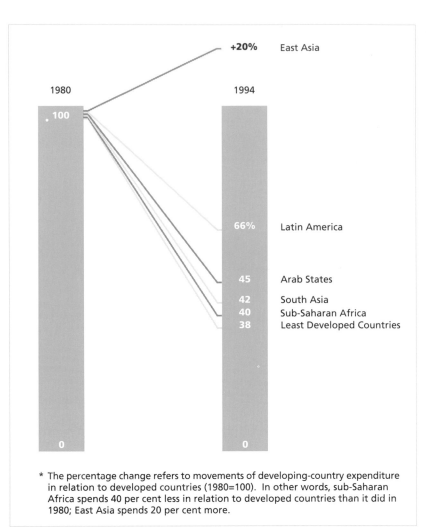

* The percentage change refers to movements of developing-country expenditure
in relation to developed countries (1980=100). In other words, sub-Saharan
Africa spends 40 per cent less in relation to developed countries than it did in
1980; East Asia spends 20 per cent more.

Financing differences are marked at all levels of education, but the
biggest gap is to be found at the primary level. Taking into account only
recurrent budgets, per capita spending on primary-school pupils in
Nepal and India is about $12, compared with $5130 in the United States.[3]
Annual spending per primary-school pupil in Britain is equivalent to
$3553 – around 130 times more than in Zambia. At one level, these simple
spending comparisons give an exaggerated picture of the problem. The
costs of materials, buildings, and teachers' salaries are obviously higher
in the developed countries, so that the same provision costs more. At
another level, financial comparisons understate the problem. They do
not, for instance, capture the high levels of private spending on education in
the industrialised countries. In the developing world, millions of households do not own a single book; the consequent restrictions on children's

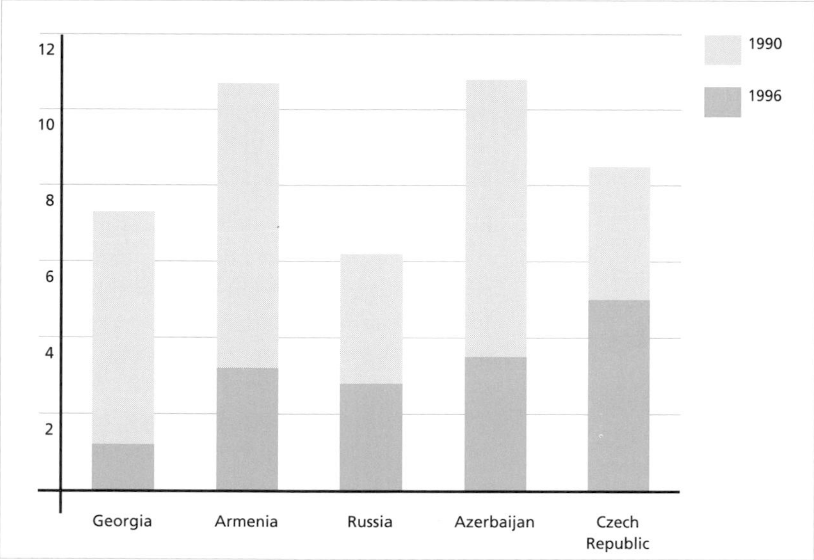

Figure 3.4
Selected transition economies: public expenditure on education as a percentage of GDP. 1990-96

Source:
UNESCO, *Education for All?*
Regional Monitoring Report 5, 1998

academic development are obvious. By contrast, recent research in Britain, the USA, and Australia found that more than 80 per cent of children of primary-school age had 25 or more books at home.[4] This illustrates how private spending capacity widens the already extreme differences in opportunity associated with differences in public spending.

Comparisons of public spending fail to capture another dimension of financial inequality. Pressure on recurrent expenditure in many of the poorest countries means that teachers' salaries often account for more than 95 per cent of spending – leaving almost nothing for the purchase of teaching materials, or the maintenance of schools.[5] Non-salary recurrent expenditure at the primary level in much of sub-Saharan Africa is less than $2 per pupil, which explains the generalised lack of textbooks and other teaching materials. This low level of public expenditure helps to explain the large share of education financing provided directly by households through cost-recovery and assorted school levies – an issue addressed in Chapter 4.

While inequalities in education provision and quality are greatest between developed and developing countries, countries in transition are also facing acute problems. They too are falling further behind the high-income industrialised countries, with a major crisis on the horizon in parts of Eastern Europe and the former Soviet Union. Highly developed education systems are collapsing in the face of declining public investment and falling living standards (Figure 3.4). Some of the major causes and consequences are discussed in the box on the next page.

The crisis of education in the transition economies

The formerly socialist 'transition' countries of Russia and Eastern Europe attained levels of access to education far beyond those of many other countries at similar stages of development. Compulsory and free basic education up to the mid-secondary level, high levels of gender equity, and, especially in the sciences, good standards of learning were among their achievements. Today, however, the education systems of the region are crumbling in a context of economic stagnation, rising inequality, and declining State provision. In education as in other areas, there is a growing danger that the positive inheritance from the past will be lost in the process of transition to market economies.

Oxfam has witnessed at first hand the collapse of education systems through its work with marginal communities in Armenia, Azerbaijan, and Georgia, the former Soviet republics in the southern Caucasus region. For these communities, the rising direct costs of schooling, such as expenditure on textbooks, meals, transport, and other services that were previously provided free, combined with wider economic pressures, notably declining wages and unemployment, put education out of people's reach. At the same time, the reduced provision of schooling, especially in areas affected by conflict, and its deteriorating quality are widely perceived as problems. The precise mix of demand and supply factors varies from place to place. But the crisis is real, and it has profound implications for economic recovery and social equity. The following are among the problems which must be addressed to prevent further decline of the education systems in these transition economies:

- **The erosion of compulsory and free basic education.** Most Central and Eastern European countries have restored enrolment to pre-transition levels. This is not the case in the former Soviet republics, which have witnessed dramatic declines in enrolment both at the primary level and in general secondary education. UNICEF has estimated that as many as one in seven children may now be out of school in Central Asia and the Caucasus. Half a million Russian children aged between 6 and 10 are now missing from each grade in the school system.

- **Rising costs.** The cost to families of educating children has risen dramatically. Budgetary constraints mean that schools are now encouraged to raise their own funds. Parents are meeting a growing share of school budgets and teachers' salaries out of their own pockets. Textbooks, once free, are now being charged for, along with notebooks and pencils. These rising costs come during a period when family incomes have been eroded by declining wages, rising unemployment, and inflation. At the beginning of 1996, the price of a package of basic materials for school in Azerbaijan was about $50. The average monthly wage was only $13.

- **Declining public provision.** For many countries, 'transition' has become a euphemism for a shrinking national economy. In 1997, real GDP in the Caucasus countries was less than 40 per cent of the 1989 level, less than 60 per cent in Russia's case. Economic decline on this scale inevitably diminishes the government's capacity to finance basic services through public revenues. Unfortunately, the problem has been exacerbated by political decisions to reduce the proportion of revenues allocated to basic services, including education. Figure 3.4 illustrates how public spending on education has all but collapsed in Georgia and in Armenia. Not only has national income shrunk by two-thirds in both cases, but the share of income going to education has fallen – by 80 per cent in the case of Georgia. Russia has reduced the proportion of national income spent on education by less, but had allocated a relatively small share of income to education in the first place.

- **Deteriorating quality of schools and schooling.** Precipitous declines in public spending have taken their toll on school infrastructure and service provision. Buildings and equipment have suffered disproportionately, with many schools in a state of chronic disrepair. One in five of Georgia's schools has been classified unsafe and unfit for occupation. In most of the former Soviet republics, teachers' salaries are now below the poverty line, forcing many to take second jobs. Low teacher morale, like deteriorating school buildings and declining public investment, is a sign of diminishing educational opportunity.

It would be wrong to conclude that the systems of education developed under central planning provided a model of uniform good practice. The quality of education often left much to be desired, with a great emphasis on learning facts by rote, rather than on child-centred development. School-management and teaching practices were generally rigid and authoritarian, with little parental involvement. There were also limits to equity, with rural areas often disadvantaged, and ethnic groups suffering discrimination. But, while reforms to central planning were urgently needed, responsibility for developing a coherent education policy and for funding equitable access seems to have been abandoned. The transition to a situation in which household income determines access to educational opportunities is inherently inefficient in economic terms. The fact that this transition is occurring at a time of rapidly rising poverty and social inequality carries grave implications for social equity and cohesion today, and for future prospects of social and economic recovery.

(Source: UNESCO, *Education for All?* Regional Monitoring Report 5, 1998)

Primary school and beyond

Good-quality primary education provides the foundation on which individuals and countries can progress to develop higher levels of skills and learning. As production becomes increasingly knowledge-intensive, the development of secure livelihoods will require not only universal primary education, but high levels of transition into secondary and higher education. Many developing countries are ill equipped to make the transition.

The combination of low enrolment and low completion rates in much of the developing world means that children spend far less time in education than children in developed countries. On average, a child entering primary school in the developing world can expect to receive eight to nine years of education, compared with the 15–17 years that can be expected in developed countries.[6] As always, however, the average conceals as much as it reveals:

- 'School-life expectancy' in sub-Saharan Africa is five to six years. It is less than three years in Burkina Faso, Mali, Niger, and Mozambique.

- In Bangladesh, 'school-life expectancy' is less than four and a half years for girls and six years for boys.

Even these cases obscure the full extent of the problem. This is because averages capture the aggregate picture for the entire population, but conceal differences between average outcomes and those for the poorest sections of society. In poor households, school-life expectancy is invariably far lower, and the proportion of children not attending school is far higher. But in many developing countries the wider consequence of poor-quality education and limited progression through the primary-school system is an exceptionally low rate of transition into the secondary-school system.

The 2015 target of universal primary education has focused international concern on the primary-school system, often to the exclusion of secondary-school education. But the quality of secondary provision is of profound importance, for at least three reasons. First, basic education alone is not enough to ensure the adoption of new production methods and diffusion of new technologies, especially those associated with information and communications. The expansion of secondary schooling is vital for the development of the higher levels of education upon which national prosperity increasingly depends. Effective secondary schooling fosters the development of more flexible and abstract reasoning skills of the type associated with high-growth sectors of manufacturing and service industries, and there is evidence that secondary schooling is positively associated with the development of export production in higher-value-added areas of production. Second, limited opportunities for progression to secondary education have the effect of reducing demand for primary education. This is because many parents see primary education as a stepping stone to the secondary education that their children need in order to maximise their income-generation and employment opportunities – a perspective supported by research that indicates high rates of return in secondary education. Third, success in accelerating progress towards universal primary education will inevitably increase demand for secondary education. At present, many secondary-education systems are unable to absorb even the trickle of students who progress through the primary-education system.

Viewed in this context, the current state of secondary education poses acute problems. At least 700 million people live in countries with gross enrolment rates of less than 40 per cent, and another one billion in countries with rates in the range of 30–70 per cent.[7] Enrolment rates in the former group of countries have not increased significantly over the last decade, and only modest advances have been recorded in the latter group. As in primary education, sub-Saharan Africa poses the greatest challenge. The region accounts for fully two-thirds of the countries with gross enrolment rates at the secondary level of less than 40 per cent, with fewer than one-third of primary-school children progressing to the secondary level. There are 19 countries in the region with gross enrolment rates of less than 20 per cent, with a large group falling far short of this level. This group includes Malawi, Mozambique, Burkina Faso, Chad, and Mali, all of which have enrolment rates of less than 10 per cent, and Tanzania, where the secondary-school enrolment rate of 5 per cent is the lowest in the world.

No developing region is yet close to achieving universal secondary-school enrolment (see Figure 3.5). East Asia, South Asia, and Latin America

Figure 3.5
Gross enrolment rates in secondary and tertiary levels of education (1995)

Source:
UNESCO, *Statistical Yearbook 1997*, Paris, 1997

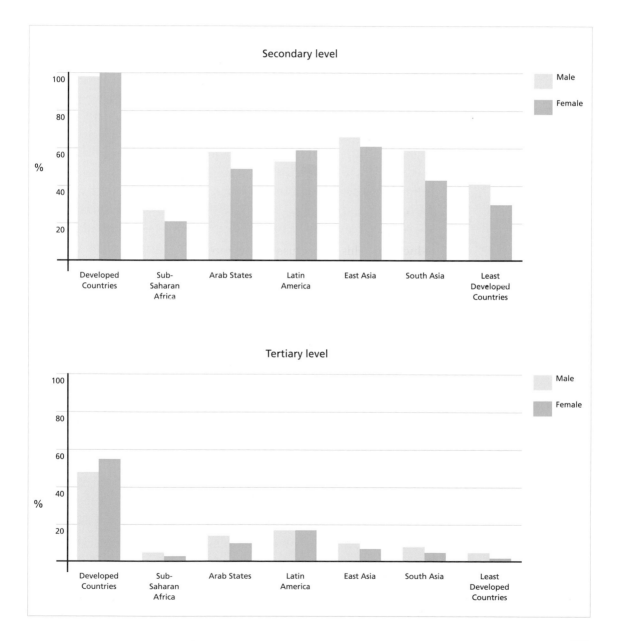

have closed the gap, but they still remain far behind the industrialised countries. Moreover, there are large gender gaps in secondary education, with girls accounting for a far smaller share of enrolment in South Asia in particular. This is the inverse of the situation in industrialised countries (and Latin America), where boys are under-represented. The transition point between primary and secondary schools is at the mid-point in a cumulative cycle of inequality. Limited progression through the secondary system produces a limited transfer into the tertiary system. Only 3 per cent of African children, 8 per cent of South Asian children, and 17 per cent of children in East Asia progress beyond secondary school. With the exception of Latin America, significant gender gaps remain at higher levels of education.

More than half of the children entering the education systems of the industrialised countries today will progress through secondary school to the tertiary system.

The contrast between developing and industrialised countries is striking. Several OECD countries have a higher rate of enrolment of young women at the tertiary level than sub-Saharan Africa has achieved for girls at the primary level. More than half of the children entering the education systems of the industrialised countries today will progress through secondary school to the tertiary system. As an OECD report puts it, 'once learning is realised on this scale in upper-secondary education, it is hard to resist the demand for tertiary studies'.[8] At the other extreme, insufficient learning at the primary level in sub-Saharan Africa means that there cannot be a sustained increase in enrolment at the lower-secondary level. Some of the differences are especially stark. While millions of girls in South Asia and Africa never step inside a school, women now account for the majority of tertiary enrolments in most OECD countries.

As the process of globalisation integrates developing countries ever more deeply into a knowledge-based global economy, differences in educational opportunity at the secondary and tertiary levels will increasingly distort the benefits of economic growth in favour of rich countries. Without a sustained expansion of coverage and an improvement in education quality at the primary and secondary levels, developing countries will fall further behind at the tertiary level. In turn, as tertiary education becomes more important to innovation, economic growth, and employment, the wealth gap and the education gap will create a vicious circle of economic decline and rising global inequality.

Unequal opportunities in access to multimedia communications technology

'Each one of our schools will be linked to the Internet by 2002,' the British Prime Minister Tony Blair pledged in 1998.[9] Similar commitments have been made by political leaders across the industrialised world. But as the communications revolution arrives in the schools of the industrialised world, there is a grave danger that developing countries will be excluded from new areas of learning. And as information technology is integrated more extensively into production systems, the risk of future marginalisation will intensify.

In the industrialised countries, telecommunications technology has already revolutionised education. Technological trends in hardware and software have increased the availability and usefulness of computers for education. Digitalisation has led to the development of computers with multimedia capacity, presenting text, image, and sound to the user.[10] On the software side, 'graphical user interfaces' have made it possible to control computer functions by pointing at pictures rather than by typing text, and to develop interactive programmes for users. Compact discs have made available a vast range of audio and visual learning devices, considerably reducing the costs of accessing information in the process.

Educationalists increasingly recognise the potential benefits of computers for improving the quality of teaching and learning, and expanding the range of information available to children. Learning opportunities are being revolutionised in particular by the Internet, a worldwide information highway, with easy access via the World Wide Web. Searching among different websites has been facilitated through simple interface 'navigation' tools, which enable schools to download documents from other computers. Increased access to user-friendly equipment that enables computers to communicate with each other has created what amounts to a 'virtual' worldwide library.

Access to computers at school is becoming increasingly widespread in the industrialised countries, starting at the primary and the lower-secondary levels. Growing numbers of children also have access to home computers – although the 'digital divide' between rich and poor house-holds is growing. In the Netherlands, more than half of all households have personal computers, 15 per cent of which are connected to the Internet. Estimates for the USA place the ratio of computers to children at the primary and secondary levels at 1:6. In the USA, Britain, and Denmark, one-third of 14-year-old science students report using computers.[11] For those with access to information technologies, there are obvious advantages. Students who are familiar with basic computing will adapt more easily to the profound changes that are happening in labour markets with the spread of information technology. They will benefit from higher incomes and wider employment opportunities, and their countries will benefit from associated gains in productivity and competitiveness.

Failure to close the information-technology gap now opening up between school systems in the rich and poor worlds will inevitably result in increasing income inequalities. But the gap cannot be closed by technology and finance alone. The problem is that the extension of computer technologies to schools requires substantial financial expenditure for the purchase of equipment and the training of staff. Governments in the industrialised world have turned to the private sector for assistance. But education authorities in the developing world face enormous financial and technical obstacles in obtaining basic computer equipment, with the result that inequalities in access to information technology will start to increase at a far earlier age.

Most schools in sub-Saharan Africa and South Asia do not have the electricity and the telephone lines needed to use computers and access international web sites, let alone the financial resources to purchase them.

Much has been written about the scope for extending computerised learning systems to the poorest countries.[12] Unfortunately, much of it is divorced from reality. The emphasis has been on the creation of international funds to transfer education technologies through partnerships between development-assistance programmes and private companies. However, many of the poorest countries lack even the most basic infrastructural requirements. Most schools in sub-Saharan Africa and South Asia do not have the electricity and the telephone lines needed to use computers and access international web sites, let alone the financial resources to purchase them. In countries such as Mali and Mozambique, where there are fewer than four telephone lines for every 1000 people, and where per capita student spending at the primary level is less than $1, the prospects for effective use of new education technologies are limited.

As the effects of inequalities in access to information technology at the primary and junior-secondary levels feed through into the higher and vocational levels of education, the knowledge gap will inevitably widen. In the era of the Information Age, described in Chapter 1, the implications for the future distribution of global wealth are profound.

Inequalities between developing countries: the Education Performance Index

North–South inequalities in access to the knowledge and skills imparted by education will shape future patterns of income distribution in the global economy. However, developing countries themselves are not a homogeneous group. There are marked inequalities in educational attainment across and within regions. These inequalities will also have a bearing, not just on income distribution and future shares of international trade, but also on prospects for human development.

Attempting to capture the extent of educational inequality poses serious methodological problems. Most reporting systems refer to data on enrolment rates, completion rates, literacy standards, and gender-based inequality. But measurements in each of these areas are treated in isolation, which can create a misleading picture of overall performance. Countries that achieve a high level of success in enrolment may perform poorly in terms of completion rates. Conversely, education systems may achieve high rates of completion for those who enter school, while large sections of the population never actually attend school.

The Education Performance Index (EPI) provides a more integrated measure of performance across a wider range of dimensions. We use the EPI to rank more than 100 developing countries on a composite indicator for education. The same countries are then ranked on the basis of income. Some of the results are predictable. The EPI confirms that deprivation in education is closely associated with overall levels of poverty. Those countries that are most desperately in need of education to escape the poverty trap have the weakest human-resource base. Of more interest are the marked discrepancies between educational attainment and average income. Income differences are an important factor in explaining human-resource differences between countries, but they are not the sole consideration. While low-income countries have lower levels of access to education, many score far higher on the EPI than would be predicted on the basis of national wealth. Conversely, many middle-income countries – especially in Latin America – score far lower. These findings suggest that good public policy in education can overcome the disadvantages associated with low income; and bad public policy will reinforce these disadvantages.

The EPI explained

The measurement of educational performance has become a highly politicised activity, especially in the industrialised countries. League tables have been developed to differentiate 'successful' from 'failing' schools, but a vigorous debate has ensued over what should be measured, and what weight should be attached to various aspects of performance. The EPI provides a different type of league table. It brings together in a composite index a range of features of deprivation in educational attainment, to arrive at an aggregate judgement on how countries are performing in relation to each other.

There are serious problems in developing a composite index. Education data are scandalously poor in many countries. For the mid-decade review of the World Declaration on Education for All, UNESCO produced detailed data on net enrolment rates, completion, and gender equity for most developing countries. However, many of the enrolment rates are little more than 'guestimates', some of which are out of line with evidence derived from household surveys. According to the World Bank, reliable net enrolment data exist for only about 70 countries.

For all their flaws, and despite problems with the data, composite indicators are useful tools. They help to simplify a complex reality on the basis of something more meaningful than a single indicator. When combined with league tables of income, they can also help to compare the performance of countries at very different levels of average income, highlighting important issues of public policy.

The EPI provides a simple composite indicator by concentrating on three aspects of educational performance: namely, coverage, completion, and gender equity. Each of these indicators has a critical bearing on the 2015 target of universal primary education. The specific measurement criteria used are as follows:

- The net enrolment rate, which captures the proportion of children aged between 6 and 11 who enrol in school. This serves as a proxy for the coverage achieved by the school system.
- The completion rate, or the proportion of students who progress beyond Grade 4.
- Gender equity, expressed in terms of the ratio of female to male enrolment.

The EPI measures the average shortfall from a perfect score (i.e. 100 per cent for net enrolment and completion, and 0 for the gender gap) across the three elements. The higher the score, the larger the shortfall. Data were compiled for 104 countries, which were then ranked on the basis of their performance in each area. An extreme deprivation line was established, representing a threshold where on average more than one-third of children were out of school, fewer than one-third were completing school, and the gender gap in enrolment exceeded 33 per cent. Finally, the EPI ranking was set alongside an income ranking, using World Bank data for purchasing-power parity in order to provide some insight into the relationship between education performance and average income levels. The technical formula for calculating the EPI is shown in Table A.1.

Two preliminary observations must be made about what the EPI is – and what it is not. First, the EPI does not capture a number of important aspects of education performance. Gender equity in enrolment is an important but limited indicator of gender discrimination in education at school and beyond. It does not capture the consequences of gender-biased teaching material, the low self-esteem associated with low expectations on the part of teachers and parents, or the excessive work burdens imposed on young girls. The EPI is of similarly limited value in measuring education quality. Completion rates are a proxy, but a weak one. As we saw in Chapter 2, many children complete school with minimal literacy and numeracy skills. In terms of coverage, gross primary-enrolment rates (showing the total number of all children enrolled in school in relation to the total cohort of children of primary-school age) are more widely available than net enrolment data (which show the percentage of enrolled children of primary-school age), but they are much less useful. All enrolment data suffer from the problem that they are only a proxy for school attendance. But the difficulty with the gross enrolment rate is that it automatically increases if grade repetitions rise, giving a misleading indicator of performance. This is why the EPI uses net enrolment indicators.

The second observation relates to methodology. One of the problems to be confronted in constructing any composite index is that of weighting.[13] Should more importance be attached to, say, increasing overall enrolment, or to completion? Should more weight be attached to completion than to gender equity? Answers to such questions will reflect personal judgement and values. In our view, there should be no difference in weighting. High net enrolment rates count for little if the vast majority of children drop out; and high completion rates count for little if they are associated with low net enrolment. To take an extreme example, a country with a 10 per cent net enrolment rate and a 50 per cent gap in gender equity should not count as a success if it achieved a completion rate of 100 per cent. Gender equity in enrolment is clearly linked to overall progress towards universal enrolment. But it is an important indicator in its own right, especially at lower levels of enrolment. For all these reasons, the EPI attaches equal weight to each indicator.

Related to the issue of weighting is that of substitutability. If a country achieves a high level in one area (say, net enrolment), should this compensate for shortfalls in other areas (such as gender equity)? Some element of substitutability is unavoidable in the construction of a composite index, but in the case of education it should be minimised.

Table 3.1 The Education Performance Index and income rankings

EPI rank		EPI Index	Income PPP($)*	Income rank	Difference in ranking
1	Bahrain	0.55	15,321	7	6
2	Singapore	0.60	20,987	3	1
3	UAE	0.94	16,000	5	2
4	Mauritius	1.04	13,172	8	4
5	Cuba	2.84	3,000	50	45
6	Jamaica	2.91	3,816	40	34
7	Sri Lanka	3.40	3,277	47	40
8	Tunisia	4.03	5,319	33	25
9	Indonesia	4.22	3,740	42	33
10	Uruguay	4.46	6,752	20	10
11	Rep. of Korea	4.51	10,656	10	-1
12	St. Lucia	4.92	6,182	21	9
13	Cape Verde	5.40	1,862	65	52
14	China	5.73	2,604	55	41
15	Iran	6.20	5,766	26	11
16	Guyana	6.43	2,729	53	37
17	Algeria	6.53	5,442	29	12
18	Costa Rica	6.99	5,919	25	7
19	Brunei Darussalam	7.28	30,447	1	-18
20	Syria	7.30	5,397	30	10
21	Mexico	8.53	7,384	18	-3
22	Botswana	8.65	5,367	31	9
23	Fiji	8.80	5,763	27	4
24	Chile	10.20	9,129	13	-11
25	Namibia	10.56	4,027	37	12
26	Trinidad & Tobago	11.09	9,124*	14	-12
27	Bahamas	11.79	15,875	6	-21
28	Jordan	12.13	4,187	36	8
29	Thailand	12.18	7,104	19	-10
30	Iraq	12.27	3,159	49	19
31	Panama	12.43	6,104	24	-7
32	Malaysia	12.80	8,865	16	-16

33	Dominica	13.23	6,118	22	-11
34	Egypt	13.52	3,846	39	5
35	Venezuela	14.42	8,120	17	-18
36	Mongolia	15.17	3,766	41	5
37	Paraguay	15.27	3,531	46	9
38	Swaziland	16.07	2,821	51	13
39	Zimbabwe	16.23	2,196	60	21
40	South Africa	16.40	4,291	35	-5
41	Argentina	16.85	8,937	15	-26
42	Qatar	17.92	18,403	4	-38
43	Philippines	17.98	2,681	54	11
44	Kenya	18.33	1,404	72	28
45	Barbados	18.87	11,051	9	-36
46	Ecuador	18.91	4,626	34	-12
47	Oman	19.08	10,078	11	-36
48	Brazil	20.75	5,362	32	-16
49	Belize	21.01	5,590	28	-21
50	Peru	21.02	3,645	44	-6
51	Cameroon	21.25	2,120	62	11
52	Zambia	21.61	962	89	37
53	Papua New Guinea	21.71	2,821	51	-2
54	Bolivia	21.81	2,598	56	2
55	Vietnam	23.39	1,208	80	25
56	Kuwait	24.95	21,875	2	-54
57	Morocco	25.42	3,681	43	-14
58	Dominican Rep.	25.49	3,933	38	-20
59	Nicaragua	25.85	1,580	71	12
60	Saudi Arabia	26.19	9,338	12	-48
61	Ghana	27.91	1,960	64	3
62	Honduras	28.76	2,050	63	1
63	Gabon	28.98	3,641	45	-18
64	Lesotho	29.24	1,109	83	19
65	India	29.36	1,348	76	11
66	Congo	29.42	2,410	59	-7
67	Nigeria	29.63	1,351	75	8
68	Colombia	30.23	6,107	23	-45

EPI rank		EPI Index	Income PPP($)*	Income rank	Difference in ranking
69	El Salvador	31.64	2,417	58	-11
70	Bangladesh	32.17	1,331	77	7
71	Zaire	32.68	429	102	31
72	Tanzania	32.86	656	100	28
73	Comoros	32.97	1,366	74	1
74	Uganda	33.29	1,370	73	-1
75	Gambia	33.75	939	91	16
76	Côte d'Ivoire	33.94	1,668	68	-8
77	Laos	34.93	2,484	57	-20
78	Togo	35.21	1,109	83	5
79	Burundi	36.17	698	97	18
80	Central African Rep.	36.55	1,130	82	2
81	Malawi	38.02	694	98	17
82	Senegal	38.97	1,780	66	-16
83	Benin	41.03	1,696	67	-16
84	Nepal	41.59	1,137	81	-3
85	Sudan	41.84	1,084	86	1
86	Guinea-Bissau	42.92	793	94	8
87	Mauritania	43.82	1,593	70	-17
88	Guatemala	44.35	3,208	48	-40
89	Rwanda	46.06	352	104	15
90	Cambodia	46.89	1,084	86	-4
91	Madagascar	47.00	694	98	7
92	Djibouti	47.68	1,270	79	-13
93	Burkina Faso	47.89	796	85	-9
95	Eritrea	51.32	960	90	-5
96	Mali	52.70	543	101	5
97	Mozambique	53.28	986	88	-9
98	Chad	53.94	700	96	-2
99	Pakistan	53.94	2,154	61	-38
100	Angola	56.71	1,600	69	-31
101	Haiti	59.43	896	92	-9
102	Bhutan	60.56	1,289	78	-24
103	Niger	61.63	787	95	-8
104	Ethiopia	67.17	427	103	-1

The achievement of gender equity at very low levels of enrolment, or relatively high rates of enrolment with wide gender gaps, should not be obscured by a simple average figure for ranking purposes. For this reason the EPI uses a weighting system that penalises countries for poor performance in each area, thereby limiting the extent of substitution.

Regional and national rankings

The EPI league table is presented in Table 3.1. It graphically illustrates the gravity of the problems facing the poorest countries. The aggregate index, summarised on a regional basis in Figure 3.6, reveals the following facts.

- The average level of deprivation in sub-Saharan Africa is 40 per cent higher than the average for all developing countries.

- Deprivation in South Asia is 32 per cent worse than the average for all developing countries.

- The average level of deprivation in the 48 least-developed countries is almost twice as bad as the average for developing countries.

- East Asia has the lowest level of deprivation, at about one-quarter of the overall average for all developing countries.

- The EPI places Latin America slightly above the developing-country average, but below the Middle East.

The EPI ranking confirms the grave state of education in sub-Saharan Africa. Of the 31 countries that fall below the line for extreme deprivation, 24 are located in sub-Saharan Africa. Fifteen of these countries are in the bottom 20, including Ethiopia, Niger, Chad, Mozambique, Mali, Sudan, Angola, Rwanda, and Burkina Faso. These countries are home to some 48 million children between the ages of 6 and 11. Other countries in the 'extreme deprivation' group include two countries in Latin America (Haiti and Guatemala); two in East Asia (Laos and Cambodia); and three in South Asia (Pakistan, Nepal, and Bhutan).

Deprivation in basic education as measured by the EPI is closely associated with income poverty and wider human-development indicators. Of course, correlation is not causation. Income poverty does not simply reflect educational attainment. Even so, with education increasing in importance as a determinant of income and wider life-chances, the interaction of deprivation in education with other aspects of deprivation will intensify. The danger is that failure to overcome educational inequalities will in turn lead to more intensive patterns of marginalisation, especially in sub-Saharan Africa.

Notes on Table 3.1
*Purchasing Power Parity (PPP) expresses the purchasing power of national income in terms of US\$ equivalence. It measures the number of units of a national currency that would be required to purchase a basket of goods that could be purchased for \$1 in the USA. The PPP makes it possible to compare income across different countries in terms of their real purchasing power.

The formula used to construct the Education Performance Index (EPI) is explained in Appendix 1.

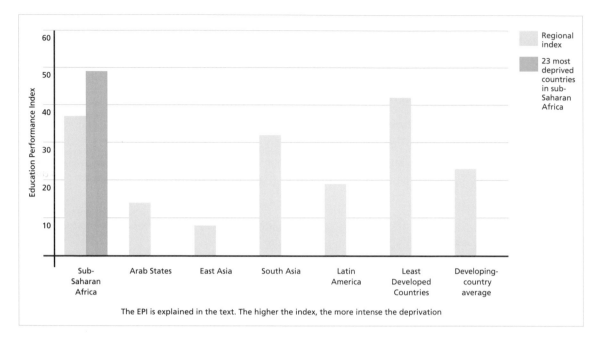

The EPI is explained in the text. The higher the index, the more intense the deprivation

Figure 3.6
The Education Performance Index: comparisons of regional deprivation

Source:
Oxfam

The EPI and income: good performers and bad

There are some obvious reasons why poor countries experience particular problems in providing basic education opportunities. Low average incomes limit the capacity of governments to finance and deliver schooling – the supply of education. Household demand for education is also linked to average income levels and the incidence of poverty. Poor households are less likely to be able to afford school fees, and more likely to depend on child labour. The overall relationship between income and educational performance is therefore entirely predictable. But the average relationship obscures a more complex picture. Large numbers of countries are under-performing in relation to their income levels; and others are achieving far more than might be expected. There is, in fact, a vast potential for educational opportunity that is being missed because of bad policy choices.[14] That potential is illustrated by the contrasting performances of good performers, who have achieved a higher EPI rank than their income rank, and bad performers, who have failed to achieve an EPI ranking commensurate with their average income levels.

Comparing EPI and income rankings confirms that, in education as in other areas of human development, some countries have performed better than others in converting economic potential into benefits for people. Several countries have achieved a high level of success in overcoming income constraints, as illustrated by Figure 3.7. Among the success stories are the following countries:

- Cuba, Sri Lanka, and China, all of whom have an EPI ranking 40 or more places above their income ranking;

- Vietnam, Indonesia, Kenya, Zimbabwe, Zambia, Tanzania, Tunisia, and Jamaica, with an EPI ranking 20 or more places above their income ranking;

- Namibia, Nicaragua, Syria, Iran, Malawi, and Iraq, whose EPI ranks at least 10 places above their average income rank.

In each of these cases, the fact that the national education ranking is higher than the income ranking indicates that public policies have, in

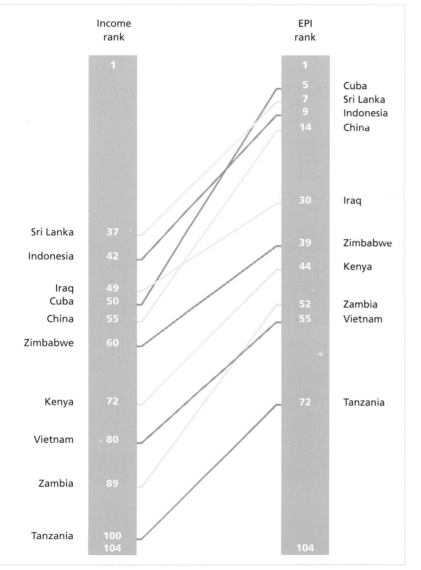

Figure 3.7
Countries with higher EPI rank than income rank

Source:
Oxfam

143

varying degrees, partly compensated for the problems associated with low income. The policies in question are discussed in more detail in Chapter 4. Typically, they have involved a combination of increased investment, reduced costs, and a strong political commitment to basic education. In some cases, the benefits of these policies are now under threat. Net enrolment rates have fallen in countries such as Zambia, Tanzania, and Nicaragua, underlining the fact that the benefits of past investments in education are fragile, and that past gains are reversible. At the same time, there are enough success stories to dispel the myth that poor countries are unable to progress towards education for all.

Unfortunately, there are also enough bad examples to dispel the myth that economic growth and increased average incomes will automatically generate human development. The benefits of economic growth and rising income in reducing income poverty and child mortality and raising the average level of educational attainment are well established. However, there are striking deviations from this relationship. These are graphically illustrated by the EPI, which shows that many countries have failed to create educational opportunities commensurate with their national wealth (Figure 3.8).

- **Latin America** has failed in a spectacular fashion to develop a basic education system with a level of coverage and performance consistent with average income levels. Several countries occupy an EPI ranking far below their income rank, among them Colombia (45 places lower), Guatemala (40 places lower), Venezuela (18 places lower), Argentina (25 places lower), the Dominican Republic (20 places lower), Brazil (16 places lower), and Chile (11 places lower). The Latin American case demonstrates the benefits of a composite indicator. In contrast to poor performers in sub-Saharan Africa, most countries in Latin America have achieved a high level of enrolment, and gender gaps are generally small. However, drop-out rates are so high that the average number of years spent in school by the poor in countries such as Brazil is less than that of the poor in countries at much lower income levels, such as Kenya and Zimbabwe. In the cases of Colombia and Guatemala, high drop-out rates are aggravated by substantial gender gaps (30 per cent and 45 per cent respectively in net enrolment). The EPI–income comparison confirms the assessment of the Inter-American Development Bank that, taking regional wealth levels into account, Latin Americans – or, more accurately, poor Latin Americans – suffer the world's worst public education systems. On average, the region's workforce has had 5.2 years of

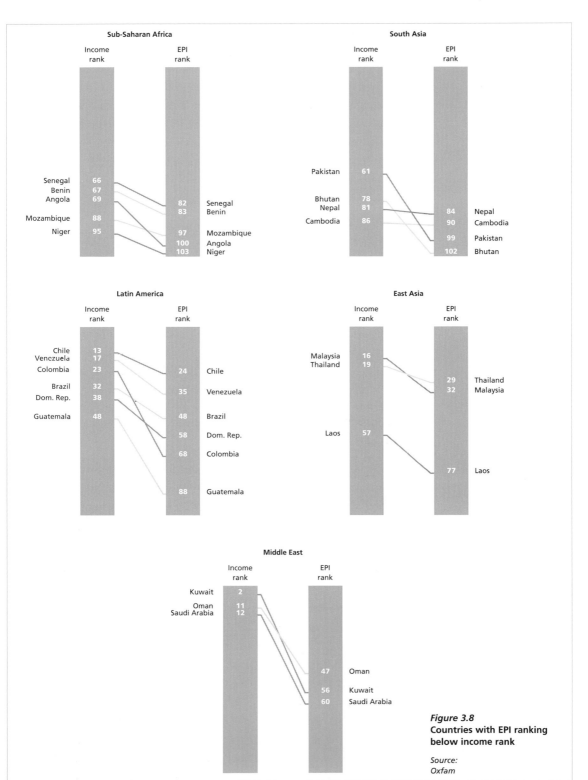

Figure 3.8
Countries with EPI ranking below income rank

*Source:
Oxfam*

schooling. If Latin America's primary-education system had been as effective as the international average for its income levels, the figure would be more than seven years.[15] Moreover, the percentage of children who drop out of primary school is twice the level that would be predicted on the basis of average-income comparisons. Under-performance in education is both a cause and a consequence of the extreme levels of income inequality in Latin America. Failure to improve performance at the base of the education system will reinforce these inequalities over time.

- Several countries in the **Middle East** have been unable – or, more accurately, unwilling – to convert national wealth into extended opportunities for basic education. In some cases, the gap between EPI ranking and income ranking is of extraordinary dimensions. Among the worst cases are Kuwait (with an EPI level 54 places lower than its income rank), Saudi Arabia (48 places lower), Qatar (38 places lower), and Oman (36 places lower). Kuwait and Saudi Arabia respectively account for the largest and second-largest differentials between EPI ranking and income ranking. The underlying reasons for the discrepancy vary. In the cases of Kuwait and Saudi Arabia, the central problem is a relatively low net enrolment rate. Completion rates for both countries are high, and the gender gap in enrolment is small. In Qatar, the gender gap in enrolment (20 per cent) is the primary problem.

For Latin America and the Middle East, the discrepancy between educational performance and potential raises some important policy questions, notably about public-spending priorities. Both regions show that relatively high levels of public spending and average income do not provide an automatic passport to reasonable levels of educational attainment. However, it is not only middle-income countries and regions that have failed to convert economic wealth into more widely shared opportunities for basic education. There is a large group of low-income countries that are under-achieving in relation to their average income levels.

The countries in sub-Saharan Africa clustered beneath the EPI 'extreme deprivation' threshold illustrate the point. Thirteen of these countries have an EPI rank lower than their income rank, including the following:

- Angola, which has an EPI rank 31 places below its income rank, demonstrating the devastating consequences of the country's civil war.

- Senegal and Benin, each of which has an EPI ranking 16 places below its income ranking.
- Côte d'Ivoire, Mozambique, and Niger, with in each case an EPI ranking 8–9 places lower than the income ranking.

Over-achievers and under-achievers

The UNDP's Human Development Report has consistently shown that poor countries can 'over-achieve' in human development in relation to their income levels. The EPI confirms this fact in relation to education. But it also shows that poor countries can massively under-achieve, highlighting the damaging consequences of factors such as bad policies, conflict, and an unfavourable external economic environment. One of the worst under-achievers revealed by the EPI is Pakistan. The country occupies 99th position in the EPI league table, or 38 places below its income ranking. Pakistan has an average income equivalent to three times that in Burkina Faso and four times that in Mali, yet it ranks below both countries. This reflects the combination of exceptionally low enrolment rates, a large – and widening – gender gap, and low completion rates.

In each of these cases, failed government policies have aggravated problems associated with low income, contributing to a significant shortfall in performance. Inadequate financial commitment, poor planning, weak administration, and, above all, failures of political leadership have contributed to missed opportunities for education. These missed opportunities imply high costs for human development. Figures 3.9 and 3.10 show the differences in opportunities provided through the education systems of China and Zimbabwe on the one side, and Pakistan and

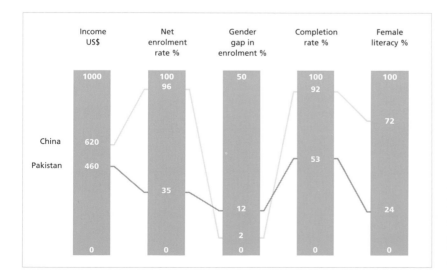

Figure 3.9
Good performers and bad performers (China and Pakistan)

Source:
UNESCO, *Education for All: Achieving the Goal*

Guatemala on the other. To summarise some of the most important differences:

- China has a slightly higher average income than Pakistan, but its citizens are three times as likely to enrol in school and almost twice as likely to complete school. The gender gap in enrolment is six times narrower than in Pakistan.

- Zimbabwe has a lower average income than Guatemala, but enrolment and completion rates are far higher. Guatemala has a 30 per cent gender gap in primary-school enrolment, while Zimbabwe has no gender gap at that level.

National inequalities in education

The EPI captures average educational attainment levels for countries. However, national averages obscure deep structural inequalities in education related to enrolment. Household wealth is the single most important factor associated with these inequalities. The poor systematically under-achieve in relation to the non-poor, although wealth gaps take different forms in different countries. They also interact with other sources of inequality, including rural–urban differences, gender disparities, regional factors, and ethnicity. These inequalities do not exist in isolation, but are overlapping and mutually reinforcing. Transmitted across generations, they shape the distribution of opportunity and perpetuate the wider structures which consign people to poverty and marginalisation.

Household wealth

Most governments in developing countries recognise the principle that

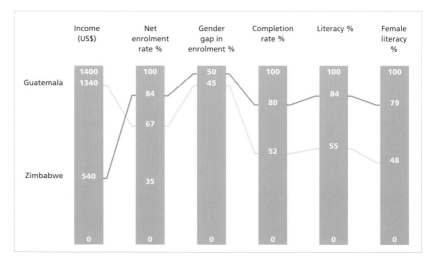

Figure 3.10
Good performers and bad performers (Zimbabwe and Guatemala)

Source:
UNESCO, *Education for All: Achieving the Goal*

education is a fundamental human right. Many enshrine that right in constitutional provisions. In practice, however, the right to education is universally enjoyed by the rich, but not by the poor. In education, as in other areas of social development, wealth matters. Differences in income shape opportunities for education, which in turn shape future patterns of wealth distribution.

This conclusion is powerfully reinforced by detailed household surveys covering a wide range of countries. One of the most comprehensive studies has used such surveys to analyse educational attainment of 15–19 year-olds on the basis of household wealth, contrasting the performance of the poorest 40 per cent with the rest of the population.[16] The results show a consistent pattern of inequality, with children from poor households less likely to go to school and more likely to drop out (see Figure 3.11). Three broad regional patterns emerge for poor households:

Figure 3.11
School-grade completion by 15–19 year olds from poorest and richest households

Source:
D. Filmer and L. Pritchett, 'The effect of wealth on educational attainment', *Population and Development Review,* March 1999

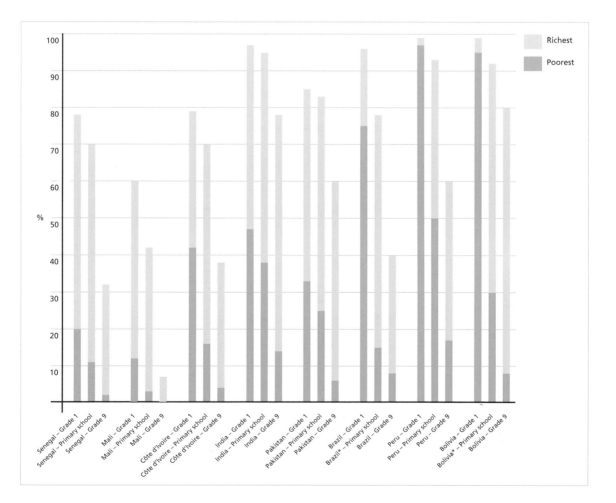

- low enrolment and high drop-out rates in much of sub-Saharan Africa (but especially West Africa);

- low enrolment and a less marked drop-out rate as far as Grade 5, followed by a sharp increase thereafter in South Asia;

- high enrolment and high drop-out rates in Latin America.

The case of sub-Saharan Africa demonstrates how high levels of poverty produce particularly intensive forms of deprivation, starting at enrolment. In Senegal, the enrolment rate for children from the richest 20 per cent of households is more than double that for the 20 per cent. Once in school, children from the wealthy households are four times more likely to complete Grade 1 and five times more likely to reach Grade 5. In Mali, four out of five children from poor households do not progress beyond the first grade of primary school. Only 2 per cent complete primary school – less than ten per cent of the national primary-school completion rate. Although wealth gaps are widest in West Africa, they are significant across a wide range of countries. In Zambia, for instance, enrolment rates for the richest households are more than one-third higher than for the poorest households.

Only 2 per cent of children from the poorest households in Pakistan complete Grade 9, compared with 60 per cent of children from wealthy households.

In South Asia, as in Africa, the proportion of 15–19 year-olds from poor households who have not completed Grade 1 is very high. Almost half fail to progress beyond this stage. Thereafter, retention in school is much higher than in Africa until Grade 5, when drop-out rates increase. In India and Pakistan, children from the wealthiest 20 per cent of households have almost achieved universal primary enrolment, while less than half of those from the poorest households enrol. Thereafter the wealth gap widens slowly until Grade 5, when it becomes a chasm. Only 2 per cent of children from the poorest households in Pakistan complete Grade 9, compared with 60 per cent of children from wealthy households. The Indian wealth gap is narrower, but still exceptionally large. Children from wealthy households are around six times more likely to complete Grade 9.

One of the advantages of disaggregated data is that they provide a clearer insight into where the main shortfalls exist in relation to the target of universal primary education. In India, there is a 38 per cent shortfall from universal completion of Grade 5. But only 4 per cent is attributable to children from the richest 20 per cent of households. Almost two-thirds of the primary-school education deficit is attributable to children from the poorest households, which underlines the need for education policy to be integrated into broader anti-poverty strategies.

The Latin American case differs from those of sub-Saharan Africa and South Asia. The pattern here is one of high initial enrolment, followed by a widening wealth gap to Grade 5 and beyond. The education gap is both created by the enormous wealth differences in Latin America and helps to sustain them. In Brazil, the initial enrolment rate for the poor is similar to that for the wealthy. But whereas four out of every five children from the richest households complete primary school, only 15 per cent of poor households do so. In some countries, wealth gaps in education reach remarkable dimensions. Completion rates for Grade 9 are some thirty times higher for children from wealthy households in Guatemala than for children from poor households. One of the most striking findings to emerge from household survey data in Latin America is that the level of attainment among children from poor households is not only lower than in East Asia, which politicians in the region typically use as a point of comparison: by Grade 5 it is lower than in sub-Saharan Africa countries such as Zambia and Zimbabwe.[17] Once again, data disaggregation helps to identify the main deficits in relation to the achievement of universal primary education. In Brazil, Peru, and Bolivia, poor children dropping out account for more than 90 per cent of the shortfall in primary-school completion.

Striking as they are, average differences between rich and poor households understate the full extent of the wealth gap in education. Differences in the median grade completed by children in differing wealth rankings reveal even wider disparities. The median represents the middle point in the survey data (i.e. with half of the households covered on either side), and thus avoids some of the problems associated with compiling simple averages. It can be used to compare attainment levels in terms of average years of education across a range of wealth groups. There are significant differences across all regions (Figure 3.12). In India, Pakistan, Senegal, Burkina Faso, Côte d'Ivoire, and Mali, the median grade completed by children from poor households is zero, because fewer than half finished at least one year of schooling.[18] In Africa and Latin America, the median wealth gap typically translates into a situation where children from poor households spend 4–7 years less in education than children from wealthier households. The wealth gap in India and Pakistan amounts to 9–10 years.

It is not only highly unequal countries that suffer from wide wealth gaps in education. Vietnam has one of the world's most equal patterns of income distribution, but the net enrolment rate for children from the poorest quintile is 10 per cent lower than for the top quintile at the

151

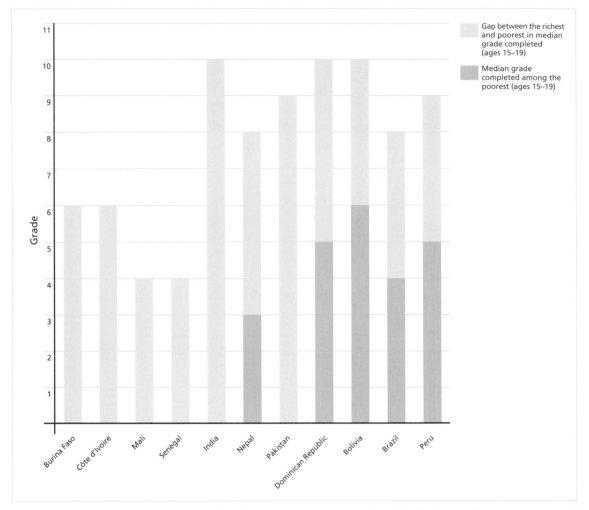

Figure 3.12
Median grade completed by 15-19 year-olds from poorest and richest households

Source:
D. Filmer and L. Pritchett, 'The effect of wealth on educational attainment', *Population and Development Review,* March 1999

primary level. At the upper secondary level, fewer than 2 per cent of children from the poorest households are enrolled, compared with 28 per cent from the wealthiest households.[19]

Overcoming wealth gaps in education is of profound importance to the achievement of the 2015 human-development targets. Bringing the average number of years spent in school by poor children up to the level of their wealthier counterparts would raise the average incomes of poor households, and produce more equitable patterns of income distribution. Both outcomes would contribute to the halving of extreme income poverty. Similarly, increasing the average number of years spent in school by girls from poor households would help to reduce child-death rates.

Different regions face different challenges if the wealth gap is to be closed. In sub-Saharan Africa and South Asia, the pressing need is to increase the coverage of education provision, while at the same time reducing drop-out rates among poor children. In Latin America, improving the physical availability of schools and the accessibility to all social classes is less of a problem than retaining the children from poor households after they have enrolled. But in all regions, the closure of wealth gaps in education and an increased emphasis on equity are the starting point for accelerated progress towards the goal of education for all.

Rural–urban disparities

There is a pronounced disparity in the provision of education in urban and rural areas. In developing countries, men living in rural areas are twice as likely to be illiterate as those living in urban areas. Differences between rural and urban women are only slightly less extreme. Such disparities reflect differences in access to basic education. Limited educational opportunities in rural areas are caused by a combination of factors, ranging from the administrative cost and difficulty of providing services to more remote areas with scattered populations, to the unwillingness of teachers to live in isolated regions, and to demands for child labour. Public-spending priorities that concentrate resources on urban areas add to the problems of rural people.

Whatever the underlying causes, in most countries the rural–urban divide is the widest of all, especially when the main city is also the national capital.

- In Peru, illiteracy rates are three times higher in rural areas than urban areas.[20]

- In Pakistan, 54 per cent of urban children aged 10–14 have completed school – twice the level for rural children in the same age group.[21]

- Niger's capital, Niamey, has a net enrolment rate that exceeds 90 per cent, but the rate is less than 20 per cent in rural areas.[22]

- Mali's national capital region of Bamako has a net enrolment rate above 80 per cent. Rural northern regions such as Kidal, Timbuktu, and Gao have enrolment rates below 20 per cent.[23]

Rural poverty and educational deprivation create a vicious circle from which poor households are often unable to escape. The case of Zambia illustrates this (Figure 3.13). Rural poverty is more pervasive and more severe than urban poverty, with around three-quarters of rural Zambians having income levels too low to meet basic their nutritional needs. Subsistence poverty is three times higher in rural areas than in urban areas, and almost half of rural children suffer from malnutrition. Educational inequalities serve to reinforce rural deprivation and transmit it across generations. Schools in poor rural areas are less accessible, less well equipped, and less able to provide an education of reasonable quality. For instance, 50 per cent of the rural poor live more than 10km from a school, compared with 10 per cent of urban poor households.[24] Rural schools have fewer qualified teachers and lower completion rates. As a result, the rural poor, who might be expected to reap some of the most significant human-development benefits of education, have the most restricted opportunities. Inequalities in educational opportunity restrict the ability of rural Zambians to work their way out of poverty.

Education can act as a great leveller, but all too often it serves to reinforce disadvantage. Even in countries marked by poor levels of overall attainment, rural populations are frequently left far behind. Only 3 per cent of pupils attending rural primary school in Tanzania proceed to secondary school, compared with 10 per cent of their urban counterparts. One reason for the discrepancy is that only 17 per cent of rural school pupils pass their primary-school leaving exam, compared with 29 per cent in urban areas.[25]

In South Asia, rural–urban disparities are particularly marked, interacting with gender differences. The province of Sindh in Pakistan demonstrates the interaction in a particularly powerful fashion. For a young girl living in rural Sindh, her chance of going to school is half that of a young girl in urban Sindh; and she is twice as likely to leave before completing school (see Figure 3.14).

Gender disparities

Inequalities in education between men and women extend across a wide

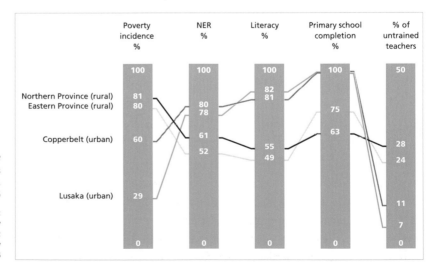

Figure 3.13
Zambia: educational indicators for urban and rural provinces, 1996

Sources:
M. Kelly, 'Education in a Highly Indebted Country', Oxfam, 1998; World Bank, Zambia Poverty Assessment, 1994

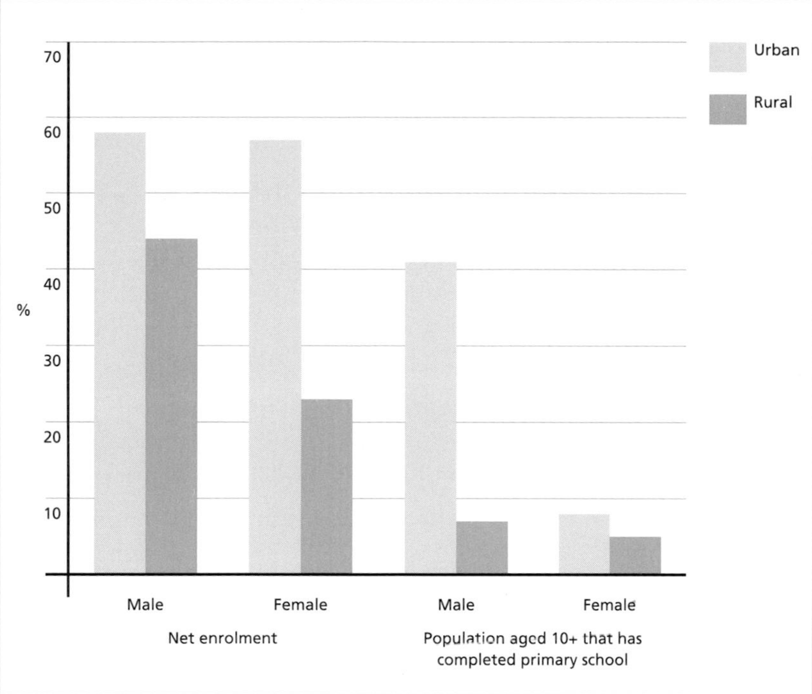

Figure 3.14
Gender differences in primary-school enrolment and completion: urban and rural Sindh, Pakistan

Source:
Government of Pakistan,
Pakistan Integrated Household Survey, 1996

range of dimensions, including enrolment, completion, and the quality of teaching. Cultural, social, and economic factors combine to place young girls and women at a serious disadvantage that starts at school and extends into adulthood. The facts of gender discrimination speak for themselves:[26]

- Women are 60 per cent more likely than men to be illiterate.

- There are 42 million fewer girls in primary school than boys.

- Gender gaps in enrolment have not narrowed significantly, even at the primary level. In South Asia, the net enrolment rate for girls is 20 per cent lower than for boys; in sub-Saharan Africa and the Middle East, it is 10 per cent lower.

- There are 12 countries in sub-Saharan Africa where the gender gap in enrolment exceeds 20 per cent.

- An average six-year-old girl in South Asia can expect to spend about six years in school – three years less than an average six-year-old boy.

Even where progress has been made towards improving equity in enrolment, disadvantages in other areas often remain intact. For instance, India has closed the gender gap in primary-school enrolment by 10 per cent since 1980, albeit to 22 per cent, which is still exceptionally high. Less success has been achieved in reducing the drop-out rate for girls.

Each year, one million more girls than boys leave school without having completed the full primary cycle.[27]

Gender disparities cannot be considered in isolation. They interact strongly with inequalities linked to household wealth and rural–urban differences. In almost all cases, poverty reinforces gender inequity, so that girls born into poor households face far more restricted opportunities for education than girls born into wealthy households. In India, nine out of every ten girls from the richest quintile of households are in school, compared with fewer than half for the poorest two quintiles.[28] This wealth-related gender gap widens over the duration of the school career. More than 80 per cent of girls from the wealthiest households complete Grade 8 – almost the same percentage as for boys from the same house-hold. In the poorest households, only one in ten girls completes Grade 8 – and boys are three times more likely to reach this level than girls.[29]

In many countries, wealth gaps aggravate already extreme inequalities between girls and boys. For instance, Nepal has one of lowest ratios of girls' to boys' enrolment in the world, and rich and poor families alike are less likely to send girls to school (see Figure 3.15). But in poor families, the enrolment rate for girls is one-third of that for boys.[30] Raising the average incomes of poor households would, in this case, almost certainly reduce gender-based inequity.

Rural–urban differences magnify gender differences almost as much as household wealth does. In Pakistan, completion rates for primary school are twice as high in urban areas as in rural areas. But in rural areas the completion rate for boys is three times higher than for girls, while in urban areas it is only 50 per cent higher. Clearly, cultural, social, and economic factors associated with life in rural areas and with rural poverty exercise a powerful influence.[31]

Important as wealth is, it cannot be taken as axiomatic that any increase in household income will improve gender equity. The relationship between income disparity and the gender gap is complex. Where the education of girls is regarded by parents as being of less value than the education of boys, economic pressures associated with low income will have adverse consequences for gender equity. Girls are likely to be the last into school and the first out when times are hard. However, this tendency is not universal. Evidence from sub-Saharan Africa suggests that, while boys are often enrolled first in school, they are often the first to be withdrawn in situations of economic adversity where local employment practices preclude the use of girl-child labour to generate cash incomes

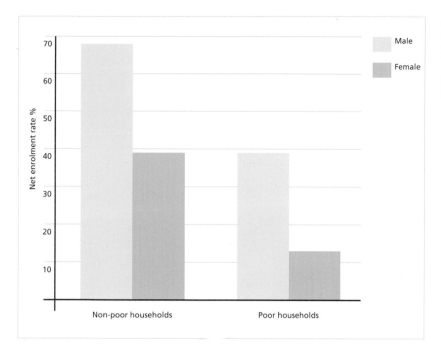

Figure 3.15
Gender-poverty gap in enrolment: Rural Hill and Tarai regions of Nepal

Source:
O. Brown and K. Wiseman,
'Primary Education in Nepal',
Oxfam, 1998

away from the home.[32] Whatever the national variations, it is clear that income growth and poverty reduction *per se* do not provide an automatic route to improved gender equity. The initial response within poor households to any increase in income may be to increase male enrolments, thus causing the gender gap to widen.

The case of Yemen graphically demonstrates the complex interaction between the gender gap and other disparities. Gender gaps in enrolment are exceptionally wide, with girls accounting for only one-third of children in Grade 1. However, the national average conceals large urban–rural differences, with girls far better represented in major urban areas (Figure 3.16). In Sana'a City, they account for more than 40 per cent of enrolments, compared with less than 20 per cent in rural Sana'a. This is consistent with the broader pattern in many countries. In contrast to many countries, however, the correlation between wealth and the education status of women appears to be weaker in Yemen. Illiteracy rates for poor and non-poor women are almost equivalent, at slightly above 80 per cent.[33] Simply raising household incomes under these circumstances will have a limited effect, a fact that indicates the importance of more deeply rooted cultural factors.

Regional disparities

Uneven progress in providing access to education has resulted in deep regional disparities within countries – disparities which, in some cases,

Figure 3.16
**Yemen: percentages of girls
and boys in Grades 1-4**

Source:
Al-Hidabi, 'Primary Education in
Yemen', Oxfam, 1998

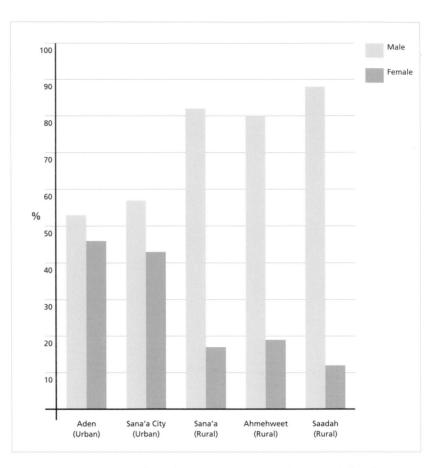

rival those between rich and poor countries. Educational disadvantage tends to be concentrated in regions with the highest levels of poverty, as the following examples demonstrate.

Brazil. While Brazil is a middle-income country, the nine States of the north-east are among the poorest regions in the world. The poorest 50 per cent of the population in these States have per capita incomes broadly in line with the average for South Asia. This is the highest concentration of poverty in Latin America, with human-welfare indicators which are far worse than in the rest of the country.[34] Inequalities in education perpetuate the human-welfare gap between the north-east and more prosperous regions (Figure 3.17). Over half the children in the rural north-east receive less than four years of schooling, and one quarter of the population has had no schooling.

The Philippines. The Philippines has achieved relatively high rates of net enrolment. Even so, almost 1 million children are not in school; and another 3 million drop out before completing Grade 6.[35] Regional differences

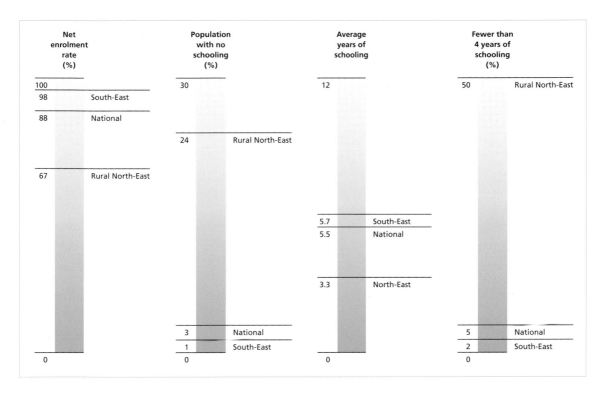

related to poverty and service-provision account for much of this deficit (see Figure 3.18). Four out of five pupils in Central Luzon complete primary school, compared with an average of one in three children in Northern Mindanao. Poverty incidence in Northern Mindanao is twice as high as in Central Luzon.[36]

Indonesia. Over the past two decades, Indonesia's progress in education has been impressive. Gender differentials have narrowed at all levels, and near-universal primary-school enrolment has been achieved. But issues of quality and progression through the secondary-school system have come to the fore, especially in the Outer Islands. Net enrolment rates vary between 100 per cent in Jakarta and 58 per cent in Irian Jaya; drop-out rates are less than 5 per cent in Central Java, but 23 per cent in East Timor.[37] The incidence of poverty on the Outer Islands is about 33 per cent, compared with 20 per cent in Java. Similar differences are observed in human-development indicators.

India. Some of the developing world's widest educational disparities exist between Indian States. In Kerala, almost all children in the 10–14 age group are literate.[38] By contrast, one-third of boys and two-thirds of girls in Uttar Pradesh are illiterate. The difference can be traced back to the

Figure 3.17
Brazil: regional differences in basic education

Sources:
S. Haddad, 'Academic Education in Brazil', Oxfam, 1998;
S. Birdsall and R. Sabat (eds.), *Opportunity Forgone*, Inter-American Development Bank, 1996

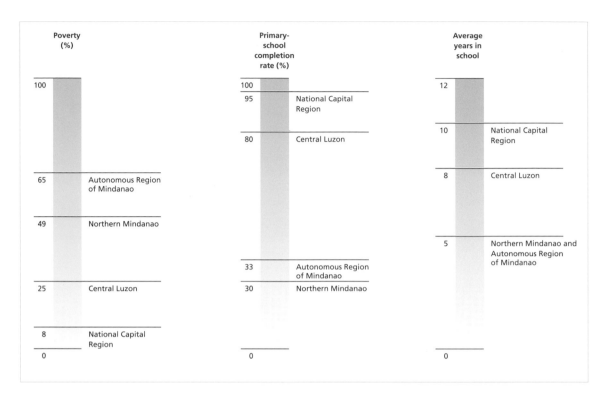

Figure 3.18
The Philippines: poverty and educational deprivation (1995)

Source:
UNDP: *Philippines Human Development Report,* Manila, 1994

primary-school system. Around one-quarter of all boys and half of girls in Uttar Pradesh have never enrolled. In the States of Bihar, Rajasthan, and Uttar Pradesh, the gender gap in enrolment is 25 per cent or more; in Kerala and Tamil Nadu it is less than 7 per cent. Inter-State differences have a profound bearing on the wealth gap in education. As noted above, there is a large national gap in enrolment between rich and poor households in India. But the wealth gap varies widely across States. In Kerala the enrolment gap between the richest 20 per cent and poorest 40 per cent of households amounts to 9 per cent; in Uttar Pradesh it rises to 56 per cent.[39] This gap extends into children's school careers. Attendance rates at school for children from the wealthiest 20 per cent of households are broadly similar for Kerala and Uttar Pradesh. However, the attendance rate of children from the poorest 40 per cent of households in Uttar Pradesh is 48 per cent – around half of the rate achieved in Kerala. Such differences starkly illustrate the fact that poverty is not an automatic barrier to higher levels of educational attainment. Public-policy choices, made in this case by State government, are capable of overcoming the disadvantages associated with low incomes. For instance, average incomes in Kerala are lower than in either Tamil Nadu or Punjab, yet nine out of ten children in Kerala complete Grade 5, compared with fewer than five out of ten in the two wealthier States. Inter-State differences also have an important bearing on gender-related wealth gaps. The gender gap in enrolment for children from the poorest 40 per cent of households is close to zero in Kerala, but reaches as high as 32 per cent for Uttar Pradesh and 44 per cent for Rajasthan.

As with other disparities, regional inequalities interact with gender disparities and urban–rural differences. In Pakistan, the proportion of the overall adult population who have completed school to primary level or beyond varies from 26 per cent in Baluchistan to 41 per cent in Sindh. However, for rural women in these two provinces, the figures fall to 6 per cent and 8 per cent respectively.

Regional inequality on this scale draws attention to the need for public action to close the gap in opportunities for households in different parts of the same country. In fact, as we show in Chapter 4, government action often does the opposite.

Ethnic and indigenous disparities

Inequalities relating to ethnic minorities and indigenous people are strongly linked to regional disparities, and to the distribution of poverty. Deprivation in this area is among the most intensive of all forms of educational deprivation. But here too averages can have the effect of obscuring cross-cutting patterns of deprivation. Within indigenous communities, inequalities based on household wealth and gender are often as pronounced as the inequalities in opportunity that separate indigenous and non-indigenous people.

East Asia has achieved some of the most impressive gains in education, increasing coverage and completion, and narrowing gender gaps. Pockets of intense deprivation associated with ethnicity remain intact, however. The case of the Philippines, which has achieved near-universal enrolment in primary school, illustrates the problem. During 1997, Oxfam conducted an education research programme in the Arakan Valley, in the eastern part of Mindanao island. The valley's highland regions have been recognised by the government as the ancestral lands of the Manobos people. While the Manobos value education for their children, not least because they learn skills that are useful in negotiating with traders, schools are usually inaccessible. In one settlement covered by the Oxfam research project in 1997, the nearest school was a four-hour walk away over rough and steep trails. As a result, more than two-thirds of children were not in school.[40]

The Philippines case is not untypical. Countries such as China and Vietnam are often held up as model performers, because of their success in achieving levels of educational attainment that compare favourably with those for countries at far higher levels of average income. In one sense, this is justified. But despite the rapid progress achieved in extending educational opportunity, ethnic minorities have often been left behind. Enrolment and completion rates in the 25 provinces with the largest ethnic-minority population are far below the national average. In Vietnam, ethnic-minority groups living in remote, mountainous, and poorer areas – such as the Northern Uplands and Central Highlands – have far lower rates of enrolment and completion than wealthier regions such as the south-east.[41] Although ethnic-minority groups account for only 13 per cent of the population, they represent half of the children who are not in school; and children of ethnic minorities make up less than 4 per cent of the school population. School-completion rates are also far lower for ethnic minorities. Nationally, just over two out of every three students complete primary education. In Vietnam's Central Highlands, the completion rate is 56 per cent. Research by Oxfam among Hmung communities in Lao Cai province in the Northern Upland region found enrolment rates as low as 40 per cent, and completion rates of only 38 per cent.[42] Differences in educational opportunities partly account for the high concentration of poverty in the Northern Upland and Central Highland regions (Figure 3.19).

India's caste system provides another stark example of education discrimination. Members of the 1091 scheduled castes and 573 scheduled tribes have historically suffered intense educational disadvantage. Often isolated both physically and geographically, these groups have lower enrolment rates, higher drop-out rates, and wider gender gaps. Past discrimination is reflected in the fact that the literacy rate for scheduled castes and tribes is more than 30 per cent lower than the national average.[43] Although there is evidence of disparities narrowing, this is happening at a slow pace.

- The enrolment gap between scheduled castes and tribes and the rest of the population is 15–17 per cent.
- The drop-out rate for scheduled tribes is 17 per cent higher than the national average.

Research carried out by Oxfam in the Indian State of Gujarat shows the persistence of inequalities related to scheduled tribes.[44] A district-level survey showed that enrolment rates for 5–10-year-old children in The

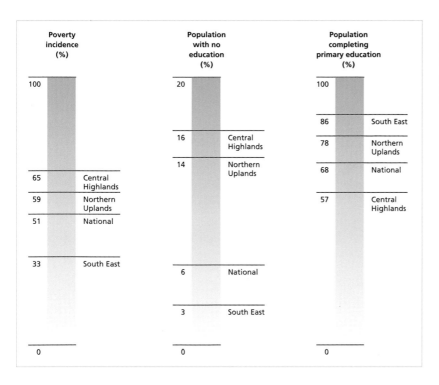

Figure 3.19
Vietnam: regional differences in poverty and educational attainment

Source:
Government of Vietnam,
Education in Vietnam, 1994

Dangs district, where more than 90 per cent of the population belong to scheduled tribes, were 8 per cent below the State average. More significantly, four out of every five children had dropped out of school by Grade 5, even though the overall completion rate for Gujarat is 50 per cent.

In Latin America, indigenous people living in remote highland areas have simultaneously suffered simultaneously from exclusion and inclusion. They have more limited access to public education systems, and these systems often represent a hostile environment in which children are taught in an alien language in an institution that does not respect their culture. Peru provides a particularly stark example (Figure 3.20). Educational opportunities in the country are concentrated in the coastal areas, with chronic under-provision in regions such as the southern highlands. By the age of ten, a child in Ayacucho, a predominantly indigenous area, will have received three years of education – one year less than a child in the capital Lima. Thereafter the disadvantages become cumulative, as the low quality of education takes its toll. Only one-quarter of children in Ayacucho complete primary school. On average, taking into account repetition and drop-out rates, it takes 15 school years per child to finish primary education in Ayacucho, compared with seven years in Lima.[45]

Figure 3.20
Percentages of indigenous and non-indigenous populations with incomplete primary schooling: Bolivia and Peru

Source:
G. Psacharopoulos, *Indigenous People and Poverty in Latin America,* World Bank, 1994

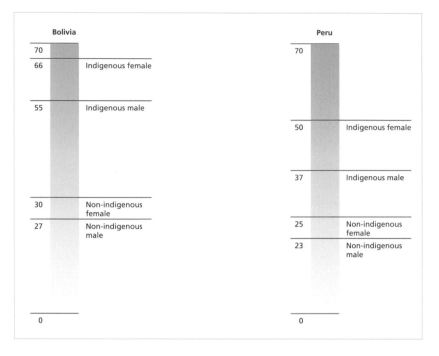

As in other regions, and with other dimensions of inequality, educational deprivation serves to reinforce poverty, with the most deprived communities experiencing the most severe exclusion. In Mexico, the 'poverty belt' states of the Pacific South account for more than 80 per cent of the incidence of subsistence poverty.[46] Some 5 million people are affected, more than the number of extreme poor in all of urban Mexico. An estimated two-thirds of those who live in the municipalities with the highest degree of poverty are indigenous people. Most of these municipalities lack access to basic amenities such as safe water and electricity – and they have the most limited access to education. Illiteracy rates for indigenous peoples are five times the national average, and net enrolment rates 20 per cent lower (see Figure 3.21). In municipalities with a proportion of indigenous people greater than 30 per cent, each adult has on average four years' less education than the national average.[47] The strong association between education deprivation and poverty among indigenous people intersects with gender disparities. Indigenous people suffer extreme disadvantages, but indigenous women are particularly affected (Figure 3.22):

- Indigenous people in Guatemala receive on average 1.3 years of schooling, compared with a national average of 4.2 years. Indigenous females receive on average half as many years of schooling as indigenous males.[48]

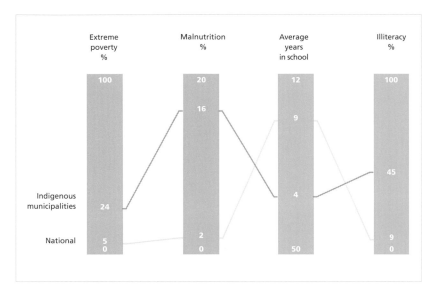

Figure 3.21
Mexico: poverty and educational deprivation

Source: K. Deininger and A. Heinegg, *Rural Poverty in Mexico*, World Bank, 1995

- In Bolivia, more than half of indigenous males and two-thirds of indigenous females do not complete primary education.[49]

- In Peru, one half of indigenous women have received only an incomplete primary education, compared with one-quarter of non-indigenous women.[50]

Education differences contribute directly to the high levels of income poverty found among indigenous people. In Mexico, average monthly incomes in non-indigenous municipalities are twice as high as in indigenous municipalities. Human-resource endowments, as well as physical-resource endowments, contribute to the gap. In Guatemala, there is direct evidence of the importance of education to income poverty. While indigenous people earn less than non-indigenous people with similar levels of education, those with the least education have the lowest incomes. Indigenous people with between 0 and 6 years of education receive less than half the average income of indigenous people who have 7–11 years of education.[51]

Capturing disparity: the disaggregated Education Performance Index

One of the disadvantages of the EPI country rankings is that they capture only the situation of society as a whole and fail to reveal the disparities and contrasts within countries. In order to address this problem, and capture the extent of national inequalities in education, we have created disaggregated EPIs for a number of countries. The same variables have been used (i.e. net enrolment rates, completion rates, and gender equity),

Figure 3.22
Guatemala: average
number of years in school

Source:
G. Psacharopoulos and H. Patrinos,
*Indigenous People and Poverty in
Latin America,* 1996

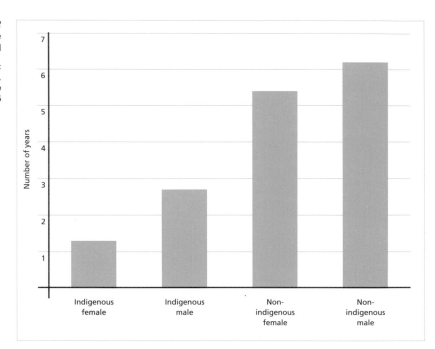

but they have been applied to different regions or social groups in the same countries. One of the advantages of a disaggregated EPI is that it facilitates comparison of educational attainment within countries. It also makes it possible to compare the performance of different groups and regions in relation to the national average.

Some of the main findings to emerge from the disaggregation exercise are summarised below and presented in Figure 3.23.

India: A disaggregation of the EPI for India's States reveals some of the widest education disparities in the developing world. The State of Kerala would rank near the top of the EPI country league table, in twelfth place alongside South Korea and above Mexico. Uttar Pradesh would rank just below Nepal. Bihar would rank 100th in the EPI country league table, fourth from bottom and below Mozambique and Chad.[52]

Pakistan: When the EPI is disaggregated for Pakistan, it reveals both the scale of overall deprivation, and the dimensions of rural–urban disparities. Urban Sindh has the best indicators, but would still fall below the extreme-deprivation threshold. It would rank 80th on the EPI league table. This is 22 places above rural Sindh, which would rank last but one on the EPI scale between Niger and Ethiopia, and one place above the rural areas of the North West Frontier Province. Both rural Sindh and rural Punjab would rank below Haiti on the EPI index.[53]

Vietnam: The disaggregation for Vietnam provides an insight into ethnic disparities. On the basis of data collected during an Oxfam research project in the Northern Upland region, we disaggregated EPI indicators for the province of Lao Cai and two communes in the districts of Sa Pa and Muong Kuong. The results highlight the continuation of extreme inequalities within an already deprived province. The Northern Uplands district of Lao Cai would rank 30 places below Vietnam, which stands in 55th place in the EPI league table. Muong Kuong would rank 33 places lower, and Sa Pa district would be four places from the bottom of the EPI table.[54]

China: Ethnic disparities in China too have remained intact. If Beijing were a separate country, it would rank fifth on the EPI index, seven places above China's national ranking. At the other extreme, the 25 provinces in which minorities constitute the majority of the population would together be in 69th position.[55]

Mexico: As with other indicators of human development in Mexico, the EPI disaggregation reveals sharp disparities between indigenous and non-indigenous people, and between different regions. For municipalities in which indigenous people account for more than 70 per cent of the population, the index of educational deprivation is 20 times higher than for Mexico City. These municipalities would rank 63 places below Mexico, in a cluster of countries that includes Benin, Sudan, and Nepal. The index of deprivation in the South Pacific region is four times Mexico's national average. These States would rank just below the extreme deprivation cut-off line, below Bangladesh and Tanzania, and 53 places below the national ranking for Mexico. The State of Chiapas has an EPI ranking close to that of Mali.[56]

Zambia: Zambia is in the upper half of the EPI league table (ranked 52nd), but the disaggregated data reflect the consequences of urban–rural disparities. Although education performance in Lusaka and the Copperbelt is deteriorating, both areas would figure ten or more places above the national ranking in a cluster of countries at higher income levels, ranging from the Philippines to Egypt. However, Eastern Province and Northern Province would be in 81st and 83rd place respectively in the EPI ranking, below the threshold for extreme deprivation.[57]

Bolivia: The disaggregated ranking for Bolivia illustrates the strong cor-relation between educational deprivation and between communities living in highland areas, rural areas, and cities. Thus, whereas urban Bolivia would rank 36th in the EPI table, alongside Venezuela, highland

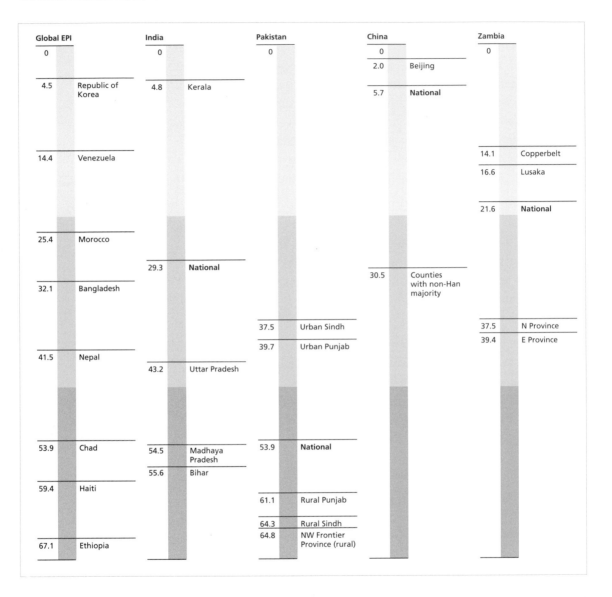

Global EPI

0	
4.5	Republic of Korea
14.4	Venezuela
25.4	Morocco
32.1	Bangladesh
41.5	Nepal
53.9	Chad
59.4	Haiti
67.1	Ethiopia

India

0	
4.8	Kerala
29.3	**National**
43.2	Uttar Pradesh
54.5	Madhaya Pradesh
55.6	Bihar

Pakistan

0	
37.5	Urban Sindh
39.7	Urban Punjab
53.9	**National**
61.1	Rural Punjab
64.3	Rural Sindh
64.8	NW Frontier Province (rural)

China

0	
2.0	Beijing
5.7	**National**
30.5	Counties with non-Han majority

Zambia

0	
14.1	Copperbelt
16.6	Lusaka
21.6	**National**
37.5	N Province
39.4	E Province

Figure 3.23
Disparity in Education Performance Index within countries

Source: Oxfam

areas would rank 100th, below Chad and one place above Haiti. Rural areas would be in 70th position, alongside Bangladesh and Tanzania.[58]

Brazil: The extreme inequality between the north-east and the south of Brazil is captured in the disaggregated EPI. The rural north-east would rank alongside Mozambique, in 97th place on the EPI index. This is 49 places below the national ranking for Brazil, and 48 places below the ranking for the south of Brazil.[59]

The Philippines: The disaggregated EPI for the Philippines illustrates the disparities between the National Capital region and Central Luzon on the

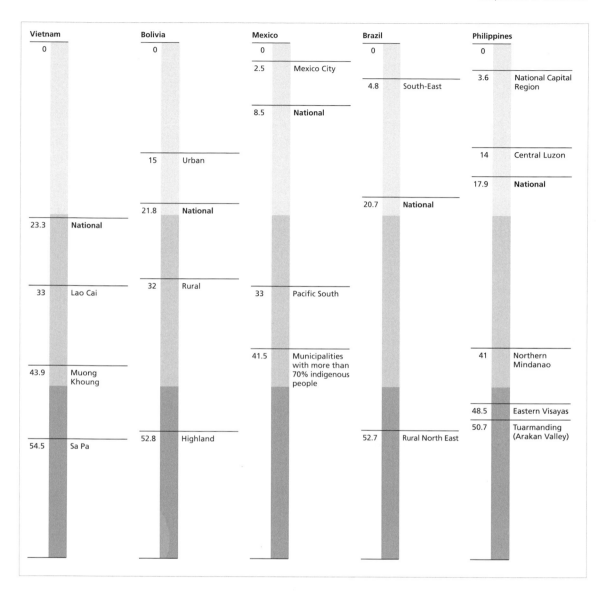

one hand, and the areas with the worst poverty such as northern Mindanao, the Eastern Visayas, and the Cagayan Valley on the other. If the Eastern Visayas were a country, it would rank lower than Burkina Faso on the EPI index, while northern Mindanao would rank alongside Nepal. The two regions would be respectively 60 and 50 places lower than the Philippines' country ranking. At the other end of the scale, the National Capital Region would rank above China, Sri Lanka, and Indonesia, in eighth position out of 104 countries. Central Luzon would be nine places above the national ranking. Beyond the provincial level, a separate EPI score was estimated for the settlement of Tuarmanding in

Figure 3.23 (continued)

the Arakan Valley, using data collected by Oxfam research with the Manobos people. Reflecting the extreme deprivation facing indigenous people, the site would rank well below the threshold for extreme deprivation and tenth from the bottom in the EPI.[60]

4

National barriers to basic education

Most of the children who do not attend primary school or who drop out early live in poor households, and they live in poor countries. These simple facts attest to the powerful interaction between poverty and educational deprivation. At a national level, low average incomes limit the financing capacity of governments, and their ability to provide their citizens with access to good-quality education. At the household level, poverty means that parents may be unable to afford the costs of sending their children to school, or unable to dispense with the labour provided by their children. It may also reinforce gender-based inequalities within the household.

This chapter examines the structural barriers that exclude poor children from educational opportunity. The first part assesses six of the major barriers to education at a household level: direct costs, opportunity costs, distance from school, gender factors, child labour, and conflict. These barriers do not operate in isolation, but interact to produce a cumulative disadvantage that locks poor households into a self-perpetuating state of deprivation that is transmitted across generations.

The second part examines the role of the State in financing basic education. Public investment can act as a great leveller in education, as in other sectors. While wealthier households are able to afford the costs of private provision, poor households depend on State provision, because they have few alternatives. In practice, State provision in many of the poorest countries is being privatised through cost sharing, or the transfer of financing responsibility from national budgets to household budgets. Far more could be done to reduce the financial burden on poor households and to extend State provision. While governments in poor countries inevitably face tough budget choices, there is ample scope for increasing public investment through the reallocation of resources.

The third section considers some broad trends in service provision, with a focus on financial decentralisation and privatisation. The former poses a threat to equity by widening the resource gap between richer and poorer regions. Private education is sometimes cited as a dynamic, innovative, more equitable, and more efficient alternative to State provision. The chapter concludes by considering such claims. It suggests that private-sector provision has a limited role to play in extending the coverage and quality of basic education, not least because the poor cannot afford private schools.

The Oxfam Education Report

Constraints on poor households

Poor households have a more limited range of choice than wealthier households. Their access to goods and services is restricted by low income, they are more heavily reliant on physical labour, they have fewer assets, and they often live in the most remote and isolated regions. All these factors influence the capacity of poor people to educate their children. Any attempt to explain in terms of single causes why children do not attend school, or drop out before completing school, would be flawed. The problems faced by poor communities vary from context to context, although there are some recurrent themes. Inability to pay is a common factor. But households do not consider education costs in isolation. The quality and perceived relevance of the education provided are also important, as are factors such as distance from school, child security, and social and cultural attitudes. Below we consider six of the main barriers confronting poor households.

The high cost of education

The Universal Declaration of Human Rights is unequivocal: *'Education shall be free, at least in the elementary and fundamental stages.'* [1] This is the legal foundation of the right to education. In principle, almost all of the world's governments acknowledge this right. Under the terms of the Convention on the Rights of the Child, now signed by all but two of the world's governments, States are required to 'recognise the right of the child to education, and, with a view to achieving this right progressively and on the basis of equal opportunity, ... they shall ... make primary education compulsory and available free to all'.[2] Despite these pronouncements, the principle that education should be free and compulsory is honoured more in the breach than in the observance. Every Indian citizen has enjoyed the constitutional right to a free education since Independence in 1947, but the poor have to spend a significant proportion of their income to secure that right.[3] In sub-Saharan Africa, the costs of getting a child through primary school can represent more than one-quarter of the annual income of a poor household. For millions of the world's poorest people, access to education is not a human right, but an unaffordable privilege. When they met at the World Education Forum in Dakar in 2000, more than 180 governments again endorsed the principle that education should be free and compulsory.[4] Yet the majority of them continue to tolerate a situation in which the poor are priced out of opportunities for education.

The principle of household financing in education is not new. Communities, families, and individuals have always met part of the cost

In sub-Saharan Africa, the costs of getting a child through primary school can represent more than one-quarter of the annual income of a poor household.

172

of education provision, whether through payments to schools, contributions in kind for school buildings, or spending on textbooks and other teaching materials.[5] During the colonial period in Africa, parents bore almost all of the costs of education services. After independence, States assumed a bigger share of financing responsibility, but the principle of cost sharing remained. The problem is that in many countries the financing burden on poor households has grown to unsustainable levels, and millions of children are consequently excluded from education.

Households face a wide range of direct costs in sending their children to school, even in countries where primary education is officially free. These costs can be divided into two categories. The first category covers official fees levied by education authorities to meet part of the cost of service provision. The second category is broader: it covers a wider range of costs met by the household budget, including the cost of textbooks, uniforms, and school meals. The full check-list of costs facing parents in most countries would include the following items:

- official fees levied by government, such as registration, tuition, and examination fees;
- levies imposed by schools and parent–teacher associations, such as school-improvement fees, building levies, charges for teaching materials, and various payments in kind;
- unofficial fees charged by schools, including 'informal' payments to teachers;
- out-of-pocket payments for uniforms, textbooks, pencils, transport, and meals;
- community contributions, such as payments in cash or kind for school construction and maintenance.

The issue of cost sharing is a source of intense debate. Most governments acknowledge that free education is desirable in principle, especially at the primary level, while at the same time denying that it is achievable in practice. It commonly argued that national tax systems could not meet the full costs of financing free primary education. What this view over-looks is the fact that cost sharing is an indirect tax on education. More importantly, it is a highly regressive tax, since it absorbs a proportionately larger share of the income of the poor than of the non-poor.

What is not in dispute is the high level of payments made by households in relation to public spending. Without these payments, the education systems of many countries would collapse. It is not uncommon in the poorest developing countries for almost the entire government budget for recurrent expenditure on education to be absorbed by teachers' salaries, leaving almost nothing for teaching materials, school maintenance, and classroom equipment. In Tanzania, for example, non-salary expenditure by government amounts to less than $1 per student, compared with an estimated minimum requirement of around $5. Payments by parents finance both the school infrastructure and the costs of providing basic teaching materials.[6]

Estimating the proportion of education spending attributable to households is notoriously difficult, partly because of the wide range of (under-reported) unofficial fees; and partly because of the prevalence of in-kind payments such as labour provisions. Figure 4.1 provides an estimate of the proportion of total expenditure in public primary schools that is borne by households and governments. In each case the household proportions are significant, rising from about one-third of total expenditure in the Philippines and Kenya to one half in Vietnam, and

Figure 4.1
Percentage of total primary-education costs met by private-household expenditure: selected countries*

Sources:
M. Bray: *Counting the Full Cost,* World Bank, 1997; national sources for countries in sub-Saharan Africa

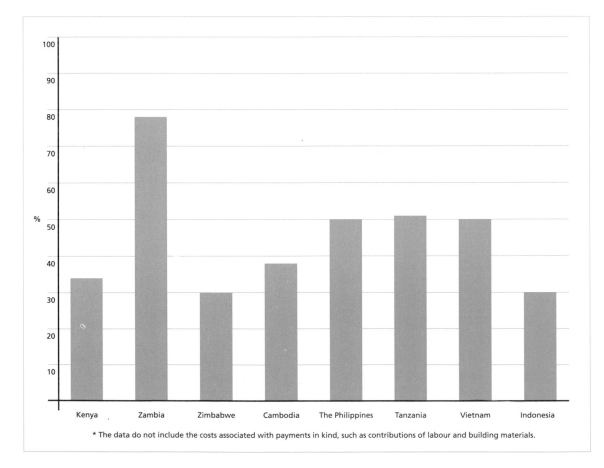

* The data do not include the costs associated with payments in kind, such as contributions of labour and building materials.

over three-quarters in Zambia, Tanzania, and Cambodia.[7] These estimates understate total household contributions, probably by a wide margin. Apart from unofficial fees, they do not take into account the cost in terms of household labour, and contributions in kind that are associated with school construction and maintenance.

Data limitations make it difficult to chart trends in cost recovery. However, such evidence as there is suggests that it has been growing in importance as a source of education financing over time. During the 1980s, per capita public spending either stagnated or went into deep decline in many developing countries. In Latin America, per capita public spending fell by more than 3 per cent a year in current terms in the first half of the 1980s, and by far more if inflation rates averaging over 60 per cent are taken into account.[8] Real spending today is still lower across much of the region than it was twenty years ago. Similarly, in sub-Saharan Africa public spending on education fell from $16bn to $15bn in current terms during the 1980s. Adjusted for inflation, real per capita spending today is probably around one-quarter less than in the early 1980s.[9]

Household budgets partly compensated for the decline in public provision. This shift was encouraged by the IMF and the World Bank, partly on the grounds that there was no alternative; and partly out of an ideological preference in favour of private financing. Cost sharing became inter-twined with an attempt to restrict the role of the State, which was deemed to be unable to finance universal basic service provision, and to be an inherently inefficient service provider. Loan conditions were used to reinforce the new ideology. One survey of structural adjustment loans for sub-Saharan Africa in the 1990s found that one-fifth included stipulations introducing or raising charges for tuition and books.[10]

Ability to pay and willingness to pay

Since the 1980s, the use of cost sharing to finance basic service provision in sectors such as health care, water supply, and education has divided the development community.[11] For some, parental contributions and school fees remain a financing imperative, and an efficient device for generating the resources needed to provide good-quality services. Wider benefits are also claimed. The World Bank frequently refers to the 'sense of ownership' created when households have to pay for services. The payment of fees to service providers, so the argument runs, not only produces more services of higher quality, but also improves the accountability of service providers.[12] While proponents of cost recovery recognise equity as a serious concern, they claim that the high level of payments made by families are indicative of a generalised willingness to pay. The following is not untypical: 'Existing payments for schooling are the most obvious indication that many parents and communities are willing (and able) to pay for schooling. This willingness seems to be particularly evident in countries where governments do not make satisfactory provision.'[13]

There is an obvious sense in which such observations are correct. By definition, parental expenditure reflects a willingness to pay on the part of those making the payment. Moreover, household surveys often reveal that a large proportion of households, including poor ones, would in principle be willing to pay for improved education services, or the construction of schools closer to villages. But the concept of willingness to pay is problematic in its application to cost sharing.

One difficulty relates to the notion of 'willingness'. It is perfectly possible to envisage a situation in which poor people may be willing to pay in principle, but unable to pay in practice.[14] An example from Zambia illustrates the point. In 1993 a national survey reported that only 4 per cent of the population were willing to pay higher fees for health care. Yet when health-care fees were increased in 1994, there was a massive decline in the utilisation of health services at all levels.[15] The reason: the increase in fees coincided with a severe drought and sharp decline in household incomes. When the World Bank carried out a poverty assessment in 1994, it found that poor households in rural areas consistently cited inability to afford health costs as the single most important problem confronting them.

Another problem is that national surveys can obscure differences in perspectives between different groups in the population. One survey in Tanzania found a majority of households indicating a willingness to pay more for education; but 18 per cent of those interviewed indicated that they would not be willing to pay anything. The poor accounted for the vast majority of those unwilling to pay.

Other things being equal, willingness to pay is likely to be substantially higher among the wealthy than among the poor, especially during periods of financial stress. Concentrating on the average costs of education for all households has the effect of obscuring differences based on wealth, for two reasons. The first, and most obvious, is that any fixed education costs will absorb a larger share of the budget of, say, the poorest 20 per cent than the richest 20 per cent. The second is that average annual payments provide a static snapshot, rather than a dynamic picture of affordability that is relevant to any assessment of ability to pay. Because poor people have vulnerable livelihoods and often live in drought-prone areas, their household income is often highly irregular. In a rural setting, for example, cash availability may peak during the post-harvest period, but there may be chronic shortages during the pre-harvest period, when families use their savings or borrow to meet consumption needs. Since the poor have limited options for averting risk, their incomes can be devastated by the effects of drought or floods. All of this has profound implications for the affordability of fees for education over time – implications that will not be captured by average, annual estimates of income and expenditure. One survey in a poor district in Kenya found that drop-out rates had quadrupled in two years because of the effects of drought and high inflation on the incomes of poor households.[16]

Claims that cost recovery engenders a sense of community ownership are not well grounded, either in evidence or in common sense. It is difficult to see why the act of payment, in and of itself, should foster greater accountability on the part of service providers, or a sense of ownership on the part of service users. Relations between providers of services such as health care and education are marked by extreme asymmetries in power and access to information; and these are far more important than the presence – or absence – of cash transfers. Household research in Tanzania found that rural parents were increasingly disenchanted with schools, because they felt that rising costs were not associated with improvements in service quality.[17] Similarly, a study in Zambia found parents expressing bitterness that their contributions were going up when government was providing less material, and when the quality of teaching was deteriorating. While participation is a necessary ingredient for good-quality service provision, the idea that cost recovery automatically enhances 'ownership' represents a crude attempt to provide a psychological rationale for a market-based approach to service provision that is inherently anti-poor in nature.

The burden on the poor

Evidence from many countries confirms that the combination of direct and indirect costs imposes a heavy burden on poor households, absorbing resources needed for investment in production and spending on food. The extent of that burden is conditioned by a wide range of factors, including the level of charges in relation to the average incomes of the poor, the timing of charges, and local factors – such as the effects of drought and seasonal labour demands – influencing household income flows.

Data on cost sharing are seldom collected on a systematic basis, and they often understate the real level of household expenditure by omitting informal fees. However, evidence from many countries suggests that education costs weigh heavily on the household budgets of the poor. The inevitable consequence is that any decline in household income or any unexpected expenditure demands – for instance, for the purchase of essential drugs when someone is sick – can render education an unaffordable option. The following cases demonstrate the impact of education costs on the budgets of the poor:

- Household surveys in **India** suggest that primary-education spending accounts on average for about 7 per cent of average household income. However, for poor households the burden is far heavier. The Public Report on Basic Education in India, which covered 1376 households in 234 villages across Bihar, Madhya Pradesh, Uttar Pradesh, Rajasthan, and Himachel Pradesh, found that the parents of children not in school cited unaffordability as the single biggest problem.[18] The average cost of sending a single child to a government primary school was equivalent to 40 days' wages for an agricultural labourer – a major financial burden for households with several children. The study also found that this average cost was well below the financing requirement for equipping children with adequate textbooks and providing them with sufficient food.

- In **Vietnam**, people in the poorest quintile have to spend 22 per cent of their non-food income to send a single child to school: almost twice the proportion spent by those in the richest quintile. At the lower-secondary level, it costs the poorest households the equivalent of 45 per cent of household income to keep a single child in school, compared with costs of 19 per cent for the wealthiest quintile.[19] Given that 28 million people in the country live below the national income poverty line, education spending clearly represents a huge burden.

- In **Nepal**, the poorest quintile spends more than 40 per cent of an average household income to send one child to primary school, twice the proportion of household expenditure as in the richest quintile.[20]

- Direct primary-school costs in **Indonesia** absorb 38 per cent of per capita incomes for the poorest quintile, compared with 17 per cent for the richest.[21]

- In **Tanzania**, direct school fees represent the equivalent of 5 per cent of the average income in Kagera, the country's poorest region, compared with 1.3 per cent of average income in Dar es Salaam, the richest region. Direct school fees account for less than one-quarter of total household costs. Taking into account indirect fees, the poorest households have to spend around one-fifth of household income to send just one child to school.[22]

Parents wanting to send their children to school face a bewildering array of costs. In Ha Tinh, one of 18 low-income provinces in Vietnam, Oxfam field surveys documented villagers paying construction fees, tuition fees, exam fees, insurance fees, 'talent fund' fees, watchman fees, and a

Mwajuma Kingu's story: cost-recovery in Tanzania

The 1995 Education Act in Tanzania confirmed the principle of free education and made it a civil offence for State officials to exclude children from school. However, large numbers of children are being excluded from education by cost factors. Oxfam research in one ward of Shinyanga Province found that more than 100 parents were being brought to court for non-payment of fees, with their children having been suspended from school.

Mwajuma Kingu lives with her three children, Hilda, Melkisedek, and Veronica, in a small rented shack in Shinyanga, Tanzania. Her story illustrates how the cost of education can exclude the poor from school.She makes her living by buying cassava and sweet potato in the market place each morning, boiling them, and selling them during the day. In an average month, she makes about TsSh7000. After paying for rent, food, and water, she has less than Tsh500 left, most of which is spent on medicine and clothes for the children. She often has to beg for water, or borrow to pay for medicines.

According to government officials, people like Mwajuma should be able to send their children to school. They point out that that the cost of registering in primary school is only Tsh1000 (equivalent to about 10 cents). But on entry to Grade 1 of the local primary school in Mwajuma's village, there is a 'desk charge' of Tsh6000, a 'building improvements' charge of between Tsh2000 and 5000, and assorted

'sports', 'scouts', and 'watchman' charges. Added to this is the cost of a uniform: Tsh5000 (without shoes) and Tsh2000 for exercise books. The total cost comes to at least Tsh15,000 per child per year – which explains why Hilda, aged ten, and Melkisedek, who is eight years old, are not enrolled in school.

In Hilda's case, there has been an element of triumph in adversity. This is her story in her own words: 'I was asking my mother to let me go to school, but she said there was not enough money. But one day I followed the teacher, Mrs Mrema, who is our neighbour, and sat at the back of her class in Standard 1. There are 100 children, so she lets me stay. I like reading and writing the best, but it would be easier if I had books.' The case illustrates how close community ties can overcome some barriers. In fact, many of Shinyanga's rural schools do not collect all of the fees required, although teachers are under considerable pressure from District Councils to do so.

Mwajuma Kingu knows the value of education – and she wants to see her children educated. 'Anyone who can't read and write in this country is going to have a lot of difficulty,' she says. But she sees school fees as a barrier that she can't overcome. Her experience demonstrates poignantly the tension between laws that make primary education compulsory, as it is in Tanzania, and practices that make it unaffordable.

variety of payments in kind, in addition to a range of official commune taxes for education.[23] There was clear evidence that cost recovery was straining household budgets and diminishing the quality of education. Almost one-fifth of parents reported attempting to reduce costs by not purchasing a full set of textbooks. Many also reported deferring payments as a last resort, but this was universally recognised as a high-risk strategy, since it risked exclusion from school. Children from approximately one-third of poor households included in the survey had been sent home from school at some stage for non-payment. Some poor households reported being forced to choose between children, keeping some at home in order to send others to school. Most poor households had developed income-raising strategies to finance education. For example, after school many children would spend the afternoon tending buffalo or working on the farms of their neighbours, in order to generate income to cover education costs.

The scale and scope of education charges facing poor households are illustrated in the boxes on pages 179 and 182, drawing on household-level research in Tanzania and Vietnam. In both cases, the real costs facing poor households significantly exceed those indicated by official figures – and in both cases cost represented a huge barrier against entry to the education system for the poor.

Official government accounts frequently understate the level of parental contributions. In Tanzania, parents are expected to pay a universal primary-education levy, equivalent to just over $2. However, a 1998 Public Expenditure Review carried out by the government found that the standard charge for entry to schools amounted to $6, once assorted building funds, sports fees, and examination fees had been taken into account.[24] Although government policy had not authorised an increase in direct charges by schools, the review noted that 'the burden of parental contributions has increased significantly over the last two years.'[25] Most schools kept no account of payments received from parents, further undermining the argument that payments help to promote accountability among service providers. Moreover, the direct school fees represented a small part of the overall cost incurred by parents. Additional parental contributions amounted to $38 on average, with around half of this amount allocated to textbooks and exercise books, and another third to uniforms. In a country where more than half the population live on an income of less than $1 a day, this represents an enormous financial burden.

Even limited moves towards increased cost sharing can have highly damaging implications in a situation of deep and widespread poverty. In the Eastern Province of Zambia, rural households spend an average of $24 a year to keep one child in primary school. This is in an area where four out of five families live below the poverty line – and where two out of three have incomes 30 per cent or more below that line. Half of all children suffer from stunted growth.[26] With so many families living on the very margins of subsistence, it is not difficult to see why cost barriers exclude so many children from school. Spending on education has to be balanced against the fact that it will leave less income for food, essential health needs, and investment in production. When school costs were increased after 1992 in Zambia, there was a marked increase in school drop-out rates.

The Zambian case is part of a broader pattern. When school fees were increased in Zimbabwe to compensate for a sharp decline in public spending under structural adjustment in 1991, the number of children not attending school rose over the next three years. About half of the parents of children not in school who were interviewed in a 1994 household survey said that their children did not attend because school was 'too expensive'.[27] Similar declines were recorded in Ghana and Côte d'Ivoire, following increases in education charges under structural adjustment programmes. In Kenya, household surveys covering eight districts showed that between one-third and two-thirds of poor households had one or more children who had dropped out of primary school. More than 80 per cent of these households reported inability to pay school fees as the main reason.[28]

While cost sharing creates pressure on the overall household budget, its specific effects on different members of the household are conditioned by social and cultural factors, especially those relating to gender. In situations where the education of girls is less valued than the education of boys, girls are likely to bear the burden of adjustment to any increase in household education costs. When Kenyan parents were asked what they would do if they had to make a choice about who stayed in school on cost grounds, 58 per cent indicated that they would withdraw daughters, and 27 per cent said they would withdraw sons, with the balance expressing no gender preference.[29] Actual behaviour has corresponded very closely with these expressed attitudes. One poverty assessment covering seven poor districts in the mid-1990s found that almost one half of poor households had taken one or more children out of school because of an inability to pay fees. Girls were twice as likely as boys to be withdrawn from school.[30]

When Kenyan parents were asked what they would do if they had to make a choice about who stayed in school on cost grounds, 58 per cent indicated that they would withdraw daughters, and 27 per cent said they would withdraw sons.

'Free' education in Vietnam

Primary education in Vietnam is ostensibly free, but in reality parents face a battery of official and unofficial charges that, in many cases, place education out of reach. Oxfam research in the Northern Upland region, where around 60 per cent of the population live below the national poverty line, found that poor households identified high cost as their single biggest problem in educating their children. In Muong Khuong district, all children were obliged to pay a variety of funds levied by their schools, along with a range of additional payments. Some of these payments – such as 'teacher holiday' funds and school festival funds – are so arbitrary as to make comparison between villages impossible. Excluding such funds, the principal costs, converted into US dollars for a child in Grade 3 of primary school, are as follows:

- School construction, repair, labour, and watchman fund $2.00
- Textbooks $5.30
- Notebooks $1.50
- Cap and scarf (uniform requirement) $0.60
- Insurance $0.50
- Compassion fund (for disadvantaged children) $4.60
- Contributions in kind (oil seeds and bamboo) $4.00

  Total costs $18.50

Modest as such costs may appear in rich countries, they represent a major burden for poor households in Muong Khuong. Moreover, costs escalate with grades, placing an immense strain on those families with several children in school.

The experience of Truong Thi Tam, her husband Nguyen Van Song, and their five children illustrates the problems facing poor families. They are one of 35 households in Ta Giang village, in the Muong Khuong district of the Northern Upland region of Vietnam. Their farm consists of small, scattered plots which produce rice, cassava, and a small amount of corn. In most years, household food stocks start to run out in March, forcing Nguyen to work as a labourer on the land of his wealthier neighbours. During this period, life is often a struggle for survival. The family will sell a few chickens, along with the remainder of their maize and cassava, in order to buy rice. All three of the household's school-age children – two daughters aged ten and 14, and one son aged 12 – are enrolled in the local primary school. Each joined at the age of ten, partly because their parents regarded the journey to school, which involves crossing a stream and a busy road, as too hazardous when they were younger.

The costs of education are high, relative to the household's resources. After the charge for notebooks, direct charges levied by the school in the form of a 'construction fund' represent the biggest single item of expenditure. The family also has to buy uniforms and contribute to a wide range of informal fees, in addition to making various payments in kind. The latter vary from the labour of the children on school-maintenance operations once a week to contributions of wood. Total household expenditure amounts to around $54 at 1998 exchange rates. To put this figure in context, it represents 67 days of work at the prevailing wage rate for day-labourers of 80 cents. The cost of the children's education represents by far the biggest item in the household budget. In order to pay school fees, especially in the pre-harvest period, Truong Thi Tam and Nguyen Van Song sometimes have to resort to borrowing, which they can ill afford, or to carrying out wage labour for wealthier neighbours, which diverts household labour.

The most serious concern for the parents is the prospect of having to meet the additional expense of the graduation tests which children must pass at Grade 5 and Grade 8, at a cost of $5.30 and $15.00 respectively. Large numbers of children drop out at this stage, because their parents cannot to afford to pay. This is part of a wider problem in Vietnam. It helps to explain why fewer than one in five children from the poorest households proceed from primary into junior-secondary school.

Given the immense financial strain, why do Truong and Nguyen attach such importance to education? The reason is summarised in an expression which many Kinh households used when asked the same question: 'tinh toan'. Literally, this means 'being able to calculate', but figuratively it is used to describe people who can trade in markets without fear of being cheated. As Truong puts it: 'Without education, my children will get bad prices from traders and they will not be able to provide for their families.' As in other parts of Vietnam, poor households such as Nguyen's would benefit from a policy that reduced formal and informal fees, and from the provision of free teaching materials to all schools.

What these various cases demonstrate is that demand for education among the poor is highly sensitive to the price at which education services are provided. Not surprisingly, it is far more sensitive than demand among higher-income groups, who are more readily able to absorb rising costs. One study in Peru found that rural households belonging to the poorest quintile were two to three times more likely than those from the wealthiest quintile to withdraw their children from school in response to a given increase in fees.[31] About half of the parents of children not in school said it was 'too expensive' to enrol their children. The impact of cost sharing on demand for education among the poor is highly seasonal, reflecting fluctuations in income levels. In rural areas, problems of affordability are exacerbated when school fees fall due during the pre-harvest period, when access to income is most restricted. Poor households in rural Zambia cite this as one of the main reasons for having to take their children out of school.[32]

Attempts have been made through various exemption schemes to protect the poor from the effects of cost sharing. Most of them provide a waiver for school fees, at least in theory. In practice, most efforts to protect the poor and vulnerable from education charges through targeted welfare systems have proved unsuccessful. For instance, while provision for exemption does exist in Vietnam, the system is highly discretionary, and remission is not well targeted towards those in most need. Even where formal exemption systems exist, they are often inaccessible or unknown, especially to remote rural populations. Oxfam research in the Shinyanga district of Tanzania found that a district-level exemption scheme for school fees had been established, but most poor families were not even aware of it.[33]

Exemption systems introduced under structural adjustment programmes have proved equally inadequate. In Zimbabwe, a Social Development Fund (SDF) was introduced in 1991 with the express purpose of protecting poor households from the effects of cost recovery. Three years later, a government survey found that only about half the population had heard of the SDF, while fewer than 5 per cent of those eligible had actually claimed assistance with school fees. Many of the poor were effectively excluded by cumbersome administrative procedures, including the authorities' insistence on formal proof of low income (seldom available to the rural poor), and the centralisation of claims offices in urban centres. For those who did succeed in navigating their way through the system, the average gap in time between application and payment amounted to eight months.[34]

One of the problems in attempting to operate an exemption system is that, in most poor countries, the costs of administration are inversely related to the financing generated by cost recovery. This creates a paradox at the heart of cost-recovery policies. Governments introduce or increase user charges as an alternative to general taxation, primarily with a view to increasing revenue. In a not untypical country in Africa with more than 40 per cent of the population living below the poverty line, an effective welfare system would limit revenue collection by exempting a large proportion of households from payments. Moreover, in countries with limited institutional capacity, the costs of exemption are likely to rise with the size of the population covered, reducing the net financial gains from cost recovery. The end result is that cost-recovery schemes with effective exemption systems are likely to provide weak financial benefits for the State. Schemes without such systems have the potential to provide more revenue, but at the cost of growing inequity in service provision.

Community financing

Even if the poor cannot afford the monetary costs of user fees, is it reasonable to require contributions in kind, such as the use of community labour to build and maintain schools? And is it unreasonable to expect wealthier communities to invest in their children's future? There are no easy answers to these questions. Community resourcing of education has long been a feature of service provision, and it is unrealistic to expect wealthier households not to invest their private income in the education of their children, even if the quality of public provision improves.[35] This is especially true of countries in sub-Saharan Africa, where – as in Kenya – village 'self-help' is built into the national education system.

However, there are serious problems with community resourcing. Community contributions to education are often perceived by the poor as an excessive burden and source of vulnerability. Material contributions impose considerable demands on household budgets. Meanwhile, the high dependence of poor households on their own labour means that contributions of labour can have grave implications for livelihood security. While wealthier households are often able to commute labour payments into cash transfers, this option is not open to poor households, so that school construction often becomes the task of the very poor (many of whom who will not send their children to school) and of women. In Vietnam, labour contributions for education lock poor people into highly unfavourable exchanges. For the wealthiest households, it costs the equivalent of three days' income to commute the labour tax levied by communes into a cash payment. In contrast, the poorest households dedicate 20 days of their labour to the commune.

The most obvious problem with community self-help arrangements is that wealthier communities are able to mobilise more resources than poorer communities. Direct financing by households and communities can perpetuate inequalities and extend them over time, because the wealthy can make larger investments than the poor can. In Indonesia, the contribution of Parent Associations has been an important source of supplementary finance for schools. The contribution is generally considered mandatory. However, while some schools in the poorest rural communities in the Outer Islands receive no parental payments at all, collections in the wealthier communities account for 20 times the government subsidy. This inevitably leads to highly unequal levels of service provision. While self-help clearly has a role to play, some are better equipped to help themselves than others.

While self-help clearly has a role to play, some are better equipped to help themselves than others.

Similar problems have emerged in sub-Saharan Africa, where community financing has often served to widen regional inequalities. For example, the relatively prosperous Kilimanjaro area in Tanzania has 20 per cent of the country's secondary schools, but only 5 per cent of its population. Similarly, Kenya's Central Province has far better school facilities than its North Eastern Province, reflecting differences in private spending.[36] Interventions by the donor community are exacerbating the problems associated with wealth inequalities. For instance, the World Bank has introduced a series of 'matching fund' initiatives, mainly in East Africa. The central idea is that the World Bank and other donors will match with cash assistance any funds mobilised by a community itself. Since wealthier communities are better able to mobilise resources than poorer communities, they can expect to capture a larger share of donor assistance, magnifying existing differences in the quality of service provision, and weakening the targeting of donor assistance on the poor in the process.

Falling costs and increased enrolments

Perhaps the most compelling case against cost recovery is provided by evidence of what happens when costs are lowered. Countries such as South Korea, Cuba, and Zimbabwe, which progressed rapidly towards universal primary education despite high levels of poverty and inequality, did so by reducing the costs to poor households through increased public investment. More recently, other countries have attempted to follow this path, in some cases with considerable success.

- **Uganda**: In January 1997, the government introduced a policy of universal primary education which removed the requirement that parents should meet 50 per cent of the fees. At the same time, the policy banned charges levied by Parent–Teacher Associations. As a result, enrolments increased from 2.9 million to 5.7 million children at the start of the 1997/98 school year.

- **Malawi:** The introduction of school fees in the mid-1980s led to a sharp decline in enrolments. In 1992, a major policy reversal abolished tuition fees for girls. Then, in December 1994, the new multi-party coalition government waived all fees for primary-school students, including tuition and construction-fund charges. By 1996, total enrolments had reached 3.1 million, more than twice the number for 1993. Relaxing the requirement that children should wear uniforms provided an additional incentive for poor parents to enrol their children.[37]

- **Ethiopia**: Fees were abolished in the East Gojam region in 1995–96, leading to a 20 per cent increase in enrolments in the following year.[38]

These examples are not intended to suggest that the elimination of cost recovery is a panacea for exclusion from educational opportunity. In both Malawi and Uganda, the surge of enrolments has created enormous problems of over-crowding and shortage of textbooks. The experience of both countries points to the importance of sequencing reforms and backing the withdrawal of fees with the increased public investments needed to raise quality. But it remains the case that a sharp reduction in cost recovery is a necessary requirement for achieving universal primary education in many countries.

Options for reform

There is an obvious problem facing policy makers who want to reduce the financial costs of education to poor households. That is, any reduction in household spending that is not compensated for by an increase in public spending will, other things being equal, reduce overall investment in education, with damaging implications for service provision and service quality. The important question is whether or not governments have the financing capacity to reduce cost sharing, while attempting to achieve the goal of universal primary education.

It is a question that goes to the heart of issues relating to political choice and equity in public financing. Advocates of cost sharing often argue that it represents an alternative to taxation. The implication is that it provides an efficient means of mobilising revenue through consumer choice – the consumers being, in this case, the parents of school children. In reality, this argument is nonsense. Cost sharing represents a system of taxation, levied through the education system, selected by governments to finance a public service. The problem is that cost sharing is less efficient and less equitable than the alternative. There are strong grounds for governments to finance basic education entirely out of general taxation. From an equity perspective this is advantageous, both because progressive general taxation links revenue mobilisation to ability to pay; and because cost sharing is excluding so many poor people from education. There is also a wider public interest in using general taxation to overcome mass exclusion from educational opportunity. While many of the benefits associated with education accrue to individuals (in the form of higher income, for instance), the costs of exclusion from education are spread across society. Slower growth, widening inequalities, and lost opportunities for improving public health have an impact on all social groups. The public interest in achieving education for all through general taxation is as powerful as the private interest.

The public interest in achieving education for all through general taxation is as powerful as the private interest.

None of this is to deny the fact that the governments of poor countries confront real budgetary constraints, just as the governments of wealthy countries do. But many of these constraints are shaped by political choices. Governments have to choose what proportion of national income to mobilise through tax revenue. They also have to balance competing budget priorities. How much of a budget is allocated to military spending rather than to education will reflect political choice, as will decisions about whether to focus education spending on primary schools rather than universities. Whether or not budgets are designed and managed in favour of the poor is as important as average income in determining financing capacity for basic services such as primary education.[39]

As we show in the second part of this chapter, political choice has the potential to widen the public-spending parameters for education in most countries. Even within existing public-spending parameters, most governments could do more to relieve the pressures on poor households caused by cost recovery. The starting point should be national and local assessments of the impact of education charges and the scope for scaling them down. In many cases this could be done without adverse consequences for education quality. Figure 4.2 illustrates the distribution of costs to parents of sending a child to school in Tanzania, Vietnam, and India. It will be immediately apparent that some of the items are of limited relevance to the quality of education. School uniforms figure prominently in household expenditure, accounting for more than one-third of the total in Tanzania and Vietnam, and rising to one half in India. In situations where education costs are imposing an intolerable strain on the household budgets of the poor, it is difficult to justify such expenditure patterns. Unfortunately, education authorities often place great emphasis on uniform requirements. Parents of pupils in government-run rural schools in Zimbabwe spend on average $4 per child on school uniforms, four times as much as they spend on textbooks.[40] Eliminating uniform requirements would reduce the pressure on household budgets, without adverse implications for education quality. Indeed, there are potential advantages for education outcomes, since some of the resources saved could be used to provide textbooks and teaching materials.

Given the critical importance of textbooks, pencils, and other learning materials for the quality of education, the withdrawal of charges for these items should also be a priority. Unlike the case of school uniforms, this will require increased public investment to maintain and extend access. Governments can also reduce the large share of costs accounted for by unofficial fees. More rigorous accounting for funds received at the school level is an urgent priority, since weak accounting systems open the door

Figure 4.2
Distribution of household education costs in Tanzania, Vietnam, and India: percentages of total spending allocated to school fees, uniforms, and textbooks

Sources:
Government of Tanzania:
Public Expenditure Review, 1998;
PROBE: *Public Report on Basic Education,* Oxford and Delhi,
OUP, 1999;
Government of Vietnam: *Education Financing Survey,* 1997

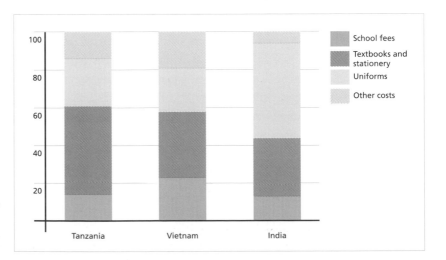

to corruption and abuse. In Mozambique's Zambezia Province, the official school fee is $1 per term. However, communities involved in Oxfam-supported projects report paying four times this amount.[41] One of the most common costs is an informal 'exam fee' charged by teachers. The children of parents who are unable to pay are not allowed to sit exams for progression to the next grade. Controlling such practices is ultimately the responsibility of local education authorities, but more democratic and accountable school management is also needed.

There are other options available to governments seeking to reduce the costs of education to poor households. Targetting by region, language group, or sex is one mechanism. Districts with particularly extreme levels of poverty, such as the 18 low-income districts in Vietnam, could be provided with free education and with additional State support on the basis of need. In Latin America, the World Bank and others have argued for free education to be provided to language groups – such as the Aymara and Quechua in Peru – that are particularly deprived.[42] Providing free education to girls could serve the dual purpose of reducing pressure on overall budgets, while at the same time supporting gender-equity goals. At the same time, governments need to consider the timing of school fees. In the Gambia, fees were demanded at the beginning of the school year, coinciding with the pre-harvest period when rural populations were at the poorest.[43] The simple act of changing the collection date helped to increase enrolment.

Finally, it should be emphasised that the removal of fees is not a universal panacea for the problem of access to education. In the highland areas of Vietnam, education is free to ethnic-minority communities, yet these communities have far lower enrolment rates and higher drop-out rates than poor Kinh households. Household-level research by Oxfam among the ethnic-minority Hmung community living in the Northern Upland region found that the need for child labour, the perceived irrelevance of education, and the use of the Kinh language were far more significant barriers to education than direct costs were. Similar patterns of variation can be found in other countries. In Pakistan, household surveys of families with children out of school found that high cost was the single most important consideration for boys in urban areas. For girls living in rural areas, distance from school, the need for household labour, and parental refusal to send children to school were much more important than cost. In rural Sindh, around 40 per cent of the parents of girls aged 10–18 who had not been to school cited the need for help at home as the main reason, while only 8 per cent said that cost was the main factor. For urban boys, this picture is reversed, illustrating the importance of gender roles in the household. (See Figure 4.3.)

Opportunity costs

When children go to school, their parents incur more than financial costs. The time and effort that children might otherwise devote to household tasks, production, or income generation are also lost. These opportunity costs are often especially high for poor households, which are heavily reliant on child labour.

Attempts to estimate the opportunity costs of child labour have often focused on the potential income losses associated with sending a child to school. Research based on this approach has reported that opportunity costs rise with the age of children, with the costs to households rising as the potential for children to generate income increases. Because wages for boys are often higher than for girls, one of the main propositions to emerge is that the opportunity costs for boys' education are higher than for girls.[44] Such conclusions are misleading. For children of primary-school age, household opportunity costs in most countries relate mainly to work in the household, rather than income generation outside the

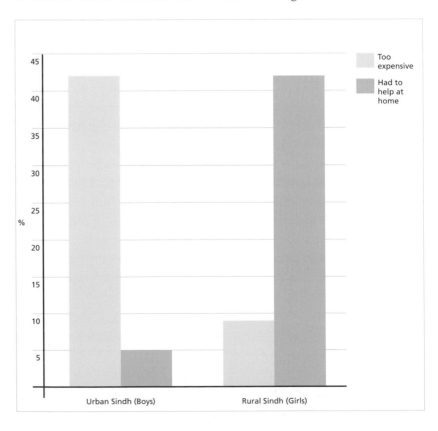

Figure 4.3
Children aged 10-18 who have never attended school: reasons given by parents for non-attendance (Sindh Province, Pakistan)

Source:
Government of Pakistan,
Pakistan Integrated Household Survey, 1996

household. In this context, labour time is more important than income. Using labour time – rather than wages forgone – as an indicator reverses the conventional picture drawn by some economists, with the opportunity costs of girls' education exceeding those for boys.[45]

Gender differences in household opportunity costs mirror inequalities in the household division of labour. Girls perform a range of tasks, from care for siblings to fetching wood and water, and cooking. In rural areas, they also contribute directly to household production by caring for animals, pounding grain, and weeding. For women, who are the primary agricultural producers in most developing countries, the labour of their daughters in the home means that more time can be spent in production and income-generating activity. Conversely, sending a girl to school means more demands on the mother's time at home.[46] There is an important poverty-related dimension to opportunity costs in education. Since poor households are more dependent on child labour and less able to hire alternative labour, the relative costs of sending children to school are higher than for wealthier households. Girls in the poorest households of rural Java work on average 94 hours a month, whereas the corresponding figure for the wealthiest households is 26 hours.[47]

The extent of child labour, and of gender inequalities in labour time, emerges from a large number of household surveys. In India, Bangladesh, and Nepal, girls assume responsibility for collecting firewood and water and caring for siblings at the age of five. By the age of ten, they may be working up to ten hours a day in productive activity inside and outside the home. Young Indian girls below the age of 14 work on average 5.5 hours each day, compared with 1.8 hours for boys.[48] Similar patterns are repeated in sub-Saharan Africa. Such facts help to explain the gender differences in enrolment at the primary level in many countries. But they also provide an insight into some of the less tangible disadvantages suffered by young girls. For example, long hours of work inevitably impair educational attainment, especially when girls also have to drop out of school during peak work seasons.

Household labour as a consequence of limited access to schools

Household demand for child labour is frequently presented as a barrier to education in its own right, with children kept away from school by parents needing their help at home. The reality is more prosaic. In many cases, children are working at home as a *consequence* of being out of school, whether because their parents cannot afford the direct costs of education, because school is too far away, or because the quality of education offered is perceived as inadequate. The Public Report on Basic

Education (PROBE) in India found that one-third of children not enrolled in school had not done any work during school hours on the day before they were interviewed. Half worked for less than three hours a day. Given that the school day in rural India lasts for only four or five hours, household labour demands can be accommodated within existing patterns of child labour in households, especially during the primary-school years. As the PROBE survey puts it: 'Unless family labour involves rigid work hours that consistently clash with school timings, it is unlikely to prevent children from attending school with reasonable regularity.'[50] So why do parents fail to send their children to school? More than 90 per cent of the parents in the PROBE survey said that they were willing to send their children to school, but could not afford to do so. In other words, most of their children were working at home by default, because they were excluded from school by high costs.

Adjusting the school term times to coincide with the agricultural cycle could significantly reduce the opportunity costs associated with education.

In other cases, household labour demands do present a barrier to school attendance. In Ethiopia, gender differences in enrolment reflect the fact that girls of primary-school age work for 14–16 hours a day on a variety of tasks. The creation of more educational opportunities for girls would clearly require an adjustment of household work patterns. Even here, however, the labour constraint is not an absolute barrier. In a USAID survey of more than 500 rural households in Ethiopia, respondents confirmed that seasonal demand for child labour was a factor in withdrawing children from school. Opportunity cost was cited ahead of direct costs as the single most important reason for children not being in school, with more than 30 per cent of parents surveyed saying that they kept their children at home to assist in agricultural production and household work. However, one in five of the parents who had withdrawn their children said that they would change their decision if the school year did not overlap with seasons of peak labour demand.[51]

Adjusting the school term times to coincide with the agricultural cycle could significantly reduce the opportunity costs associated with education in such cases. In Colombia, the Escuela Nueva programme (discussed in Chapter 6) has adjusted the school term and day to the seasonal labour patterns of local communities. The Community Schools programme in Egypt has done the same. In both cases, community participation in the education planning process enabled school authorities to increase enrolments and reduce drop-out rates.

Opportunity costs in education are not immutable and unchanging facts of life, as these examples demonstrate. They can be reduced – or increased – through public policies. Research in Ghana has shown that distance from a source of drinking water has a significant impact on school attendance.[52] The findings suggest that, as in other countries, the opportunity costs of sending girls to school could be reduced by improving water supply. Because girls spend more time than boys caring for siblings, improving pre-school provision would have a similar effect. The availability of community-based child-care centres can relieve girls of responsibility for looking after siblings during school time. While some cost is inevitably involved, materials, staff, and financial resources can be mobilised within communities. In Nairobi, Oxfam is working in the Korogocho slum area with a community-based group, providing places in pre-school groups for 40 children. The centre is staffed by local women who have been trained in basic child development and are paid a small fee. Pre-school groups have the additional advantage of preparing children for primary school by raising nutritional standards and introducing children to the school environment.

Distance from school

Each day millions of children in the developing world embark on long journeys to their schools. These journeys add enormously to the opportunity costs of education, since they result in children being away from home for long hours. They also create security fears for parents, especially concerning young girls. Excessive distance frequently results in parents enrolling children later and – especially in the case of girls – ending their school careers earlier.[53] In most societies, distance from school is inversely related to the prospects of girls going to school, especially after puberty. In Egypt, for example, for communities located within 1km of a school, the average enrolment rate is 94 per cent for boys and 74 per cent for girls. Where the distance is increased to 2km, boys' enrolment barely falls, while girls' enrolment drops by 10 per cent.[54]

Gender segregation and distance in rural Pakistan

The implications of distance from school vary from society to society. In countries where cultural practices place a premium on female seclusion, the association between distance and gender equity in school attendance is particularly strong. This is the case in much of rural Pakistan, which has some of the largest gender-equity gaps in the world.[55] Cultural barriers to education are exacerbated by an official policy of gender segregation in a situation where there are fewer schools for girls than boys. In the North West Frontier Province, more than 40 per cent of villages lack a government-funded girls' school – and only one-fifth of government primary schools are for girls. Similar gender inequities prevail in Baluchistan, where there are ten times as many boys' schools as girls' schools.

One-third of villages in rural Baluchistan have no girls' school within 6km, compared with one-tenth for boys' schools. In rural Sindh, barely 50 per cent of all villages have a girls' school in their locality, compared with 94 per cent for boys' schools.[56] Gender segregation in an environment marked by chronic shortages of schools for girls is a prescription for exclusion.

In Pakistan, gender segregation has served not just to exacerbate the problem of distance, but also to introduce enormous inefficiencies across the education system. Given that a typical village requires only one school, the inefficiency of single-sex teaching is self-evident. In fact, many parents have been willing to send their girls to mixed schools, as witnessed by the presence of girls in many boys' schools. In 1995, a UNICEF survey found that as many as 3000 rural schools taught fewer than ten children.[57] Parents in many villages are rejecting segregation by enrolling their girls in boys' schools, regardless of official policy. As many as one-third of rural schools are now *de facto* co-educational. However, many parents are unwilling to send female children to schools that do not have separate toilets for girls.

Parental concerns

Parental fears about security are closely correlated with the distance that children have to travel to school. For rural communities in Zambia, school journeys often imply distances far in excess of 2km. According to the 1996 Living Conditions Measurement Survey, 16 per cent of rural children live more than 6km away from a school.[58] In many cases, the journey to school will mean traversing swollen rivers during the rainy season, or negotiating other hazards. Villagers in one area of Zambia's Eastern Province which borders on a game reserve reported to Oxfam staff that their fear of wild animals attacking the children was a major reason for keeping them at home. In Mozambique, another Oxfam survey revealed that parental concern over fatigue caused by long-distance travel led them to defer enrolling their children until the age of ten. Fear of exposing girls after puberty to sexual molestation on the same journey resulted in many girls being taken out of school at the age of 13.[59] Distance factors frequently intensify regional disparities in opportunity. In Mali, the capital region of Bamako has an enrolment rate above 90 per cent. Distances to school average less than 1km. In Timbuktu, by contrast, the average distance to school exceeds 7km – and only one-quarter of children enrol. The situation is not untypical of the Sahelian region, where low population density and a widely dispersed population make distance from school one of the biggest factors behind non-attendance.[60]

Much can be done to address the problems associated with distance. Support for village schools or satellite schools – small units linked logistically and administratively with larger schools in the area – can help to bring education services to children, instead of requiring children to travel long distances. Such schools have been successfully developed in remote rural areas of Bangladesh, and are now being developed in highland areas of Vietnam. More generally, the long-term problems associated with long journeys to school need to be addressed through a combination of better planning of local facilities, support for local community initiatives in developing village-level schools, and increased public provision. These issues are discussed in more detail in later chapters.

Cultural barriers to gender equity

Some of the difficulties facing young girls in education lend themselves to relatively simple solutions, at least in principle. Schools can be built, scholarships granted, pencils and books provided, costs reduced, and so on. However, some of the greatest obstacles to equity are located not in financial or material constraints, but in the minds of parents, teachers, and political leaders.

Disadvantage begins in the home. In many societies, customary practices and attitudes result in female education being assigned a lower value than male education. Patrilineal inheritance and patrilocal residence are two such practices. For parents, they can mean that the benefits of their investment in a daughter's education will be transferred to the husband's household on her marriage, since she will leave the parental home. There is a popular Telugu expression in South Indian which says that 'educating a daughter is like watering another man's garden', summarising in stark terms a widespread attitude that ascribes a low value to girls' education.[61]

In some cases, investing in the education of a girl is seen not as a basic right or as a source of high returns, but as a potential liability. In Zambia, the marriage of daughters is regarded as a source of bride-wealth. One participatory poverty assessment in Northern Province illustrated how this could work against girls' education. Most families take their girls out of school after Grade 4, not only because it is seen as wasteful to continue, but also because of a perception that bride-wealth payments will diminish for an educated girl.[62] Maternal education can have a significant bearing on this perception. The education of a daughter can often seem pointless to households where the mother has traditionally spent her life doing domestic work, and may have had limited encounters with other views.

In some cases, investing in the education of a girl is seen not as a basic right or as a source of high returns, but as a potential liability.

The cultural practice of early marriage places another major restriction on educational opportunity. In the East Gojam area of Ethiopia, girls start to marry at the age of eight, by which stage few have even started school.[63] The onset of puberty creates further problems, as many parents cite fear of pregnancy outside marriage as the reason for keeping pubescent girls at home. Such fears, associated with shame, bride-wealth rights, and simple parental concern, surface most strongly when pubescent girls have to walk long distances to school. Economic pressures often interact with cultural practice to disadvantage girls still further. In Tanzania, several researchers have noted not only that parents stop sending their daughters to school for fear of losing a dowry in the event of unwanted pregnancy, but also that they pressurise them to marry early in order to secure bride-wealth sooner rather than later.

In the Tanzanian case, 6o per cent of the girls who do proceed to the secondary level are eventually expelled on account of pregnancy.

Because girls in many of the poorest countries start primary school late, early marriage and pregnancy can cut short an already brief education. School systems often fail to take into account the consequences of early marriage. In the Tanzanian case, 6o per cent of the girls who do proceed to the secondary level are eventually expelled on account of pregnancy.[64] Changing attitudes to early marriage and dowry systems, and developing more flexible attitudes towards pregnant teenagers who have not completed their education are key ingredients for reform.

Perceptions of the value, role, and abilities of young girls are brought into the classroom. Girls are often expected to conform to the values and norms of a male-dominated society, in which little or no encouragement is provided for them to develop their own aspirations. Gender differences are often reinforced by teachers. Surveys of teachers' attitudes, in a variety of settings in Africa and South Asia, consistently show that most believe girls to be less able than boys, especially in mathematics and science. Classroom surveys show that, in many schools, less time is spent in asking questions of girls and involving them in school activities.[65] Negative self-images inevitably follow, with adverse implications for performance in school tests. Biased textbooks reinforce the vicious circle, typically presenting young boys and men as adventurous, inquisitive, and dominant, with girls portrayed as passive, admiring, and equipped only to play traditional roles. Analysis of teaching materials in Africa has shown that women and young girls appear predominantly in domestic roles and are often characterised as ignorant.[66] A survey carried out by the Swedish International Development Agency analysed the gender images in 42 primary-school textbooks in Zimbabwe. It concluded: 'Gender stereotyping and prejudice against women in virtually any role outside the home is a continuous thread ... "Happy women" are those performing the domestic role in an exemplary fashion. Where women do leave the home, they always seem to become nurses. There are only one or two presentations of women as farmers ... There are no examples of women-headed households, women in professional, entrepreneurial or cultural pursuits, or males in a domestic role.'[67]

Strategies for change

What can be done to remove cultural barriers to gender equity? Self-evidently, there are no easy answers. Changing household attitudes and practices is an obvious starting point. High-level political campaigns, supported by local leaders, can help to improve parental awareness of the value of education and restrict early marriage. But this requires a political commitment at the highest levels of governments – and such commitment is often sorely lacking. Earlier enrolment is also vital, in order to maximise the pre-puberty years spent in education. Education systems in countries where early pregnancies are a fact of life need to provide support to young girls, rather than punitive sanctions in the form of summary expulsion.[68]

Women teachers can provide a role model for girls, a source of security for parents, and a more sympathetic ear for young girls going through difficult times in their lives. In several countries with large gender gaps at school, there is a close correlation between the presence of female teachers and the attendance of girls in classrooms. Figure 4.4 demonstrates the relationship for selected regions in Ethiopia and Yemen. Unfortunately, women teachers are most scarce in the rural areas, where gender divisions are deepest. South Asia and sub-Saharan Africa – the two developing regions with the largest gender gaps in enrolment – have the lowest proportion of female teachers. Some of the successful micro-level strategies for increasing numbers of female teachers, discussed in more detail in Chapter 6, have focused on local recruitment and training.

Cost reduction is another strategy for reducing gender inequity. Because the education of girls is insufficiently valued and the opportunity costs of girls' labour are high, household demand for girls' education tends to be weaker. Other things being equal, where the costs of education for girls and boys are similar, but girls' education is deemed less important, economic pressures will affect young girls most immediately. As we saw earlier, one of the side effects of cost recovery is to reinforce gender inequity. Reducing the costs of education can reduce the incentive for households to keep children out of school. The success of various

Figure 4.4
Relationship between presence of female teachers and percentage of girls attending school: selected regions, Yemen and Ethiopia

Sources:
P. Rose, *Gender and Primary Schooling in Ethiopia,* Institute for Development Studies, 1997; D. Al-Hidabi, 'Basic Education Baseline Research in Yemen', Oxfam, 1998

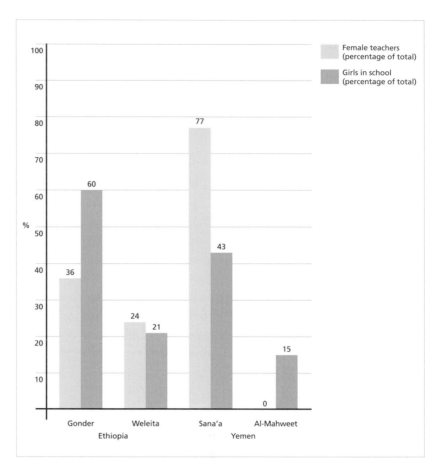

schemes that provide incentives for girls' education through bursaries, fellowships, or vouchers illustrates how the removal of economic pressures can stimulate demand for girls' education.

Ultimately, however, the challenge is to raise awareness of gender-specific barriers to education. Without fundamental changes of attitude and a conviction that individuals, households, and society as a whole can benefit from gender equity, the impact of specific policies is likely to be limited. Changing attitudes is inherently more difficult than changing policies, not least because it requires the development of alliances that span political divides. This challenge is being addressed by a wide range of non-government organisations, such as the Forum of African Women Educationalists (FAWE) in sub-Saharan Africa.[69] Founded by five women Education Ministers in the early 1990s, today FAWE is active in 31 countries, providing research and strategic resource-planning to advance the cause of girls' education.

Child labour

A young girl in India collects water or firewood with her mother after school, and later cares for her siblings while her mother cooks; a boy of primary-school age in Vietnam tends the family's buffalo, while his father ploughs a field; street children hawk goods in Nairobi or Mexico City; young girls from Nepal and Thailand are enslaved in the sex industry; and thousands of children crouch behind looms in the carpet factories of Bangladesh, working in dusty and dangerous conditions. Children carry out a vast range of jobs in a variety of conditions, some of which are far more damaging for educational attainment – and for child health – than others.

Any evaluation of the interaction between child labour and educational opportunity must take into account the diversity of child labour. Work involving degrading or psychologically damaging conditions must be seen for what it is: a crime against children. Long hours of work, leading to fatigue and impaired intellectual development, are also inconsistent with the right to education. Yet not all child labour is harmful. Many children are working in stable and safe environments, in which labour is part of family socialisation; and in which desperately poor parents are trying to balance their children's need for education with the household's need for labour.

According to the International Labour Organisation (ILO), about 250 million children between the ages of 5 and 14 are working in developing countries. Most of these live in Asia, but the proportion of working children is highest in Africa, where one in three is estimated to be engaged in some form of economic activity, principally in agriculture.[70] Premature and extensive labour is depriving many of these children of their only chance to acquire the literacy, numeracy, and learning skills that they need to escape poverty. Just under half of the global number of child labourers are thought to be in full-time work.[71] It is these children who suffer what amounts to a clear breach of the internationally recognised right to education. Unacceptable forms of child labour are symptoms of poverty, exploitative social and economic relations, and (increasingly) family breakdown caused by AIDS-related deaths. The problem cannot be legislated out of existence, but it can be addressed through practical action at the community level, combined with supportive action by local authorities, national governments, and the international community.

Poor communities themselves have often taken the lead, working with local NGOs. One example is to be found in the Kenyan capital of Nairobi, where an Oxfam partner agency, Mungano Wa Wanavjiji, is working with the residents' association to support a small training and literacy centre. Most of the pupils are adolescents who missed their chance for a primary education and now survive by hawking and scavenging. The school day and curriculum are geared to fit the realities of these vulnerable livelihoods. Classes are conducted over a three-hour period in the morning and in the early evening, with children learning numeracy skills to equip them for trading. During 1998, the first pupils made the transition to government schools, illustrating the potential for partnerships between governments and non-government agencies.

The MVF Foundation

Some non-government initiatives are being expanded and integrated into national plans. An example is a programme set up by the M Venkatarangaiya Foundation (MVF) in the Indian State of Andhra Pradesh.[72] Working with local communities whose high levels of household debt have forced families to supply child labour to large-scale cotton plantations, MVF has developed practical responses. Its programme has now been integrated into a State-wide strategy for reducing child labour. The MVF has grown from small beginnings in five villages, to provide educational opportunities for more than 80,000 children from 500 villages. The Foundation is working in an area with high levels of child labour and exceptionally low rates of female enrolment. The immediate priority was to get young children from households perceived as likely to use child labour into primary school. Then, a new programme was developed for children aged 9–14 who had not been to school because they were working, and were now too old to start at the primary level. The 'bridging programme' provided for these children, now mostly run in village schools, prepares them for progression into government schools.

Most of the children enrolled in MVF schools were either already working as agricultural labourers on cotton farms, or destined to follow their brothers and sisters in this line of work. Large household debts owed to the cotton farmers as a result of high-interest loans taken up during the 'hungry season' had created a cycle of life-long debt bondage, which was in turn providing the farmers with a steady stream of child labour.

The success of the MVF has been built on local foundations. The starting point was a campaign of mass political mobilisation, targeting the owners of cotton farms, as well as the parents of child labourers. More than 1500 teachers joined a Forum of Teachers Against Child Labour, going out to villages to talk to the parents of out-of-school children about the pressures facing the household, and to identify ways of releasing children for education. These teachers also helped to train large numbers of 'para-teachers', most of them from local villages. Parent–Teacher Associations were established in every village, with parents helping to develop the curriculum and to design the schedule for the school day.

Since its inception, the MVF approach has been scaled up through action by State education authorities. The government of Andhra Pradesh has developed its own 'Back-to-School' programme, which borrows from many of the ideas piloted by MVF. More recently, MVF has agreed to work under the umbrella of the donor-funded District Primary Education Programme (DPEP), which now covers eight districts of Andhra Pradesh, including the Ranga Reddy district, where MVF began. One of MVF's conditions for participating, which the authorities accepted, was that the government should extend support to all alternative schools by bringing them into the mainstream of the education system.

From local to global initiatives

Child labour is rooted in household poverty and the social and economic environment that causes it. Change at the local level to reduce the pressures associated with poverty is the first requirement for ensuring that labour demands do not deprive children of their opportunity for an education. Local action can be supported through international measures, but there is an intense debate about the most effective strategies for change.

Some initiatives are using economic incentives to counter child labour and get children into school. In Brazil, the Federal District of Brasilia established a system of stipends during 1995 for every low-income family with a child aged between 7 and 14. Only the poorest 20 per cent of families are eligible. Already operating across nine cities and covering about 44,000 children – equivalent to 12 per cent of enrolments – the scheme has dramatically reduced drop-out rates. The State provides $90 for the education of each eligible child progressing through primary school. The District has now applied to donors and creditors for funds to extend the scheme, partly through a debt-conversion programme under which resources released through debt relief will be invested in the stipend programme.[73] International support for such schemes is exemplified by UNICEF, which has helped to pioneer partnerships through which employers are given incentives to educate children employed in their industries. In Bangladesh, a 1995 agreement between the ILO, the Bangladesh Garment Manufacturers' Association, and UNICEF stipulates that children under the age of 14 should be removed from the workplace, enrolled in school, and provided with a monthly stipend financed by donors.[74]

One alternative to international incentives is disincentives, in the form of trade sanctions against countries that tolerate child labour or goods produced by it. This issue generates much heat in international debate. Some organisations, such as the ILO and a number of trade unions, have argued for a social clause, outlawing child labour, to be introduced into the rules of the World Trade Organisation.[75] This would have the effect of penalising child-labour practices by allowing countries to withdraw trade preferences and impose punitive sanctions. Successive administrations in the USA have broadly supported this approach, reflecting the strength of a bi-partisan Congressional view in favour of sanctions against child labour. Congress itself has frequently threatened action outside multilateral trade rules. UNICEF's initiative in Bangladesh was in part a response to the Harkin Bill, a law adopted by the US Congress that threatened unilateral trade sanctions against any exporter employing child labour.[76]

Some opponents of trade sanctions see such actions as an attempt to impose unrealistic standards on developing countries, primarily in the interests of protecting jobs in the industrialised world.

Some opponents of trade sanctions see such actions as an attempt to impose unrealistic standards on developing countries, primarily in the interests of protecting jobs in the industrialised world.[77] Others point out that trade sanctions, even when introduced with good motives, can have unintended outcomes. One effect of the Harkin Bill in Bangladesh was to prompt widespread dismissals of child workers. In the absence of alternative opportunities for income generation or employment, such outcomes are likely to compound the very poverty and vulnerability that causes child labour. Even so, while the threat of trade sanctions may be a blunt instrument, it can be an effective one. In Sialkot district of Pakistan, large numbers of children are employed in stitching footballs for export. The threat of a consumer boycott in advance of the 1998 European Championships, combined with targeted incentives for employers, resulted in a reduction of children's working hours and the provision of educational opportunities.[78]

Whatever the benefits generated by trade sanctions in specific cases, they do not offer a long-term solution to the problem of child labour, for several reasons. Their focus on traded products in the formal sector runs the risk of displacing child labourers into the informal sector, where working conditions are more hazardous and exploitative. Moreover, most child labour is employed not in export production, but in the domestic economy. It follows that a focus on trade and the formal sector will not address the problems facing the vast majority of child labourers operating in informal sectors. Finally, trade sanctions invariably raise issues of *realpolitik*: they are far more likely to be targeted at smaller countries with limited retaliatory capacity, such as Bangladesh, than at large countries, such as Brazil and India, with more bargaining power in trade negotiations. Many developing countries see efforts to put child labour on the WTO agenda as a further attempt to exploit a multilateral trading regime that is already structured to serve the interests and concerns of the rich world. For all of these reasons, there is a need for an international framework with clearly agreed multilateral rules which will provide a basis for action but avoid arbitrary and discriminatory measures, and which will protect the interests of working children. The threat of trade sanctions can make a difference, even in the absence of such a framework, by persuading governments to legislate against child labour, or to enforce existing provisions more effectively. Ultimately, however, the eradication of child labour will depend on progress towards poverty reduction, and on public action to raise the political profile of the issue.

Raising awareness of the problem is one of the most important roles for international action to increase educational opportunities for child labourers. During 1998, the Global March on Child Labour brought millions of people on to the streets of India, Pakistan, the USA, Spain, Mexico, and many more countries.[79] This event has helped to strengthen the political impetus behind the ILO's proposed new Convention on extreme forms of child labour. The new Convention will, if adopted, go beyond existing provisions contained in Conventions 138 and 146. While these already outlaw the worst forms of child labour, including bonded labour, slavery, and prostitution, the new Convention will also cover hazardous employment (including, for example, work that does not allow children to return home at night).[80] An important feature of the Convention is that it will demand the immediate elimination of the worst forms of child labour. It will enjoy the status of a 'core Convention'. This means that even those countries among the 173 ILO member states that do not ratify it will be held accountable for its implementation. It is therefore important that the Convention is strengthened and the definition of 'worst forms of child labour' extended to include any work that systematically deprives children of access to basic education.

Conflict as a threat to education

In parts of the developing world, the absence of conflict has been one of the greatest barriers to achieving the goal of basic education for all. It destroys lives, undermines education infrastructure, and reduces the capacity of States to finance basic education. It is impossible to estimate the educational costs of conflict. The number of direct victims is enormous. According to UNICEF, almost 2 million children have been killed in wars over the past decade, and another 4.5 million have been disabled.[81] Many millions more – from the south of Sudan to Afghanistan – have suffered malnutrition as a consequence of conflict. In countries such as Angola, Sierra Leone, Sudan, Liberia, and Uganda, the proliferation of light weapons has resulted in armed factions forcing children to fight in the front line, with devastating psychological effects.

The impact of conflict on education extends beyond children. Education services, and service providers, are often targets in conflict situations. In Mozambique and Ethiopia, Oxfam is working with local communities who are reconstructing schools destroyed during civil wars. In both countries more than two-thirds of school buildings were destroyed. In Rwanda, more than 60 per cent of teachers were murdered during the genocide in 1994.[82] Of the 15 countries identified under the UN Special Initiative on Africa as requiring urgent support because they have enrolment rates of less than 50 per cent, ten (Angola, Chad, Eritrea, Ethiopia, Guinea Bissau, Liberia, Mali, Mozambique, Rwanda, and Somalia) are either experiencing or recovering from serious civil conflict. Evidencing the sensitivity of girls' enrolment to the physical threats implied by conflict, the enrolment range for girls in these countries is 13–31 per cent, compared with 23–49 per cent for boys.

One of the most striking features of Oxfam's work with communities affected by conflict is the high priority that they attach to maintaining access to education. Education is seen as a way of restoring normality to children's lives, and ensuring that their opportunities are not destroyed.

- In the Ikafe region of northern **Uganda**, where Oxfam has carried out a resettlement programme with refugees from the south of Sudan, communities have prioritised the establishment of schools and day-care facilities. In fact, the availability of education in a situation where children are free from the risk of abduction is cited by refugees as one of the main reasons for wanting to remain in the camps.

- In south **Sudan**, Oxfam is working with communities in conflict zones who, although they constantly have to move home, establish schools under trees to maintain continuity in education. There are an estimated 1500 primary schools in areas held by one of the two main rebel groups. Displaced people from the south are also attempting through their own efforts to reconstruct educational opportunities in camps for displaced people in Khartoum (see the box on page 205).

- In **Afghanistan**, Oxfam works with the Afghan Development Association (ADA), a local organisation that has employed 575 teachers and rebuilt 26 schools. ADA is now directly engaged in dialogue with the Taliban, aimed at restoring the right of girls to attend school.

Inadequate humanitarian responses

International humanitarian responses have failed to reflect the importance attached to education by communities suffering the consequences of armed conflict. All too often, emergencies serve as a green light for the mobilisation of food and medicines, while the maintenance of education takes a back seat. This was acknowledged in a 1996 report of the Inter-Agency Consultation on Humanitarian Assistance and Refugees, which conceded: 'Education is rarely addressed adequately, and educational activities are often cut back in times of crisis.[83] Given the presence of 3.7 million people who are either refugees or displaced people in Africa alone, this is a serious failing.

Another problem, given insufficient attention, is that gender inequities are intensified by conflict. Research by ActionAid in several war-torn countries concluded that girls in camps for refugees and displaced people seldom participated in schools, even where they were available. One of the main reasons was a fear of rape and other forms of violence.

Reconstructing education: conflict and displacement in Sudan

Mayo Camp for displaced people sprawls across the densely populated settlements in the south of Khartoum. The poverty is immense. There is no sanitation; clean water is in short supply; and the basic health services are grossly inadequate. This camp is home to 80,000 of the estimated 4 million people who have been forced from their homes during Sudan's long-running civil war. The majority are Dinka people from Bahr el Ghazal and the Upper Nile, two of the areas worst affected by the war. Most have lost everything: their homes, their animals, their land, their savings, and in many cases family members. But they have not lost the desire to see their children educated.

Aok Duku left Bahr el Ghazal in south Sudan after a military operation and an ensuing famine in 1991. She cares for seven children, four of her own and three of her sister, who is dead. The children are aged between four and 16. She survives by selling small amounts of spices and groundnuts in markets, and using the income to buy food, pay for water and medicines, and to educate her children. Aok Duku herself never had an education. But today she is a member of the Parents' Association of Mercy School, attended by four of her children. The school is the result of efforts by Aok and other residents of Mayo camp to reconstruct their communities. They built the school in 1992; they paid the teacher, bought the books, and went to the Ministry of Education and non-government organisations – including Oxfam – for financial and technical support to expand the school. Today, more than 1000 displaced children attend Mercy School. Why make such an effort in the face of such overwhelming adversity? 'Because education will help my children to build a better life away from this place. Literacy will make them more confident with strangers. It will help them to get better prices from traders, and they will know how to ask for health services,' says Aok.

For children living in situations of conflict, or in the aftermath of conflict, education can help to overcome the effects of violence. In Rwanda, more than 90 per cent of children witnessed violence and killing during the 1994 genocide. More than one-third saw family members murdered. School can provide an environment in which such trauma is addressed. More broadly, education is one of the few means of healing wounds and reconstructing the social fabric. Working with national education authorities, UNICEF has developed a peace-education curriculum, based on teaching materials about communication, co-operation, and conflict management. It has been widely used in Burundi, Liberia, and Sri Lanka, among other countries. The aim is to provide children with the skills and attitudes needed to support non-violent conflict resolution, using the school as a 'zone of peace' in which children have an opportunity to work together. Teachers have been trained in techniques aimed at fostering mutual tolerance and acceptance.[84]

For children living in situations of conflict, or in the aftermath of conflict, education can help to overcome the effects of violence.

The role of the school is critical in peace building. In many cases it is the only institution in which children from communities riven by conflict and suspicion can overcome their fears. After the 1994 genocide in Rwanda, the destruction of schools and security fears resulted in the virtual collapse of formal education. In the rural Mushabati community in Gitarama, an area that had witnessed vicious fighting before the genocide and appalling levels of killing during 1994, the closest school was a two-hour walk away. In 1996, Oxfam funded a satellite-school project designed to bring education to some 3000 children in the area. After mapping exercises in individual villages, a pattern of school distribution was designed to ensure that no child would have to walk more than 3km, or traverse areas regarded as dangerous. Today, the seven newly constructed schools are part of the National Programme for Scholarly Support (NPSS). More than 80 per cent of the population in the project area are Hutu, but the NPSS has started supporting efforts to enrol Tutsi children in the schools. The process will require careful management and teacher support, which is being provided through the Gitarama Re-education Centre. Properly managed ethnic mixing in schools is one of the most effective strategies for avoiding future conflict.

Public investment in education

Public investment in education is among the most cost-effective ways of reducing poverty, boosting economic growth, and promoting basic human rights. In many countries, the benefits of public spending are reduced by inefficiencies and inequitable spending patterns. But government budgets hold the key to improving the coverage and quality of education services available to poor households. These households are less able to finance private expenditure than their wealthier counterparts, and more likely to be excluded from private markets. Progress towards the goals of universal and free basic education therefore requires an enhanced role for publicly financed services.

The absolute level of spending on basic education is determined by three variables: the share of GDP accounted for by government revenue; the proportion of that revenue allocated to education; and the share of the education budget allocated to basic education. The level of State commitment in each of these areas will reflect political judgements about appropriate levels of taxation, national priorities, and the commitment of governments to the development of pro-poor patterns of budget allocation.[85] As we show below, political decisions taken in many developing countries do not reflect a commitment to the international development target of universal primary education. While low income is a constraint on public investment, most developing countries could do far more to increase public investment in basic education, either by shifting resources between sectors, or by improving the allocation of resources within the education sector. Chronic under-financing is often a product of flawed approaches to public spending. Insufficient resource mobilisation, highly inequitable patterns of expenditure, and misplaced budget priorities all figure prominently.

One of the consequences of under-investment by governments has been a proliferation of private-sector initiatives, some of which are supported by donors. The inadequacies of public education systems have driven many poor households into private systems. In some cases these offer cheaper and better-quality alternatives to State provision. While this fills a vacuum, it does not offer a route to universal primary education, because poverty often excludes the poor from private markets. Ultimately, governments have the responsibility to carry out the public expenditure reforms needed to support free and compulsory primary education.

National resource mobilisation
National wealth and rates of economic growth exercise a powerful influence on the capacity of States to finance education, as illustrated by Figure 4.5. This shows that sub-Saharan Africa spends a higher proportion of its GDP on education than any other developing region. Yet this effort translates into the equivalent of only one-fifth of the per capita spending

on education achieved in Latin America, where the share of national income spent on education is far lower. Comparisons between countries at different levels of wealth are striking. Burkina Faso spends the same proportion of GDP on education as South Korea, but this translates into $6 per capita, compared with $390 per capita in South Korea.

Differences in economic growth over time account for the inverse relationship between the share of national income invested in education and current spending levels. In 1970, South Korea was spending approximately the same sum per child in receipt of basic education as Mexico was spending. By the end of the 1980s, it was spending three times as much. This was despite the fact that public spending on education had fallen as a share of GDP in South Korea, while it increased in Mexico.[86] Economic stagnation in the 1980s and slow recovery in the first half of the 1990s left Latin America's per capita spending on education 30 per cent lower in real terms in 1995 than in 1980.[87] As in other areas of human development, there is a high price to be paid for slow economic growth.

The importance of economic growth to education financing is powerfully evident in Africa – and not just in terms of comparisons with higher-growth regions. In 1970, Sudan was spending more per capita on education than Botswana. Today, Botswana is spending four times as much, not because of an increased public-expenditure ratio, but because of much faster growth. Even good performers in sub-Saharan Africa have suffered

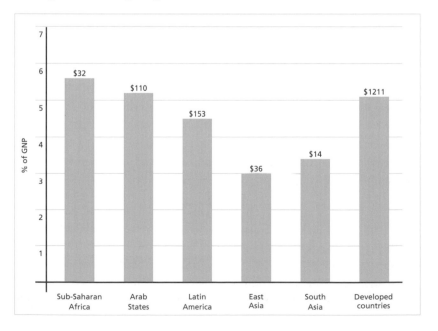

Figure 4.5
International spending on education: as a percentage of GNP and per capita

Source:
UNESCO,
Statistical Yearbook, 1997

the consequences of slow growth. Zimbabwe has one of the world's highest proportions of GDP allocated to education; but even so, real per capita investment remained static during the 1980s, as a consequence of economic stagnation. If Zimbabwe had matched Thailand's rate of growth since 1990, real per capita spending levels would be almost double the current levels.

The share of national wealth collected by government through taxation has an important bearing on financing capacity. The higher the level of average income, the smaller the share of GDP that the government has to capture to meet a fixed level of spending in education. In the poorest countries, high levels of poverty, low disposable incomes, and weak tax-administration systems result in relatively low levels of revenue collection. Countries such as Uganda and Tanzania channel around 12–13 per cent of their national wealth through the government budget. This rises to more than 16 per cent for countries such as Brazil and Indonesia, and over 20 per cent for high-income countries.[88]

There are no hard and fast rules on appropriate levels of revenue collection. High taxation can act as a disincentive to investment and undermine growth (limiting the scope for future public investment in the process). By the same token, inadequate public investment in basic services also has damaging consequences for growth, and for poverty reduction. Political choices, rather than average income levels, determine the financing capacity of the State. Pakistan mobilises a smaller share of national income through taxation than Vietnam, despite having much higher average income levels. Peru collects about half as much tax revenue in relation to GDP as Indonesia, despite having average incomes that are twice as high. In both of these cases, higher taxation has been associated with a stronger growth performance *and* better public provision of basic services.[89] In both Pakistan and Peru, public under-investment has had adverse consequences for economic growth as well as for social equity. The fact that both countries lag far behind Vietnam and Indonesia in terms of education and other human-welfare indicators is, in part, a consequence of limited public financing for basic services.

All governments have to make complex choices when balancing the need to raise revenue for public investment in basic services and the need to maintain an economic environment capable of sustaining growth. Policies associated with globalisation and liberalisation are limiting the range of choice. The presumption that low levels of taxation are good for growth, coupled with the increased scope for tax evasion as capital becomes more mobile, is restricting the potential for revenue mobilisation (see the next box). To a greater or lesser degree, this problem afflicts all countries. But developing countries are most severely affected, because their revenue base is so limited in relation to the financing requirements for providing universal primary education and other basic services. The policy choices that confront these countries are complex. If high taxation restricts growth, it will undermine the future financing capacity of governments. But inadequate provision of basic education is itself a constraint on growth, as we saw in Chapter 1. Tensions between tax reductions on the one side and the provision of basic education services on the other need to be carefully considered. Where such reductions reduce government financing capacity in education, they have the potential to reduce future prospects for growth and investment, while at the same time undermining the potential for poverty reduction. In Ghana, tax reforms introduced during the 1990s have provided extensive tax breaks for foreign investors, especially in high-value extractive industries such as gold mining.[90] The revenue forgone could be used to extend educational opportunities to the millions of poor households that are denied access to even the most minimal good-quality education services.

Allocation of resources to education

National wealth may be the primary determinant of overall spending levels, but the national expenditure effort in education – measured as a proportion of GDP – is still important. Most of the developing countries that have achieved rapid progress towards universal basic education from a weak starting point have spent 5–7 per cent of GDP on education.[91] Measured against this yardstick, many countries with huge deficits in education are falling short not just of this target, but also of the minimum requirements for achieving progress towards the 2015 goals (see Figure 4.6).

- In **South Asia**, the percentage of GDP spent on education is exceptionally low by international standards: less than 3 per cent in Pakistan, Nepal, and Bangladesh, and just over 3 per cent in India. This is only slightly higher than half of the average for sub-Saharan Africa. The lack of commitment to education is reflected in the fact that Pakistan and Bangladesh allocate only 8 per cent of their national budgets to education. India allocates more, at around 11 per cent, but even this is just over half of the regional average for sub-Saharan Africa.

- In **sub-Saharan Africa**, countries such as Chad, Mali, Tanzania, and Zambia are spending less than 3 per cent of GDP on education: far too little to meet basic education needs.

Globalisation: a threat to public investment in education?

Ten years ago, the term 'globalisation' was almost unheard of. Today, it is a central theme in almost any debate on human development. Enormous increases in capital movements, the emergence of international production systems under the auspices of powerful transnational companies, and the sustained expansion of world trade are among the defining features of economic globalisation, which has entailed a process of policy change. The liberalisation of trade, the removal of controls on capital flows, and low taxation are widely seen as necessary ingredients for policy reform in countries that want to reap the benefits of integration into a global economy.

Globalisation has important implications for the ability of governments to finance investments in basic education and other priority social sectors, although these are seldom considered. There is a real danger that the combination of liberalisation, the increasing mobility of capital, and tax reform will erode the financing capacity of poor countries, with adverse implication for progress towards the 2015 human-development targets. From the perspective of social-sector financing, the impact of globalisation on taxation has been particularly important. Most developing countries urgently need to improve the efficiency and equity of their tax and public-spending regimes if they are to progress more rapidly towards universal primary education. But, especially in the poorest countries, domestic revenue-raising capacity is often limited, and the tax base is small – and globalisation could further erode it. Its proponents advocate that governments should limit the share of global GDP that they mobilise through taxation, in order to promote investment. As taxes fall, the ability of States to maintain basic services declines, especially in a context of low economic growth. One of the consequences is an unequal distribution of benefits from globalisation, as the ability of the State to provide poor people with access to education, health care, and economic infrastructure diminishes.

The growing ease with which firms can shift their operations from one part of the world to another presents another problem. It has fuelled a process of tax competition. Governments have been reducing tax rates on high-income groups and foreign investors in a bid to attract investment. The result is that the poor are shouldering a bigger share of a declining tax base, which is in turn constraining efforts to extend basic service provision. Between 1986 and 1988, 67 out of 69 countries reviewed in a recent study had reduced taxes on high-income groups.

The corrosive effects of tax competition have been reinforced by tax evasion, although the distinction between the two is becoming increasingly blurred. Electronic commerce, corporate secrecy, and the growing mobility of capital have left all governments facing problems of revenue collection. High-income groups and foreign investors can avoid tax, either by using off-shore accounts, or through complex corporate accounting techniques to understate tax liability. This is a problem for rich countries as well as poor, as witnessed by the efforts of industrialised countries to regulate off-shore centres. But the consequences of tax evasion are more severe in developing countries, both because of their limited revenue bases, and because they lack the regulatory capacity to limit tax evasion. In some cases, off-shore accounts can provide a convenient outlet for plundered public finances, diverting resources that could be invested in areas such as education and health. The former Nigerian dictator, General Abacha, was accused in 1997 of illegally transferring funds of around $800m – roughly equivalent to his country's spending on education, health care, and community services.

The limited income-tax base in poor countries has been one of the reasons why other tax instruments are favoured, in particular trade taxes; but trade liberalisation is eroding this part of the revenue base. In Chile, a planned reduction in import tariffs was not implemented, because potential revenue losses would have undermined the capacity of governments to maintain basic services. The problem is that many governments have committed themselves to radical trade-liberalisation measures to which they are bound under the rules of the World Trade Organisation, without considering the implications for public financing.

The challenges posed by globalisation extend beyond taxation. The expansion of capital markets has been facilitated by the removal of government controls on capital flows in developing countries. In East Asia, a surge in capital flows was swiftly followed by huge outflows when investor confidence collapsed, leaving a crisis in public finance. During 1997-98, the education and health budgets in Indonesia were cut by one-third.

(Sources: I. Grunberg: 'Double jeopardy: globalisation, liberalisation and the fiscal squeeze', *World Development* 26(4), 1998; Oxfam: 'Tax Havens: Releasing the Hidden Billions for Poverty Reduction', Briefing Paper, Oxford, June 2000.)

- In **East Asia**, the Philippines and Indonesia are among the worst performers, allocating just over 2 per cent of GDP to education. If the Philippines were to match the proportion of GDP allocated to education by Zimbabwe, it could increase per capita spending by a factor of more than three. This would enable it to extend educational opportunities in more remote areas, reduce the burden on household budgets, and invest in some of the major qualitative improvements that are needed.

There are no public-expenditure blueprints for achieving universal primary education, although many countries fall far short of the standard of 5–7 per cent of GDP (Figure 4.6). More important from the perspective of education financing is the extent to which States are failing to make the investments needed to achieve universal primary education. The financing requirements for achieving this goal are more modest than is often assumed. These are in the range of 1–2 per cent of GDP for countries such as Indian and Pakistan in South Asia, and slightly higher for sub-Saharan Africa.[92] For some countries, international action in the form of debt relief and increased aid is a necessary condition for achieving the financial targets for universal primary education – an issue that is addressed in Chapter 6. Most, though, have the potential to mobilise the resources that are needed through public-spending reforms in two areas:

- improving the equity of public spending in education by changing intra-sectoral allocations, with an increased emphasis on primary education;

- switching expenditure from non-productive areas such as military budgets into basic education.

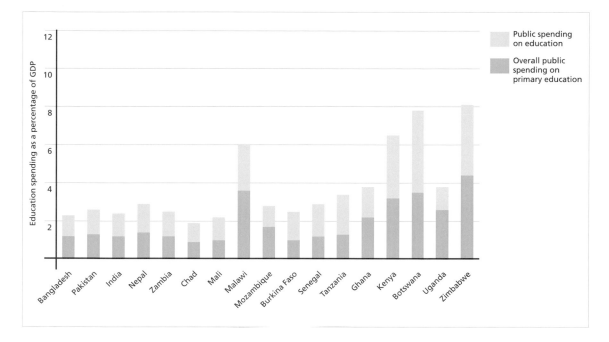

Equity in education spending

The way in which resources are allocated within social sectors shapes the distribution of benefits across society. At any given level of overall education spending, the amount spent on basic education will be determined by the pattern of expenditure across different parts of the education system. The intra-sectoral allocation of education spending has important implications for achievement of the 2015 targets. Because poor people use basic social services such as primary education and primary health care more than they use higher levels of provision, public spending will have more progressive outcomes; that is, the poor will reap a larger share of the benefits. Where public finance is biased towards higher levels such as universities, wealthier households will be the prime beneficiaries, since fewer children from poor households progress to higher levels of the education system. All too often, the prevailing pattern of public expenditure favours wealthy households, who can afford to meet higher private costs, rather than poorer households, who cannot.

One way of identifying overall levels of equity in social-sector spending is by measuring the incidence of benefits among a range of income groups. Briefly summarised, this considers the relationship between the amount spent on services at various levels and the users of these services.[93] The bigger the share of overall usage accounted for by the poor, the larger the incidence of benefits for this group. Benefit-incidence analysis is

Figure 4.6
Public spending on education as a percentage of GDP: selected countries

Sources:
World Bank, *World Development Indicators,* 1998;
UNESCO, *World Education Report,* 1998;
M. Ul Haq, *Human Development in South Asia,* UNDP, 1998;
national data

particularly revealing in a study of education expenditure. It shows that the richest quintile captures on average more than half of the benefits of public spending in tertiary education, while the poorest quintile captures less than 5 per cent.[94] The reason for this discrepancy is the under-representation of children from poor households in higher levels of education. In the case of primary education, the picture is reversed, with the poorest 20 per cent of the population capturing a larger share of benefits than the wealthiest 20 per cent (Figure 4.7).

Intra-sectoral allocations in education influence the overall level of provision for basic education, as shown in Figure 4.6. Several countries – among them India, Pakistan, Zambia, and Chad – achieve outcomes that are the worst of all worlds: low levels of overall expenditure, combined with a spending bias against basic education. Others – such as Malawi and Ghana – partly compensate for low overall levels of spending with a distributional bias in favour of primary education. As in the case of overall expenditure, there is no set yardstick for good performance. However, for low-income countries facing major problems in terms of coverage and quality in education services, expenditure levels in the range of 3–3.5 per cent are probably a minimum requirement for achieving the 2015 target.

Weighting budgets against the interests of the poor
While poor households, who are the least able to pay for education services, stand to derive the greatest benefit from spending on the primary-school system, governments often prioritise the interests of higher-income groups. This is reflected both in a relatively low share of primary education in the overall education budget, and in marked discrepancies between per capita investment in primary education and investment in the tertiary level:[95]

- **India** allocates just 46 per cent of its (under-financed) education budget to primary education. For the cost of educating one university student, it would be possible to educate 39 pupils in primary school.
- The government of **Nepal** spends 20 times as much per capita on tertiary education as it does on primary education, in a country where only half of the children enrolled in primary school complete four years of education.
- **Zambia** spends $27 on every pupil in primary education, compared with $3688 on every university student – a multiple of 135. Theoretically, the resources released by shifting the funds spent on two university students could guarantee the recurrent budget for an entire seven-grade primary school, with 35–40 pupils in each class.

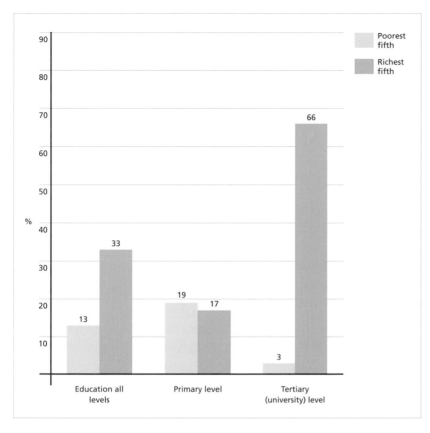

Figure 4.7
Education: the distribution of public-spending benefits

Source:
UNDP/UNICEF/World Bank,
*Implementing the 20/20 Initiative:
Achieving Universal Access to
Basic Services,* 1998

- The case of **Niger** demonstrates that it is possible to combine high levels of poverty and education deprivation with public-spending patterns which favour the rich. Only 43 per cent of the education budget is allocated to primary education. The 900,000 rural children who are not in school do not benefit at all from this budget, while 4700 university students receive scholarships equivalent to ten times the average national income.

- **Bolivia** allocates over half of the national education budget to the tertiary sector and just 32 per cent to primary education, one of the lowest levels of provision in the developing world.

- **Venezuela** has the worst record in terms of inequity, allocating less than one-quarter of its national education budget to primary and secondary education combined, and three-quarters to the tertiary level.

Improving equity

Improving equity is an important part of the education-reform process, because it has the potential to redistribute public investment towards the poor, improve the quality of service provision, and reduce the pressure on household budgets. Clearly, redistributive policies cannot compensate

215

for the effects of low average incomes in the poorest countries, but they can enlarge the envelope of resources available for basic education. The experience of Malawi and Uganda is instructive. During the second half of the 1990s, both countries combined a sustainable increase in the share of GDP allocated to education with a strong redistributive shift in favour of primary education. Five years ago, the two countries were spending less than half their education budgets on the primary sector. Today, both allocate about two-thirds of their expenditure to this sector. As shown in Figure 4.6, this is a far higher level of equity than has been achieved in many other developing countries. Increased public investment has facilitated the withdrawal of school fees, which has contributed to rapid increases in primary-school enrolments. If countries such as India and Pakistan followed the example of Malawi and Uganda in raising to two-thirds the share of the education budget allocated to primary education, it would be possible for them to increase spending at this level by between 15 and 20 per cent.

In the case of Uganda, the redistributive shift in public spending has been doubly effective, because it has taken place in the context of rapid economic growth, accompanied by a broader shift in budget priorities in favour of education. The education sector has been absorbing a growing share of a growing economic cake, with primary education the main beneficiary. In other countries, public-spending reform has been less successful, because it has taken place in a low-growth environment, in which education is accorded a low priority in public spending. The case of Tanzania illustrates the point. As in Uganda, the share of the education budget allocated to primary education rose from around one half to two-thirds in the 1990s, but only 2.5 per cent of Tanzania's GDP is allocated to education. Failure to increase this share, coupled with sluggish economic growth rates averaging only 1 per cent per annum in the second half of the 1990s, means that real public spending per primary-school child was lower in 1998-99 than it was in 1994. This underlines the critical importance of economic growth for successful public-spending reform.

The smaller the share of any given population that progresses through the primary-school system to higher levels of education, the more regressive public spending at these levels becomes. This is not to suggest that post-primary spending is 'anti-poor'. Financing for education has to be developed in an integrated fashion, with primary schooling seen as part of the broader system. It also has to be acknowledged that failure to invest sufficiently in secondary-school systems undermines the potential for poor households to reap the full benefits of investment in primary education. But in a situation where large sections of society are excluded from a basic education system, partly because of inadequate public spending, heavy transfers of funds to university students are not appropriate. Most of these students are drawn from high-income groups who are subject to limited taxation and, in contrast to poor households, able to pay. The generalised move across most developing countries towards lower tax regimes for high-income groups has increased the regressive character of public spending in many countries. One way of correcting this is for governments to introduce cost recovery at higher levels of the education system. Paradoxically, however, governments have been less than enthusiastic about such measures. One survey of 15 African universities in the first half of the 1990s found that only half charged student fees, producing revenues averaging about 10 per cent of the annual university recurrent budget (compared with a figure of 80 per cent for primary-school budgets!).[96] Countries such as Nepal and India recover only 5–10 per cent of higher-education costs, and Pakistan even less. Cost recovery is also minimal in Latin America. The contrast with East Asia is striking. In this region, governments have maintained a strong commitment to cost recovery at the higher levels of the education system, in order to release public-investment resources for the lower levels. Successful reformers in sub-Saharan Africa – such as Uganda and Malawi – have followed the East Asian model. For instance, the introduction of cost-sharing policies into the tertiary sector has reduced the share of universities in Uganda's national education budget from over 20 per cent in the mid-1990s to 15 per cent today, and a projected 12 per cent for 2002.[97]

Countries such as Nepal and India recover only 5–10 per cent of higher-education costs, and Pakistan even less.

Shifting the balance of education spending in favour of poorer households and poorer regions of countries can potentially accelerate progress towards universal basic education. In 1980, the poorest quintile in Chile captured around 22 per cent of total education spending, and the richest quintile attracted 20 per cent. By 1992, a shift in public-spending priorities had resulted in a smaller proportion of the education budget going to higher education (where cost-recovery measures were strengthened), and a larger share going to primary education.[98] As a result, the poorest quintile saw their share of education spending increase by around one half, while the richest quintile's share fell by a similar amount.

In other cases, governments have shifted spending priorities in the wrong direction. In the Philippines, the share of elementary-education expenditure financed out of the government budget has fallen sharply over the past decade, pushing up household costs (see Figure 4.8).

Meanwhile, the share of higher-education spending funded by Government has increased.[99] Public investment in a variety of voucher schemes has increased the share of secondary schools in the education budget from 10 to 17 per cent. Most of the adjustment has been borne by the primary sector. Households now meet almost one-third of the total costs of primary-education spending – three times more than in the mid-1980s, and 50 per cent more than the proportion of the tertiary-education budget financed by households (Figure 4.8). As one Oxfam evaluation of the policy change puts it: 'The downside of the government taking on more responsibility for secondary education is that it is subsidising students who would have gone to private school even without the subsidy. Even worse, the government is subsidising a higher percentage of the unit costs of college education, and the share is increasing. While it is an undeniable fact that student costs are higher at the tertiary level, the government is heavily subsidising households who can afford to pay, while under-financing basic education systems in the poorest regions.[100]

Despite a large deficit in primary education, Vietnam has also moved towards less equitable public-spending patterns. More than in most developing countries, the poorest households in Vietnam used to benefit disproportionately from primary-education spending. This was a result of high overall enrolment, coupled with the fact that poor households have more children. This pro-poor pattern is reversed at the lower-secondary level, where most children from poor households drop out. However, there has been a distinct shift of expenditure priorities away from the primary sector, with its share falling from 38 per cent of education expenditure in 1991 to 27 per cent in 1997.[101] Part of the failure to progress beyond high levels of enrolment towards high rates of completion and qualitative improvements can be traced directly to this change in priorities.

Much of the analysis of equity in public financing has tended to focus solely on the distribution of resources between different levels of the education system. As indicated above, this provides an important indicator of equity. But it cannot be assumed that all spending on primary education is automatically 'pro-poor'. This is especially true when a large proportion of poor households are unable to send their children to school – or when their children drop out of school during the early grades. One of the perverse consequences of a high drop-out rate is that public spending can become strongly pro-wealthy, even at the primary level. Pupils who stay in the system, mostly from wealthier families, benefit from a rising per capita subsidy, in addition to lower teacher–pupil ratios. To demonstrate this effect, Oxfam disaggregated per-pupil spending per grade in the Sa Pa district of Vietnam. The exercise showed that, whereas $24 was spent on each pupil in Grade 1, more than $150 was spent in Grade 5, raising serious questions about the distribution of funding within the primary sector.[102]

Expenditure switching: from military waste to investment in basic education

Reforming public spending is fundamentally about rethinking the role of government. Debate on this subject has been dominated by ideologically charged exchanges concerning the relative merits of public versus private provision. The dominant view in the 1980s was that the State was inherently inefficient. This replaced the previously dominant view that States should play a central role in guiding development. Neither perspective helps to address the real challenge of defining the role of government. The real issue is not whether there is too much or too little

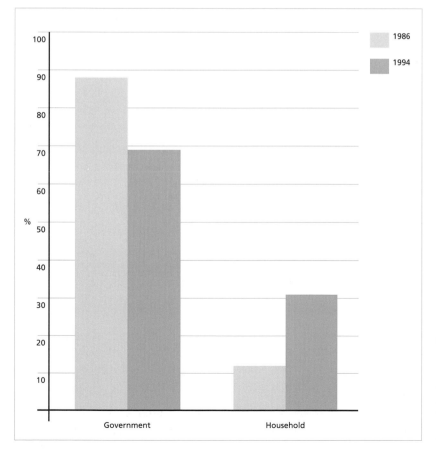

Figure 4.8
The changing distribution of costs between government and households: primary education in the Philippines (1986 and 1994)

Source:
World Bank,
The Philippines: A Strategy to Fight Poverty, 1997

State activity, but whether that activity contributes effectively to poverty reduction and the wider public good. Measured against these criteria, the role of the State is often variable. Often there is too much activity in areas that generate few social benefits, such as subsidising loss-making enterprises and military expenditure, and too little activity in other areas with far greater social benefits, such as the provision of basic education services. The problem is not that States are too big, or too small. It is that they are often over-active in areas where they do not have a clear advantage over the market, and under-active in areas where markets do not produce equitable and efficient outcomes. Basic education is an example of widespread under-activity. Perhaps the most egregious example of excessive State financial activity relates to military budgets.

In Pakistan, military spending is currently 25 per cent higher than the health and education budgets combined.

Governments in sub-Saharan Africa, the world's most disadvantaged region in terms of access to education, are spending some $7 billion annually – 2 per cent of their combined GDP – on imports of military equipment.[103] South Asia is spending approximately $10 billion (Figure 4.9). One way of assessing the opportunity costs of this spending is to measure it against government social-sector expenditure. As shown in Figure 4.10, military expenditure represents almost half of total spending on health and education in Africa, increasing to almost two-thirds in South Asia – the two developing regions with the worst human-development indicators. The costs of military spending, in terms of opportunities forgone in education, go far beyond the immediate consequences of failing to invest in schools, teachers, and adult education. They extend to the future losses incurred in terms of lost growth, lost opportunities for reducing child mortality, and widening income inequalities.

Nowhere are the opportunity costs more visible than in India and Pakistan. Taken together, these countries account for a large proportion of global illiteracy problems – and both deny millions of children access to a good-quality education. Yet, in both cases, education budgets are static at low levels, while military expenditure is soaring. The two countries are worth considering in more detail, if only because they both illustrate that financing education for all concerns political choice as much as it concerns affordability.

In **Pakistan**, military spending is currently 25 per cent higher than the health and education budgets combined.[104] While the entire education budget accounts for only 2.7 per cent of GDP, the defence budget absorbs almost twice this amount. The difference is more striking still when public spending on primary schools is compared with spending on armaments. Whereas 25 per cent of government expenditure is directed towards defence, primary education receives only 4 per cent. In other words, political choices made by the government of Pakistan result in the country spending six times more on its military forces than on the education of its children. This is in a country that is falling further and further behind in education (it ranks 98 out of the 104 countries listed in the Education Performance Index), and where there are 150 soldiers for every 100 teachers.

What does this military extravagance mean for the 11 million Pakistani children who are not in school and the further 4 million who drop out before they have finished primary school? One way of addressing this question is to compare actual military spending with the estimated costs of achieving universal primary education, which are estimated at around $1bn per annum, or approximately one-quarter of the annual military budget.[105] While successive governments in Pakistan pay lip-service to the need for a concerted effort to end the country's education deficit, their financial priorities tell a different story. For instance, the $943m deal signed in 1997 for three French submarines would almost cover the additional costs of financing universal primary education for one year.[106]

Until recently, military spending in **India** had been declining as a proportion of government expenditure. This trend has now been reversed. In mid-1998, the Indian government announced a 14 per cent increase in defence expenditure, to accommodate an enlarged nuclear

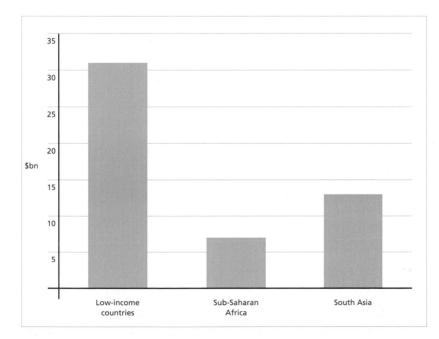

Figure 4.9
Military expenditure in developing countries (US$bn)

Source:
Stockholm International Peace Research Institute,
SIPRI Yearbook, 1998

Figure 4.10
Military spending (in dark tint)
as a proportion of total
spending on health
and education

Source:
UNDP, *Human Development Report,*
1998

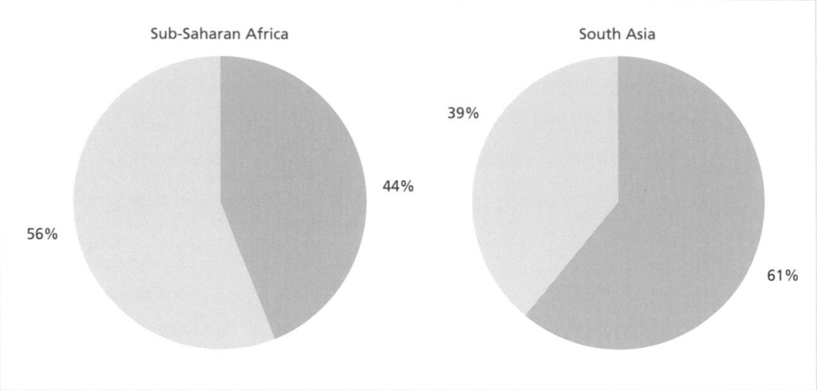

Sub-Saharan Africa

South Asia

56%

44%

39%

61%

programme and an expansion of conventional armaments.[107] The new budget will undermine the government's ability to raise education spending as a proportion of GDP, in a situation where military budgets already absorb considerably higher proportions of public expenditure than do all levels of education. This warped prioritisation becomes even more obvious when primary education is considered separately. It consumes the equivalent of 1.4 per cent of GDP, compared with the 2.4 per cent represented by military spending.[108]

While India ranks in the lower half of the Education Performance Index (see Chapter 3), it has aspirations to join the world's military elite. The Indian government spends a larger share of its budget on military research and development than most industrial countries (see Figure 4.11), notwithstanding the fact that 30 million children of primary-school-age, almost one-quarter of the global total, are not in school. Much of the $1.8 billion spent in this area during the first half of the 1990s contributed to the development of the Light Combat Aircraft.[109] This project, hatched ten years ago, is a classic example of mis-spending. Costs have been massively inflated by technological advances, production is several years behind schedule, and there is a growing view that the plane will be militarily redundant at the point of take-off. Yet the project continues to absorb millions of dollars each year, diverting desperately needed financial resources from education.

Some indication of the wider opportunity costs associated with military spending can be summarised in three simple, but damning statistics:[110]

· The extra $1.3 billion allocated to India's defence budget in 1998 would be sufficient to construct the one million schools and hire the additional 600,000 teachers necessary to achieve universal basic education by 2005. If only half this sum were spent on primary

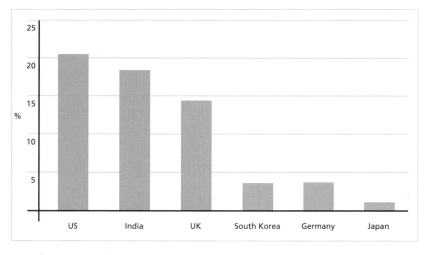

Figure 4.11
**Government spending on
military research and
development (R&D)
as a percentage of national
R&D spending**

Source:
UNDP, *Human Development Report,*
1998

education each year, universal basic education would be a reality within seven years.

- $58m, less than 5 per cent of the addition to the defence budget, would have financed a package of essential educational items (costing $1 per pupil) for the poorest 50 per cent of children, and an enhanced package (costing $1.15) for the poorest 20 per cent.

- The $490m spent on military research and development in 1996 could have been converted into investments of $15 for each one of the 32 million children not in school – investment that could have taken the form of textbooks, school meals, bursaries for girls, or classroom facilities.

It would be wrong to assume that South Asian governments are alone in their attachment to military overspending. In all, there are 25 countries that spend more on what is euphemistically described as 'defence' than on health and education combined. Many more countries with large education deficits have military budgets that are equivalent to their primary-education budgets. Countries in conflict inevitably have highly distorted public-spending allocations: Sudan spends four times as much on its military budget as on education, as does Angola. Similarly, post-conflict countries and those vulnerable to conflict often maintain high levels of military spending. For example, Rwanda and Burundi both have military budgets which are twice the size of their primary-education budgets. Ethiopia had succeeded in reducing military spending from the equivalent of 20 per cent of GDP in 1992 to 2.2 per cent in 1996. However, the share rose again rapidly in response to border tensions with Eritrea and it has now overtaken spending on education.

Aid donors are justifiably critical of public-spending policies that attach more priority to wasteful military spending than to basic services. Unfortunately, many of the same donors are only too happy to encourage demand for their military exports, thereby contributing to the very practices that they condemn. Between them, the industrialised countries accounted for 97 per cent of major exports of conventional arms in 1997, while developing countries accounted for just under 75 per cent of imports.[111] This trade has ruinous implications for human-development efforts. South Asia's poor cannot afford the $1.3 billion in resources transferred to arms suppliers in industrial countries. In sub-Saharan Africa, the $224m spent on arms imports each year represents waste on an equally epic scale. All the leading arms exporters have signed up for the international targets on 'education for all' and poverty reduction. Yet they continue to support and encourage patterns of budget expenditure which conflict with the attainment of these targets. Ultimately, responsibility for the expenditure reforms needed to convert military spending into investment in education rests with developing countries. But reforms are needed on both the supply and demand sides. The industrialised countries, as the world's leading arms suppliers, must also establish rules and regulations that prevent arms transfers to countries where they are damaging the prospects for human development.[112]

South Asia's poor cannot afford the $1.3 billion in resources transferred to arms suppliers in industrial countries.

Military expenditure is not the only form of wasteful expenditure that diverts resources from education and other priority areas. In much of sub-Saharan Africa, public subsidies paid to loss-making enterprises continue to absorb a large share of limited budget resources. It has been estimated that around 11 per cent of GDP in India is allocated through national and State governments to subsidies in sectors such as power, irrigation, and credit.[113] The bulk of these subsidies, which dwarf expenditure on primary education, are captured by wealthier producers and richer States. In Zambia, support for loss-making copper-mines accounts for more than 10 per cent of government revenues, again limiting the resources that are needed for education. Both cases powerfully demonstrate the need for governments to consider more carefully the equity effects of public-spending choices.

Financial decentralisation and privatisation

The role of government as a provider of basic services is under constant review in almost all countries. While the contexts vary, two recurrent themes consistently emerge: decentralisation and privatisation. **Decentralisation** is one of the most powerful trends in public-service provision across the developing world. Many developing countries have been devolving authority away from central government to local service providers, in an attempt to improve the efficiency and equity of service provision. While this creates the potential for more accountability among service providers, serious equity-related problems have emerged. Where decentralisation weakens the redistributive role of the State, it can widen already extreme inequalities in education linked to wealth. **Privatisation** is happening at different levels. While the State continues overwhelmingly to dominate education provision, especially at the primary level, private-sector providers are growing in importance. More importantly, education financing is being transferred from States to households by default. As we saw earlier, 'cost sharing' has become a euphemism for a process of privatisation fuelled by public under-investment.

Decentralisation

The case for decentralisation is well known. Administrative and political decentralisation can bring decision making closer to the communities most directly affected, making providers more accountable and more responsive to local needs. However, from an equity perspective, decen-tralisation can be a double-edged sword. Poor regions with the greatest needs in terms of public-service provision are likely to have the most limited revenue-raising potential. To the extent that decentralisation limits the capacity of the State to undertake redistributive transfers, it will have damaging consequences for the quality and availability of service provision in poor areas.[114]

Unequal spending in Brazil

The regressive effects of decentralisation on public spending in education are graphically illustrated by the case of Brazil, which has the most decentralised financing system in Latin America. Twenty-three states and more than 45,000 municipalities share the responsibility for providing basic education with the federal government. About one-third of Brazil's primary-school education is provided by municipal authorities. State bodies account for another half, and the federal government the remainder. There are wide discrepancies in financing associated with this structure. In rural areas, however, municipal authorities run almost two-thirds of primary schools. The budgets of these authorities are chronically under-financed. In the rural north-east, spending per pupil averages $50 in municipal schools, compared with $300 in (mainly urban) State schools. The gap between municipal schools serving poorer districts in the rural north-east and State schools in the south-east is even wider, with the latter spending about 20 times more per pupil. One of the reasons for the high level of variation in basic-education indicators for Brazil (see Chapter 3) is that the decentralised system of education financing reinforces the income inequalities between States, communities, and rural and urban areas.[115]

The highly unequal spending patterns that characterise the education system in Brazil are the consequence of unequal resource mobilisation. State-level authorities raise almost half of all taxes in Brazil, mainly through sales taxes. Inevitably, tax revenues are highest in States with the highest levels of disposable income (i.e. the south and the south-east), and lowest in the States with the lowest incomes and highest poverty levels. Revenue is thus inversely related to need. Municipal spending is funded principally by transfers from the federal budget and by local taxes, but although there are redistributive mechanisms designed to reduce inequalities between rich and poor States, these remain weak. The transfer has been insufficient to compensate for the financial advantages enjoyed by wealthier States. Moreover, transfers from the federal government to the municipal level have been gradually declining. In 1996 a Fiscal Stabilisation Fund was established to finance the national fiscal deficit. More than one-fifth of government revenues is now automatically transferred to this fund. Part of the adjustment has been borne by the federal education budget, so that transfers to municipalities have fallen by 18 per cent – a sum equivalent to 0.3 per cent of GDP. As the pressure to reduce the fiscal deficit intensifies with the current financial crisis, further cuts are in store.

The redistributive role of the State

It is not just countries marked by high levels of inequality that have experienced widening human-development gaps as a result of decentralisation. Those with more egalitarian patterns of income distribution have displayed similar problems. In China, the share of central government in overall revenues has declined sharply since the move to financial decentralisation in the early 1980s, limiting the scope for redistributive policies. As a consequence, disparities in social provision between rich provinces and poorer provinces are widening, along with urban–rural divisions. Many schools and health clinics at the local level have introduced charges for basic services, in order to recover costs and raise revenue, which has had further adverse consequences for equity.[116] The Chinese case demonstrates the threat to social equity that emerges when the redistributive role of the State is weakened.

One of the ways in which governments with a commitment to equity attempt to maintain a redistributive role is by transferring revenue raised from general taxation to poor regions, either through equalisation grants or by other transfers aimed at matching resources to needs. In practice, however, such arrangements are difficult to implement. About one-third of government expenditure in Vietnam is administered at the local level.[117] Communes and provinces play an important role in tax collection, although central government establishes strict rules when setting tax and expenditure levels. It is also responsible for setting 'financial norms' that provide higher levels of transfer to poorer regions – such as mountainous areas – and are intended to avert inequalities in service provision. Partial success has been achieved. Average income in the high-income provinces in Vietnam is three times greater than in low-income provinces, but per capita public expenditure on services is only 57 per cent higher. This underlines the importance of central-government transfers in correcting for regional inequalities in financing capacity. Even so, the three wealthiest provinces – Hanoi, Ba-Ria, and Ho Chi Minh City – have achieved average per capita expenditures three times higher than the average for the rest of the country. With only 10 per cent of the national population, these rich provinces account for almost 25 per cent of total public spending.[118] Here too, fiscal decentralisation is contributing to adverse distributional outcomes that threaten to widen social inequalities over time.

Evidence from many countries points to a far weaker relationship between central-government allocations and local needs than has been achieved in Vietnam. In Tanzania, the government allocates resources to the 20 regions of the country to cover the costs of administration and service delivery. These allocations, accounting for around one-third of the national budget, are supposed to be weighted on the basis of need. Yet in the case of education there are some striking inverse relationships between need and provision. For example, the pupil–teacher ratio in Shinyanga, one of the poorest regions, is 1:56, compared with 1:30 in Ruvuma, a slightly wealthier region. However, the per capita budget allocation for Shinyanga is 30 per cent below the national average, while the allocation for Ruvuma is 23 per cent above.[119] The reasons for this pattern are unclear, but the allocation of funds may reflect the relative bargaining power of different localities, rather than local needs – a common problem in decentralised financial systems.

One of the requirements for overcoming some of these adverse effects is to maintain a redistributive national tax system. The problem with meeting this requirement is that it conflicts with one of the central aims of decentralisation: namely, a reduction in the share of national revenue distributed through central government. There are relatively few cases in which redistribution and decentralisation have been successfully combined. One of them is Bolivia. Under the tax-reform law of 1993, the decentralisation process includes fiscal arrangements that transfer resources from the three richer departments – La Paz, Cochabamba, and Santa Cruz – to the rest of the country; and from urban to rural areas.[120]

Even where governments are committed to redistributive goals, decentralisation can weaken their ability to control spending outcomes in line with such goals. Local-government financing in most developing countries depends heavily on transfers from the centre as the main source of revenue. Central governments can use this control over financing to influence decentralised spending patterns. For example, education legislation in Colombia and Ecuador requires municipalities to use 30 per cent of the resources transferred for education purposes. But central-government control over revenue does not provide an effective guarantee of control over expenditure. There are often tensions between central and local government bodies over spending priorities, and local-government priorities may – or may not – reflect locally expressed needs. In Uganda, the government used a block-grant system to facilitate decentralisation in the mid-1990s. However, it has been estimated that less than one-quarter of the capital budget for education allocated by central ministries actually reaches local schools. Corruption accounts for part of the discrepancy. More significant has been the transfer of resources into activities that are perceived as having a higher priority at the local level, notably the construction of rural feeder-roads.[121]

Decentralisation can undermine equity in situations where local authorities seek to increase their revenue efforts. Central-government policy in Tanzania is that schools should keep the contributions made by parents in order to provide textbooks and maintain buildings. In practice, this policy directive is ignored by most district councils, with parental contributions being absorbed into the general district budget, where they may or may not be used for the purposes of education. Local authorities have also introduced a wide range of levies on smallholder producers, eroding the incentives created by the liberalisation of agricultural marketing. Similar problems are reported from China, where local authorities have resorted to cost recovery in order to mobilise funds for expenditure on items that fall outside the scope of the grants provided by central government.

One of the guiding principles of decentralisation is that it will help to create service-delivery structures that mirror local needs and aspirations.

In practice, however, this is less a function of decentralisation *per se* than of the extent to which local political decisions are influenced by the voices of the poor. State power in India has often been captured by elites who, in many cases, have little interest in the needs of the poor. This is apparent from existing patterns of expenditure on education at a State level. Per capita spending varies from $61 in Kerala to $30 in Uttar Pradesh and $26 in Bihar. In other words, education spending across the three States is inversely related to need.[122]

The privatisation of education financing

For much of the nineteenth century, private financing and philanthropy dominated the provision of education in the industrialised countries. During the twentieth century, as awareness of the importance of education increased, most governments prioritised public provision, especially in basic education. At the dawn of the twenty-first century, the wheel has turned again. Advocates of an enlarged role for the private sector are gaining in influence. They point to the potential of private provision in extending choice, increasing accountability within the school system, and reducing pressure on over-stretched budgets.[123] In place of an unequivocal commitment to universal public provision of good-quality basic education, donors and governments are emphasising the virtues of private–public partnerships. The potential erosion of State responsibility in this area raises important questions about equity in service provision.

The private sector as an education provider

The private sector is becoming an increasingly important provider of education across much of the developing world. While it plays a smaller role at the primary level than the secondary level, it is growing in importance. The notion that private schools are servicing the needs of a small minority of wealthy parents is misplaced. One household survey in rural India found that about 10 per cent of children were enrolled in private unaided schools, compared with an official figure of 2 per cent. In Uttar Pradesh, one-quarter of all children were enrolled in such schools.[124] Such findings indicate that private education is a far more pervasive fact of life than is often recognised.

Private education providers range from community-run schools to schools run as a commercial business. But service provision is only one dimension of privatisation. Education financing is already privatised to a high degree, with households increasingly covering gaps left by inadequate public provision. In some cases, the costs of supposedly 'free' public education make private education a competitive option. In Lahore, average annual expenditure for parents sending their children to private primary school in 1996 was about $112 – double the level for children in public schools. It is interesting to note that a lower-cost private sector has emerged to meet the demands of poor households. One-quarter of the private schools in the city were charging less than $20 per annum, which was less than one-third of the cost of sending a child to a government school.[125] Thus, although the likelihood of a child attending private school rises with parental income, more than half the families in the lowest income group were choosing private education for their children. Household surveys found that poor households cited teacher absenteeism in government schools as the main reason for choosing private schools. In this case, the unaffordability of State provision and the under-performance of public education have created a growing market for private education among poor households.

While private schools are filling part of the space left as a result of the collapse of State provision, their potential to facilitate more rapid progress towards universal basic education has been exaggerated. They are unable to address the underlying problems facing poor households, not least because their users must be able to pay, which the parents of most children who are out of school often cannot do. The case of Zambia illustrates the problem. Between 1990 and 1996, the number of private schools increased three-fold without any discernible effect on the decline in enrolment rates.[126] The reason: the poorest households who were not sending their children to school were being excluded by high cost. In Latin America, private schools now account for more than 14 per cent of primary-school enrolment, and considerably more in many countries. Here too, however, the expansion of the private sector has had no discernible influence on the educational status of poor communities.

Turning to the issue of quality, there is no doubting the appalling standard of provision in public education systems across much of the developing world. But crude contrasts between 'low quality' public systems and 'high quality' private systems are misleading. The private sector covers a range of providers of variable quality, including many that are of exceptionally low quality. In many countries, only the wealthy can afford good-quality private schools.[127] Private schools of inferior quality are more affordable to the poor, but they do not offer the advantages often assumed for private education. Surprisingly, in view of the confident assertions made in some quarters, there is little hard evidence to substantiate the view that private schools systematically outperform public schools with comparable levels of resourcing. In Peru, private primary schools produce far better education outcomes and, eventually, higher rates of return for their graduates in labour markets; but average household spending per pupil in these schools is more than ten times higher than in State primary schools. Private schools also offer lower pupil–teacher ratios and have a far higher proportion of trained teachers.[128]

Nor is there any evidence that private schools are inherently more accountable than public schools. Top–down planning and hierarchy are indeed central features of many public education systems, but there are many examples of highly accountable public school systems (see Chapter 6). As in the case of cost recovery, the idea that payment for services automatically generates a sense of ownership is little more than an attempt to disguise an ideological preference for market provision in a pseudo-psychological rationale.

Where private schools provide a high-quality service compared with the public sector, they inevitably widen existing disparities related to income and region. In Bolivia, 60 per cent of non-poor households now send their children to private schools, whereas 94 per cent of the extremely poor send their children to public schools.[129] Most private schools are located in urban areas and more commercially developed rural areas. Wealthy Bolivians have choices about whether or not to use these schools; but those living in poverty have no choice, other than to send their children to a public school of vastly inferior quality. Where private schools are more accessible to the poor, they tend to offer a low-quality service that will restrict children's future opportunities.

The idea that payment for services automatically generates a sense of ownership is little more than an attempt to disguise an ideological preference for market provision in a pseudo-psychological rationale.

Estimates of the relative efficiency of private and public schools often overlook a further problem with regard to financing. In many countries, private schools receive extensive support from the State sector. For example, one study in Indonesia found that most rural private schools were as dependent on subsidies from government as were schools in the public sector. Hidden subsidies are also extensively present, especially in Latin America. Several countries in the region – including Peru – provide significant tax advantages to parents who send their children to private schools, and to the schools themselves.

Public under-investment and privatisation

Perhaps the greatest stimulus to the development of private school provision has been under-investment in public provision. There is a political dimension to this problem. As the public education system deteriorates, those with the purchasing power to choose private education will do so. The end result is that those with economic power perceive no self-interest in defending a public education system that their children do not use. In much of Latin America, elite groups have almost no interaction with the public education system. This makes it more difficult to mobilise the resources and develop the tax regimes needed to improve the quality of public education, thus creating a vicious circle of decline.[130]

None of this is to suggest that private provision has no role to play. Demand-led support for the private sector can sometimes generate gains in terms of equity. The Urban Girls Fellowship Programme, set up in Quetta, Pakistan, by the World Bank in 1995, is an example.[131] A community-based organisation was contracted to work with parents in low-income neighbourhoods with low levels of enrolment for girls. Public provision was absent, and distances from public schools were identified as a major barrier. Where enough parents indicated that they would be willing to send their children to school with some support, a small subsidy – about $3 per month – was made available, with government support, to stimulate the establishment of new private schools. Special incentives were provided for the enrolment of girls. The extent of unmet demand was reflected in the fact that girls' enrolment increased by 33 per cent, while boys' rose by 27 per cent. In this case, support for private-sector provision had positive outcomes. Voucher schemes supported by the World Bank in Colombia have also generated equity benefits. Targeted at poor neighbourhoods and poor households through strict eligibility criteria, these have extended access to the secondary-school system for children who would otherwise have dropped out after primary school. As a transitional arrangement in countries where public education systems are failing to reach the poor, support for good-quality private providers can create equity gains, as these examples illustrate. By contrast, attempting to legislate against private providers when State systems are failing offers few such gains. This has happened in countries such as Tanzania, where the government retained a strong political commitment in principle to public education, while failing to extend it in practice to large sections of the population. The result is that the public education system is becoming increasingly privatised, with wealthier communities supporting schools of far higher quality than are available in poor areas.

In terms of achieving the 2015 target of universal primary education, there is no alternative to comprehensive public provision of good-quality basic education. Private–public partnerships have a role to play in some countries, but only at the margin. They do not solve the problem of mass exclusion, and do not diminish State responsibility for providing education for all.

5

International co-operation: the record since Jomtien

International co-operation was a central theme at the World Conference on Education for All, held in Jomtien in 1990. It was recognised that many of the world's poorest countries lacked the financing capacity that would be necessary to ensure more rapid progress towards universal primary education. Increased support was acknowledged to be essential if the targets set were to be met.

Northern governments made three substantive commitments at Jomtien. First, they promised 'increased international funding (...) to help the less developed countries implement their own autonomous plans of action'.[1] No specific aid targets were set, but the statement of intent was unequivocal. Second, it was acknowledged that repayments of foreign debt were undermining the ability of many countries to protect, let alone increase, spending on basic education. The final declaration called for 'the adoption of measures (...) to relieve heavy debt burdens'. At a time when debt relief for the poorest countries did not figure prominently on the international agenda, it went on: 'Creditors and debtors must seek innovative and equitable formulae to resolve these burdens, since the capacity of many developing countries to respond to education and other basic needs will be greatly helped by finding solutions to the debt problem.'[2] The third commitment was, in many respects, the boldest of all. At the time of the Jomtien conference, the economic policy environment in developing countries was dominated by IMF–World Bank structural adjustment programmes. The Jomtien Declaration sent a clear message that these programmes were failing to protect education budgets. In future, it stated, 'structural adjustment policies should protect appropriate funding levels for education'.[3]

The commitments made at Jomtien reflected a renewed commitment to education as a basic human right. Under the Covenant on Economic, Social and Cultural Rights, adopted in 1966, every State had agreed to 'take steps, individually and through international assistance and co-operation ... to the maximum of its available resources with a view to achieving progressively the full realisation of rights recognised'.[4] This established the clear principle that universal human rights implied universal responsibility in mobilising the finance to protect them. But the Jomtien conference was one of the first attempts to translate this into practical policies.

This chapter examines the record of international co-operation, measured against the commitments made at Jomtien. The record is a shameful one. After promising increased aid, donors have cut their aid budgets to their lowest levels for more than thirty years. Development assistance for education has not been spared in the process of retrenchment. The effectiveness of aid has been further undermined by gross inequities in the distribution of aid spending on education. In Chapter 4 we saw that many developing countries allocate public spending disproportionately to the higher levels of the education system, where the benefits accrue mainly to the wealthy. Yet few governments in these countries operate budgets that are as unfavourable to the poor as are the aid budgets of the donor community, which overwhelmingly prioritise higher levels of education. The first part of this chapter reviews the international community's post-Jomtien performance on aid and assesses some of the more recent developments in aid policy.

Spending on debt has continued to exceed spending on basic education, especially in sub-Saharan Africa.

The second part of this chapter addresses the issue of debt. Its focus is on heavily indebted low-income countries. Contrary to the commitments made at Jomtien, creditors have failed to develop the 'equitable and innovative formulae' needed to end the debt crisis in these countries. Spending on debt has continued to exceed spending on basic education, especially in sub-Saharan Africa. The Heavily Indebted Poor Countries (HIPC) Initiative, announced at the end of 1996, marked the beginning of a more positive approach to debt relief. But it has delivered too little, too late, to a very limited number of countries. Apart from its financial failings, the Initiative has also failed to establish a mechanism that links debt relief to effective poverty-reduction initiatives. Instead, it has created a cumbersome process under which governments must produce comprehensive Poverty Reduction Strategy Papers (PRSPs), in order to be eligible for the HIPC Initiative. This process is delaying debt relief, and depriving poor people access to the education, health-care, and other facilities that could be financed with savings from debt reduction. As in the case of aid, the Jomtien commitment has been broken.

The third part of the chapter surveys developments in the design and implementation of structural adjustment programmes, concentrating on the role of the IMF. These programmes are at the centre of a major debate about reform, the outcome of which remains uncertain. The evidence of this chapter is that IMF-inspired policies have continued to undermine the access of poor people to education, not just by cutting basic social-service budgets, but also by intensifying household poverty.

At Jomtien, governments recognised that co-operation to achieve international targets in education required more than development assistance. It also needed better management of international economic relations in matters such as trade and finance, in which developing countries were often vulnerable to forces beyond their control. The fourth section of this chapter shows how the failure to manage economic relations in one crucial area has led to devastating setbacks for basic education. The financial crisis in East Asia, and the international community's response to it, had the effect of increasing poverty and undermining poor people's access to education.

The record on aid: declining budgets with inequity

International aid plays a modest role in financing education. Even in sub-Saharan Africa, the most aid-dependent region of the world, development assistance accounts for only 4–5 per cent of total expenditure on education.[5] However, this average figure obscures important variations. In some countries, especially those emerging from conflict, aid represents a far larger share of spending on education. Development assistance also plays a vital role in financing some of the more ambitious national education strategies. It represents one-third of the projected financing for the development of five-year education plans in Mozambique and Uganda, rising to half of the total in Zambia.[6] These cases suggest that aid has the potential to play a far more significant role in education financing than it does at present.

Aid-spending patterns

The level of aid spending on basic education is function of three factors: overall aid flows, the share of aid directed towards education, and the distribution of spending between various layers in the education system. Since 1990, international aid to education has constituted a fixed proportion of a diminishing aid budget, with basic education accounting for a small share of the total spending. Aid spending on basic education has fallen in real terms, which is the opposite of what was promised at Jomtien. The decline in aid over the past ten years is not what was expected at the start of the 1990s. The World Conference on Education for All coincided with the beginning of a new era in East–West relations. It was hoped at the end of the Cold War that development assistance would reap a 'peace dividend' from reductions in military spending and improved international relations. In the event, development assistance peaked in 1992 and then went into steep decline. Sixteen of the 21 OECD countries providing development assistance were spending less on aid at the end

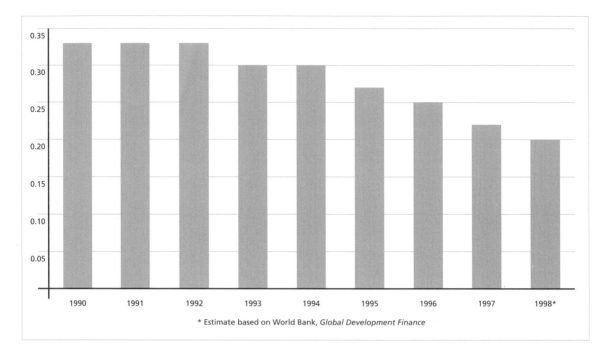

* Estimate based on World Bank, *Global Development Finance*

Figure 5.1

Trends in aid as a percentage of OECD Gross National Product

Source:
The Reality of Aid, Earthscan, 1998

of the 1990s than at the start.[7] In 1998, development assistance hit a historic low, falling to 0.20 per cent of donors' gross domestic product (GDP), compared with 0.35 per cent in the mid-1980s (Figure 5.1).[8] In absolute terms the decline was even more spectacular, because some of the largest donors in the Group of Seven (G7) made the deepest cuts. Collectively, the G7 countries now allocate 0.19 per cent of their GDP to aid, which is less than half of the average for other OECD countries.[9] As a share of GDP, the USA halved its aid budget in the 1990s. The outlook for aid flows continues to remain poor. The world's two biggest aid donors, Japan and the USA, both announced further aid cuts in 1998. Only three donors – Britain, Sweden, and Ireland – announced increases during 1998–99.

The decline in aid spending as a proportion of donor GDP was accompanied by a diversion of assistance away from the poorest countries. Competing demands from Europe and Central Asia meant that the share of the (diminishing) aid budget allocated to low-income countries fell from 45 per cent of the total in 1991 to 28 per cent of the total in 1996. The end result was a massive loss of financial resources for some of the world's poorest countries. In 1997–98, sub-Saharan Africa was receiving $4bn less in aid than it did in 1992–93.[10] These trends in aid have combined to make the UN target (for donor countries to commit themselves to aid levels equivalent to 0.7 per cent of their GDP) appear wildly optimistic.

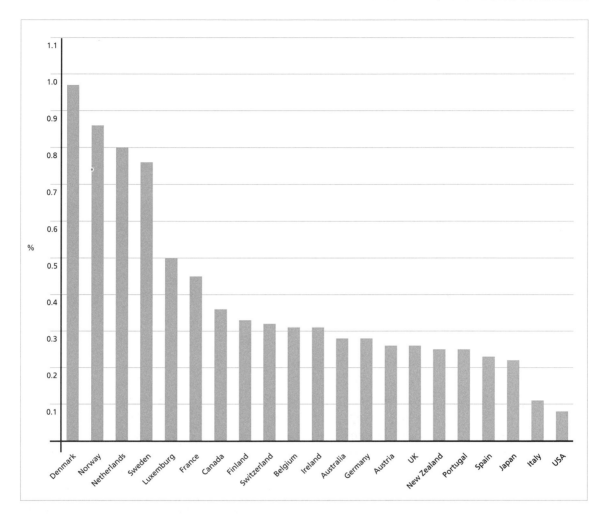

Only four countries currently meet this target (Figure 5.2).[11] Raising aid levels to the 0.7 per cent target would require an additional $100bn in development-assistance budgets. Simply restoring aid levels to the proportion of donor GDP that they represented in 1992 would require an additional $24bn. To put the latter figure in context, it is three times the estimated annual cost of providing universal primary education.

Because donor spending on education has not changed significantly as a proportion of donor budgets, it has suffered in proportion to the overall decline in aid. Averaging out expenditure patterns for 1992–1996, we can see that the donor community allocated just over 10 per cent of its collective aid budget to education – the same as in 1990.[12] Translated into financial terms, this fixed share of a declining budget represents a loss of approximately $2bn per annum by 1997. There were important variations in donor performance during this period. Several major

Figure 5.2
Aid as a percentage of the GNP of OECD countries

Source:
Development Assistance Committee Report, OECD, 1998

237

donors – including Canada and the Netherlands – made cuts in education spending that were proportionately larger than the overall decline in aid. Others – notably the World Bank – increased their funding.

Efforts to mobilise international resources in support of universal primary education have suffered both from the overall decline in aid and from the distortion of development-assistance programmes towards higher levels of education. Less than 2 per cent of total aid flows are directed towards primary education – a category that broadly covers primary, junior-secondary, and adult literacy programmes.[13] Donors allocate less than one-fifth of their education budgets to this sector, which is supposedly the highest priority in terms of poverty reduction. Donors spend ten times more on support for transport infrastructure than they do on primary education: a spending pattern that is hard to square with donors' official statements on the importance of education for reducing poverty.[14] Any developing-country government following the OECD example by spending less than one-fifth of its education budget on primary education would face strong criticism from the donor community.

Equity in aid budgets

There are marked differences between donors in how aid is allocated to various levels of the education system. Capturing these differences is made difficult by the inadequacies of donor reporting. Several govern-ments – including Sweden and Denmark – appear to understate their real spending on basic education by excluding support for non-govern-ment initiatives. Others have improved their performance dramatically over the past two years, and the figures have yet to register in the reporting system of the Development Assistance. To take one example, Britain spends an estimated 5 per cent of its aid budget on basic education, which is double the level reported by the Development Assistance Committee (DAC) of the OECD.[15] There are also large annual fluctuations linked to the financing cycles for big programmes that can distort reporting figures.

With all of these provisos in mind, we turn to Figure 5.3, which summarises the position on the basis of DAC data for the year 1997–98. It shows that some countries, such as the USA, direct a relatively large proportion of a small aid budget for education to the primary sector. This raises questions about the poverty focus of the national development-assistance effort. For every $1 that the USA spends in education, another $24 are spent on military assistance. Other countries, such as Australia, allocate a small part of a large education programme to primary education. Despite these variations, the overall picture is one that is far removed from the commitments made at Jomtien to basic education. At least eight OECD countries allocate less than 1 per cent of their aid programmes to education, while only three – Denmark, Germany, and Sweden – allocate 5 per cent or more. In some cases, the bias in favour of higher education is of striking proportions, with Australia leading by bad example. While this country directs a larger proportion of its aid spending towards education than any other OECD donor, more than 80 per cent goes to post-primary education – the bulk of it to scholarships for foreign students studying in Australia. The average cost of one of these scholarships amounts to around $60,000 – enough to finance the (non-salary) recurrent costs for ten primary schools in Mozambique in the same year. In 1997, an official Committee of Review criticised these scholarship programmes, on the grounds that they were diverting resources from initiatives that would have a much bigger impact on poverty.[16] The review argued that, as with most scholarship programmes, few of the beneficiaries would return to their country of origin, so that most of the benefits associated with their education would be transferred to other OECD countries. Despite these criticisms, Australia's distribution of education spending has yet to change.

Donor countries themselves tend to benefit disproportionately from spending on higher levels of education. The large share of the Japanese aid programme that is directed towards universities limits the financial

Figure 5.3
Aid to education and basic education as a percentage of bilateral ODA (1995-96)

Source:
OECD Development Assistance Committee reporting system

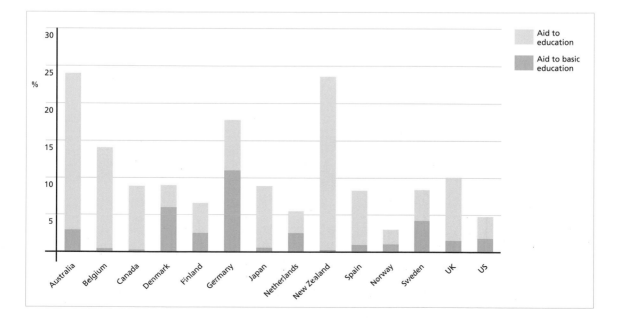

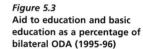

benefits of development assistance. This is because aid is tied to the use of Japanese goods and services, creating lucrative contracts for large construction firms and other suppliers.

The World Bank

The World Bank occupies a central position in the development-assistance effort in support of education. It is the largest source of external finance for education, typically accounting for between 30 and 40 per cent of total aid to education. In contrast to other donors, the World Bank increased its overall commitments to education after the Jomtien conference. The share of lending directed towards primary education also increased, and now accounts for around half of the World Bank's education portfolio – almost double the figure for the late 1980s, and far in excess of the level achieved by any other donor.[17] Aggregate resource transfers from the World Bank conceal a complex pattern of regional variations, some of which cast its post-Dakar performance in a less favourable light. Figure 5.4 shows that most of the increase in lending since 1990 has taken the form of loans from the International Bank for Reconstruction and Development (IBRD) – the World Bank's hard-loan

Figure 5.4
World Bank: IBRD and IDA loan commitments to the education sector (1988-98)

Source:
'The World Bank Education Sector Investment Lending', World Bank, 1998

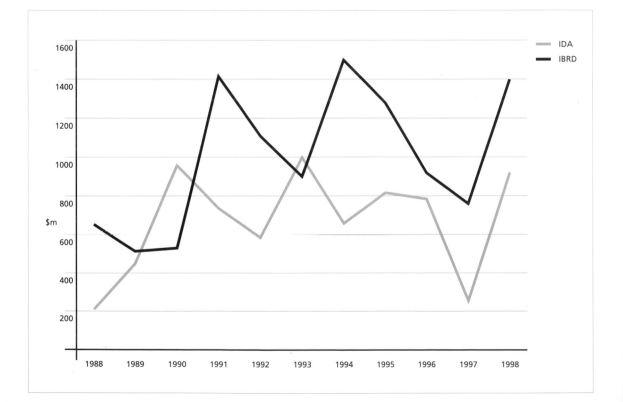

facility. The loans, provided at near-market interest rates, have been made to a relatively small group of middle-income countries. Future spending will continue this trend, with Korea, Brazil, Mexico, Turkey, Argentina, and Thailand figuring prominently among the beneficiaries.

In contrast to IBRD transfers, lending to the poorest countries, which takes place through the World Bank's soft-loan affiliate, the International Development Association (IDA), followed a generally declining trend (despite fluctuations) during the 1990s. IDA commitments for the period 1996–98 averaged $653m, compared with $713m for the period 1989–91.[18] The end result of these two trends is that World Bank assistance to education has been growing most rapidly in wealthier countries that, whatever their other problems, do not lack the financing capacity to achieve the targets agreed at Jomtien, with or without World Bank support. Conversely, World Bank disbursements have been virtually static in countries with the largest education deficits and most acute financing problems. The reason for this discrepancy can be traced to the World Bank's operations in sub-Saharan Africa – the region that is furthest off-track in relation to the 2015 goal of universal primary education.

Figure 5.5
World Bank: education sector 1986-99 – new commitments and disbursements to sub-Saharan Africa

Source:
A Chance to Learn, World Bank, 2000

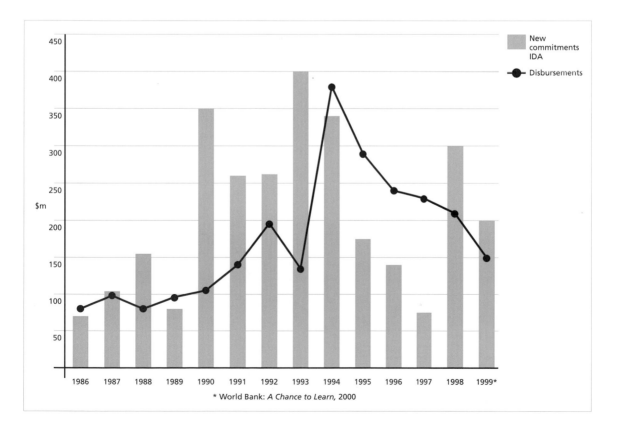

* World Bank: *A Chance to Learn*, 2000

IDA commitments to sub-Saharan Africa increased slightly in the three years after the World Conference on Education for All (Figure 5.5), but then fell sharply. By 1997 they were no higher than in the mid-1980s. The increase in commitments to the region since 1994 is a misleading indicator of performance: actual spending has fallen consistently since 1994. Total spending on education in Africa stood at $150m in 1998[19] – at best a modest contribution to eliminating a financing gap of around $3bn per annum that impedes progress towards achieving universal primary education. At the end of the 1990s, sub-Saharan Africa accounted for about 11 per cent of total World Bank assistance to education, and Latin America absorbed 33 per cent, underlining again the discrepancy between need on the one side and resource allocation on the other (Figure 5.6).

Part of the reason for under-spending in Africa can be traced to problems in the region, including civil strife, the limited capacity of national institutions, and the failure of governments to develop a policy environment conducive to education reform. Large loans to several countries have been delayed for one or more of these reasons. Even so, the low level of disbursements, and the large gap between commitments and actual spending, raise important questions about World Bank programme planning. In particular, the policy conditions required for disbursement may be unrealistic in relation to the institutional capacity of governments.

Figure 5.6
World Bank: disbursements for education by region

Source:
'The World Bank Education Sector Investment Programme',
World Bank, 1998

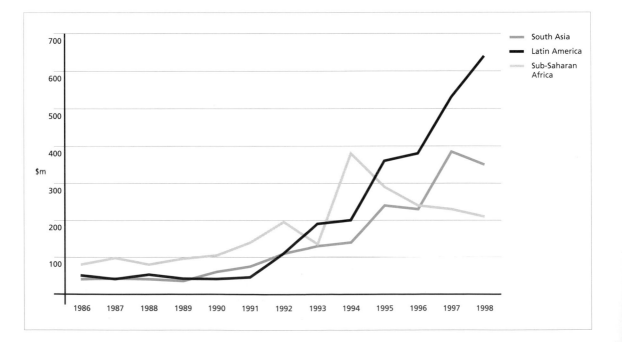

The quality of aid: a mixed record

The decline in the quantity of development assistance over the past decade has been accompanied by growing concerns over the efficiency of aid. It has been argued that aid is effective only in a favourable policy environment, and that many governments lack the capacity to absorb and use aid resources efficiently. Such arguments have provided donor governments with a convenient rationale for reducing their overall levels of aid, or for not matching the commitments that they made at international conferences with actual increases in aid.

It is obvious that investments of aid, like any investment, will be more effective in a good policy environment than in a bad one. High levels of inefficiency, lack of capacity, and corruption do not make for efficient use of resources, whether they are provided through aid or from public revenues. The problem is that many of the arguments used to challenge aid efficiency lack credibility. All too often they are used to advance the case for a particular set of reform policies, many of which are unproven in terms of outcomes for growth and poverty reduction. Much depends on how a 'good' policy environment is defined. In one influential study, economists in the World Bank claimed that aid was most efficient in countries with a specific macro-economic regime based on market-based exchange rates, low inflation, and openness.[20] Using exactly the same data for slightly different reference years, another study found that aid produces similar benefits for economic growth under a variety of different macro-economic regimes, with no clearly discernible pattern emerging.[21]

In the case of education, international aid has generated very tangible benefits across a wide range of policy environments. Inevitably, some of the strongest results have been achieved in countries characterised by high growth and a strong government commitment to education. But this does not represent a case in itself for diverting aid from 'weaker' to 'stronger' performing countries in the name of efficiency. Aid has increased opportunities for education among poor communities in countries – such as Pakistan – that lack either a credible macro-economic reform framework or a government that is seriously committed to poverty reduction. In some cases, aid programmes have acted as a catalyst for improved education policies, especially where they have provided the resources needed to scale up local initiatives into national plans. The start-up costs may be high, but initial investments with limited immediate returns can generate high returns in the long run. Any definition of aid efficiency needs to take into account the potential benefits of such programmes over the long term, rather than focusing narrowly on immediate benefits.

Uganda provides an example of a strong policy environment for development co-operation. The government has developed a strategic investment plan for education, geared towards reaching well-defined goals, including the achievement of universal primary education by 2003 and improvements in education quality (see Chapter 6). Government commitment to primary education has been reflected both in public-spending reforms and in a bold initiative to end school fees. Inputs required for achieving these goals have been identified and costed.[22] Projected expenditure for classroom construction and measures to facilitate access for those with special needs is estimated at $316m over five years. Another $150m has been budgeted for achieving qualitative improvements through teacher-training programmes, curriculum development, and textbook supply. Government contributions to these programmes are reflected in annual budgets and a medium-term financing plan. The strength of the education plan, the government's commitment to education, and the existence of a credible budget and national poverty-reduction strategy have created an environment in which aid investments are likely to yield strong returns in terms of human development.

At the other extreme, successive governments in Pakistan have failed to provide credible leadership on education reform. Education planning in the country has suffered from weak institutional capacity, a lack of government commitment, and an unfavourable macro-economic environment. Primary education has been a low priority in public spending, and the country is marked by extreme regional and gender inequalities (see Chapter 3). The province of Baluchistan has some of the worst indicators for girls' education and gender equity in the developing world. In the mid-1980s, only one-third of villages had primary schools within a distance of one kilometre, and less than one-tenth had a school for girls within this distance. Despite this unfavourable environment, donor interventions under the Primary Education Development (PED) have produced positive results.[23] The PED began with a human-resource survey which showed that the majority of villages wanted schools for girls, contrary to received wisdom among policy makers. Using the survey results to identify areas of special need, an extra 2000 schools were built between 1989 and 1993, 60 per cent of them for girls. To allay parental fears about their daughters' health and safety, security walls were built around schools. Another finding to emerge from the survey was that households viewed the presence of female teachers as an important criterion when deciding whether to send girls to school. Chronic shortages of teachers in Baluchistan made it difficult to address this problem within the existing resource base, and restrictions on women's freedom to travel made it hard to train local women and girls. To address this problem, a mobile teacher-training unit was established in rural areas. More than 900 girls and women were trained in the first five years of the programme.

Two important considerations guided the design of donor policies in PED. First, a strong emphasis was placed on institutionalising community participation through a local non-government organisation, the Society for Community Support to Primary Education in Baluchistan. Founded in 1993 and staffed predominantly by women, the Society has promoted support for education in villages through outreach work, and encouraged the development of village education committees. It plays a crucial role in designing teacher-training programmes. The second feature of the PED programme was the development of a strong institutional relationship between communities and government, mediated by the Society for Community Support. Working with the Society, local communities have taken the lead in constructing schools, while government has provided an incentive for women to enter the teacher-training programme by covering the budget costs of teachers' salaries. The PED has not resolved the education crisis in Baluchistan. It has, however, made a real difference to the lives of many people – and it has helped to identify potentially beneficial reforms. While girls' participation in primary school is still low – at less than one-third of enrolment in the mid-1990s – the number of girls in school increased by more than 50 per cent between 1990 and 1995. Community schools created under the PED accounted for almost the entire increase. The gender gap has narrowed, with the ratio of boys to girls in areas served by community schools falling from almost 3:1 to 1.7:1. Children in community schools consistently outperform their counterparts in tests administered for Urdu and maths, pointing to significant improvements in the quality of education. The PED has helped to develop a curriculum geared to meet local needs, and to produce gender-sensitive teaching materials.

Aid is at its most effective when it supports local initiative, builds on local institutions, and links these institutions to government structures.

One of the lessons to emerge from such programmes is that aid is at its most effective when it supports local initiative, builds on local institutions, and links these institutions to government structures. In the Indian State of Rajasthan, the Shiksha Karmi and Lok Jumbish programmes (described in more detail in Chapter 6) were developed by NGOs working in Rajasthan as a response to severe shortages of schools and teachers to serve poor communities in remote areas. The programmes emphasised the local recruitment and training of teachers, and the development of curricula perceived by the community as being directly relevant to their needs. Initially, this took place independently of government programmes, so that the benefits were restricted to relatively small enclaves. However, the Swedish Development Agency (SIDA) has worked with the government to integrate some of the strategies developed by NGOs into State-level planning. In turn, State-level planning has influenced the design and implementation of the national District Primary Education Programme, illustrating how local interventions can, with the assistance in this case of aid donors, act as levers to achieve wider change.

In some cases, donors have worked with the government to develop local initiatives into wide-ranging reform strategies. In the late 1980s, the National Council of Women and the Ministry of Education in Malawi developed a strategy for addressing the problem of low enrolment rates, poor teaching quality, and extreme gender inequality. The government's failure at the time to prioritise education blocked the implementation of this strategy. But in 1994 a new government announced a radical shift in policy under the Girls' Attainment in Basic Literacy and Education Programme (GABLE), which drew on the main elements of the strategy developed by the National Council for Women.[24] School fees were eliminated for all children, plans were established to double the number of primary teachers, school policies banishing pregnant teenage girls from primary school were abolished, and an extensive classroom-construction programme was launched. One of the more innovative features of the programme was the extensive use of theatre to take messages about the importance of girls' education into rural communities. The Gender Unit, established as part of GABLE in the Malawi Institute of Education, helped to identify strategies for reforming school practices that had adverse implications for the educational attainment of girls, including streaming by gender, the exclusion of girls from mathematics classes, and teacher attitudes that devalued girls' education. The development of the GABLE programme was supported by donors' commitments of $130m. This helped to reduce the pressure on schools to charge fees, to facilitate classroom construction, and to support the development of new curricula. GABLE has not resolved Malawi's education problems, especially in terms of education quality; nonetheless, its results have been impressive. Within two years of its inauguration, the number of children in primary school increased from 1.8 million to 3.2 million, and girls' education has been established as a priority issue on the national political agenda.

Problems of aid quality

Each of these examples demonstrates the positive role that aid can play in generating progress towards good-quality primary education for all. Government ownership and commitment to education reform is a key ingredient of success (as in Malawi and Uganda), but local initiative, supported by donors, can also drive the reform process (as in Baluchistan) and help to enrich government efforts (as in India).

Aid for education does not have an unblemished record, however. Programmes have often failed to achieve their expected results, sometime because national policies and institutions have failed; and sometimes because of doors' shortcomings. One of the most serious of these has been a failure to co-ordinate aid programmes. In the past, donors concentrated their aid resources on specific projects. Often they sought to bypass what they saw as inefficient national government structures, working instead with local NGOs. In the process they created parallel administrative systems, reinforcing the problem of weak government capacity. Much of the spending associated with donor-funded projects did not pass through the national budget, adding to the lack of transparency and accountability.[25] Over-stretched line ministries in education were faced with complex reporting and budgeting procedures for hundreds of different projects, with each donor insisting on separate requirements. An intolerable strain was placed on limited human resources, reinforcing a vicious circle of institutional decay. Because donors concentrated their (largely unco-ordinated) efforts on local projects, there was little dialogue with governments over the development of overall education-sector programmes.

Some of the problems associated with project-based aid were the result of inappropriate budget-management policies, notably the artificial distinction that was drawn between investment budgets (for activities such as school construction), and recurrent budgets (mainly for teachers' salaries). Most donors have been willing to finance investment costs, but unwilling to finance recurrent costs. Such distinctions are arbitrary and highly damaging. Support for teachers' salaries can be one of the most effective strategies for improving school effectiveness. Too often, however, donors' investments have produced good-quality school buildings that provide bad-quality education, because teachers are underpaid and demoralised. For governments, the distinction drawn by donors between investment and recurrent spending had the additional disadvantage of undermining budget management. When donors build schools or health clinics, governments have to cover the recurrent costs of providing staff

Support for teachers' salaries can be one of the most effective strategies for improving school effectiveness.

247

and equipment through the annual budget. Yet donors have seldom considered the long-term budgetary implications of their project spending, much of which does not even pass through the national budget.

Project design has failed in other respects. In sub-Saharan Africa, nearly one-third of the World Bank's education projects do not meet the criteria for minimum performance standards set by the Bank's Operations Evaluation Department – twice the average for all regions.[26] Unfavourable policy environments account for part of the problem; but project design and implementation have also been found wanting. One World Bank review of 26 of its projects in Africa identified a catalogue of problems. Almost all the projects included a textbook-supply component, recognising the critical role of textbooks in education performance and an equally critical shortage in textbook provision. The problem was that the projects focused on supply, rather than on the capacity of schools to use the materials. Many of the schools lacked even the most rudimentary storage capacity, few teachers were trained to use the materials supplied, and no provision was made for in-service support. Many of the potential benefits of textbook supply were lost, as were many of the books. The review concluded that the World Bank was justified in prioritising text-books, but that insufficient consideration had been given to ensuring their effective use. This was part of a wider failing that the review traced to a focus on inputs, which provided a simple and quantifiable bench-mark for performance, rather than on outcomes. It concluded: 'The assumption that selecting the right mix of policies will inevitably lead to changes in student performance must give way to the realisation that an integrated approach that combines inputs, process and climate in individual schools is the key to improving the quality of education.'[27] Similar comments could be applied to a far wider group of donors.

Patterns of aid spending have important implications for the quality of aid. Many donors are now attempting to direct their aid efforts to areas of special need. The World Bank has prioritised programme expansion in 31 countries in which it is active where the 2015 target of universal primary education will not be met at the current rate of progress. Fifteen of these countries have been targeted because they have exceptionally wide gender gaps (among them Pakistan, Yemen, Chad, and Guatemala). All the African countries in the group of 31 are also covered by the UN's Special Initiative for Africa. UNICEF and the British government's Department for International Development (DFID) have taken the lead in developing a multilateral framework for co-ordinating donor efforts in countries with large gender gaps. Meanwhile, most bilateral agencies are consolidating their programmes to focus resources more effectively. USAID is using gender-related indicators of disadvantage to redefine its programme, and DFID is developing a medium-term strategy that will direct more than 80 per cent of education spending to a group of approximately ten countries. These various processes will help to improve the efficiency and equity of aid allocations, although serious problems remain. The proliferation of multilateral initiatives and consolidation of national programmes are taking place in the absence of a co-ordinated international strategy designed to identify resource needs in terms of the 2015 targets. In many cases, programme development is being guided more by history than by an assessment of need, with donors specialising in countries to which they are linked by a common language and past investments. There is a pressing need for a global education-financing plan, designed to target donors' resources more effectively.

There is a pressing need for a global education-financing plan, designed to target donors' resources more effectively.

Donors have also failed to improve the quality of their aid programmes in one crucial respect. Technical assistance continues to dominate aid spending on education, accounting for around three-quarters of the total.[28] The problem is that a large share of this technical assistance – estimated at between 20 and 40 per cent – is spent in donor countries, where it buys the services of assorted consultants, instructors, and construction companies. Such spending may be justified where local alternatives are not available; but in many cases more cost-effective and more efficient alternatives are available.

Sector-wide approaches

Recent years have witnessed a distinct shift in approaches to development co-operation. Donors have been moving away from project-based strategies and towards sector-wide approaches, or 'SWAps', as they are known in development jargon. The shift is an important one, because it is redefining the respective roles of donors and recipient governments in development co-operation.[29] The development of SWAps has taken place for four reasons.

- First, donors have become increasingly aware that individual projects – even good ones – will have a limited effect if the overall policy environment is not conducive to successful education reform.

- Second, donors now acknowledge that the administrative demands associated with project-based approaches have placed undue stress on Education Ministries in developing countries, hampering the development of effective national strategies in the process.

- Third, sector-wide approaches emphasise the importance of rational 'ownership' – the current buzz-phrase in donor discourse. In principle, this is supposed to mark the end of attempts to engineer policy reform through loan conditionality; sector-wide approaches are therefore premised on the principle of government ownership.

- The fourth factor behind the development of SWAps relates to the role of aid in public financing. Northern governments have become increasingly concerned with the problem of 'fungibility' in relation to the way in which additional resources are accommodated in national budgets. In this context, fungibility derives from the fact that any money provided through aid may pay not just for the specific item against which it is allocated, but also for the marginal expenditure that it makes possible. By giving money for, say, primary-school construction, donors might be enabling governments to use the resources that they would have used for this purpose to finance spending in other areas, such as the military budget.

The fungibility problem is a real one. Research carried out by the World Bank in 1997 found that each dollar in aid provided by donors for education had the effect of increasing overall public spending in recipient countries by a similar amount, but without any discernible impact on spending on education.[30] The issue was further highlighted by the 1998 report of the Chairman of the OECD's Development Assistance Committee, which observed that an increase in spending on education by donors had been accompanied by a decrease in education spending in recipient countries. Because of the fungibility problem, donors now place far more emphasis on recipient governments having budgets that reflect a broad commitment to poverty reduction. These sector-wide approaches, and their integration into national budget planning, are a key requirement.

Briefly summarised, a SWAp is supposed to provide an integrated programme, setting out policy objectives, a comprehensive policy framework, a detailed investment plan, specific expenditure plans, and detailed funding commitments for government and donors. It follows that one of the requirements for a successful SWAp is the development of a medium-term expenditure plan, setting out annual budget provisions on a rolling basis. For instance, Uganda's Education Strategic Investment Plan (ESIP) sets out a five-year strategy for achieving clearly articulated objectives within a financing framework provided by a medium-term financial strategy, upon which annual budgets are based. Although experience with sector-investment programmes is so far limited, they do seem to have considerable potential. At their best, they can provide a coherent framework for defining the shared policy-goals of donors and recipient governments, and the financing commitments needed to achieve them. They can also create a mechanism through which donors can channel resources through the national budget, rather than through specific project budgets, thereby reducing administrative demands on government. However, sector-wide approaches do not provide a 'quick fix' solution to the many problems associated with aid effectiveness – and, in many respects, donor rhetoric on SWAps is related only weakly to practice on the ground.

Problems with sector-wide approaches

Perhaps the most obvious point to make about SWAps is that they are very complex undertakings. In Ethiopia it took over five years of intensive work to develop the sectoral plans for health and education. Implementation has involved co-ordination between the Federal Government and eleven regional entities in the context of far-reaching public-sector and civil-service reform.[31] This is not an untypical case. Evidence from several countries suggests that a typical planning cycle for the development of SWAps takes five–seven years, whereas there is an urgent need for increased donor support to take immediate effect.[32] One of the challenges is to balance the need for rigorous SWAp planning with the need for speed in aid disbursements.

Donors themselves have made much of the demise of old-style conditionality under SWAps. In many countries, however, old-style conditionality has emerged in a new guise, often with a distinct bias towards serving donors' interests. In Zambia, the key trigger for donors to release funds during the second phase of the country's education-sector strategy, starting in 2001, is that the government must spend at least 20 per cent of its budget on education, after debt-servicing claims have been met. Within this overall requirement, the government is required to allocate at least 60 per cent of the budget to primary schools. Some donors monitor compliance by placing staff in social-sector ministries.[33]

From a financing perspective, the most efficient SWAp strategy would involve donors placing their resources at the disposal of a government by pooling their resources in the national budget.[34] By committing funds for two-three years without conditions, donors could in theory define the total aid resources available to government for the financing of development plans. This would be good for national ownership, and it would also help to resolve budget problems associated with unpredictable aid flows. However, any movement towards the transfer of pooled resources would require a high level of confidence in national budget processes. Donors are accountable to their taxpayers and have an obligation to ensure that aid resources are put to effective use; and they must have sufficient confidence in national authorities to relinquish effective control over their aid funds. The result is that some of the problems associated with project-based aid have resurfaced. In Ethiopia, the Swedish International Development Agency channels resources for SWAps through line ministries, but insists on separate reporting requirements, including district-level budgets, for the various projects against which its funds are earmarked. This has resulted in serious tensions with central ministries, which argue that national reporting systems are sufficient.

The practice of earmarking funds against specific elements in SWAps is widespread. In the Zambian case, each of the 14 external agencies involved in the education-sector strategy link their financial support to specific programmes. The same applies to the health sector. The World Bank is one of the few donors in Zambia to provide funding for the health sector as a whole. Others operate stringent reporting require-ments. For instance, the US contribution to district-level health programmes has come through a basket of funds, granted in the form of debt relief. The Zambian government is required to submit monthly statements to USAID, showing expenditure activity on a daily basis. One of the ways in which donors have retained operational control over their aid budgets is through technical assistance. Only 3 per cent of Britain's aid for the health programme in Zambia is provided through pooled funds at district level, while more than 55 per cent is provided in the form of technical co-operation.[35] Several governments in Africa have complained that the implementation of SWAps has been held back by the continuation of what they see as unrealistic donor requirements, and by the absence of any predictability in aid flows linked to donor conditionality.

There are no easy answers to any of these problems. SWAps highlight a serious dilemma facing the donor community: namely, how to promote national ownership, while at the same time retaining the ability to account for funds in countries with weak budgeting systems. Unconditional development assistance is not a serious prospect, despite donors' protestations to the contrary; but continuing to tie aid to specific projects and programmes defeats the whole purpose of SWAps. Donors themselves could do far more to translate their new principles into operational practice. An obvious starting point would be the development of a common reporting system. Such a system could be integrated into the national budget, as it has been in Uganda, providing a framework for reporting to donors on the same basis as governments report to the general public. Some donors, including the USA, have expressed reservations about the loss of donor control that is inherent in such an approach. But if developing-country officials have to deal with only one set of procedures, they will be better able to develop capacity and build up their own administrative systems.

Ultimately, the success of SWAps will depend on government capacity. Donors can play an important role in financing and supporting the development of institutional capacity, but qualities such as 'ownership' cannot be generated through conditionality, whether of the old or new variety. There is a tendency on the part of some donors to see success in planning for sector-wide approaches as the key to sustained poverty reduction. It would be more accurate to say that good sectoral planning depends on initial governmental commitment to poverty reduction, backed by strong political leadership. In Uganda, such leadership has provided donors with sufficient confidence to increase the space available to government. Elsewhere, donor perceptions of SWAps have reflected their assessments of the reform credentials of key ministers. Three years ago, the Zambian health-sector strategy was viewed as a potential model, and the education-sector strategy was regarded as being exceptionally weak by comparison. This changed when the Minister of Health was replaced by a successor lacking credibility in the eyes of donors, and when a former Vice-President with strong reform credentials was appointed to lead the education-sector strategy. The episode demonstrated the importance of donors' perceptions of political leadership in their assessment of sectoral programmes.

Good sectoral planning depends on initial governmental commitment to poverty reduction, backed by strong political leadership.

The debt crisis as a barrier to education for all

In the mid-1980s, Julius Nyerere, then President of Tanzania, confronted his country's creditors with a stark question: 'Should we really let our children starve so that we can pay our debts?'[36] The answer came back in the affirmative. The failure of Northern governments to address the deepening debt crisis in poor countries had devastating consequences for poor people, and for the capacity of States to maintain basic services. Education systems were badly affected by the debt crisis. In many countries – including Tanzania – the gains achieved over two decades after Independence were rolled back in the space of a few years.

Today, the debt problems of poor countries figure far more prominently on the international agenda. In late 1996, a major new initiative was launched to resolve these problems; but, four years after its adoption, and one year after a major reform, the Heavily Indebted Poor Countries (HIPC) Initiative is failing to provide debt relief on the scale required. Debt relief has the potential to release resources that could be used to finance basic education and poverty-reduction initiatives. The same resources could, of course, be used to finance an increase in military spending. It is important that the HIPC Initiative directs resources to human-development investments that will make an immediate and tangible difference to people's lives. So far, however, it has failed to provide an effective link between debt relief and poverty reduction.

The human-development deficit in heavily indebted countries

There are 41 low-income countries classified by the IMF and the World Bank as 'heavily indebted'.[37] Collectively, they suffer from some of the worst human-welfare indicators in the world. In the UNDP's *Human Development Report*, which ranks countries on the basis of a composite indicator covering income and non-income dimensions of poverty, of the 44 countries ranked in the 'low human development' category, 33 are in the HIPC group. Deprivation extends across all aspects of human welfare (Table 5.1). Average life expectancy in HIPCs is 51 years – 12 less than the average for all developing countries. The under-five mortality rate is 156 deaths per 1000 live births. This translates into 3.4 million child deaths annually, most the result of poverty-related infectious disease and malnutrition. Education indicators are similarly bleak. There are 47 million children of primary-school age in the HIPCs not attending school – more than one-third of the worldwide total.[38] The quality of schooling in most of these countries is wretchedly low, with chronic shortages of teaching materials, and the education infrastructure in a parlous state.

It is not just the current state of development that raises cause for concern. The rate of progress in improving human development is exceptionally slow. Some of the main international development targets may now be beyond the reach of the HIPCs, including those for education.

Using the model described in Chapter 2, we took trend data for enrolment and population growth for the 41 heavily indebted countries and projected them forward to 2015. The projection indicates that the number of children not in school in these countries will rise to 57 million by 2015 (Figure 5.7). They will represent three-quarters of the total worldwide number out of school in that year. This projection refers only to

Table 5.1: Human-development indicators in heavily indebted poor countries

Source: UNICEF, *Children in Jeopardy,* 1999

Indicator	Industrialised countries	Developing countries	HIPCs
Child mortality rate (deaths per 1000 live births)	7	96	156
Life expectancy	78	63	51
Literacy rate (%)	98	71	55
Access to safe water (%)	100	70	53

enrolment, the first step on the ladder to good-quality, universal primary education. It takes into account neither the rate of completion for those who start school, nor the quality of education provided.

Projections for child mortality are equally disturbing. The two-thirds reduction in child death rates by 2015, envisaged under the international development targets, implies a target rate of 52 deaths for every 1000 live births in the HIPCs. If current trends continue, the actual rate in 2015 will be 134 deaths for every 1000 live births (Figure 5.8). Only three of the 41 HIPCs are on track to achieve the 2015 target.[39] At the other end of the spectrum, child-mortality rates are either stagnating at high levels (as in Côte d'Ivoire and Chad) or increasing (as in Zambia).

There are no projections available on income-poverty trends. At present, it is probable that slightly more than half of all people living in the HIPCs are surviving on less than $1 a day. Halving poverty by 2015 in line with

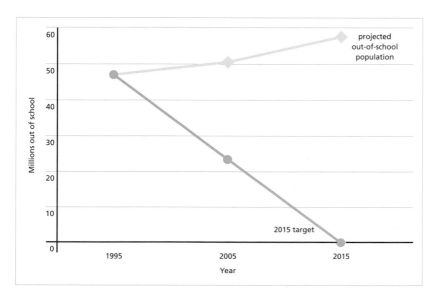

Figure 5.7
Projected numbers of children not enrolled in school in Heavily Indebted Poor Countries, 1995-2015

Source:
Children in Jeopardy, UNICEF, 1998

255

the international development targets would require per capita economic growth rates in excess of 2–3 per cent a year, provided that future patterns of growth were more equitable than past patterns. Given that per capita income growth for sub-Saharan Africa during the second half of the 1990s was less than 1 per cent per annum, and that there is little evidence of improved income distribution, prospects for achieving the poverty-reduction targets are not good.[40] Changing the dire human-development prospects for the HIPCs will require concerted action across a wide spectrum of policies. As indicated in Chapter 1, education has a critical role to play, not just as a development goal in its own right, but also as a catalyst for economic growth and improved public health.

Debt servicing as a barrier to human development

The debt stock of the HIPC countries – $206bn in 1996 – represents the small change of overall developing-country debt, accounting for no more than 12 per cent of the total. However, relative to ability to pay, the debt burden is enormous.[41] Figure 5.9 shows that the debt stock of the HIPCs is far larger in relation to export earnings and GDP than for other developing countries. In relation to national income, average debt stock is more than three times the average for all developing countries. This has important implications for economic growth, and hence for the capacity of governments to finance investment in education. Excessive debt stock undermines growth by creating disincentives for investors, domestic and foreign, in the form of uncertainty over future tax rates, inflation, and exchange rates.[42] The annual repayments made to meet

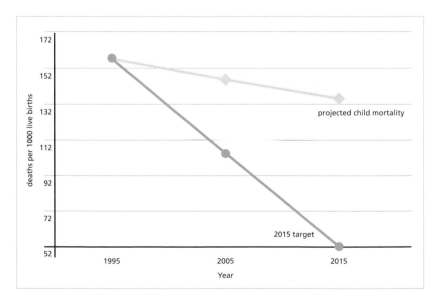

Figure 5.8
Projected child-mortality rates for Heavily Indebted Poor Countries, 1995-2015

Source:
Children in Jeopardy, UNICEF, 1998

creditors' claims also undermine growth by diverting foreign exchange from essential imports, and by depriving governments of the revenue that they need in order to maintain economic infrastructure.

The impact of slow growth on social-sector financing is cumulative, as we saw in Chapter 3. It progressively erodes the capacity of governments to improve the quality and coverage of the basic services that they provide. But debt servicing also creates more immediate problems. Traditionally, measurements of debt sustainability have tended to focus on the capacity of governments to meet their debt-service payments through export earnings. This is an important indicator, but a partial one. From the perspective of social-sector financing, what matters is the impact of debt on the national budget – and it is here that the most immediate effects are felt.

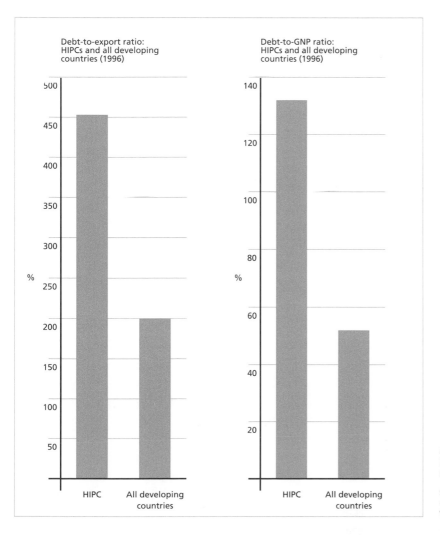

Figure 5.9
Debt sustainability in Heavily Indebted Poor Countries

Source:
Global Development Finance,
World Bank, 1998

One of the features of debt servicing in the HIPC countries is that it has been consuming a large share of the very limited public revenues available to governments. In 1996, external debt servicing was absorbing more than one-quarter of government revenue in Ethiopia and Niger, and more than half in countries such as Tanzania, Nicaragua, and Honduras.[43] The consequence is that creditors' claims have been displacing high-priority social-sector investment. At a time when millions of children are denied their right to an education, and when millions more fail to survive childhood because of poverty and inadequate health services, governments in the HIPC countries are spending far more on repaying creditors than on basic social services. Among the outcomes not captured in financial data on debt are hunger, disease, and mass illiteracy.

Sub-Saharan Africa is the worst-affected region. Between 1990 and 1998, debt-service payments averaged around $12bn per annum – more than double the annual spending on basic education. In several countries, spending on debt has far exceeded spending on primary education. As Figure 5.10 shows, countries such as Honduras, Nicaragua, and Zambia have been spending four times as much on debt servicing as on basic education. In some cases, debt-service payments exceed spending on basic health care and education *combined*. It should be emphasised that this is happening year in and year out. Figure 5.11 summarises the relationship between debt servicing and government spending on basic social services for Tanzania, Zambia, and Nicaragua over several years. It shows that debt payments were absorbing more than twice the combined expenditure on basic education and primary healthcare for much of the 1990s. It is difficult to square these budget realities with the bold commitment to 'innovative and equitable' solutions to the debt crisis promised at the World Conference on Education for All in Jomtien.

Some economists maintain that the absolute level of debt servicing is not relevant to the financing of basic social services, provided that net resource transfers are positive.[44] In other words, if the HIPCs have been receiving more in aid than they have been repaying in debt, then there is no debt problem. The HIPCs have indeed been receiving a net transfer, amounting to around 5 per cent of their GDP, but the argument that such transfers negate the impact of debt servicing is deeply flawed. Even if bilateral aid appears to offset debt repayments in theory, it does not do so in practice. This is because donor assistance is directed mainly towards areas such as balance-of-payments support, or to specific projects that are financed off-budget. It does not automatically find its way into the national budget. However, the financial burden of debt does fall

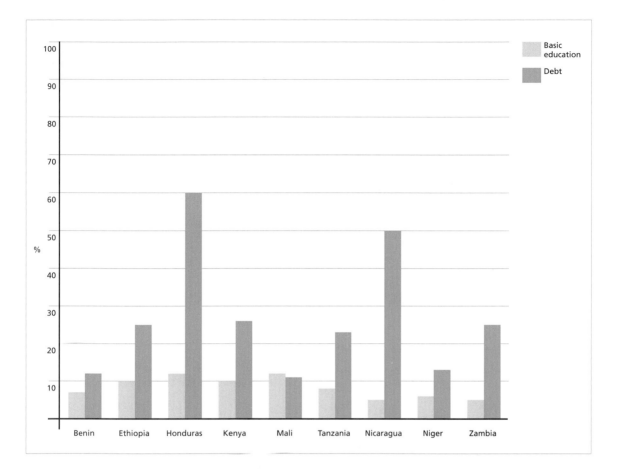

directly on the national budget and allocations to line ministries.[45] It follows that the two types of financial transfer (i.e. debt repayments on the one side and aid transfers on the other) are not strictly comparable, and that aid transfers do not compensate for the budgetary effects of debt repayments. Another problem is that aid transfers are not only erratic, making long-term planning in areas such as health care and education difficult: they are also declining over time. In 1998, development assistance to the HIPCs was 40 per cent lower than in 1990. The following examples illustrate the enormous burden imposed by debt servicing on six countries, each of which faces enormous challenges in relation to the 2015 target of universal primary education.

- **Ethiopia**: Although the proportion of recurrent government expenditure on education has increased from 12 per cent of the budget in 1989 to 18 per cent today, with a parallel increase in allocations to the primary sector, these gains are relatively modest when set against reductions in defence spending. Before the armed conflict with

Figure 5.10
Percentages of budget allocated to debt and basic education (1997)

Source:
World Bank national budget data

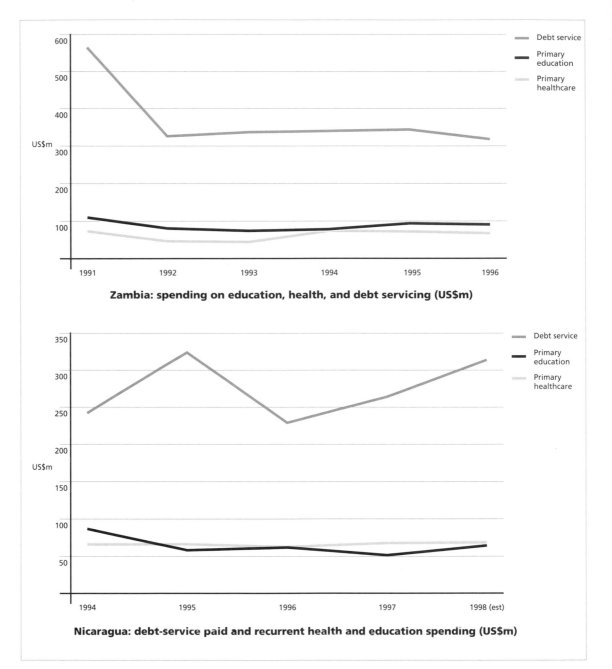

Zambia: spending on education, health, and debt servicing (US$m)

Nicaragua: debt-service paid and recurrent health and education spending (US$m)

Figure 5.11
Spending on debt, basic education, and primary health care: Zambia, Nicaragua, and Tanzania

Source: national budget data

Eritrea intensified in 1998/99, defence spending had fallen to 12 per cent of government spending, compared with more than 42 per cent in the late 1980s. Unfortunately, the 'peace dividend' mainly benefited Ethiopia's creditors. Over the period 1989–95, the share of government expenditure allocated to debt servicing increased

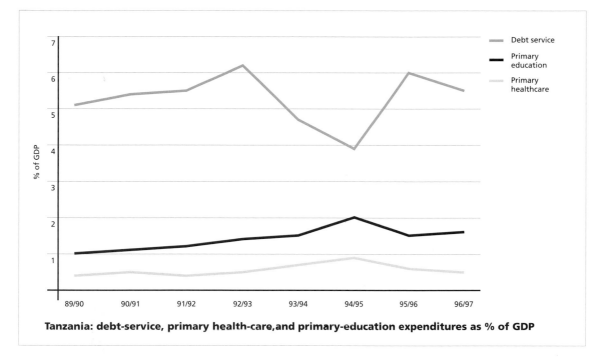

Tanzania: debt-service, primary health-care,and primary-education expenditures as % of GDP

fourfold to 28 per cent. Debt repayments represent 2.5 times the government's spending on basic education: about $2.50 per capita is spent on primary education and more than $6 per capita on debt. This is in a situation where three-quarters of the population of primary-school age – 9 million children – are not in school; where fewer than 10 per cent of girls enrol in primary school; and where one-quarter of the children who do enrol drop out before reaching Grade 2.

Figure 5.11 continued

- **Zambia**: Education expenditure has recovered slightly since 1993, but it remains far lower as a proportion of GDP and per capita than in the mid-1980s. Actual spending per primary student was $28 in 1996, compared with $36 in 1985. There are chronic shortages of class-rooms in urban areas, and most public schools are in a state of grave disrepair. Debt servicing is hampering efforts to address these problems. In 1993–96, average annual spending on education was $82m, about 2.5 per cent of GDP. Average expenditure on debt servicing over the same period amounted to $335m – more than 10 per cent of GDP. These debt-service payments have been maintained, although an estimated 560,000 children are not in school, enrolment rates are declining, and the incidence of illiteracy is rising. Rising costs have forced many of the poorest households to withdraw their children from school.

- **Tanzania**: There are some 2.2 million Tanzanian children not in school, and illiteracy is rising at the rate of 2 per cent a year. The country has one of the lowest rates of progression from primary to junior-secondary levels in the world, with fewer than 5 per cent of children enrolling in secondary school. Public spending on debt in 1997/98 amounted to $275m, or $9 per capita. This is twice the per capita expenditure on education, and four times the spending on primary education. Recurrent spending per pupil, net of teachers' salaries, is pitifully low, at about $1.

- **Niger**: Ranked 173rd out of 174 countries on the UNDP Human Development Index, Niger is one of the world's poorest countries. More than half of the population live in poverty. Enrolment rates are low, especially in rural areas, and the country has one of the world's widest gender gaps in enrolment. Only 12 per cent of girls aged 6 to 11 attend school, compared with 48 per cent of boys. Most schools lack books and supplies, education quality is poor, and the direct costs of sending a child to school are high relative to income. Although education spending has risen as a share of GDP, spending on primary education is less than half of government expenditure on debt.

- **Nicaragua**: With a per capita debt of more than $1300, Nicaraguans have one of the highest ratios of debt to income in the world. The problem is not simply one of debt stock. Debt servicing absorbs more than two-thirds of government revenue, $55 per person in 1997. By comparison, spending on primary education amounts to less than $10 per capita. During 1990–95, debt servicing increased from $50 to almost £300m. Over the same period, spending on education as a proportion of GDP fell by 25 per cent. Spending per pupil has also fallen. In 1993, recurrent spending per primary-school pupil was $34, compared with $43 three years before.

Debt relief in perspective: from 'special terms' to the reformed HIPC Initiative

The continuation of the debt crisis in poor countries into the first decade of the new millennium testifies to the failure of successive debt-relief measures. These started in the 1980s, culminating in the announcement of the HIPC Initiative in 1996. Reform of this Initiative in 1999, following intense public campaigning, raised hopes of more rapid progress towards debt reduction on the required scale. So far, these hopes have been thwarted by a failure to move towards rapid implementation. There are also doubts about the extent of debt relief provided for under the reformed Initiative.

As the debt crisis evolved in the early 1980s, most creditors took the view that debtors were facing temporary liquidity problems. Their debt-relief strategy reflected this mistaken premise. The aim of the strategy was to provide continued financial flows, enabling countries to maintain debt repayments, while rescheduling small amounts of debt stock as payments fell due. Creditors hoped that full payments would eventually be made as economic recovery got underway.[46] Innovations came slowly. Multi-year rescheduling was introduced in 1984. In 1987, creditors began to concede 'special terms' that provided for longer-term rescheduling and introduced the option of debt forgiveness. Levels of debt forgiveness were gradually increased through a series of initiatives. By 1994, the Naples Terms had provided for a reduction of 67 per cent in eligible debt stock. 'Eligible' was the operative term. Multilateral debt owed to the IMF and the World Bank was excluded from debt relief. Given that these two institutions accounted for about one-quarter of debt stock and over half of debt servicing by 1996, their omission was significant.[47] Much of the bilateral debt owed to governments was also excluded, since any stock accumulated after a country had applied for debt relief was deemed ineligible.

The failure of creditor strategies in the 1980s and 1990s was reflected in deteriorating debt indicators. Over the decade to 1996, the debt stock of the HIPCs increased by a factor of three (Figure 5.12). Although actual levels of debt servicing did start to fall in the first half of the 1990s, this owed less to debt relief than to a widening gap between *scheduled* payments and *actual* payments. By 1996, less than half of all scheduled payments were being met, with the rest accumulating as arrears and driving up total debt stock.[48] Payments on arrears accounted for two-thirds of debt repayments to bilateral creditors by 1997.

The HIPC Initiative, announced at the end of 1996, marked a major departure from previous creditor strategies in several crucial respects. For the first time, it extended the principle of debt relief to multilateral creditors. It also established debt ceilings, or 'sustainability thresholds'. Any country with a debt stock exceeding these thresholds would be provided with debt relief, subject to its compliance with two successive IMF programmes. Finally, the HIPC Initiative increased to 80 per cent the level of debt reduction provided by bilateral donors. Progress under the initial HIPC Initiative proved disappointing. In the two years after its announcement, only four countries – Uganda, Bolivia, Guyana, and Mozambique – received any debt relief. One of the major reasons for the slow progress was the requirement that debtors should comply with two IMF programmes.[49]Although the framework allowed some scope for

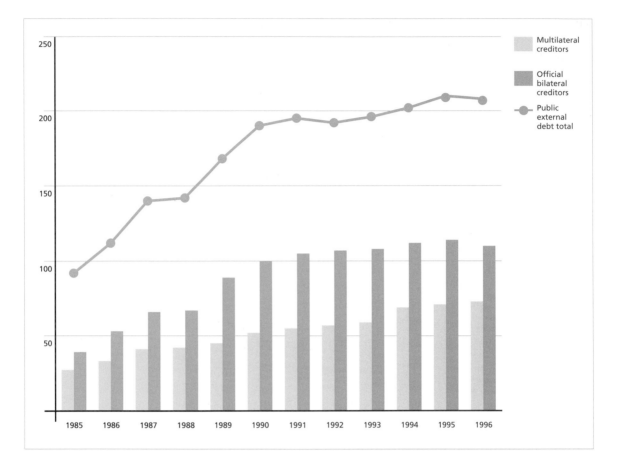

Figure 5.12
**Developing countries:
public external debt by creditor
– Heavily Indebted Poor
Countries (in US$bn)**

Source:
World Bank,
Global Development Finance,
various years

flexibility, this translated into a six-year track record in economic reform, provided that the programmes were not interrupted. Since only one-third of IMF programmes were completed without interruption, this created the potential for considerable delay. Moreover, little flexibility was shown in practice. In 1997, when Uganda became eligible for debt relief, it had a strong track record in economic reform, stretching back over a decade. Yet creditors insisted on its complying with an IMF programme for a further year before it received HIPC Initiative debt relief.

The failure of the HIPC Initiative to deliver on the promise of an end to the debt crisis fuelled an unprecedented international campaign for more effective action, and an official review. In 1999, the Group of Seven industrial countries, meeting at the Cologne Summit, set out a new strategy for providing deeper, earlier, and more comprehensive debt relief.[50] Two important innovations were introduced.

- *Additional debt reduction.* The reformed HIPC Initiative lowered the debt-sustainability threshold by around 25 per cent, thereby increasing the level of debt relief provided.[51] Bilateral creditors will reduce eligible debt stock by up to 90 per cent, and more if needed to achieve the debt-sustainability targets. Lowering the debt-sustainability threshold had the effect of increasing the number of countries eligible for debt relief from 26 under the previous regime to 33.

- *Earlier debt reduction.* Under the previous framework, debtor countries qualified for bilateral debt relief after undergoing one IMF programme. In HIPC Initiative jargon, the end of this first programme marked the so-called 'Decision Point', at which point the IMF and World Bank would undertake a debt-sustainability analysis. If this analysis showed that bilateral debt relief was insufficient to leave countries with a sustainable debt, countries became eligible for deeper debt reduction and multilateral debt relief. First, however, they had to implement their second IMF programme in order to reach the so-called 'Completion Point', at which they qualified for full HIPC Initiative debt reduction. Hence, in total, it could take up to six years to qualify. The new framework addressed this problem by introducing a 'floating Completion Point'. The gap between Decision Point and Completion Point can now be narrowed – or extended – depending on whether or not governments meet requirements for macro-economic reform and poverty reduction. But countries become eligible for interim debt relief after the Decision Point, so that a reduction in *debt-service* payments is possible with immediate effect, although the stock of debt is not reduced until after Completion Point.[52]

Performance under the reformed HIPC Initiative

What are the prospects of the reformed HIPC Initiative ending the devastating impact of debt on social-sector provision and human welfare? On paper, it represents an ambitious step forward. The overall level of debt relief envisaged under the new Initiative is more than double that initially provided for. The costs of debt reduction to creditors will rise to $27bn in net present-value terms, equally shared between bilateral and multilateral creditors.[53] Apart from deepening debt relief, creditors have also set ambitious targets for country coverage. When the new framework was adopted, 25 countries were targeted for receiving debt relief by the end of 2000.

It is too early to assess the effectiveness of the new Initiative. However, serious problems have emerged in the year since it was announced. Implementation remains painfully slow. By August 2000, only eight countries – Bolivia, Burkina Faso, Mauritania, Mozambique, Uganda, Honduras, Senegal, and Tanzania – were receiving debt relief under the HIPC Initiative.[54] Prospects for meeting the target of 25 countries by the end of 2000 appeared to be limited. The willingness of several key creditors to finance their contribution to the debt-relief package has also been called into question. Early in 2000, the US Congress refused the Administration's request for the $600m needed to cover America's contribution. Other creditors – including Japan – have used this as a convenient pretext for withholding their full financial contribution.[55]

There are further problems relating to the level of debt relief provided for under the reformed HIPC Initiative. Headline figures tend to create an exaggerated impression of the real budget savings that governments will make, because they refer to reductions in debt stock (much of which was not being serviced), rather than debt payments. Budget savings on repayments are larger for some countries than for others. If government spending on debt after enhanced HIPC Initiative assistance is compared with the spending that would be required after traditional debt relief, Zambia's debt-service bill may be predicted to fall by half in 2000–01, and Tanzania's by nearly one-fifth. But what matters in terms of social-sector financing is the proportion of government revenue that will be directed away from domestic priorities and towards debt servicing. In many cases the proportion will remain large. For example, both Zambia and Tanzania will be allocating more than one-fifth of government revenue to debt repayments in 2001.

Such outcomes raise important questions about the debt-sustainability criteria used under the HIPC Initiative. These criteria provide an indication of the ability of governments to meet creditors' claims, but only in a narrow financial sense. They do not provide a measure of the appropriate balance to be struck between these claims and the human-development claims of poor people in heavily indebted countries. Nor do they establish a benchmark against which to assess what level of debt repayment might be consistent with the public-investment requirements for achieving the 2015 development targets. Figure 5.13 shows that several heavily indebted countries will emerge from the HIPC debt-relief process still spending far more on debt servicing than they are spending on education. Very high opportunity costs are implied by this imbalance between public investment in a sector that is vital to poverty reduction and unproductive spending on debt, as the following cases illustrate.

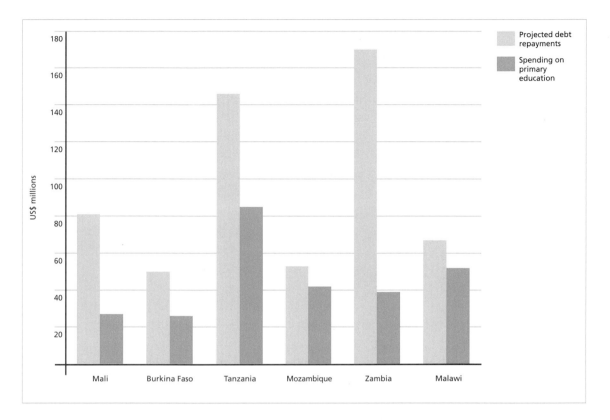

Figure 5.13
**Public spending on primary
education (1997-98) and debt
(projected after HIPC debt
relief)**

Source:
World Bank debt-sustainability
analysis and national budgets

- **Tanzania**: Under the reformed HIPC, Tanzania will receive debt relief amounting to $2.1bn. Translated into average annual budget spending terms, this will reduce debt servicing from an average of $174m between 1997 and 1999, to $146m between 2001 and 2003.[56] The end result, however, is that the government will still be allocating one-fifth of its revenue to debt servicing. In 2001, spending on debt will be twice as high as current spending on basic education in the 1998 budget. This is in a country with 2 million children out of school, one of the lowest rates of transition from primary to secondary school in the world, and chronic shortages of basic teaching materials. Such public-spending patterns are clearly not compatible with a commitment to the rapid achievement of universal primary education.

- **Zambia**: Under the reformed HIPC Initiative, Zambia will make large budget savings, amounting to more than $200m in 2001 and 2002. Viewed from the perspective of social-sector financing, however, these savings are wholly inadequate. In 2001, Zambia will be spending around five times more on debt servicing than it currently spends on education. Indeed, its expenditure on debt will exceed the total combined budgets for education and health care. As in Tanzania, this diversion of resources will severely compromise national poverty-reduction efforts. In education, enrolment rates are still lower than in the early 1980s, and more than one-quarter of the country's schools are in a state of serious disrepair. Zambia is one of the few countries in the world in which literacy rates are falling. The national crisis in education is part of a wider human-development crisis. More than half of the population live in extreme poverty, and several human-welfare indicators are deteriorating. Malnutrition in children under the age of five has risen from one-third of the child population to more than half. The HIV/AIDS crisis is having a devastating impact on health and education. The incidence of tuberculosis increased five-fold in the 1990s, and around 13 per cent of Zambian children under the age of 14 are orphans – the highest rate in the world. For a country in this position to be spending more on debt than on health care and education raises fundamental questions about the commitment of the creditor community to the 2015 human-development goals.

- **Burkina Faso**: Human-development indicators for Burkina Faso are among the worst in the developing world. The country ranks third from bottom on the UNDP Human Development Index. Just over one-third of boys and around one-quarter of girls are in school. In the Sahelian provinces of the north-east, fewer than one in ten girls go to school. In the country as a whole, more than one million children aged 6–12 are not in school. The quality of education for those who are in school is extremely poor. Class sizes in excess of 100 are common, as are chronic shortages of textbooks. Despite this, the post-HIPC Initiative debt-service bill will amount to around twice the level of government spending on education.

- **Mali**: Preliminary estimates suggest that, like Zambia, Mali will emerge from the HIPC Initiative still spending more on debt relief than on health care and education *combined*. Once again, this will divert public spending from areas of desperate need. Mali has the seventh-highest child-death rate in the world (220 deaths for every 1000 live births), and some of the lowest enrolment rates for primary education. Only one in ten boys and one in twenty girls progress to lower-secondary school.

It might be argued that the imbalance between debt servicing and spending in sectors such as basic education owes less to creditors' debt-relief policies than to the spending priorities of national governments. There is an element of truth in this view. Governments in countries such as

Zambia, Burkina Faso, and Mali do under-invest in primary education. However, the same cannot be said of Malawi, which will also emerge from the HIPC Initiative spending more on debt than on primary education. This is a country that invests more of its GDP in education than almost any other developing country, and allocates almost two-thirds of this spending to the primary sector. Even if Zambia matched Malawi's commitment to education and equity in public spending, its primary-education budget would still fall far short of spending on debt.

This brief review of the prospective debt profile of heavily indebted countries demonstrates the urgent need to establish new criteria for debt sustainability. Public investment in primary education and basic health-care has the potential to generate high returns in terms of economic growth, poverty reduction, and public health. The same cannot be said of financial transfers to external creditors. What is required is a new approach that sets an upper ceiling on debt-service obligation, consistent with a country's human-development needs. Oxfam has proposed a ceiling of 10 per cent on the amount of government revenue allocated to debt servicing. For most HIPCs, this would have the effect of increasing by 50 to 100 per cent the annual budget savings provided through debt relief.

Debt relief and poverty reduction: still the missing link

Unsustainable debt has been part of problem facing poor countries that are attempting to progress towards the target of universal primary education. It follows that debt relief has the potential to become part of the solution. If the resources released as a result of HIPC Initiative debt reduction can be used to invest in poverty-reduction initiatives, the benefits should be reflected in improved prospects for human development. This is what the heads of government of the G7 countries had in mind at the 1999 Cologne Summit, when they reformed the HIPC Initiative. According to their communiqué, 'The central objective of this initiative is to provide a greater focus on poverty reduction by releasing resources for investment in health, education and social needs.'[57] The problem is that the mechanism developed to achieve this goal is deeply flawed in design, jeopardising the enormous potential gains in human welfare that could be generated through debt relief.

The link between debt relief and poverty reduction under the reformed HIPC Initiative is provided by Poverty Reduction Strategy Papers (PRSPs). These are documents that debtor governments have to submit at Decision Point to the boards of the IMF and the World Bank. Their scope is enormously ambitious. They are supposed to set out comprehensive strategies for reducing poverty and increasing growth over an annually updated three-year time-frame, all within a coherent macro-economic framework. PRSPs are expected to set clear goals, linked to the 2015 international development targets for poverty reduction, and to include appropriate monitoring indicators. The process envisaged for the development of PRSPs is equally ambitious. There is a premium on national ownership and design, but governments are expected to develop their poverty-reduction strategies, 'taking into account the views of Parliaments and other democratic bodies, where they exist, the donor community, civil society and specifically the poor themselves'.[58] Progress to Completion Point and ultimate debt relief will depend on government performance in implementing the PRSP. Debtor countries will be obliged not just to prepare a poverty-reduction strategy document, but also to show that interim debt relief is being fully integrated into the national budget. Recognising that a fully fledged PRSP will take time to prepare – one or two years, according to estimates by IMF–World Bank staff, creditors have agreed that debtor countries may initially prepare an Interim PRSP. These documents are supposed to set out broad principles, describe the main elements of macro-economic policy and poverty-reduction strategies, provide a timeline for the development of full PRSPs, and indicate what measures will be taken to facilitate participation.[59]

At one level, the PRSP approach is a triumph for non-government organisations and the popular campaign for debt relief. That campaign has been motivated as much by a concern to ensure that the benefits of debt relief went to the poor as by the conviction that Northern governments had failed to address a major financial problem. The PRSP model also provides an opportunity for civil-society organisations – NGOs, churches, trade unions, business, and professional groups – to influence the design and implementation of poverty-reduction strategies. But it also raises a number of problems. Some of these relate to tensions inherent in the PRSP process, among them the following.

- *National ownership*: Creditors claim that the defining feature of the PRSP exercise is 'national ownership'. Yet the fact remains that the concept was developed by creditors and is being implemented under IMF–World Bank auspices. The premium on national ownership is ultimately backed by stringent conditionality: governments that are unwilling to prepare a PRSP need not apply for debt relief. Some developing countries view the PRSP as the latest form of aid conditionality, repackaged in the donor rhetoric of the late 1990s.

- *Speed and quality*: There is an unavoidable tension between the needs of debtor countries and poor people in those countries for immediate debt relief, and the demands of creditors for a high-quality poverty-reduction document. This tension has become apparent repeatedly in relation to the participation of civil society in the development of PRSPs. In Tanzania and Honduras, local NGOs have claimed that government has rushed through the development of Interim PRSPs, with IMF–World Bank approval, in order to receive early debt relief. In Bolivia and Honduras, NGOs claim that government and the IMF have subordinated the participation process to the dictates of IMF programme scheduling.

- *PRSP design*: All participants in the PRSP exercise are committed in principle to poverty reduction. In practice, however, there is not much consensus on what a good poverty-reduction strategy is – and less still on who should judge it. Key questions relate to the diagnosis of the underlying causes of poverty, the consistency of budget allocations against poverty-reduction goals, and the design of macro-economic reform. The IMF occupies a central position. This is because creditors attach considerable weight to budget stability, and because they see the IMF as the best arbiter of policy design for achieving this goal. However, the IMF has been criticised by some donors and NGOs for placing an undue emphasis on the achievement of low inflation through policies that are inherently damaging for employment and social-sector provision. In Bolivia, one of the reasons for the breakdown in dialogue over the PRSP was the refusal of the IMF and the government to include in that dialogue the reform of the country's macro-economic framework.

There is an unavoidable tension between the needs of debtor countries and poor people in those countries for immediate debt relief, and the demands of creditors for a high-quality poverty-reduction document.

- *Confusion over Interim PRSPs*: Interim PRSPs were developed as a response to a real dilemma: namely, how to provide early debt relief on the one hand, while insisting on strong poverty-reduction strategies on the other. In practice, it is difficult to see that they serve any purpose at all. In Tanzania, the Interim PRSP was developed early in 2000, following limited consultations with non-government organisations.[60] The document does little more than restate the macro-economic reform objectives defined in the country's IMF programme. Some of these objectives, including measures to allow foreign investors to acquire equities in the stock market, and the commercialisation of land rights, are of dubious benefit for poverty reduction. More broadly, there is no attempt in the Interim Tanzanian PRSP to identify new initiatives or policies through which debt-relief financing could be used to achieve specific human-welfare gains. In the case of education, the only specific commitment is to carry out a 'school mapping exercise' to determine the quality of provision in about half of the country's districts. On poverty reduction more generally, the document offers only the promise of continued human-welfare monitoring.

The interim PRSP in Tanzania illustrates some general flaws in the current strategy for linking debt relief to poverty reduction. As presently conceived, PRSPs are designed to achieve an enormous range of macro-economic reforms, many of which already figure prominently as targets in existing IMF programmes. These reforms are supposed to be integrated into a national poverty-reduction strategy. For countries such as Uganda that are already implementing strong macro-economic reform and poverty-reduction programmes, it is difficult to see what PRSPs are supposed to add. But the institutional context for poverty reduction in Uganda has been developed over more than a decade. In countries such as Tanzania, with a far weaker track record both on economic reform and poverty reduction, PRSPs are being presented as a new departure. In practice, however, they are merely contributing to a long-term process, using debt relief and aid conditionality as a mechanism for ensuring reform. Neither the interim PRSP, nor the full version, addresses the immediate question of how to ensure that savings from debt relief are directed towards public investments that will reduce poverty. From a HIPC Initiative perspective, the entire exercise is in grave danger of becoming a profound irrelevance. This has political as well as financial ramifications. When the HIPC Initiative was announced in 1996, the World Bank's President, Jim Wolfensohn, described it as 'good news for the poor'. Four years on, the tangible advantages for the poor are difficult to discern. Without early evidence that the HIPC Initiative is capable of generating human-development gains, its credibility, already stretched to breaking point, will continue to suffer.

Without early evidence that the HIPC Initiative is capable of generating human-development gains, its credibility, already stretched to breaking point, will continue to suffer.

An alternative to Poverty Reduction Strategy Papers: debt-relief funds

The alternative to the PRSP approach, especially in countries with weaker macro-economic policy environments, is the development of national debt-relief funds dedicated to well-defined poverty-reduction goals.[61] Financed through the savings generated by debt relief, these funds could be channelled through the national budget to priority areas such as education, health care, and rural infrastructure. To be effective, such arrangements would have to be integrated into sectoral planning strategies. In countries where sectoral plans establish clear policy goals and a time-frame for achieving them, backed by investment plans for specific programmes, debt-relief funds could be integrated into their budget provisions. They would provide additional resources that could be used either to accelerate implementation (for example, by shortening the planned period for achieving universal primary education), or to improve the quality of service provision (for example, by increasing the supply of books to schools, or essential drugs to health clinics). The sectoral planning targets and time-frame would be adjusted to reflect the increase in resource allocation.

Objections have been raised to such an approach. It is variously claimed that it would be unworkable, ineffective, and incapable of addressing the fungibility problem. In fact, the government of Uganda, the first country to receive debt relief under the HIPC Initiative, has pioneered a highly successful poverty fund, partly financed through debt relief. The Poverty Action Fund (PAF) was initiated in 1998–99 to provide a mechanism for disbursing budget savings released as a result of debt relief. These amounted to around $37m per annum during the first two years.[62] The PAF was used to finance public spending in five key areas central to poverty reduction: namely, primary education, primary health care, water and sanitation, rural feeder roads, and agricultural extension. Financing was earmarked against specific objectives. For example, the Primary School Facilities Grant, provided through the PAF, was directed towards the refurbishment or reconstruction of around one thousand classrooms as part of the national programme to provide free, universal primary education.

In many respects, the Ugandan PAF embodies the key principles of the PRSP approach. Goals have been identified through a process of consultation with civil society, and the PAF itself is subject to stringent monitoring and independent auditing. Although resources are channelled through a separate account, all expenditure falls under the oversight of Parliament and the Auditor General's office. The funding provided through the PAF is directed towards clearly articulated goals set out in the national poverty-reduction strategy, which are in turn embedded in both annual budgets and a medium-term financial framework. The difference between the PAF and the PRSP concept relates to the practicability of the former in terms of generating real and immediate human-welfare benefits from debt relief. While the PRSP approach locks the debt-relief project into complex national reform processes that will stretch over many years, the PAF model offers the prospect of more immediate benefits. It provides a transparent device for directing savings from debt relief towards increased public investment in areas that will enhance the health status, education, and livelihoods of the poor.

Dedicated poverty-action funds financed through debt relief could make a real difference in relation to the 2015 target of universal primary education. They could be used to increase supplies of basic teaching materials, or to reduce the financial burden on poor households wanting to send their children to school. For example, governments could earmark savings from debt relief for grants to replace the revenue generated by cost-recovery. Such an approach could make a real difference to millions of poor households. As we saw in Chapter 3, cost sharing, or the practice of charging parents for basic education, is excluding millions of poor children from an opportunity for education. Tanzania was cited as an example. Households in the country are currently financing about one-third of recurrent spending on education, which places an enormous strain on the budgets of the poorest households. Yet the household contribution represents only around 3 per cent of the resources currently allocated by government to debt servicing. In this case, the government could use a debt-relief fund to finance an increase in grants to schools against the specific objective of reducing – or eliminating – cost recovery, perhaps with an initial focus on the poorest districts. Including such an objective in the Interim PRSP would indicate a more serious commitment to poverty reduction than the reiteration of IMF macro-economic targets set out in the current PRSP.

Dedicated poverty-action funds financed through debt relief could make a real difference in relation to the 2015 target of universal primary education.

The use of debt-relief funds to replace the education tax levied through cost sharing is only one option. Governments could develop other strategies, indicating how they would use debt-relief funds to accelerate progress towards universal primary education. One of the problems facing Zambia, for example, is that it has a long track record of weak economic reform, matched by equally weak governance. This has delayed progress towards debt relief. However, the country has developed a strong education-sector strategy. The Basic Education Sub-sector Investment Programme (BESSIP) has set the target of universal primary-school enrolment by 2005. The BESSIP provides the umbrella for an integrated strategy, incorporating programmes aimed at increasing the supply of instructional materials, improving school health and nutrition services, developing the skills of teachers, and decentralising authority and responsibility. Annual government spending under the first phase of the programme (1999–2002) amounts to about $56m, with donors providing a similar amount.[63] Among the quantified targets for 2002 are the construction of 2000 additional classrooms, the creation of bursary schemes for children for poor households, and an increase in the number of trained teachers in rural schools. In each of these areas, the contribution of finance generated through debt relief would make it possible to adjust the targets upwards. Existing investment and costing plans would make it possible to link debt relief to (for example) a specified number of additional classrooms constructed, or teachers trained. Of course, more ambitious options would also be possible. Spending by households on primary education currently represents the equivalent in financial terms of around 10 per cent of government spending on debt. There is no reason, in principle, why government, donors, and civil society could not develop a strategy for eliminating cost recovery through debt-relief financing.

Leaving aside the specific targets and policy options chosen, the guiding principle for debt-relief funds should be a clear commitment to poverty-reduction goals, defined through dialogue with civil society. Budgets should be subjected to independent auditing, with the reports published. While none of this will resolve the theoretical problems associated with fungibility, it will help to deliver a poverty-focused debt initiative, as promised by the HIPC Initiative.

Structural adjustment and the role of the IMF in poor countries

Structural adjustment programmes have had an important bearing on the policy environment for education since the 1990 World Conference on Education for All, especially in the poorest countries. Unsustainable debt, large budget deficits, and balance-of-payments problems have forced many of these countries to turn to the IMF and the World Bank for loans. Policy conditions attached to these loans have defined the macro-economic environment in which education planning takes place. Within the structural adjustment framework, the IMF enjoys a special authority.[64] Bilateral donors and other financial institutions – including the World Bank – require an IMF 'seal of approval' before providing aid or loans. This places the Fund at the apex of a hierarchy of policy conditionality, with the power to decide whether or not developing-country governments merit assistance. The delegation of this degree of authority reflects the primacy attached by Northern governments to the IMF's core remit: namely, short-term macro-economic stability and low inflation.[65]

In 1997, 31 low-income countries were implementing IMF programmes. These programmes have systematically undermined progress towards universal primary education and other human-welfare targets. While macro-economic stability is vital to the sustained growth on which poverty

275

reduction depends, IMF programmes have sought to achieve stability through policies that have had the effect of undermining the provision of basic services, exacerbating inequalities and, in many cases, increasing household poverty. The record of these programmes in relation to economic growth is poor, which has had further adverse implications for government financing of basic services.

The impact of IMF programmes on access to education and other basic services

It is useful to distinguish between the two main ways in which adjustment policies influence the access of poor households to basic services: namely, through their impact on public spending and through changes in household income. In practice, the two effects are inter-related. Household incomes have an important bearing on whether or not households can afford access to basic services, and the provision of such services influences household income, for example by influencing the health risks to which poor people are exposed.

During the 1980s, IMF–World Bank adjustment programmes were severely criticised for their failure to protect public spending on basic services. Public-expenditure targets were set with scant regard for the budgets for health care or education, which were frequently cut very severely. Although the IMF claims that its programmes are now designed to protect, or increase, social-sector spending, this is difficult to square with the evidence. Part of the problem with assessing IMF claims is that the institution is highly selective in its use and interpretation of data. In 1998 it presented evidence on social-sector spending for 66 countries over a ten-year period, covering the period before, during, and after IMF programmes.[66] The evidence purported to show that governments in low-income countries with IMF programmes had been able to increase social-sector spending by almost 3 per cent a year – more than double the rate of increase for higher-income countries. As the IMF survey concluded, 'Spending on education and health, on average, fared reasonably well.'

Unfortunately, the term 'on average' was more than usually ambiguous in this context. As with any human-development statistics, average trends conceal wide variations, especially when they are extended over a decade and a large number of countries. The average rate of increase discovered by the IMF was in fact the result of very large gains in per capita spending in a small group of countries (including Georgia, Sao Tome and Principe, and Cambodia), modest gains elsewhere, and

Although the IMF claims that its programmes are now designed to protect, or increase, social-sector spending, this is difficult to square with the evidence.

deep cuts in a large group of countries. Disaggregation of the IMF's own data showed that per capita spending on education in the sub-Saharan African countries with IMF programmes fell, on average, by 0.7 per cent a year. Thirteen of the 18 African countries covered in the sample reduced their education spending in per capita terms, in some cases by exceptionally large amounts. Several – including Zambia, Côte d'Ivoire, and Zimbabwe – reduced per capita spending under IMF programmes by 8 per cent or more per annum.[67] Public-spending cuts on this scale inevitably inflict serious damage on poor communities. They erode the quality of service provision and increase the financial burden on poor households, which are left to cover through user fees the financing gap that is created by the withdrawal of State spending.

In some respects, exercises comparing public spending before and after IMF programmes are of limited relevance. The really important question is whether or not spending levels are compatible with a commitment to achieving social goals such as universal primary education, or good-quality public health care. In countries where average spending on basic healthcare is less than half of the amount required to provide access to health clinics and essential drugs, marginal movements in per capita spending are, at best, a limited indicator of progress. The same principle applies to education. It may be justified for the IMF to point out that, in recent years, the Tanzanian education budget has been protected under its programmes. But this budget is providing for levels of spending per student of less than $1 – far too low to meet even the most basic requirements for good-quality, universal primary education.

The broader consequences of the IMF macro-economic programme on household incomes are of crucial importance for education. Overall economic-growth performance ultimately determines the financing capacity of governments. Combined with income distribution, it also has a powerful bearing on household poverty. There are formidable problems in addressing the impact of IMF programmes in these areas, not least among them the problem of assessing what might have happened in the absence of an IMF programme. Cross-country comparisons can provide some insights, but the results that emerge depend heavily on the selection of countries and reference years. Such evidence as there is suggests that any benefits for economic growth have been exceptionally modest.

In 1997, an IMF review of its programmes in low-income countries found that growth rates had increased by only 0.5 per cent a year. Many of the core targets set had been missed. For instance, only about half of the targeted reduction in budget deficits was achieved, and progress in reducing inflation was limited.[68] More recently, in 1999, the IMF produced a more upbeat assessment covering the period 1995–1998. This claimed that per capita incomes were rising at an average of over 2 per cent a year in African countries with IMF programmes.[69] The problem is that much of this increase can be traced to the exceptionally strong performance of just two countries – Mozambique and Uganda – and to a marked improvement in world prices for primary commodities, on which most countries with IMF programmes depend. The decline in world commodity prices in 1998 had the effect of reducing average per capita income growth for the period 1995–1999 to around 1 per cent per annum.

It is in fact hazardous to arrive at any conclusion from the highly politicised use of statistics that characterises debate on IMF programmes. The most thorough independent review reaches the conclusion that the benefits of these programmes in terms of increased growth have been modest, and that investment levels – the key to future growth – have stagnated.[70] What is absolutely clear is that growth performance under IMF programmes in Africa has been far too weak to halve income poverty by 2015, as envisaged under the international development targets. It has also been too weak to generate the revenues needed to sustain public investment in education at the levels required to achieve universal primary education by the same date.

Data limitations have made the debate on the relationship between IMF programmes and income distribution even more confused than the debate on growth. However, there is little evidence to support the view that improved income distribution has counteracted the effects of low growth by disproportionately raising the incomes of the poor. Distributional problems appear to have hampered progress towards poverty reduction, even in some of the stronger-performing countries. For instance, the incidence of rural poverty in Uganda fell by 10 per cent between 1992 and 1996 as a result of rapidly rising average incomes. However, whereas poverty-reduction rates among cash-crop producers in the Central region fell at twice the national average rate, they fell at less than one-third of the national rate among food-crop producers.[71] Similar distributional patterns have been reported for Ghana, where poverty rates among staple-food producers in the northern Savannah region are declining far more slowly than the national average. These distributional outcomes cannot be directly attributed to IMF policy. They reflect a more generalised failure on the part of governments to focus on the macro-economic requirements for growth, to the exclusion of distributional considerations. But the IMF itself is a key part of this problem, since its programmes have been built almost entirely around macro-economic targets, with scant regard for issues of distributional equity.

Adjustment in operation: the cases of Zambia and Zimbabwe

Adjustment programmes are not developed in a vacuum. They are introduced into countries suffering deep economic problems, often including large budget deficits and declining incomes. There are seldom pain-free options for resolving these problems. But the degree of pain associated with IMF policies in the 1990s was intensified by poor programme design, with devastating implications for progress towards the targets set at the World Conference on Education for All. This can be illustrated by reference to two countries that were seen as flagship programmes in the first half of the 1990s.

One of the core objectives in IMF programmes is to achieve low inflation. Policies designed to achieve this end place a premium on reducing government budget deficits, through a combination of expenditure cuts and increased revenue. These short-term budgetary objectives are integrated into a wider structural reform agenda developed by the IMF and the World Bank. While the objectives vary from country to country, loan conditions typically prioritise the liberalisation of agricultural markets, reduced taxes on higher-income groups, trade liberalisation, and privatisation. The IMF programme adopted in Zambia in 1991 reflected these priorities.[72] Under the programme, the government was required to reduce public expenditure by an amount equivalent to 4 per cent of GDP. Loan conditions also required the rapid liberalisation of agricultural markets and financial markets. From the outset, the programme was plagued by poor planning, a flawed sequencing of reforms, and inadequate attention to the protection of basic services.

Actual cuts in public spending were far deeper than initially planned, partly because of over-optimistic projections about inflation (which soared with the removal of price controls and financial liberalisation). Public spending on activity not related to debt servicing or drought fell by more than 5 per cent of GDP between 1992 and 1994. By 1995, the education budget was 25 per cent lower than it had been at the start of the adjustment programme in 1991. Cost recovery at the school level was increased in an effort to maintain financing. Even in remote rural areas with the most intense poverty, entry costs for school, taking into account various payments in kind, were increased to the equivalent of around $5. Cost recovery was also increased in the health sector, placing further demands on household incomes. These were falling, partly as a consequence of drought, and partly because the withdrawal of the government from agricultural markets led to the collapse of the marketing system. The government and the World Bank had intended to facilitate the emergence of private-sector alternatives by expanding the supply of credit to traders. In the event, most of this credit found its way into government Treasury bills, which were being issued at high interest rates (another consequence of financial liberalisation). For poor producers, one-third of whom live 20 kilometres or more from the nearest market-trading centre, the collapse of the marketing system was devastating. Many were left unable to market their crops in the year after the drought, and this fact intensified their poverty. Between 1991 and 1994, small-holders' incomes are estimated to have fallen by an average of one-third, and by considerably more in remote rural areas. At the end of 1993, the World Bank conducted a national poverty assessment which found that 'the issue of rising costs of education was frequently raised as a problem at the level of the household'. In terms of Zambia's progress towards the goal of universal primary education, the impact of the IMF programme was devastating. Over the period 1990–96, the enrolment rate fell by 14 per cent, leaving the estimated out-of-school population at over half a million.

Many of the mistakes made in Zambia were repeated in Zimbabwe. Here, too, ambitious targets were set for reducing the size of the budget deficit. Under the Framework for Economic Reform, a national budget deficit that was equivalent to 10 per cent of GDP was to be halved between 1991 and 1995.[73] Tax rates on high-income groups and companies were to be reduced at the same time, in an effort to boost investment. The implications of the tax cuts for government revenue meant that the budget-deficit target would have to be achieved mainly through expenditure reductions. These turned out to be far more severe than expected. So steep were the tax cuts (equivalent to 4 per cent of GDP) that government revenue fell by more than was planned.[74] At the same time, financial-market liberalisation resulted in increased payments of government debt. Since payment of this debt was a statutory obligation, government spending on this item had to rise, while government revenue was falling. Wildly optimistic projections for economic growth built into the IMF framework (5 per cent per annum, as against an actual performance of 1 per cent per annum) further reduced the revenue available to governments. It followed that the burden of adjusting to the target for reducing the budget deficit would fall heavily on unprotected budget areas, including healthcare and education. The impact on the education system was devastating. The two halves of Figure 5.14 show the impact of declining government revenue and rising debt payments on education spending. They show that real spending per student in primary school fell by 40 per cent over the period 1990–1995, to the lowest level in real terms since the early 1980s.[75] The budget for primary health care was also cut by one-third in per capita terms, leading to chronic shortages of drugs and rising costs of health treatment.

The fact that growth rates did not match expectation was partly attributable to drought. But from the perspective of education financing, the important point was that no attempt was made to adjust either the budget-deficit target or the reduction in tax rates to protect social-sector provision. Discounting debt repayments, government spending fell by the equivalent of 7 per cent of GDP in the first half of the 1990s.[76] In a context marked by drought and stagnation, the consequences were inevitably severe. As in Zambia, the squeeze on public spending increased the financing burden on poor households. Cost recovery was introduced for primary health clinics, leading to a catastrophic decline in attendance among the poor. In education, cost recovery was introduced for urban primary schools. Officially, rural schools were exempted, but household surveys captured a sharp increase in costs associated with informal fees and rising prices for uniforms and textbooks. By the end of 1992 these costs were estimated at over $11. Given that around 40 per cent of Zimbabwe's population was living on an income below the poverty line of $1 a day at the start of the adjustment programme, and that per capita incomes in rural areas were lower in 1995 than in 1991, this represented a huge burden.[77]

Six rounds of household surveys carried out by UNICEF in Zimbabwe between 1991 and 1996 dramatically illustrated the financial pressures experienced by poor households, partly as a consequence of IMF programme design. The surveys found a marked increase in the number of children out of school, along with clear evidence of financial distress linked to school fees. In 1993, almost one-third of households with children cited unaffordability as the reason for their absence. By 1995, 44 per cent cited high cost as the reason for not sending their children to school.[78] The importance of cost increased with the age range covered, with two-thirds of parents of out-of-school children in the age range of 13 to 17 years reporting financial problems as the main factor.[79] Many other households reported having to deplete household savings in order to meet the costs of sending their children to school – a fact reflecting the high value placed on education by poor rural communities.

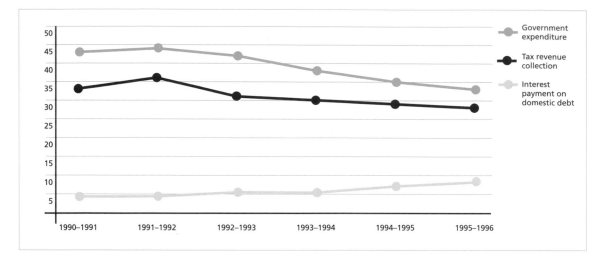

Figure 5.14(a)
Zimbabwe: revenue collection, domestic-debt repayments, and budget expenditure, 1990-96, as percentages of GDP

Sources:
Zimbabwe: Recent Economic Developments, IMF, 1996;
The Public Sector and Poverty Reduction Options,
World Bank, 1996

Social hardship would have been a feature of any adjustment process in Zimbabwe, even under more favourable economic conditions. But, as the External Review of IMF programmes concluded in 1998, 'Social hardship was avoidably severe because of poor programme design.'[80]

Issues in IMF programme design for low-income countries

Reform of the IMF is seldom off the international agenda. However, in recent years the reform debate has intensified – and nowhere more so than in relation to the IMF's role in low-income countries. The outcome of this debate will have important implications for progress towards the international development targets for human development.

Poverty reduction has become a central theme on the IMF reform agenda. The Fund will play an important role in defining the macro-economic elements required in the Poverty Reduction Strategy Papers (PRSPs) discussed earlier. By the same token, IMF programmes and loan conditions will have to take into account the poverty-reduction goals and strategies adopted in the PRSPs. Some of the changes introduced so far may be more cosmetic than real, including the decision to rename the Enhanced Structural Adjustment Facility (ESAF), the lending programme for low-income countries, as the Poverty Reduction and Growth Facility. But there is a real sense in which the PRSP process has brought the issues of poverty and human development to prominence in the IMF's remit.

There is one view, strongly held in the US Treasury and Congress, as well as among some non-government organisations, that the IMF should not be involved in lending to low-income countries. It is argued that IMF programmes are not appropriate in countries contending with long-term development problems. In fact, the lending issue is almost completely

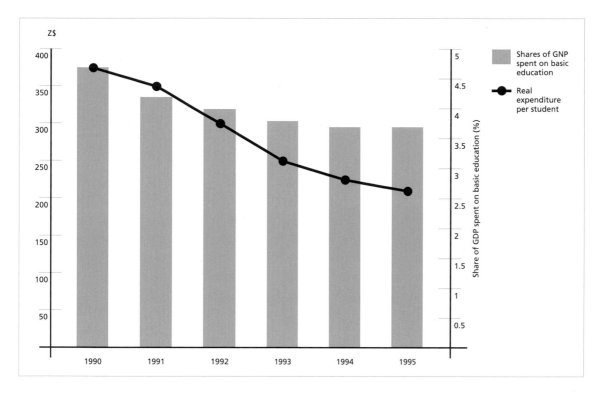

Figure 5.14(b)
Zimbabwe: Trends in per capita primary-pupil spending and shares of education in GNP (1990-95)

Sources:
Zimbabwe: Recent Economic Developments, IMF, 1996;
The Public Sector and Poverty Reduction Options, World Bank, 1996

irrelevant to the real debate. The transfer of finance from the IMF to low-income countries is modest, and in some years negative (with repayments exceeding new loans). What gives the IMF its unique authority is not its lending, but the view of Northern governments that it remains the most effective judge of policies for achieving macro-economic stability. This view is unlikely to change in the near future. It follows that the real debate should be about the substantive reforms needed to make the IMF more effective in addressing the challenge of poverty reduction.

Some of these reforms emerge clearly from the previous analysis. Setting budget targets that lead to deep cuts in social-sector provision is not an acceptable practice at a time when the Fund's major shareholders in the G7 are signing up to ambitious international development targets. But the IMF needs to go beyond safeguarding priority social-sector budgets. If the international development targets are to be achieved, they have to be reflected in budget provisions. That means placing poverty reduction at the heart of IMF programming – a place previously occupied by narrowly defined monetary goals. Gearing budgets towards the international development targets involves more than reviewing trends in public spending. It also demands that public spending should reflect a commitment to the provision of free primary education and affordable

283

public healthcare. As the interlocutor in dialogues between donors and governments on budget priorities, the IMF has a key role to play. Learning from the mistakes made in countries like Zambia and Zimbabwe, the Fund also needs to build into programme design an element of risk assessment and contingency planning. Public-spending plans need to be constantly reassessed in the light of revenue shortfalls, slower than expected growth, and other unexpected outcomes that threaten government capacity to maintain basic services.

There is a strong case to be made for tolerance of modest budget deficits in the interests of increasing public spending on aspects of social and economic infrastructure that are vital to growth.

One of the main problems with IMF programmes as they are currently designed is that they set over-stringent targets for reducing budget deficits, usually with a view to achieving budget surpluses. These targets result in excessively high interest rates and the compression of demand, both of which are partly responsible for the low investment and weak growth achieved under structural adjustment. While the IMF's programme approach may be justified in countries suffering chronic macro-economic stability, its continuation into the post-stabilisation period creates serious problems.[81] There is a strong case to be made for tolerance of modest budget deficits in the interests of increasing public spending on aspects of social and economic infrastructure that are vital to growth. For instance, Tanzania's IMF programme targets a budget surplus equivalent to 2 per cent of GDP. In a context where school infrastructure is in a dire state and where the quality of education is suffering for want of the most basic teaching materials, the costs of meeting the IMF target may out-weigh any benefits in terms of reduced inflation. One recent government review of public expenditure concluded that the budget target represent-ed 'a harder budget constraint than is necessary at present'.[82] The IMF itself has acknowledged the case for more flexibility on targets for budget deficits, but it remains to be seen what this means in practice.

One of the most contentious issues in IMF programme design concerns the treatment of foreign aid. This relates to the problem of budget deficits. In broad terms, the objective under IMF programmes has been to ensure that government spending does not exceed revenue. The problem is that the IMF does not include foreign aid as revenue, partly on the grounds that aid flows are uncertain; and partly because high levels of aid spending today may leave governments with schools and health clinics that they cannot afford to run tomorrow. In countries where aid transfers can amount to 4–5 per cent of GDP, as they do in Africa, the Fund's approach severely restricts the public-spending capacity of governments. This has been a source of tension between the IMF on the one hand and many donors, governments, and the World Bank on the other. As a former Chief Economist of the World Bank has argued, in countries that have an assured supply of development assistance, 'it may make sense for the government to treat aid as a legitimate source of revenue, just like taxes'.[83] This view has powerful implications for education policy, where relatively modest increases in public investment can produce very large gains in terms of improving access and the quality of service provision.

The problems facing the IMF as it seeks to define a role for itself in the development of poverty-reduction strategies are complex. In the past, it has focused its efforts on budget-management policies designed to achieve low inflation. This will remain an important task, because high inflation is bad for macro-economic stability, and for long-term social-sector financing. But judgements on inflation have to be based on a broader set of criteria. Increased spending on, say, rural feeder roads, might have the effect of increasing inflation initially, but later, as increased output comes on stream, it can reduce inflation, boost growth, and reduce household poverty. Similarly, increasing investment in education may mean that more children leave school with the skills they need to increase productivity and reduce vulnerability, again generating important benefits for growth and distribution. These trade-offs must be considered as part and parcel of any public-spending planning exercise. In the past, however, there has been no public debate about what criteria should be used to make decisions, and no public assessment of what any decisions made might mean for poverty reduction. Whatever its other shortcomings, the PRSP framework could provide a mechanism for addressing this problem.

East Asia's experience provides a timely reminder that financial problems in global markets have a human dimension.

Lessons from the East Asia crisis

The failure of Northern governments to address the debt crisis in Latin America during the 1980s contributed to a 'lost decade' for human development, with poverty increasing and social infrastructure deteriorating. In the 1990s, failure to resolve the debt crisis in the poorest countries has hampered progress towards universal primary education and poverty reduction. More recently, the financial crisis in East Asia has revealed new threats to human welfare, to which Northern governments have again failed to respond. These threats can be traced to the extraordinary increase in private-capital flows and the instability of the international financial system.

East Asia's experience provides a timely reminder that financial problems in global markets have a human dimension. What started as a financial crisis rapidly became a social crisis, as economic collapse was transmitted to households in the form of rising unemployment, declining incomes, and cuts in public spending. Education systems have not been insulated from the social consequences. Rising poverty and the diminishing capacity of States to maintain education infrastructures has stalled progress towards universal basic education, intensifying pre-crisis problems in the process. There is now a grave danger that widening inequalities in education will reinforce income inequalities and restrict prospects of economic growth, with damaging implications for poverty reduction. Reform of global capital markets represents one of the greatest human-development challenges facing the international community. Social-policy problems seldom figure prominently in debates over the reform of international financial markets. Yet it is increasingly clear that more efficient – and more equitable – management of globalisation is a prerequisite for achieving the 2015 human-development targets. The question is whether international co-operation is capable of producing a more effective response than it did to the debt problems of Latin America and Africa.

The impact of the financial crisis on education

Over the three decades before the financial crisis struck, East Asia had been more successful than any other developing region in reducing poverty. It was the only region on track for achieving the international development goal of halving the incidence of income poverty. Other indicators for human welfare were also improving. Economic-growth rates averaging more than 6 per cent a year, relatively equal income distribution, and increasing public provision of basic services were behind the social progress achieved in the region.[84]

The financial crisis changed the social and economic landscape in East Asia with dramatic effect.[85] During 1998, the economies of Indonesia and Thailand contracted by 14 per cent and 8 per cent respectively. Inflation became rampant. Unemployment in Indonesia, South Korea, and Thailand rose from 5 million in 1996 to 15 million in 1998. As national economies went into rapid decline, household incomes fell. In Indonesia, average incomes fell by 25–30 per cent during 1997–98. Estimates of the impact on income poverty vary, but it is probable that the incidence almost doubled in Indonesia, leaving another 18 million people below the poverty line.

Before the financial crisis, rapid increases in average incomes had been accompanied by sustained improvements in education. By 1994, two-thirds of all Indonesians had at least a primary education, compared with fewer than one-quarter in the early 1970s.[86] Access to primary school among children aged 6–11 was almost universal both in Indonesia and

Thailand. In Thailand, enrolment rates for lower-secondary school had reached 72 per cent by the mid-1990s. Despite these achievements, both Indonesia and Thailand faced acute problems, which were to be exacerbated by the economic crisis.

Although the increased enrolment rates in junior-secondary school in Indonesia had been impressive, one-third of the children completing primary school did not go on to junior-secondary school in the mid-1990s. Another 20 per cent of those children enrolling in primary school did not complete their education. Drop-out rates were especially high in Outer Islands such as Irian Jaya and West Kalimantan, reflecting the failure of the education system to overcome problems associated with poverty.[87] Improvements in education quality had lagged behind improvements in the coverage of the education system. One national literacy test in the early 1990s found that only about half of junior-secondary school students met minimum standards.

In Thailand, the National Education Development Scheme, introduced in 1992, was an attempt to address structural weaknesses that had intensified during the 1980s as the rapidly growing high-technology sectors of the economy generated demand for an increased supply of skilled workers. The education system had been unable to meet this demand. While enrolments at the junior-secondary level had increased dramatically, only one-quarter of children progressed through to the upper-secondary level. One of the consequences of the mismatch between labour-market demand for skilled workers and the supply of secondary-school graduates was a widening wage gap, with the unskilled being left behind. Between the mid-1970s and 1995, Thailand had one of the world's fastest-growing rates of inequality, with the national Gini coefficient increasing by 10 percentage points. According to the World Bank, one-third of the increase in inequality was directly attributable to education differences between the skilled and unskilled.[88]

Consequences for education

Some of the most severe effects of the financial crisis on education were experienced in Indonesia. Primary-school enrolments were affected, with the number of children of primary-school age not in school increasing by 3 per cent in 1998.[89] But the impact was far stronger at the secondary level, where enrolment rates for children aged 13–19 fell by 11 per cent. Drop-out rates also increased. At the primary-school level, rural areas were affected worse than urban areas, with this picture being reversed at the secondary-school level.

Figure 5.15
Drop-out rates in Indonesia, 1997-98: differences based on gender and income

Source:
Education in Crisis: the Impact and Lessons of the East Asian Financial Shock, World Bank, 2000

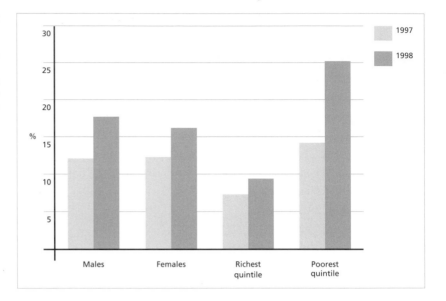

Economic crises hurt both the poor and the non-poor, but their consequences are far more devastating for those who live already under or just above the poverty line. Poor people lack the savings to help them through bad times, and they lack access to insurance schemes. In Indonesia, the differential effects of economic crisis on the poor and non-poor were particularly marked in education.[90] For the poorest quintile of children aged 13–19, the drop-out rate almost doubled between 1997 and 1998, increasing from 14 per cent to 25 per cent (Figure 5.15). Among children from the richest quintile, the increase was far more modest, with the drop-out rate rising by 2 per cent from a much lower starting point. These differences underlined the inability of poor households to absorb the rising costs of education in declining budgets. Even before the crisis, the cost of sending a child to junior-secondary school in Indonesia represented the equivalent of 40 per cent of average household expenditure among the poorest quintile of the population.

Assessing the impact of the regional financial crisis on education in Thailand is very difficult, because data for pre- and post-crisis years were inadequately reported. While the effects were less powerful than in Indonesia, they were still severe. According to the Asian Development Bank, almost one-fifth of children dropped out of lower-secondary in 1998, while fully one-third dropped out of upper-secondary school. The drop-out rate for the poor during the 1998–99 school year was almost double that for the non-poor.[91]

Enrolment and drop-out data capture only one aspect of the impact of the financial crisis on education. Rising household poverty had far wider implications. One of the most alarming aspects of the crisis in Indonesia was a marked deterioration in public health and nutritional status. One survey in 1998 found that iron-deficiency anaemia, which impairs the immune system and the intellectual development of children, affected two out of three children – far more than in the mid-1980s. In Thailand, household surveys found poor parents resorting to increasingly desperate strategies to keep their children in school, including the sale of assets, borrowing money, and reducing consumption in other areas. One such survey, carried out by the Foundation for Children's Development, included intensive interviews with 143 poor rural households.[92] It found that prices for notepads and uniforms had increased by more than 50 per cent and that school-lunch provisions had been cut, thus raising the costs of education to parents. More than one-third of the households reported having fallen into debt as a consequence of rising education costs.

Government budgets for education were slashed by the financial crisis, especially in Indonesia. Real spending on education fell by more than one-third during the two years after the crisis.[93] The health-services budget was cut by a similar amount.[94] In education, the reductions in public spending were absorbed in declining salaries for teachers, reductions in textbook provision, and fewer school meals. In the health sector, spending on essential drugs for health centres fell by more than 40 per cent, at a time when inflation was placing alternative supplies beyond the means of the poor. This retrenchment in public spending meant that the ability of the State to protect the poor was being eroded, at the same time as rising poverty made State action more essential.

The impact of the financial crisis on the education systems of East Asia draws attention to the severe human-development risks associated with failure to manage globalisation more effectively. Sustained improvements in the access of poor people to education have been among the most important reasons for the rapid poverty-reduction achieved in the past. They have contributed to more rapid and more equitable patterns of economic growth than have been achieved in other developing regions, and to advances in public health. There is now a real danger that this virtuous circle will be pushed into reverse. The exclusion of poor people from education poses the risk of lower economic growth, with increasingly unequal distribution of the benefits. This underlines the importance of managing global capital markets far more effectively, not just to protect international financial stability, but also to advance human development in the poorest countries.

Underlying causes and the international response

The financial crisis in East Asia was only one in a series that marked the second half of the 1990s. It was preceded by the Mexican crisis, which Michel Camdessus, then Managing Director of the IMF, pronounced as 'the first banking crisis of the twenty-first century'. He was referring to the onset of a new systemic risk to the global financial system, linked to the emergence of a highly volatile international capital market. Events in East Asia, and the subsequent contagion effects across Latin America, confirmed the extent of that risk. The fuel for the East Asian crisis was provided by weak domestic policies, including weakly regulated banking systems, over-valued currencies, and unaccountable governments. But the torch was applied by institutional investors in global capital markets. More effective – and more equitable — management of these markets is vital if more rapid progress towards the international development targets is to be achieved.

During the 1990s, most countries in East Asia opened their financial systems to foreign investors. Attracted by a combination of high growth and currencies that were fixed against the US dollar (thereby removing exchange-rate risks), capital flooded in. Some of it was directed towards long-term investment, but short-term speculative flows became increasingly important. Between 1993 and 1997, dollar lending to Indonesia doubled, with almost two-thirds of the new funds coming in the form of short-term loans directed towards the corporate sector and stock markets. The surge in capital flows was reflected across the region in speculative stock-market bubbles, spiralling property prices, and rapid increases in short-term debt. Exchange-rate appreciation, another consequence of heavy capital inflows, undermined export competitiveness and generated large current-account deficits.[95] It was the combination of rising debt and large current-account deficits that led to speculative attacks on East Asian currencies. The fragility of the system became evident as these collapsed like dominoes, causing investors to panic in the process. In 1996, the inflow of funds into East Asia amounted to $97bn. In 1997, the outflow was $12bn – a turnaround equivalent to 11 per cent of GDP.[96] Local financial systems were left with a huge dollar-denominated debt burden, while the costs of servicing the debt were escalating as the value of local currencies fell. The deeper problem was not so much that underlying macro-economic conditions were weak. These were still high-growth economies characterised by low inflation, sound budget management, and strong investment. The catalyst for collapse was the herd mentality of foreign investors, who generated a self-perpetuating financial panic based on changed perceptions of risk.[97]

The extent of the crisis posed Northern governments with an enormous challenge. What was needed was an international response aimed at preventing a financial crisis from becoming a deeper social and economic crisis. There were three immediate requirements. First, the creation of an expansionary economic environment, with public spending used to protect employment and basic services. Second, action to prevent the emergence of a debt crisis. Third, measures to protect the poor during a difficult adjustment period. The international response failed on all three counts.

Any industrialised country facing a recession in a climate of low inflation would respond by reducing interest rates and increasing public spending, as both the United States and Japan did in the 1990s.[98] In East Asia, the IMF was given responsibility by Northern governments for responding to the crisis, both by using its own resources, and by acting as the gatekeeper for the wider international rescue effort. Unfortunately, the lending conditions defined by the IMF were entirely inappropriate, with a bias towards economic austerity, reduced public spending, and high interest rates. In Thailand and Indonesia, governments were instructed to target budget surpluses equivalent to 1–2 per cent of GDP. This measure prolonged and deepened the recession, with the devastating implications for household poverty and education summarised above.[99]

Given that unsustainable foreign debt was one of the most immediate causes of the crisis, early action to reschedule or reduce creditors' claims was essential.

Given that unsustainable foreign debt was one of the most immediate causes of the crisis, early action to reschedule or reduce creditors' claims was essential. Here too the IMF failed to provide leadership. Between 1996 and 1998, Indonesia's external debt stock rose from a level equivalent to 60 per cent of GDP to 146 per cent. As in the low-income countries discussed earlier, one of the consequences of unsustainable debt is the diversion of public spending away from high-priority basic services. During 1998, the Indonesian government allocated more than one-fifth of its revenue to debt servicing, at a time when the budgets for education and health were being subjected to deep cuts.[100] Efforts were made to protect poor households from the effects of the crisis, through targeted social-welfare interventions. These met with varying degrees of success. In Indonesia, the World Bank and the Asian Development committed around $400m to the government's Back-to-School Campaign. This is intended to provide scholarships to more than 6 million children, and block grants to more than 60 per cent of primary and junior-secondary schools.[101] One of the problems with the campaign is that it was not launched until one year after the onset of the crisis. While some interim efforts were made, serious problems were reported in targeting, with many of the poorest regions – especially the Outer Islands – being neglected. The response appears to have been more effective in Thailand, where international assistance was channelled through already well-established scholarship funds for primary and secondary-school children, and various subsidised loan schemes. In 1999, subsidised loans were being provided for almost 700,000 children – four times as many as in 1996. Targeted transfers through the education budget meant that overall public-spending cuts in Thailand were far less severe than in Indonesia, and that poor households were less severely affected.[102]

Reform of global financial markets

Reform of the global financial system is not a subject commonly associated with international debate on the 2015 targets for human development. In the immediate aftermath of the East Asian crisis, there was much talk of the need for 'a new global financial architecture'. As the perceived threat to Western financial systems has receded, so has political interest in developing this agenda. Yet financial crises continue to present a powerful – and increasing – threat to sustained progress in poverty reduction.

Several lessons emerge from the policy mistakes made in East Asia. The first is that crisis prevention is better than crisis response. For poor households, the losses of income, assets, and opportunities for education that they suffered during the crisis cannot easily be recovered. Restoring stability is also costly, as evidenced by the $100bn spent by Northern governments in East Asia. One of the requirements for crisis prevention is the protection of capital markets in developing countries. Of all the economic reforms implemented in the 1990s, financial liberalisation stands out for having generated the fewest benefits, while causing the most serious disruption. The combination of open capital accounts, weak regulation of the financial sector, and volatile short-term capital flows has been responsible for a succession of financial crises. Several countries – such as Chile and Malaysia – have responded to the threat posed by surges of speculative capital, either by taxing short-term capital transfers or by restricting market access.[103] However, the US Treasury is strongly opposed to capital controls and favours reforming the IMF's mandate to give it more authority to liberalise financial markets and open them to foreign investors. From a poverty-reduction perspective, this is short-sighted in the extreme. There is no evidence to support the view that capital-account liberalisation is beneficial for economic growth, and considerable evidence that it is bad for economic stability.[104] Most of the potential beneficiaries are located on Wall Street and other financial centres; most of the potential victims are poor households in developing countries, who bear the adjustment costs associated with reduced public spending, slow growth, and rising unemployment.

Northern governments themselves have a central role to play in regulating markets, since the major institutional players are banks and financial institutions located in Northern countries. Measures are needed to reduce the scope for speculative lending, for example by imposing more stringent requirements on banks to back high-risk investments with reserves.[105] One measure that might help to dampen excessive speculative activity is taxation on activity in currency markets. The introduction of a small tax of around 0.1 per cent on foreign-exchange transactions would act as a disincentive to speculative activity, while at the same time generating potential revenues in the order of $200bn.[106] Capturing even a small share of this revenue for priority investments in education and health care could help to accelerate progress towards the 2015 target.

At present, the main beneficiaries of debt relief in the event of financial crisis are the commercial banks and foreign investors who are being 'bailed out' by IMF loans, most of which are recycled to repay creditors.

When financial crises strike, a rapid, well-co-ordinated response is essential. At present, there are no international financing mechanisms available with resources on the scale required. The mechanisms that are available are provided under IMF auspices, a fact that has been damaging for economic recovery and poverty. As with its programmes in low-income countries, the IMF needs to reform its programmes so that they do not apply a single blueprint, based on financial austerity and deflation. Effective debt relief is another vital ingredient for successful crisis-response. At present, the main beneficiaries of debt relief in the event of financial crisis are the commercial banks and foreign investors who are being 'bailed out' by IMF loans, most of which are recycled to repay creditors. New rules are needed to ensure that private creditors accept the consequences of unsound high-risk investment decisions, by providing debt reduction when markets prove those decisions to be flawed. This, after all, is how markets are supposed to work. Allowing poor populations to suffer the consequences of unsustainable debt through rising poverty and diminishing opportunities for education is not an acceptable alternative.

Finally, targeted social-welfare funds clearly have a role to play, but poverty-reduction strategies need to be integrated far more carefully into macro-economic design. In East Asia, the development and implementation of social-welfare programmes did not really take effect until well after the event, and long after the IMF loan conditions had defined the macro-economic environment in which these programmes would operate. The division of labour that emerged was one in which the IMF assumed responsibility for macro-economic reform, while the World Bank assumed responsibility for social welfare. The fact that IMF loan conditions were reinforcing the very problems that social-welfare programmes were designed to address graphically underlined the need for a more coherent and comprehensive framework.

6

Partnerships for change: States and NGOs in education reform

Ultimate responsibility for securing the right to education rests squarely with national governments. International aid has an important role to play, especially in the poorest countries, but it cannot substitute for effective State action. The same is true for non-government organisations (NGOs). These play an important role in providing educational opportunities to communities and social groups that might otherwise be excluded, filling the gap left by the State. But no country has achieved universal primary education in the absence of effective State action.

The proposition that governments have primary responsibility for education is not a defence of existing approaches to education reform. In many countries, the education sector has been blighted by over-centralised planning. Communities have been seen not as active participants in the reform process, but as passive recipients of education services designed and delivered by unaccountable bureaucracies. There are few other services for which poor people pay so much, but over which they have such limited influence. The results have been predictable. Ignorant about the constraints and specific problems facing communities that are excluded from the system, education planners have often been unable to respond to their needs. Oblivious to the constraints of gender, they have failed to remove the barriers that exclude young girls from school. Unwilling to develop curricula that correspond to the perceived needs of poor people, they provide an education that many see as profoundly irrelevant. Instead of developing child-centred approaches to learning, teacher-training programmes are often designed to transmit information through rote-learning, with children seen as passive recipients of knowledge, rather than as active participants in an education process.

Reforming education is a complex process. School systems are not insulated from the wider social system, or from the poverty, power relations, gender-determined differences, and wider inequalities that permeate it. Schools themselves are a point of contact between a diverse array of actors: governments, communities, parents, teachers, and children. Collaboration between these actors is crucial to successful policy reform. It is sometimes forgotten that education reform is also a political process. It implies changes in public attitudes, policy priorities, and power relations in education, and it has implications for the distribution of benefits in areas such as taxation and public spending. Success in education reform is not just about identifying 'good policies': it is also a matter of building the broad democratic alliance and consensus needed to underpin the reform process.

The role of the State is central to education reform. Disenchantment with centralised, bureaucratic, and inflexible State planning led, in the 1980s, to a global tendency to reduce the role of the State. Concern over the inefficiency of governments as service providers prompted many donors to place an emphasis on the development of NGOs and the private sector as an alternative.[1] In the 1990s, the pendulum began to swing back again, as it became increasingly evident that private initiative could not deliver progress on the scale required. There is today a broad recognition that the achievement of good-quality universal primary education requires a balanced approach in which States are revitalised by drawing on innovative actions developed by non-government providers. Conversely, effective action by NGOs requires a strategy for scaling up local intervention through State action to achieve a wider dispersal of benefits.

The achievement of good-quality universal primary education requires a balanced approach in which States are revitalised by drawing on innovative actions developed by non-government providers.

The real challenge, therefore, is to enhance the performance of public institutions by improving their accountability, increasing their efficiency, and making them more open to public participation; and to improve the efficiency of non-government interventions by expanding small-scale initiatives to reach a far wider group of beneficiaries. Such partnerships are already emerging. They are improving the quality and efficiency of State agencies, enabling them to develop innovative strategies that are reaching communities previously excluded from education services, while at the same time increasing the impact of non-government interventions.

This chapter examines the changing relationship between governments and civil society. The first part considers what States have done, and what they can do, to make universal primary education possible. It describes examples of successful State action to overcome constraints associated with poverty and low income. The second part examines the changing relationship between States and non-government organisations, pointing out the dangers inherent in the emergence of parallel systems of education provision. The third part reviews a number of cases where partnerships between government and NGOs have been successful. The common feature of these partnerships is that they have been built on community participation, with governments scaling up imaginative and innovative ideas developed at the community level into district-wide and national plans, thus improving the coverage and quality of education systems.

State action for universal primary education

The goal of achieving universal primary education poses a daunting challenge. Tens of millions of new school places must be created, educational opportunities must be extended to marginalised social groups, and the quality of education must be dramatically improved. All of this has to happen in countries with high levels of poverty and scarce public finance. Faced with the gap between resources and needs, it is unsurprising that the capacity of States to deliver universal primary education has been called into question.

Debate about State responsibility and capacity to provide mass education in societies marked by extreme poverty is not new. There was one country which had a protracted debate about the desirability of introducing free and compulsory universal primary education, extending over almost 50 years. Millions of children from poor households were not in school. Those who were in school received education of very poor quality. Successive governments took the view that mass public education was beyond the financial capacity of the State, leaving voluntary providers to maintain services. The argument that education should be wholly funded through general taxation was regarded as preposterous, and potentially ruinous of national prosperity. Yet when the foundations for a national school system were finally established, the results were extraordinary. Within the space of ten years, the number of children in State schools increased from fewer than 10,000 to more than one million. Over the next ten years, numbers doubled again. True, the education was of a scandalously poor quality and – for the poor – of short duration, but the political decision to make universal primary education possible had, within a few short years, established the foundations of a national education system.

The country in question was Britain, during the 20 years after the introduction of the 1870 Education Act.[2] Comparisons with the challenges facing developing countries today may seem far-fetched. After all, Britain was at that time the world's pre-eminent industrial power. But the British example is germane for at least two reasons. First, notions about the appropriate role of the State and the affordability of universal primary education changed dramatically over a relatively short space of time. Social reformers, trade unions, and some of the country's more forward-looking industrialists succeeded in changing public attitudes and political priorities. Second, education became part of a wider social reform movement, linked to the development of political rights.

The case of Uganda

As argued in Chapter 4, what is feasible in education is determined as much by political choice as by average income levels. If poverty were the main determinant of State capacity, a country such as Uganda ought to be a poor performer. Until the mid-1990s it was so: almost one in three children of primary-school age were not in school. Drop-out rates were high, with only one-quarter of girls progressing to Grade 6. High education costs – equivalent to about one-fifth of average income – were excluding poor children from school. Government spending reflected a low level of commitment to education, and a high level of inequity. Just over 1 per cent of GDP was allocated to the education budget, almost half of it to higher education. From this unpromising starting point, in the space of the two years between 1996 and 1998, the number of children enrolled in primary school almost doubled, with more than two million additional children coming into the system. The net enrolment rate increased from 54 per cent, less than the sub-Saharan African average, to more than 80 per cent.[3] Large numbers of over-age children who had dropped out of school have registered again.

The catalyst for change was the government's Universal Primary Education (UPE) programme. Introduced in 1997, the programme provides free primary education for four children from every family, significantly reducing cost barriers. This is part of a wider strategy aimed at achieving universal primary education by 2003, allied to a 65 per cent transition rate from primary to lower-secondary school. Ambitious goals have been set for the 2003 target date, including the construction of 25,000 class-rooms, the provision of water and sanitation for all schools, a free set of primary-school textbooks for all children, and an extensive teacher-training programme. Strong economic growth has helped to mobilise new financial resources, but the targets have been backed by a reorientation of public-spending priorities. Public spending on education has increased from 1.6 per cent of GNP in the early 1990s to almost 4 per cent today.[4] Most of the additional resources have been directed towards basic education, which now accounts for around two-thirds of the education budget, compared with only half in 1990. Development co-operation has played an important role. Donors have pledged $70–80m per annum throughout the plan period – equivalent to around one-quarter of total spending. Budgetary resources released through debt relief under the IMF/World Bank's Highly Indebted Poor Countries (HIPC) Initiative have also played an important role, enabling the government to divert resources from debt servicing into education.[5]

Immense challenges remain. The rapid increase in enrolment has placed a huge strain on the education infrastructure, with potentially damaging implications for the quality of education. But the Ugandan example demonstrates what is possible with strong political leadership. President Museveni has made the achievement of universal primary education one of the core objectives of the Ugandan government's policy, identifying this as a key requirement for sustaining high growth. Education-policy objectives have been placed at the centre of the macro-economic planning framework, ensuring that they are backed by resources. At the same time, education has been brought to the fore of national policy debate through a high-profile campaign aimed at changing attitudes and informing local communities about their rights in education.

Broader lessons from 'high-achieving' countries

The Ugandan case is part of a broader historical pattern of successful State intervention in education. Public-policy interventions have enabled a wide range of States to achieve rapid educational transformations under very different policy conditions. Today, South Korea is thought of as a development success story. It has combined high growth with rapid poverty reduction over some four decades. What is sometimes forgotten is that this achievement followed rapid progress towards universal primary education at a time when poverty and illiteracy were widespread. In 1950, more than three-quarters of South Korea's population were illiterate. By 1960 that figure had fallen to one-quarter. In the 15 years up to 1960, primary-school enrolments increased by 265 per cent.[6] This process, it should be noted, preceded the rapid rise in average incomes during the 1960s. Gains in education helped to create the impetus for sustained high growth, which in turn generated new resources for investment in primary education.

Not all of the development success stories in education are in East Asia. In sub-Saharan Africa, both **Botswana** and Zimbabwe achieved rapid advances in education over short periods. At independence in 1966, most of Botswana's population was illiterate. Fewer than half of the country's children of primary-school age were in school. Within two decades, universal primary education had been achieved, and more than two-thirds of children were making the transition from primary to secondary school.[7] Behind this achievement was a rapid expansion of the primary-school infrastructure, financed by diamond exports. In terms of enrolment and completion rates in the sub-Saharan African region, Botswana is now second only to Mauritius.

President Museveni has made the achievement of universal primary education one of the core objectives of the Ugandan government's policy, identifying this as a key requirement for sustaining high growth.

Improving the quality of education in Uganda

The success of the UPE programme in Uganda depends on the government's capacity to combine increases in the coverage of the education system with improvements in quality. An obvious problem is that of sequencing: qualitative improvements cannot be achieved overnight, but parents are concerned with the standard of education that their children receive today. The danger is that failure to achieve rapid qualitative improvements will result in increased drop-out rates. The Ugandan government is aware of this danger and is co-operating with donors in an intensive effort to avert it. Even so, the problems associated with more than two decades of under-investment cannot be eradicated overnight, especially in a situation where the same school infrastructure is having to cope with twice as many students. Among the main challenges and policy responses are the following.

- *Overcrowding.* The average pupil–teacher ratio has increased to 110:1 in Grade 1 and 1:55 in Grades 3–7. These high ratios are the result partly of a failure to prepare for UPE through an expansion of the teacher-training programme; and partly of an under-estimate of the numbers necessary to meet increased demand. An additional 10,000 teachers must be recruited over and above current levels in order to reduce the average ratio to 55:1 by 2003. This target is far higher than the internationally recognised ceiling of 40:1 for good-quality instruction. Donors are supporting a major increase in funding for teacher-training and teacher-upgrading programmes, such as the Teacher Development Management System (TDMS). The Netherlands is providing $45m for the expansion of the TDMS. However, the Ugandan government must urgently develop strategies for extending multi-shift teaching in order to reduce classroom pressures.

- *School construction.* The school-construction programme is running behind schedule. At least 26,000 new classrooms need to be rebuilt and 11,000 refurbished. Bureaucratic delay in the Ministry of Education, allied to a preference for the construction of high-cost schools, has acted as a brake on action in this area. Britain's Department for International Development is supporting a low-cost, community-led classroom-construction project in four districts.

- *Textbook shortages.* The government's target is to have one book per child for each subject by 2003. The major difficulty is costs (each book costs $4) and the inability of poor households to afford them. Financing for textbook provision increased by 300 per cent between 1996 and 1997, but serious problems have emerged in the delivery of books to schools.

- *Gender equity.* One of the problems facing the government is to sustain progress towards parity between boys and girls. Following a dramatic increase in girls' enrolment, new initiatives have been developed to enhance their performance and progress through a full primary cycle. For example, the Education Strategic Investment Plan is providing support for girls in the most deprived regions of the country, through grants made to schools. Another initiative, the Alliance for Community Action, developed by UNICEF and the Forum of African Women Educationalists, is providing grants to local NGOs and community-based organisations for girls' education. However, serious problems have emerged in the recruitment of female teachers (who represent less than one-third of the total), especially in rural areas.

Uganda provides some important policy lessons for other poor countries. The UPE programme was introduced into a policy context in which the primary-education system had been eroded over time through financial neglect. Increased investment, phased in over two to three years in advance of the UPE initiative, could have reduced some of the transitional pressures that have emerged. Finance for that investment could have been generated through additional domestic resource mobilisation, and through earlier debt relief.

Unlike Botswana, **Zimbabwe** did not enjoy the benefits of high growth after independence in 1980. The post-independence government also inherited a society fractured along racial lines and one of the world's most unequal education systems. Large sections of the rural population were excluded from an education system that was geared both financially and geographically towards the interests of the white minority. Within five years, however, the system had been turned on its head. A further one million children had been enrolled in primary school. Within ten years, Zimbabwe had one of the highest adult-literacy rates in Africa.

As we saw in Chapter 3, Latin America has an appalling record in education. Taking into account levels of national wealth, the region is comprehensively under-achieving. There are, however, significant exceptions to the rule of poor public policies, one of the most spectacular being **Cuba**. At the time of the 1958 revolution, more than half a million children were not in school. Those who were in school received on average three years of education. Within one year, an additional 300,000 children had been enrolled; and within five years universal primary education had been achieved.[8] By the mid-1970s, two-thirds of the population were receiving at least six years of education. Another exception to the Latin American rule is **Costa Rica**, which progressed rapidly towards universal primary education over the two decades following the 1948 civil war. High growth was accompanied by high levels of public investment in areas such as basic health care and education, generating rapid improvements in a wider range of social indicators. Today, the education performances of both Cuba and Costa Rica present a striking contrast with those of countries such as Brazil and Venezuela which boast far higher levels of average income.

It is sometimes argued that rapid progress towards universal primary education has been achieved in developing countries only under favourable economic conditions. The above cases demonstrate that such assessments are wide of the mark. In Zimbabwe, progress towards universal primary education was maintained during a period of economic stagnation. The rapid advances achieved by South Korea happened *before* the surge in growth that started in 1960. It is true that Botswana has sustained one of the highest growth rates in the world; and that revenues from diamond exports made it possible to maintain exceptionally high levels of public spending (equivalent to 40 per cent of GDP by 1990). But Botswana is not the only country in the world to have enjoyed windfall gains from the export of natural resources. Nigeria, to take an obvious example, has generated enormous wealth from the export of oil. Instead

Zimbabwe: transforming education in a racially divided society

At Independence in 1980, Zimbabwe's education system bore all the hallmarks of a racially divided and fragmented society, with more than half of the country's children excluded from school. In 1980, fewer than one million children, of an eligible population of more than two million, were enrolled in primary school. Inability to afford school fees, and inadequate facilities, especially in rural areas, were the main barriers to entry. Within five years of Independence, the number of children in primary school had doubled, before climbing to 2.4 million in the early 1990s. Previous gender biases in enrolment were removed, with parity achieved at the primary level by the end of the 1980s.

How was this transformation achieved? Zimbabwe's school infrastructure was dramatically expanded during the ten years after 1980, with the number of primary schools increasing from 2400 to 4500. Community mobilisation was central to this process: more than 1000 rural schools were built without government support. A parallel expansion took place at secondary level, where enrolment increased by a factor of ten during the decade after independence. Opportunities for secondary education played an important role in stimulating demand for primary education. Increasing demand for education was met through a range of innovative strategies. The Zimbabwe Integrated National Teacher Education Course (ZINTEC) pioneered new approaches to teacher training, shifting the training site from colleges to classrooms. By 1987, 4000 more trained teachers had been recruited. Extensive use was also made of untrained teacher assistants, 20,000 of whom were working in classrooms by the end of the 1980s. Double-shift and multi-grade teaching methods were also introduced. So successful were these approaches that, despite the surge in enrolments, the pupil–teacher ratio actually fell during the 1980s from 43:1 to 39:1. Finance was mobilised through a combination of redistribution and increased revenue collection. Before Independence, average expenditure for each white pupil was about 20 times higher than for a black pupil. The reallocation of resources in favour of rural areas decisively shifted this imbalance. At the same time, the share of GDP allocated to education increased by 3 per cent between 1980 and 1985 to almost 10 per cent, one of the highest levels in the developing world. Education has consistently been the single biggest item of budgetary expenditure, accounting for an average of 18 per cent of total spending in the 1980s. Distributive equity has been consolidated by concentrating resources on the primary sector and poor communal farm areas; and by withdrawing school fees in communal areas. Real per capita spending on primary education rose by one-quarter in the 1980s.

However, serious problems have emerged during Zimbabwe's educational transformation. Because of the heavy reliance on community mobilisation, the quality of schooling has been strongly influenced by household incomes and the prosperity of communities in school-catchment areas. Drop-out rates have remained relatively high, with one-quarter of the intake into Grade 1 failing to progress to Grade 4. Almost one in ten of rural children leave school before completing Grade 2, without attaining even functional literacy. These problems have intensified under the national programme of economic structural adjustment (see Chapter 5). Severe budget cuts have eroded the quality of education, and drop-out rates have increased as a result of greater recourse to cost recovery and community financing. Inevitably, people living in poverty have suffered most. The post-Independence gains in education remain under threat. Even so, the experience of the 1980s remains a testament to what can be achieved in education by governments with a strong political commitment and vision for the future.

of investing the proceeds in social infrastructure, governments have converted that wealth into military hardware, invested in dubious infrastructure projects, or transferred revenues to foreign bank accounts. Similarly Brazil, like Costa Rica, enjoyed three decades of relatively strong growth until 1980. But successive governments failed to ensure that the benefits of growth were converted into public investment in education, partly because of an unwillingness to reduce the private consumption of high-income groups through taxation; and partly because public spending was highly inequitable. As a result, the benefits of growth were captured disproportionately in the form of income gains for the wealthy, instead of being invested equitably in public welfare, as they were in Costa Rica. Such outcomes reflect the failure to develop a political consensus in favour of extending educational opportunity. Given the high costs associated with mass exclusion from education in terms of low growth, they also point to the inability of political elites to develop even the most rudimentary sense of enlightened self-interest.

The record of high-achieving countries has not been the product of a common ideology, any more than it is the outcome of economic advantage. In Cuba and Zimbabwe, socialist governments saw educational reform as part of a commitment to nation-building and social justice. In Costa Rica, the achievement of universal primary education was a central element in the social democratic consensus that evolved after the 1948 civil war. In South Korea, education underpinned an ideology of economic modernisation embraced by an authoritarian government. If there was a common element unifying these diverse experiences, it was a political conviction that universal primary education was an imperative for government policy. One recent UNICEF study covering nine countries, as well as the Indian State of Kerala, has identified six broad requirements for the attainment of universal primary education. Beyond this common starting point, these were other common policy themes.[9]

- *Political commitment.* In each case, governments made the achievement of universal primary education a political priority at the highest level. Political choice was a necessary requirement for progress.
- *Financial commitment.* Political commitment was reflected in financial allocations to basic education during the period of transformation. Over the period 1950–70, Costa Rica doubled the share of public spending allocated to basic education. Cuba increased the share of GDP allocated to education by 3 per cent over the decade up to the mid-1970s. Zimbabwe achieved the same increase over the period 1980–88. Botswana increased spending on primary education at the rate of 11 per cent per annum during the 1970s.

303

- *The central role of the public sector.* Countries that have achieved rapid transformation in basic education have done so through public action, rather than private provision. There was no private provision at the primary level in Cuba after the revolution. Despite the strong free-market ideology in Korea, private providers were absent from basic education. More than 90 per cent of primary-school children attended public schools in Costa Rica in the mid-1960s. Similar levels of public provision were recorded in Botswana during the 1970s and in Zimbabwe during the 1980s.

- *Equity in public finance.* During the decisive periods of progress towards universal primary education, investment resources for education were concentrated in this sector. In the mid-1980s, the ratio of public spending per pupil in primary education to spending on each university student was 1:7 in Cuba, compared with an average of 1:33 in sub-Saharan Africa. Until South Korea achieved universal primary education, it allocated more than 60 per cent of public spending to primary education, allowing the private sector to play a more significant role in secondary education, and recovering a large share of expenditure on higher education from charges on students.

- *Reducing the costs of education to households.* Increased public expenditure was used in each case to reduce the cost of education to households. Free primary education was introduced in Sri Lanka immediately after independence. Similarly, Cuba made free education a right of citizenship. Botswana lowered primary-school fees in 1973 and removed them altogether in 1980. In Zimbabwe, rural fees for primary education were withdrawn after independence.

- *Integration of education reforms into wider human-development strategies.* Education reforms were supported by wider strategies which reduced poverty. In Zimbabwe, Cuba, Botswana, and Costa Rica, for example, health-sector reforms led to improvements in child health and nutrition, thereby enhancing the capacity of poor households to benefit from education reforms.

Political commitment and the right to education

Political commitment, the first and most important requirement for success, requires more than government declarations in favour of universal primary education, and pronouncements affirming the right to education. All too often, constitutional and legislative rights are of limited relevance to poor communities, who lack access to legal recourse and for whom would-be constitutional rights are unenforceable. There are, in fact, only 23 countries lacking legislation that makes education compulsory.

Article 45 of the Indian Constitution famously declared that: 'the State shall endeavour to provide within a period of ten years ... free and compulsory education for all children until they complete the age of 14 years'.[10] After half a century of independence, and despite the pledges of the Planning Commission, Parliament, and State governments, there are still more than 30 million children out of school. Many Latin American countries have even older constitutional commitments to education. The right of all citizens to a free primary education was recognised in the Brazilian constitution of 1824. More recently, the 1996 National Law on Directives and Principles for National Education established the State's duty to provide 'obligatory fundamental education, at no cost, for all, including those who did not have access to the same at the appropriate age'. As in India, constitutional principle has proved at best a weak guide for State action, especially in relation to the poor.

This is not to suggest that legal provisions are unimportant. In many countries, local communities have succeeded in using legal rights as a lever for gaining access to basic education. The community-schools movement in Brazil emerged in the poor neighbourhoods and districts of the north and the north-east during the 1970s. They were a response to failures of the public education system and the demands of poor households for education. The schools were not legally recognised, and they received no support from governments. By the early 1990s, however, associations of community-school educators had emerged as an important political force in the popular movement.[11] Supported by non-government organisations such as the Centre of Luis Freise and the Centre of Popular Education, urban slum communities in Recife and Salvador and rural communities in the States of Bahia and Pernambuco mobilised behind the associations to demand legal recognition and financial support for community schools. In 1998, a constitutional amendment recognised the schools in law, and State and federal budget provisions were amended to allow for financial support. Born during a time of political strife, the community-schools movement has contributed to the wider struggle for democratisation in Brazil, and at the same time has enabled poor communities to gain access to a publicly financed education system from which they were previously excluded.

The experience of community schools in Brazil illustrates the importance of the dynamic interaction between legal provisions and political mobilisation. Community-based associations have been able to use legislative provisions to advance their claims. In other contexts, legal frameworks have been too weak, and too inaccessible to provide effective support for local action. In India, constitutional provisions on basic education consist merely of a Directive Principle giving States the authority to enforce compulsory education, if they so choose – and many do not. There is limited recourse for challenging inaction, although this could change. Under a constitutional amendment proposed by the Saika Committee in 1997, free and compulsory basic education would become a fundamental right, enforceable through law.[12] Familiar objections have been raised. It is claimed that such a provision would be unaffordable, unenforceable, and potentially damaging to the poor (who would be deprived of household labour). Almost exactly the same objections were voiced by the British colonial administration in the last century, when Indian social reformers such as Gopal Krishna Gokhale proposed free, compulsory education. The arguments against it, especially those relating to affordability, have not gained in force over the past hundred years.

The international human-rights machinery is too opaque, too distant, and too cumbersome to make a real difference to the lives of poor communities.

Constitutional and legal rights to education are important as a source of political empowerment. They are not a substitute for effective State action, however. In 1990, the government of Bangladesh introduced the Primary Education Compulsory Act. Ambitious programmes have been developed to make its objectives attainable, including extensive collaboration with NGOs. But in the absence of an increase in public funding for primary education, which needs to grow from less than 1 per cent of GNP to at least 3 per cent, good-quality and universal primary education will prove an elusive goal. It is likely to prove even more elusive in Pakistan, where the National Education Policy (NEP) covering the period 1998–2010 has set ambitious targets, including 90 per cent enrolment by 2002. Unfortunately, the NEP abounds in vague platitudes about the merits of education, but offers few details, financial or administrative, about how its goals are to be achieved. As the late Mahbub ul Haq, the prominent Pakistani economist, wrote of his country shortly before his death, 'Political commitment for a spirited campaign to universalise primary education in the shortest possible time is still lacking in the country.'[13]

It is not just at a national level that legislative provisions have failed to empower local communities. Education is recognised as a fundamental human right in international treaties, some of which – such as the Convention on the Rights of the Child – entail legally binding obligations on States. In practice, however, the international human-rights machinery is too opaque, too distant, and too cumbersome to make a real difference to the lives of poor communities.

Planning for education for all

One of the features of successful State planning in education has been the development of comprehensive strategies for achieving well-defined goals, including strategies for implementation. Since the 1990 World Conference on Education for All, there has been a proliferation of national plans, but these plans have often lacked concrete mechanisms for implementation. India is a case in point. Central and State governments have developed a wide range of policies ostensibly aimed at achieving commitments made at Jomtien, starting with the central government's 1992 National Policy of Education. Key themes in the latest planning documents are decentralisation, social mobilisation, and the integration of non-formal education programmes into national schemes.[14]

There is no doubt that action in these areas is desirable. However, many of the concrete elements in the overall strategy involve little more than a repackaging of past initiatives, most of which have failed in spectacular fashion. One example is the long-established Non-Formal Education (NFE) programme, which is supposed to target communities neglected by the formal education system. In theory, there are now 250,000 NFE centres, roughly one for every two villages in the country. However, one recent survey in the northern Hindi-speaking States, covering 188 rural villages, found fewer than ten functional centres. Operation Blackboard, another tried-and-tested programme now integrated into the Education for All planning process, was started in 1987 to provide financial assistance and teaching equipment for more than half a million primary schools. But a lack of political commitment in States such as Uttar Pradesh, Bihar, and Madhya Pradesh has meant that the benefits have been negligible.

India's District Primary Education Programme (DPEP) has been more effective. Launched in 1994, it represents the most ambitious government initiative in education to date. Covering 64 districts in 12 States, DPEP aims to provide universal access to school and to reduce drop-out rates by 10 per cent. There is much to commend in the DPEP's approach. It provides a unifying structure through which donor support can be channelled, but which is highly decentralised at the same time. Proposals for achieving the programme's goals can be submitted by districts, and participating States are required to ensure that DPEP funds are additional to existing financing provisions. More importantly, DPEP provides, for the first time, substantial support for expanding community-level initiatives such as those discussed below. The problem is that the

Indian government has failed to develop a concerted political strategy for universal primary education, or (as we saw in Chapter 4) to set public-spending priorities that reflect a commitment to this objective. While there are obvious merits in operating through decentralised State structures, many of the States with the most pressing needs have failed to prioritise education, often reflecting the political indifference of State-level elites. There is consequently a danger of DPEP initiatives being mediated through State-level structures that are unresponsive to the basic education needs of poor people.

The importance of political commitment is apparent in some of the more successful Indian States. The case of Kerala is relatively well known. More recently, Himachel Pradesh has achieved rapid progress, making the transition from mass illiteracy to universal primary education over a relatively short period of time.[15] What makes this achievement even more impressive is the fact that it has taken place in a State marked by high levels of child labour and a highly unfavourable settlement pattern, with small villages spread over a large geographical area. State-level planning has been responsible for much of the success. This has included a consistent emphasis on the development of rural infrastructure, with roads and schools being accorded a high priority. Per capita spending in education is about twice the all-India average, contributing to a pupil–teacher ratio that is half the national average. Special incentives have been provided for disadvantaged households, including free textbooks for all Scheduled Caste children. In contrast to other States, Himachel Pradesh has also taken seriously the commitment to improve the ratio of female to male teachers, with attendant benefits for gender equity.

Himachel Pradesh has achieved rapid progress, making the transition from mass illiteracy to universal primary education over a relatively short period of time.

Part of the problem in education planning, at the national as well as the international level, is the prevalence of targets that are presented separately from the strategies needed for their attainment. Education planning in Zambia illustrates the problem. Clear and impressive targets have been set for achieving universal basic education:[16]

- all 7 year-olds will be in Grade 1 by the year 2000;
- all 7–13 year-olds will be in Grades 1–7 by 2005;
- all 7–15 year-olds will be in Grades 1–9 by 2015.

Less impressive than these targets are the strategies for achieving them. By 1999, fewer than half of Grade 1 pupils were aged seven or below. The numbers of over-age children attending school, and still entering the system, were so large that there was not the slightest prospect of this target being met. The 2005 target for universal primary education is equally unrealistic under prevailing conditions. Achieving it would require an annual increase in enrolment of 96,000 pupils, almost ten times the actual increase achieved during the first half of the 1990s. For purposes of comparison, it is also twice the rate of increase achieved during the expansion of the primary-education system in the 20 years after independence, at a time when public investment was increasing. As noted in Chapter 5, Zambia's under-performance has been the product of a crippling debt burden, as well as domestic policy failures.

States and non-government organisations

Public policy in basic education provision was once regarded in most developing countries as the sole preserve of the State. Private provision, independent of support from government planning, was typically viewed with indifference or outright hostility.[17] Countries such as Tanzania and Vietnam banned private provision. Others saw private-sector delivery as a mechanism for filling gaps left by the State, whether through mission schools or commercial ventures. Service provision by NGOs outside formal State structures was seen as unacceptable by many governments. Despite the prevailing view, however, many NGOs were getting involved in education, often independently of State auspices. In some cases they provided welfare assistance to poor households. In others, NGOs developed education initiatives that were intended to overcome the failures of government policy. In Latin America, support for non-formal education with marginalised social groups such as indigenous people and communities displaced by conflict was developed in overt opposition to government. Similarly, in South Asia and, to a more limited degree, in sub-Saharan Africa, NGOs became increasingly involved as service providers in basic education, attempting to reach specific sections of society (for example, women in South Asia) or regions ignored by government.

While the precise relationship varied from country to country, relationships between governments and NGOs in matters of education were often fraught. For NGOs, governments were often part of the problem. Their education planners displayed all the worst characteristics of over-centralised bureaucrats: they were indifferent to local needs, insensitive to gender concerns, and unable to deliver an effective service. Governments often saw NGOs as unprofessional 'fly-by-night' operators, in many cases motivated largely by political convictions hostile to government interests.

During the 1980s, the relationship between NGOs and States underwent a significant change. Crippled by slow growth, a deteriorating trade environment, and foreign debt, governments were increasingly forced to acknowledge the need for alternative sources of finance and service delivery. Conditions attached to loans provided by the IMF and the World Bank further restricted the authority of the State. Bilateral donors too came to see NGOs as an alternative to the State in providing more efficient services at lower cost. Within the NGO community itself, a powerful counter-trend was gathering momentum. Having been drawn into service delivery, many saw the limitations of a project-based approach. At best, good projects in a bad policy environment could provide islands of excellence, but their potential for promoting wider change was limited. Recognition of this fact led a growing number of NGOs to seek partnerships with the State, aimed at influencing national policies by establishing good practice at a local level.

The evolution of ActionAid, a UK-based NGO, is instructive. The agency has worked in basic education for more than 25 years, and its early programmes stressed input provision. As in other areas of NGOs' work, ranging from health care to irrigation, the idea was that the provision of physical inputs would help people living in poverty to overcome their relative disadvantage. This rationale was challenged by a review of ActionAid's school-infrastructure programme in Kenya.[18] The review, carried out in 1994/95, concluded that, while many schools had been constructed and stocked in response to requests for support, there was little evidence of an increase in enrolments, or of improvements in the quality of education. Several problems were identified. ActionAid's assistance had not reduced the costs of education to parents, because government had increased recourse to cost-recovery. Macro-economic factors, linked to the country's structural adjustment programme, had undermined micro-level efforts. While the quality of schools had improved, parents and poor households had been marginalised in decision-making processes. Head-teachers had prioritised expenditure on classrooms and buildings, despite evidence that parents favoured investment in textbooks. The ActionAid review suggested that a deeper failure to empower parents in the school-management system was behind their inability to influence decisions. It recommended an end to funding for school construction, and more investment in developing innovative strategies for school management.

Through its willingness to make public a document which offered forthright criticisms of its own programme (a practice as rare among

NGOs as among major donors), ActionAid was able to contribute to a wider shift in policy. Instead of attempting to 'direct' development, the lesson from Kenya was that NGOs should adapt their interventions to the needs of local communities, as expressed through participative processes. Participation is now a central theme of NGO involvement. It is increasingly recognised that community involvement is one of the most critical requirements for successful education reform. But effective community involvement in the management of schools and education planning involves complex political processes and power relations, as witnessed by Oxfam's experience in Mozambique. It is a complex process, because of the heterogeneous nature of communities, their histories, and the problems confronting them.

Other lessons emerge from a broad array of NGO experiences. One is that non-formal education does not, except in rare cases, offer a genuine alternative to State action. Uganda's experience illustrates this point. Not even the most powerful coalition of NGOs could have achieved in 50 years what the government's UPE achieved in two years. The Bangladesh Rural Advancement Committee (BRAC) is the world's largest non-formal education provider. It employs 34,000 part-time teachers and operates in 66,000 villages. Even so, it reaches fewer than 10 per cent of children of primary-school age.[19] Parallel non-formal education systems have their own shortcomings, in addition to those associated with coverage. In the absence of strong national supervision, there is a danger of proliferating quality standards. While non-formal systems may serve the minimum purpose of getting poor children into classrooms, in the absence of effective State regulation they may also provide a third-rate education. Interventions by NGOs outside a national planning framework can also result in the uneven delivery of services, with a weak link between provision and need. That link can become weaker still as a consequence of changes in NGO priorities. Non-formal systems maintained by voluntary funding from national or inter-national NGOs are inevitably subject to the whims of donors. If basic education goes out of fashion on the NGO agenda, services are prone to collapse. The potentially more serious problem is that parallel education systems can have the unintended effect of absolving States of their responsibility to meet their citizens' basic learning needs. Finally, failure to develop organic links between formal and non-formal education systems is likely to exclude children from poor households from mainstream schools – a problem that is especially pronounced in the transition from non-formal primary to public secondary school, for example.

Parallel education systems can have the unintended effect of absolving States of their responsibility to meet their citizens' basic learning needs.

311

Parents' management committees in Mozambique

Mozambique has some of the world's worst education indicators. Fewer than half of all boys and one-third of girls enrol in school. Drop-out rates are high, and education quality is low. Much of the school infrastructure was destroyed during the country's civil war, but achieving universal primary education will require more than an increase in the number of schools. More accountable and better-quality service provision is also essential.

NGOs belonging to Oxfam International support several education programmes in Mozambique. One of them is in the province of Zambezia, where the education system was devastated during the civil war. It has three components: school building, teacher training, and support for parents' management committees. Schools have been built in eight villages, in an effort to address problems of supply. Demand-related factors are being addressed through teacher-training programmes and, crucially, through the parents' management committees. The committees – Ligação Esacola Comunidade (LECs) – are recognised in law and encouraged by government. Their role involves helping to maintain and manage school compounds, monitoring teacher performance, and providing support for extremely poor children. In the eight communities where Oxfam has built primary schools, an Oxfam community-development worker has supported the committees and organised exchange visits, where parents can meet other committees which are functioning well.

How successful have the LECs been? The record is mixed: some village committees have helped to establish genuine partnerships between community and school, providing parents with a voice in the school's management, while others barely function, and some have been co-opted by corrupt staff. In Nipive village, Gurue district, the consensus among parents is that the LEC has brought about real benefits. It has enabled parents to challenge policies that result in teachers being transferred to other areas after short periods. They are also pressing for the provision of free school meals, textbooks, and pencils. Meetings with teachers take place on a regular basis, and there are no reports of bribes and corruption. Thirty miles away, the LEC in Mangone village has a very different track record. The committee had organised the construction of the school, but was disbanded after it was built. There are no elections for committee members, who are not accountable to other parents. The staff in Mangone were reported to charge parents unofficial fees before their children could progress to the next grade, a factor that helps to explain extremely high drop-out and repetition rates. Fewer than a third of the children who enrol in Mangone are still attending school by the fifth grade.

A key lesson from these experiences is that the social context strongly influences the effectiveness of the LECs. In Mangone, most of the population stayed in the village during the civil war, and relations have remained polarised between supporters of the conflicting parties, Frelimo and Renamo. The principle of working with parents has not been accepted by the school staff and village leaders. Many of the villagers are afraid to criticise the school staff openly, and corruption is a serious problem. In contrast, most of Nipive's population fled from the village during the war, either to camps in Malawi or to relatives in government-controlled areas. When families returned from the camps in Malawi, where their children had received a basic education, many were keen for them to continue their schooling.

Partnerships and participation

Any attempt to address the task of achieving universal primary education solely through central State planning, or through non-formal initiatives, is unlikely to succeed: broad-based partnerships are needed. In order to encourage such partnerships, governments must move beyond espousing the rhetoric of participation, to developing collaborative approaches which draw on the strengths of local communities. For their part, NGOs need to find points of contact between the non-formal education system and government structures, so that the approaches developed at a community level can be scaled up and their benefits multiplied. Participation, like education itself, is an important end in its own right. Human development is partly a matter of people and communities improving their own lives and taking greater control over their destinies. But apart from its intrinsic value, there are good reasons for education policy makers to encourage more participative approaches. They provide mechanisms for identifying the education needs and problems of local beneficiaries, and they provide a mechanism for assessing the quality and relevance of service provision.

Nothwithstanding these potential benefits, it cannot be assumed that participation is a panacea for overcoming the problem of exclusion for educational opportunities. Highly participatory institutions are perfectly capable of generating highly unequal outcomes. These can result from inequalities in the abilities of various kinds of actor to articulate their demands, or to transform demands into decisions.[20] In India, Village Education Committees have provided a forum for expressing local needs, but the very poor and low-caste groups often have the weakest voices.[21] Elsewhere, parent–teacher associations often reflect the demands and aspirations of wealthier households, especially with regard to payments for school buildings and textbooks. There are also differences of interest between service providers and users. Teachers and health workers may see cost-recovery as essential to their own welfare and the quality of the services they provide, but poor households may see it as a source of exclusion. In some cases, the notion of participation has been subjected to widespread abuse, with perfunctory consultation or material contributions to service provision treated as evidence of ownership.

Similar caution is needed in assessing the relative strengths and weaknesses of State and non-State actors. Non-government organisations and private providers are often seen as the most efficient agents for facilitating participation, often on the basis of preconceived theory rather than empirical evidence. State agencies are seen as inherently unresponsive to local needs. This is unwarranted. In fact, there are successful examples of State interventions. One study of a highly successful maternal and child health-care programme in north-east Brazil found that extension workers were motivated by a strong sense of mission and common purpose with local populations.[22] The scheme created career incentives linked to success in gearing services towards local needs through extensive participation. In Uganda, the government has developed a rolling, participatory poverty-assessment exercise, covering all aspects of livelihoods and access to social services. The assessment is conducted under the auspices of the Ministry of Finance, which has adjusted a number of macro-economic reform measures and public-spending plans to reflect local needs. What these cases demonstrate is that the effectiveness of States in facilitating participation is conditioned by wider political processes.

Simply transferring authority from central to local and community-level structures in the absence of a coherent national strategy is not a prescription for overcoming the exclusion of the poor.

Counter-examples of unsuccessful State intervention are not in short supply. With some notable exceptions, top–down adult-literacy programmes have failed, despite the great financial and political efforts often associated with them. The National Literacy Movement in India, for instance, has mobilised 10 million volunteers, but outside India's southern States it has achieved limited success. By contrast, smaller-scale NGO programmes, such as the REFLECT approach developed by ActionAid, described below, have achieved high levels of success through a bottom–up approach in which, through intensive participatory work, literacy-training methods are adapted to the specific needs of local communities. In primary education, micro-level initiatives, such as the BRAC programme in Bangladesh, have often been far more effective than government action in increasing the enrolment and performance of girls. But for NGOs to move beyond local initiatives, and for governments to build on the innovation that such initiatives provide, partnerships are essential.

Developing such partnerships entails difficult processes. Each of the actors involved has strengths and weaknesses. Governments may lack local understanding, but local communities are not homogeneous and their decision-making bodies seldom prioritise the needs of the poor. Simply transferring authority from central to local and community-level structures in the absence of a coherent national strategy is not a prescription for overcoming the exclusion of the poor. Partnership requires a recognition of the capacities and comparative advantages of each actor, which is often difficult to achieve in practice. Added to the difficulties created by the different institutional ethos and political

The REFLECT approach to adult literacy

Adult-literacy programmes have a chequered history. Some countries – China in the 1950s, Cuba in the 1960s, and Nicaragua in the 1980s – have achieved major advances in a short period of time. Others have been less successful. The National Literacy Mission in India has involved a huge mobilisation, but its successes have been local rather than national. Some of the more recent successes have owed less to top–down national programmes than to partnerships between States and non-State actors. In Senegal, the government is implementing the national literacy programme by contracting local NGOs, community groups, and church organisations working at the grassroots.

One of the most innovative literacy programmes is REFLECT, an approach which builds on the theories of Brazilian educator Paulo Freire, fusing these with the participatory methodologies developed by practitioners of Participatory Rural Appraisal (PRA). In a REFLECT programme, each community generates its own learning materials by constructing maps, matrices, calendars, and diagrams to analyse local life and to systematise local knowledge. Reading and writing are developed on the basis of these different visual representations ('graphics'). Initially developed in 1993 by ActionAid in Uganda, Bangladesh, and El Salvador (with success rates of 60–70 per cent), REFLECT is now used by more than 100 organisations, working in more than 30 countries. Several government programmes are now experimenting with REFLECT. One of the keys to its success appears to be the way in which it fuses a literacy-learning process with an empowerment process, based on people doing their own detailed and systematic local analysis. Participatory approaches to literacy, such as the REFLECT programme, have integrated a vast range of techniques from theatre to socio-drama, role play, song, dance, proverbs, poetry, oral history, games, codifications, collective writing, community printing, and even video and television. However, there is a growing recognition that the essence of a participatory approach lies not so much in the tools and techniques used as in the attitudes and behaviour of facilitators.

This flourishing of alternative approaches at the local level arises from some important theoretical work which, challenging the assumption that there is a static condition of 'literacy', emphasises the diversity of cultural meanings of literacy. As well as informing REFLECT, this has led to work on 'real literacies': an approach that stresses the need to take literacy training out of the classroom and to focus on the real contexts in which people need to use literacy. A new community literacy programme in Nepal is presently adapting these ideas. There is growing evidence that these methodological developments and learning from recent adult-literacy programmes and campaigns can lead to more effective work in the future. However, most governments and international donors remain reluctant to invest their resources for education in anything outside the core formal system. This could prove to be a serious mistake. It is parents who decide whether to send their children to school and who, in practice, have to pay, either directly or indirectly. Non-literate parents are less likely to make the necessary sacrifices. The home environment is probably the biggest single factor in determining a child's success in school. Children with non-literate parents are the first to drop out and they very rarely excel, because there is no reinforcement or support for school at home.

(Source: D. Archer and S. Cottingham: *Action Research Report on REFLECT*, Overseas Development Administration, London, 1996.)

perspective of NGOs and States are those associated with the social, ethnic, cultural, and geographic distance between various actors. It is a long way in each of these respects from village-based work with, for example, scheduled tribes in Bihar to the Education Ministry in New Delhi.

For all these problems, collaboration in achieving shared goals can help to overcome mutual suspicions. In Vietnam, for example, Oxfam has developed close working relationships with government authorities. On Oxfam's side, the catalyst has been a growing recognition, based on experience of project work, that exclusion from basic-education opportunities is reinforcing the poverty and marginalisation of indigenous communities. The government is also concerned that the problems of more marginal communities are not being addressed, despite a strong political commitment to universal primary education. The result of this shared concern has been co-operation in devising practical strategies for improving the quality and accessibility of education services.

Many of the benefits of participation and partnership are difficult to measure, although some are immediately apparent. For example, NGO involvement can make it possible to hire and train more teachers, especially female teachers, through local recruitment, with government meeting recurrent salary costs. Community involvement in school management makes it possible to develop schedules which take into account the reality of seasonal labour demands, thereby reducing drop-out rates and increasing the efficiency of public spending. Qualitative improvements in the relevance of curricula, the standard of teaching, and the development of teaching materials can also be generated through collaboration, and there is often a demonstrable impact in terms of enrolment, attendance, completion, and improved gender equity. Successful participative partnerships between State and non-State actors have been based on six core achievements, illustrated in the next section of this chapter and summarised here:

- *Identifying problems.* Involving parents in the education process is an essential starting point. National planners are ill-equipped to understand barriers to education at community level. The Lok Jumbish project in India involves communities at the outset in a school-mapping exercise. Through a participatory process, parents identify what they perceive as the main obstacles that prevent their children attending school, including the problems associated with existing provisions. Information from the mapping helps to frame policies

Supporting pilot activities in education: Oxfam in Vietnam

Vietnam has made impressive gains in education in the last several decades, with national education indicators exceeding what would be expected from a country with such low income levels. This is due largely to the great importance ascribed to education by the people and the government of Vietnam. Yet serious challenges remain. While enrolment rates are high, primary-school completion rates are still low. The progress required for Vietnam to achieve its target of universal basic education is daunting. Beyond access, there is also the issue of quality, in particular how the education system can provide Vietnamese children with knowledge and skills that will be relevant, worthwhile, and useful to prepare them for the challenges of the future. This is especially necessary for the children of ethnic minorities, who often have special difficulties learning in a language that is not their native tongue.

In 1994, after working in the education sector over several years, Oxfam in Vietnam started to support a small pilot project that fostered innovative teaching methodologies. These had been developed successfully in other poor countries, including Bhutan, where they had enhanced the educational attainment of children. A small group of teachers, identified by the Irish voluntary Agency for Personnel Overseas (APSO), was brought in to train Vietnamese teachers in child-centred, activity-based methods. The foreign teachers worked directly with Vietnamese teachers and education officials over several weeks, to demonstrate how these methods could be used to motivate and engage children who might otherwise find the lessons uninteresting.

A decision was taken to focus on teaching mathematics and the Vietnamese language at the early primary level (Grades 1–3). In each case, pupils learn by doing, and through creative play. One method uses materials that enable children to develop a greater understanding of mathematical concepts. Another supplements traditional rote-learning with more effective methods of language teaching, which use purposeful application of words and games to encourage the understanding of whole texts and the meaningful use of words. Moreover, pronunciation and spelling are taught by using words children that are already familiar with, and by using whole texts to develop reading skills. When lessons relate to children's own experiences, they are understood better. During teacher training, modest sets of materials are used, which are given to the teachers who pass through this curriculum.

Teachers are also encouraged to be innovative in other aspects of their teaching. For example, instead of standing in front of the classroom talking at the students, teachers are encouraged to go to individuals or groups of children and guide them, responding to their needs. Sometimes students are seated in small groups facing each other or in a large circle, instead of in rows facing the teacher, so that the children learn through interacting with each other. In addition, parents are encouraged to have more contact with the teacher and school, and take an active role in their child's learning. Thus, Oxfam's education-support programme in Vietnam brings together three components: teacher training, using simple equipment; improved facilities, including more and better classrooms; and community-development work.

Both pupils and teachers have been pleased with many aspects of the new teaching methods. From the outset, Oxfam has worked with staff at the Vietnamese Ministry of Education and Training (MOET) and relevant donors, UNICEF in particular, to identify parts of the methodology training that were proceeding well, or faltering, and to adjust the activities accordingly. At the end of the initial demonstrations in 1994, the Vietnamese and foreign specialists together identified the areas of potential success and failure at a large workshop. A booklet was published to disseminate the information more widely in Vietnam. There was sufficient interest on the part of the partners at local and central levels to initiate a two-year project to bring back one of the trainers to work with a Vietnamese counterpart, mainly in order to continue working with teachers in the poor mountainous province of Lao Cai. Two major activities were initiated. First, two small teams of 'key teachers' were trained intensively, so that they could work with a large number of less experienced teachers who were posted to remote schools in two districts. Second, Oxfam staff worked with teacher trainees at the Lao Cai Teachers' Training College. Experiences have been shared regularly through a Vietnam Education Forum, organised by UNICEF and a number of NGOs, to provide feedback to MOET staff at central and local levels, and to staff and partners in relevant international institutions.

Many issues remain to be resolved in Oxfam's programme, such as identifying the best methods to develop groups of 'key teachers', deciding on the most appropriate mix of training methods, and finding ways to involve local departments of education. Moreover, because of the long-term nature of the work, results are gradual and difficult to perceive and measure. Oxfam and its educational counterparts have agreed on another two-year period for teacher-training input. Following the successful placement of a volunteer from the British agency Voluntary Service Overseas (VSO) in Oxfam's Mekong Delta programme, now there are two VSO volunteers responsible for teacher training in the three provinces where Oxfam has on-going programmes. Interim reviews and evaluations have identified successes on which the new team can build, and problems that remain to be solved.

Oxfam believes that providing funding and 'pilot classrooms' for such innovation is a small but valuable contribution to the development of education in Vietnam, especially as MOET has now endorsed the idea of new teaching methodologies. Whereas the Ministry might be reluctant to use its own scarce resources for pilot activities of this nature, it can learn through Oxfam's support, especially in seeing what is feasible in the very poor communities where Oxfam works. Moreover, there are lessons to be learned by larger donors who support innovations in education, including the British government's DFID and the World Bank, from the on-going partnership between Oxfam and MOET.

about where schools should be located. But the mapping exercise is also a source of empowerment, because it engages communities in debates about education provision: debates from which they are usually excluded. More broadly, participatory assessments can identify the specific reasons why girls are kept at home.

- *Adapting schools to community needs.* As shown in Chapter 4, household-labour demands have an important influence on school attendance. Yet school timetables and term times are often set in national capital cities, with scant regard for factors such as harvest dates. The Escuela Nueva programme in Colombia turned conventional approaches on their heads and adapted the school term to rural life, instead of attempting to make rural life fit the school day. Central to the programme is a system of continuous assessment, in which learning modules replace the traditional curriculum. Instead of having to pass an examination at the end of each school year, children can complete the modules and move to the next grade at their own pace, when they meet a certain standard. This avoids the stigma and financial waste of children being held back because they fail an examination. It also means that students can drop out for brief periods, whether as a result of sickness or because they have to work, and return when they are ready.

- *Developing child-centred learning.* Teachers in BRAC schools in Bangladesh place strong emphasis on engaging with children, who are encouraged to ask questions, design, draw, and engage in co-operative learning activities with other children. Building the self-esteem of young girls is one of the most important aspects of the BRAC approach. Its success is reflected in the fact that three-quarters of its pupils are young girls, over 90 per cent of whom complete a primary cycle. In Egypt, community schools have developed techniques, based on the approaches of BRAC and the Escuela Nueva programme, which achieve better examination results than government schools in the process.

- *Improving teacher recruitment and standards.* Poor parents consistently complain about the inferior quality of teachers, their indifference to the needs of children and the community, and their absenteeism. Each of the initiatives discussed below has developed new teacher-training programmes, with a strong commitment to in-service support. BRAC and the Shiksha Karmi project in Rajasthan recruit local people who have completed 8–10 years of education. Evidence strongly suggests that these teachers are more highly motivated and more strongly committed to serving poor communities than many professional teachers. The recruitment of local teachers also makes it possible to bring schools to communities, reducing the distances that children have to travel. In Pakistan, the Busti programme has increased female enrolment by recruiting local teachers who hold classes in their homes. Parents of young girls aged between 5 and 10, who would not be allowed to make the journey to a government school for security reasons, place greater trust in this arrangement.

- *Enhancing local control.* Success in education reform is more likely when parents and pupils are given a greater say in education policy, at various levels. Involvement in identifying problems is an obvious, if insufficiently recognised, starting point. Setting up schools without knowledge of local labour patterns, language needs, and gender issues is a prescription for failure. Parents' engagement in diagnosing problems can help to involve them more deeply in local education. Participation in education also means structured involvement in the management of schools, including decisions about financing. School governance, like national governance, should be built upon the foundations of democracy and accountability. It extends from the school itself to district-level planning and implementation.

- *Scaling up.* Community initiatives can generate far wider benefits where they are integrated into national programmes. Alternatively, projects can develop as enclaves which have minimal contact with the formal education system. Most of the projects described below are distinguished by the fact that they involve genuine partnerships between government, NGOs, and donors. In Bangladesh, BRAC schools teach children up to a level where they have the skills and confidence to make the transition to government schools. The Lok Jumbish project in Rajasthan, developed as a co-operative venture between the State government, NGOs, and local communities, is now being integrated into India's national plan for achieving universal primary education. In Baluchistan in Pakistan, the community schools are the result of co-operation between the State and local NGOs. Partnerships are important for governments, because they can generate the community mobilisation that is needed to meet the targets set in national plans.

Partnerships in action: five case studies

Collaboration and partnership cannot be developed in the abstract. There are no blueprints for success, although there are some recipes for failure, such as governments developing plans for building partnerships by decree, with local communities used as vehicles for service delivery. More successful approaches have evolved from practical co-operation, flexibility, and a willingness to learn in the pursuit of shared objectives. The five case studies below illustrate some successful approaches.

Two programmes in Rajasthan: Shiksha Karmi and Lok Jumbish

The State of Rajasthan is one of the poorest in India, with some of the country's worst educational indicators. Only 20 per cent of women are literate, half the level for men. Fewer than 60 per cent of children are in school. Infant-mortality rates are high. Problems of access to education are compounded by the fact that the population of the State is widely dispersed, with about one-third living in small remote hamlets. The Shiksha Karmi and Lok Jumbish projects have developed pioneering responses to deep-rooted educational problems in Rajasthan.[23] Beginning as small-scale micro-level initiatives, both have been integrated into State-wide strategies for meeting the educational needs of deprived rural communities.

Shiksha Karmi

One of the central problems facing communities in Rajasthan, especially in more remote areas, is absenteeism on the part of teachers. Professional teachers may appear on the books of the State's Education Ministry for salary purposes, but they are often absent from classrooms. The basic strategy developed by the Shiksha Karmi, or 'education workers' project, has involved substituting absentee professional teachers with locally recruited teachers. The initial project was based on the work of a small NGO, the Social Work and Research Centre (SWRC). During a pilot project in 1975–78, SWRC ran three experimental primary schools, using local teachers and providing continual in-service training. The curriculum and textbook design related directly to life in a rural environment. When the project was evaluated, the Shiksha Karmi schools compared favourably with government primary schools.[24] As a result, the government of Rajasthan, in co-operation with SWRC, extended the project to 13 more villages where teacher absenteeism was particularly high.

Following the success of this expanded project, the government of Rajasthan launched a much wider initiative, with financial and technical support from the Swedish International Development Agency (SIDA). The project was extended in two phases to cover 300 villages by 1991, and 2000 remote villages in 140 'blocks' by 1995. Some impressive results have been achieved:

- More than 1300 previously unused day schools are now functioning. In addition, almost 3000 'schools of convenient timing' have been established, with a flexible daily schedule to accommodate household labour demands.

- More than 120,000 children are being educated through the programme.

- Retention rates are still low, at 50 per cent between Grades 1–5, but this compares with a 30 per cent retention rate in 1989. More than 40 per cent of children now successfully complete Grade 5.

- More than half of the children in Shiksha Karmi schools are from Scheduled Castes and tribes.

The Shiksha Karmi project has been expanded with a high level of local participation, allied to strong logistical support. Villages are selected on the basis of requests from Panchayat Samiti (the block administration). Candidates for teacher training are selected after intensive discussions with local households, sometimes extending over several weeks. The selection procedure has been one of the main bottlenecks during efforts to expand the project, but success depends on finding the right candidates. Once chosen, the education workers are initially trained on a 37-day residential course by another NGO, Sandhan, which has developed specialised courses tailored to the needs of rural Rajasthan. This is supplemented by refresher courses and regular in-school training, totalling 54 days a year.[25] This in-service support is stronger than that provided to teachers trained in the formal system. The government pays stipends to the teachers, but their management and supervision is delegated to local communities and non-government organisations.

Many problems remain to be addressed. It has proved difficult to recruit female teachers, who still account for only one in ten of the total. The limited presence of women teachers has in turn hampered efforts to improve gender equity. While overall enrolment levels have increased, the gender gap in enrolment remains wide. Enrolment of boys has increased from 50 per cent to 88 per cent; girls' enrolment has risen from 21 per cent to 65 per cent.[26] Participatory assessments involving the community have identified a range of measures to address the problem of recruiting female teachers. The target is to have at least one female Shiksha Karmi teacher in each school, to develop girls-only 'courtyard schools', and to provide escorts for girls who have to walk significant distances to school.

The Shiksha Karmi project illustrates how partnerships between NGOs and government can generate benefits which extend far beyond isolated grassroots projects. Expanding the programme from three villages has enabled the NGOs involved to reach a far wider community, and it has facilitated improvements in government education services. Inevitable tensions have emerged between participatory approaches that are geared towards local consultation and approaches that emphasise the speed of service delivery; further tensions are apparent between the desirability of fostering local experimentation and the need for accountability to the Ministry in charge. But the project has developed innovative responses which are changing the face of education across Rajasthan.

Lok Jumbish

The Lok Jumbish (People's Movement) programme is another joint initiative developed by the government of Rajasthan, in co-operation with local NGOs and financed by SIDA. Launched in 1992, it has the ambitious aim of establishing a decentralised education system, with Village Education Committees (VECs) taking a central role. Each VEC numbers about eight people, who are nominated by community assemblies. In addition to these village-level structures, Lok Jumbish has established block-level committees, including government, NGO, and VEC appointees. These committees, covering 100–150 villages, are vested with the power to open and up-grade schools, and to appoint new teachers.

By 1998, the initiative had extended to 75 blocks, or one-third of rural Rajasthan. About 1000 elementary and 300 upper-primary schools fall under its administration, along with more than 1000 non-formal education centres. The project has developed its own teacher–training modules, which have been used to train 2300 teachers.[27]

One of the most important Lok Jumbish innovations has been the village-mapping exercise. More than 4000 villages have participated in developing 'maps' which go beyond identifying the location of schools and roads, to establishing the social and cultural problems faced by local communities in accessing schools. Issues of school quality, curriculum relevance, distance, and teacher attitudes all figured prominently. Women's groups identified the major deterrents to girls' education. As a source of information, these exercises have helped to mould Lok Jumbish programme responses. More importantly, they have provided an entry point for local people to participate, for the first time, in discussions about education problems and needs. As with the Shiksha Karmi programme, major advances have been made:

- Over the first four years of the project, enrolment rates in Lok Jumbish villages increased by one quarter.

- Enrolment of girls has increased faster than that of boys (from a net enrolment rate of 29 per cent to one of 59 per cent). The gender gap is closing, even though girls still account for only about one-third of enrolment.

One of the most important concerns identified by women in the mapping exercises was the shortage of female teachers, as in the Shiksha Karmi programme. This problem persists, but a Women's Teachers' Forum has been established to attract new recruits. Considerable emphasis has also been given to teacher training. Two-week motivational courses are run every year, and 900 'master trainers' provide constant in-service assistance. At the same time, Lok Jumbish has contracted external organisations to help develop textbooks in language and mathematics for Grades 1 and 2. In contrast to the practices in the government system, prototypes were tested on parents and children, and amended in the light of their comments. Surveys show that children find these books more interesting and comprehensible than standard texts.

Integration into DPEP

These two programmes illustrate what can be achieved by concerted co-operative action between local communities, NGOs, government, and international donors. Many of the Shiksha Karmi and Lok Jumbish

323

blocks are now being integrated into the national District Primary Education Programme that became operational in Rajasthan in 1998. Another positive feature of both programmes has been the high standard of evaluation carried out by participants in Lok Jumbish and Shiksha Karmi. These have helped to identify problems and shortcomings, notably in relation to gender equity. Finally, both projects have avoided the trap of dependence on donors. From providing more than 90 per cent of financing in the early stages, SIDA now funds less than half of the project's costs, while the State government has assumed responsibility for a growing share of funding.

The Bangladesh Rural Advancement Committee (BRAC)

Bangladesh has made considerable progress in basic education over recent years. There is a large unfinished agenda, however. About 4 million children never go to school, almost half of those who do attend drop out in the early grades, and education quality is poor. According to one World Bank study, four out of five children completing primary school fail to meet a minimum standard of performance in test scores. The net enrolment rate for girls (78 per cent) is 10 per cent lower than for boys, threatening to extend gender inequity in literacy into the next generation.

The Bangladesh Rural Advancement Committee (BRAC) has developed some of the best-known, and most effective, strategies for addressing the education problems of poor rural communities.[28] These strategies have built on the foundations of intensive community participation, local recruitment of teachers, an emphasis on girls' education, the development of a relevant curriculum, flexible hours, and cost effectiveness.[29] BRAC currently runs 35,000 schools, providing education to 1.2 million children. Three-quarters of the pupils are girls. One of the reasons for this success in countering the national gender bias is a strong emphasis on the recruitment of local female teachers. Two-thirds of the teachers are women. Teachers are required to have undergone nine years of schooling themselves and to complete a 15-day training course, supplemented by monthly in-service training. Most are locally recruited and paid a modest stipend of about $12 per month.[30]

There are two types of school. The first offers three years of education for children aged between 8 and 10 who have never attended primary school. The second provides a two-year course for 11–16 year-old children who have dropped out of government primary schools. After completing BRAC courses, children are equipped to begin, or return to, formal primary schools at Grades 5 or 6. Educational attainment in BRAC schools compares favourably with government schools (see Chapter 2) at all levels.[31] Each child receives a set of basic teaching materials, including a slate, pencils, notebooks, and textbooks. This better teaching environment is produced at lower cost. The average cost per child educated in a BRAC school is approximately $20 per annum, compared with $51 in State elementary schools.

Before establishing a village school, BRAC staff engage with parents to identify seasonal labour demands. This enables the school calendar to be adjusted to fit local needs. Schools teach a simplified curriculum and use flexible scheduling, suited to rural life. The community and local landowners help to choose the site for the school, and provide labour and materials to build classrooms. Lessons last three hours a day, six days a week, 270 days a year. This compares favourably with government schools, which have shorter hours and two long vacations. A distinguishing feature of BRAC education is its child-centred approach. The classrooms are brightly decorated with posters and children's work. Pupil participation is encouraged, with a strong emphasis on children asking questions, reading, designing, drawing, singing, and undertaking joint project work. Rote-learning is limited to short periods. Each school has a chalk-board and charts, picture cards, and counting sticks. BRAC schools do not use physical punishment of pupils, which is rife in State schools.

BRAC's work demonstrates what is possible when education systems are adapted to local needs. It also shows the power of demonstration effects. The government of Bangladesh is now adopting many of the curriculum ideas and teacher-training methods pioneered by BRAC. In the past, co-operation between BRAC and other NGOs on the one side, and government on the other, has been weaker than it should have been. Some officials have been critical of the development of alternative curricula and teacher-recruitment strategies, but this too is changing. The programme designed to get older children back into school has been developed in dialogue with the government. This dynamic interaction between the formal State system and the informal NGO system under-lines the danger of artificial distinctions between formal and non-formal education.

Egypt: the Community Schools Project
Egypt is one of nine high-population countries targeted for improving literacy under the Education for All initiative. More than 30 million Egyptian adults are non-literate, and each year another quarter of a million are added to the total. The failure to stem the tide of increasing

illiteracy is rooted in extreme regional and gender-linked inequalities that start in the primary-school system. Almost 1 million girls are estimated to be out of school. The official net enrolment rate is about 80 per cent for girls and boys, but household surveys tell a different story. In Upper Egypt, school-attendance rates vary between 67 per cent in cities such as Assuit and Sohag, and less than 55 per cent in surrounding rural areas. Problems are especially pronounced in more remote rural areas, where young girls in particular are excluded from educational opportunities.

In 1992, UNICEF and the Ministry of Education piloted a community-school model in four of the most remote rural hamlets in Upper Egypt.[32] The aim was to provide universal access to school (with a focus on girls' enrolment), to select and train facilitators and teachers from local communities, to develop a curriculum suited to local learning needs and preferences, and to emphasise child-centred development. Under the partnership arrangement, the government was to provide the finance for books, teachers' salaries, and a school nutrition programme. The local community was to provide space for the school, establish an education committee to manage the school, and advise on curriculum development. UNICEF assumed responsibility for training staff and providing schools with furniture and equipment. Integration with the national education systems was ensured through a provision which made graduates from the community schools eligible for examinations in government schools at the end of Grades 3 and 6. The village education committee selects teachers from among local women with an intermediate school certificate. These women are then trained through a combination of intensive residential work on child-centred development, classroom teaching, and in-service training. Teachers meet fortnightly with the school-management committee to discuss problems.

Within four years of the pilot project's establishment, it was already clear that the community schools were far more successful than the formal education system in reaching remote and marginalised communities. By the end of 1995, there were 125 schools, catering for 1650 children. In hamlets where the enrolment rates for girls were often as low as 15 per cent, the community schools were achieving girls' net enrolment rates in excess of 70 per cent. Each of the four pilot schools achieved a 100 per cent success rate in the test for passing from Grade 1 to Grade 2, compared with a 33 per cent failure rate in government schools. Apart from improving education at the primary level, the community schools have provided adult-literacy classes.

There is little doubt that community schools have the capacity to expand the coverage of the national education system, and to reduce illiteracy, but therein lies one of the dilemmas. The government of Egypt has announced ambitious plans to establish more than 3000 community schools over the next few years. But the very success of the experiment has been the product of intensive and painstaking collaboration at community level, where cultural discrimination against girls remains deeply entrenched. Transforming the experiment into a national policy will, in the absence of a change in institutional norms in central government, undermine the local conditions for achieving success.

Colombia: the Escuela Nueva programme[33]

Colombia is an example of much that is bad about education policy in Latin America. The share of primary education in overall spending has declined since the 1970s, and per capita spending is 12 times higher in the tertiary sector than the primary sector. This is despite the fact that the country has one of the lowest enrolment rates for girls (65 per cent, compared with 95 per cent for boys) in the region. But in a country not regarded as a leader in the field of innovative policies in education, the Escuela Nueva (New School) programme provides a model for extending opportunities to the rural poor which is being adapted in other countries.

What makes the Escuela Nueva programme exceptional? Unlike many of the other initiatives discussed in this report, it started as an innovation launched by a group of reform-minded teachers within the formal education system in the mid-1970s. The programme placed an emphasis on the development of a relevant curriculum and flexible school schedules, long before these approaches were fashionable. Moreover, the initiative's survival over almost a quarter of a century is an impressive testament to its durability and relevance. A group of teachers in poor rural areas began the initiative after a process of intensive dialogue with local communities to identify the reasons for low enrolment and high drop-out rates. Three concerns emerged: the curriculum, teacher training, and school management. Out of the response has developed a movement which now covers over 17,000 rural primary schools – almost half of the total in Colombia.

The Escuela Nueva curriculum, like that developed by BRAC, is geared towards rural areas. Because many of the communities involved live in remote areas, where there may not be enough children for a full school, a new multi-grade approach to teaching was developed, with one or two teachers covering all grades. Learning guides were developed for use by children in groups, with detailed instructions for how to use them.

The guides were designed to encourage 'learning-by-doing' through a range of activities which develop in children an ability to think for themselves, rather than simply receive information. Another integral part of the school is a small library, stocked with dictionaries and about 70 children's books.

One of the distinctive features of the Escuela Nueva programme is the system of grade promotion. Assessment takes place on a continuous basis, and promotion to successive grades is flexible, but not automatic. This means that children do not have to re-take a whole year if they fail an examination at the end of a grade. Each child is moved to the next grade when he or she achieves the required academic standard. One advantage of the approach is that children can interrupt their studies, for instance during a harvest period, without being required to go back to square one. Given the huge disincentives and opportunity costs created by repetition, this is a major advantage.

A strong emphasis is placed on teacher training. Initial training for new teachers involves three workshops which focus on child-centred development and the portrayal of the school as an integral part of community life. In-service training takes place through 'Rural Micro-Centres', where groups of 10-15 teachers meet to exchange ideas and upgrade their skills. The teacher-training process stresses the importance of involving parents in their children's education, while the school itself is designed to operate as an information centre for the entire community. One of the learning modules involves children working with parents to develop seasonal calendars for agricultural cycles, as well as social, cultural, and economic maps of the community.

One of the strengths of Escuela Nueva institutions is that they get results. Recent evaluations show that they outperform conventional rural schools in most academic tests (Grade 5 mathematics being the exception). Children also complete the primary education cycle earlier than the national average for rural schools. Attitudes and life-skills are less easy to evaluate. However, a World Bank comparison of Escuela Nueva and conventional schools concluded: 'The analysis of self-esteem which shows that girls equalled boys in this dimension demonstrates the equalising effect of a participatory methodology.'

Pakistan: community initiatives in a hostile environment
Education reform in Pakistan has been hampered by a failure to develop strong partnerships between national government and NGOs. The financing of education has been highly politicised, with decisions linked

to systems of patronage and clientelism. As a consequence, central government has failed to devolve control to local bodies, or to engage with community-based organisations. This has resulted in chronic problems of implementation, partly due to an inability to examine realities on the ground, and partly due to the activities of corrupt and unaccountable State bodies.

The costs of failure to develop more participative structures are reflected in high levels of waste. In 1995, a UNICEF survey revealed that the simple act of clearing classrooms used to store broken furniture could increase school capacity by 10 per cent.[34] The absence of any meaningful mapping exercises involving local communities has resulted in a situation where there are more than 3000 rural schools with fewer than ten students, and another 2000 with no students at all! Despite this bleak picture, however, there are islands of hope. A growing recognition of the importance of education on the part of communities, allied to political indifference on the part of central government, has led to a proliferation of community-led schemes.

The Society for Community Support for Primary Education

The province of Baluchistan has some of the lowest enrolment rates and widest gender gaps in Pakistan. Female literacy is only about 10 per cent, and 2 per cent among rural women. The combination of cultural obstacles to girls' education, such as seclusion and early marriage, and chronic under-provision is at the heart of the problem. The Society for Community Support for Primary Education in Baluchistan, known as The Society, is attempting to improve the access of girls to education through a process of community mobilisation. During 1993–94, teams from The Society, more than 80 per cent of whose staff are women, visited 900 villages to discuss educational problems and identify needs. Village Education Committees (VECs), mainly comprising the fathers of school-age children, and Mothers' Education Committees (MECs) were established as contact points.[35] The MECs have been instrumental in fostering new attitudes to the value of education; and in a society where seclusion is the norm, monthly women's meetings are helping to create opportunities for discussion.

The community-mobilisation efforts undertaken by The Society have been accompanied by an intensive dialogue with government. One tangible expression of this co-operation has been the development of community schools. These have been set up in villages where a woman educated to Grade 10 is willing to teach at primary-school level, and where there is a primary school. Surveys are carried out by The Society to determine the numbers of children in the village. The VECs are required to apply to government for a school to be established, and to provide land for a temporary school facility. Government then tests, trains, and appoints the teacher, and sends materials to the school. In-service support for the teacher is provided through the Society's Mobile Female Teacher-Training Unit.

There are now almost 300 community schools, with approximately 12,000 girls enrolled: about 8 per cent of total female enrolment in Baluchistan. Management of these schools is vested in the VECs. Drop-out rates in the schools are far lower than the average level for girls, as is absenteeism. The lessons from the community schools are informing dialogue between the World Bank, NGOs, and government under the $100m Baluchistan Primary Education Programme.

The Busti Programme

The Busti (community) programme, which is a collaboration between a Karachi-based NGO and UNICEF, aims to provide basic education to children who can then be admitted to formal schools. The age group covered is 5–10, and about three-quarters of pupils are girls. The Busti initiative has succeeded in reversing the normal gender bias, partly by providing education in homes. It has set up more than 200 home schools, enrolling more than 6000 students, at a per-unit cost of $6 — far lower than average costs in public elementary schools.[36] This approach was adopted after community discussions revealed that journeys to school were a major deterrent to female education. Local women are recruited as teachers, who in turn set up a school in their homes. Parents pay the teacher up to $1 per month, less than they would pay in the State system. There is no requirement to wear school uniform, and school timings are flexible. While there is some criticism of a failure to develop teaching techniques which go beyond rote-learning, the Busti initiative does demonstrate what can be achieved when education provision is adapted to community needs.

7

An agenda for action

More than half a century has passed since the Universal Declaration of Human Rights made free and compulsory basic education a fundamental human right. Enormous advances have been made. Yet at the start of the new millennium, the right to education continues to be violated on a widespread and systematic basis. The exclusion of millions of poor people from the opportunities promised in the Universal Declaration is one of the most potent sources of poverty and inequality in the world today.

The first decade of the new millennium began in the same style as the 1990s, with a major international conference on education. The World Education Forum, convened in Dakar, Senegal in April 2000, marked the tenth anniversary of the World Conference on Education for All. Like its predecessor, the World Forum reaffirmed the commitment of all governments to education as a basic human right. The challenge now is to move from the rhetoric of reaffirmation to the policies needed to make the universal right to education a reality for all people. Governments do not lack the resources or the capacity to achieve this goal. What is lacking is the political will and vision needed to accelerate progress. The time has arrived for a fundamental review of what went wrong after the bold commitments made at the 1990 World Conference on Education for All in Jomtien, and for a forthright assessment of the challenges ahead. Many of the problems can be traced to Southern governments. Basic education continues to suffer from chronic under-investment and highly unequal spending patterns. The result is that poor people are offered education services of poor quality, often at high – and unaffordable – cost to themselves.

The damaging consequences of under-investment for the quality and accessibility of education are reinforced by other problems. In many countries, education planning continues to suffer from a production-line mentality, in which children are processed through school systems that are unresponsive to local needs. Centralised planning continues to dominate, with local communities often excluded from meaningful participation. Unsurprisingly, parents often perceive the school curriculum as being irrelevant to the needs of their children. Classroom practices frequently reflect a limited vision for education, with teaching methods geared towards rote-learning, rather than the development of creative potential. It is true that some of the world's poorest countries have shown what can be achieved through ambitious reforms programmes, backed by political will – but these are small islands of success in a sea of failure.

International co-operation has a vital role to play in mobilising resources and supporting national strategies for change. Northern governments promised much in this respect, but have delivered little. Aid budgets for education have been cut, the debt crisis has been allowed to continue, with devastating consequences for school budgets, and structural adjustment programmes are undermining the access of poor people to good-quality education. New forms of co-operation between rich and poor are needed, if the 2015 goal of universal primary education is to be achieved. Ultimately, however, solutions to the global crisis in education will have to be built on the foundation of partnerships between Southern governments, local communities, and organisations working with the poor. As we showed in Chapter 6, these partnerships are starting to emerge. Northern governments can help to create an enabling environment in which education reform can succeed. But the political momentum and the strategies for change needed cannot be imported from outside. That is why action to mobilise for change at the national level holds the key to successful reform.

From Jomtien to Dakar

The World Education Forum, held in the Senegalese capital of Dakar in April 2000, marked the first great UN summit of the new millennium. One hundred and eighty eight governments met to review the progress achieved over the previous decade, and to adopt a new 'framework for action'. Some of the outcomes were entirely predictable, including the reaffirmation of principles adopted at previous summits. But the Dakar *Framework for Action* marked a step forwards in two important respects. First, it bluntly acknowledges that 'without accelerated progress towards education for all, national and internationally agreed targets for poverty reduction will be missed, and inequalities between countries and within countries will widen'. Second, it identifies some of the mechanisms and strategies needed to translate the commitment to universal primary education into reality. It would be wrong to exaggerate the importance of the *Framework for Action*, and much will depend on how governments use it, but it does have the potential to generate change. There are four substantive innovations in the Dakar *Framework for Action*:

- **Free education**. The 1990 World Conference on Education for All did not produce a commitment to free and compulsory primary education.

This reflected an increasing requirement on the part of governments and donors that part of the cost of basic education should be met by households. The Dakar *Framework* strongly reasserts the right of all children to 'have access to (...) free and compulsory education of good quality'.

- **The development of national plans.** Governments have been requested to develop national plans, or strengthen existing plans, for achieving education for all. The plans are expected to address problems associated with under-financing, and to establish budget priorities that reflect 'a commitment to achieving education for all goals and targets at the earliest possible date, and no later than 2015'. They will also set out strategies for overcoming the problems faced by those currently excluded from educational opportunities, with an emphasis on gender equity. It is envisaged that the national education plans will be integrated into a wider poverty-reduction and development framework. Finally, there is a strong emphasis on public participation: 'These plans ... should be developed through more transparent and democratic processes, involving all stakeholders, especially people's representatives, community leaders, parents, learners, NGOs, and civil society.'

- **Guaranteed financing.** At previous UN summits, social-development targets have been set without any reference to the mobilisation of international resources needed for their attainment. The Dakar *Framework for Action* does not wholly depart from this tradition. No specific goals have been set for resource mobilisation; but Northern governments have acknowledged that many countries currently lack the financial resources needed to achieve education for all within an acceptable time-frame. The *Framework* therefore establishes the principle of 'guaranteed financing'. It states that 'no countries seriously committed to education for all will be thwarted in their achievement of this goal by a lack of resources'. If this commitment is converted into practice – and it is a big 'if' – it could have profound implications for international financing of national education initiatives.

- **The development of a global initiative.** Translating the principle of guaranteed financing into practice will require a coherent international plan of action. The World Forum on education could have provided such a plan, and its failure to do so was a major setback. On a more positive note, the Dakar *Framework for Action* makes an unequivocal commitment to develop a plan. It states: 'The international community will deliver on (its) collective commitment by developing

No countries seriously committed to education for all will be thwarted in their achievement of this goal by a lack of resources.

with immediate effect a global initiative aimed at developing the strategies and mobilising the resources needed to provide effective support to national efforts'. A range of financing options is listed, including increased aid; earlier, deeper, and broader debt relief; and the strengthening of sector-wide approaches.

It should be emphasised that the Dakar *Framework* is just that: a framework. It is not a coherent plan of action, or an initiative backed by resources. It does, however, establish some important ground-rules. The commitment to develop national plans of action that set clear budget priorities and involve civil society provides a yardstick against which to judge the actions of national governments. Similarly, the commitment to develop a global initiative to ensure that no national strategy fails for want of adequate finance establishes clear standards for Northern governments. Perhaps most importantly, the Dakar Framework provides a potential focal point for the political alliances and partnerships needed to bring about change at the national and global levels. Indeed, the Framework itself reflects the influence of a global campaign on education, mounted in advance of the World Education Forum. The post-Dakar challenge is to develop more effective strategies and policies at the national level, and, through international action, to provide the financial resources necessary to ensure that such policies succeed.

Action at the national level

There are no national blueprints for achieving education for all. Different countries face different problems, although inadequate and unequal access, high drop-out rates, poor-quality education, and the persistence of deep gender-linked inequities are recurrent themes. While national strategies must be developed in a way that takes account of local realities, there is tremendous scope for learning from, and adapting, good practice. By the same token, there are enough bad policy examples to identify strategies that will not deliver more rapid progress.

The national education plans envisaged under the Dakar *Framework for Action* could provide a catalyst for focusing political attention on the 2015 targets, provided that some potential pitfalls are avoided. It is important that the plans do not become token exercises in the production of documents designed to meet donors' reporting requirements, rather than to address real problems. Substantive commitments have to be made and acted upon – and the planning process needs to meet the public-participation criteria established at Dakar. By the same token, the national education plans should not simply duplicate existing efforts.

The Global Campaign for Education

'Education For All' was the motto of a dilatory inter-governmental process that monitored progress towards universal basic education during the 1990s. In the early months of 2000, it became the rallying cry of an impatient new campaign – the Global Campaign for Education (GCE) – demanding an end to the scandal of mass illiteracy and exclusion from basic education. The campaign brought together a powerful coalition of forces. It includes Education International, an umbrella group of unions repre-senting 23 million teachers, and a diverse array of non-government organisations, among them Global March Against Child Labour, Oxfam, ActionAid, and coalitions of NGOs from 40 countries.

Within months of its official launch in October 1999, the campaign was making headway. In the run-up to the World Education Forum in Dakar, it organised public protests in India, Brazil, Tanzania, Britain, Spain, and more than 20 other countries. The aim was to raise awareness of the scale of the challenge facing the government representatives heading for the Dakar conference – and their lam-entable record of achievement over the past ten years. Inspired by the big single-issue campaigns of the 1990s on landmines, international debt, and other development issues, the Campaign greeted the new millennium with a week of action around the world. In India, children marched on Parliament and staged two hours of street theatre. In the United Kingdom, 1000 life-size cardboard cut-outs of Prime Minister Tony Blair marched on Parliament. In Sierra Leone there were television debates and celebrity football matches involving children. Across 90 countries there were press conferences, lobbying meetings, newspaper articles, demonstrations, marches, opinion polls, seminars, video screenings, fingerprint petitions, and human chains.

Government delegates arriving in Dakar in April could not have helped but notice the NGO presence. Campaign billboards with French and English texts asking *Will they never learn?* appeared in city streets. Ten thousand Senegalese schoolchildren marched through downtown Dakar in support of the campaign. The Global Campaign's candidates were elected to nearly all the seats allocated to NGOs on the Forum's drafting committees. And throughout the meeting, campaigners stalked the corridors, lobbying delegates and talking to journalists. When the Dakar conference began, the impact of the campaign was immediately in evidence. UN Secretary General Kofi Annan, in his address to the opening plenary session, welcomed the formation of the GCE and promised that its voice would be heard. Surrounded by a crowd of journalists and TV reporters, Annan walked out of the conference hall to witness a demonstration, with more than 1000 Senegalese students waving yellow cards in the manner of soccer referees giving a final warning. The target of the cards was the official government delegations attending the conference.

Apart from receiving the endorsement of the UN Secretary General, the GCE was enthusiastically welcomed by the heads of other UN agencies such as the United Nations Development Programme (UNDP) and the United Nation Children's Fund (UNICEF), and by the representatives of several developing-country governments. Although the final communiqué adopted by governments in Dakar included some of the GCE's main demands, it fell far short of expectations. It included new commitments to free and compulsory primary edu-cation of good quality, and the principle that no country committed to education for all would be allowed to fail for lack of resources. Neither of these commitments would have been made in the absence of the GCE. But the details of how the international community would actually implement these promises were vague. Campaigners had been calling for a global action plan to mobilise resources to support the efforts of developing countries.

Since the World Forum on education, the GCE has been growing in strength. Campaign activists have increased their efforts to convince govern-ments and the big agencies that a global action plan is needed to deliver on the promises made at Dakar. If they were disappointed with the reluctance of governments to make hard commitments, campaigners had at least registered a strong presence at the Dakar Forum. The challenge facing the GCE's members now is to build on what was achieved there. That means engaging with Southern governments as they develop their national education strategies – and it means holding Northern governments to account for the commitment they have made.

In his final address to the Forum at Dakar, the Global Campaign's Tom Bediako put the governments and institutions on notice: 'In the last few months we have seen a flowering of a world-wide movement of civil society dedicated to the fight for quality education for all ... I want to tell you we will not go away. We will continue to campaign at local, national, and international levels.'

In particular, they should not be used to create another layer of bureaucracy. Many governments are already developing or implementing strategic plans for their education sectors. These establish targets and strategies for achieving universal primary education, overcoming inequalities, and improving education quality. They also provide indicative financial estimates that should be integrated into national budgets and medium-term financing strategies. The national plans requested by the World Forum on education should be governed by the principle of *additionality*. That is, they should seek to establish what more could be done with an increase in public investment and a renewed political effort. The costs of accelerating progress towards the 2015 targets by a variety of measures (for instance, bringing forward the date for the provision of universal primary education, stepping up provision in the poorest districts, or increasing classroom construction or textbook supply) should be established. Once established, these indicative costs could be used to allocate spending under the proposed global initiative.

As with existing sectoral planning, the new national education plans will not succeed unless they are built on genuine partnerships between the various actors involved, with local communities themselves having a real voice in their design. Priorities will vary from case to case, but there are some fundamental and non-negotiable requirements that could be established in key areas such as public spending, cost-sharing, gender equity, exclusion, and education quality.

Changing public-spending priorities

Improved efficiency in the allocation of resources has the potential to generate education benefits in all countries, rich and poor. But in many of the poorest countries, efficiency gains within the education system cannot overcome the problems associated with inadequate public invest-ment. Insufficient funding has as its corollary shortages of essential teaching materials, dilapidated school buildings, demoralised teachers, and high costs to parents. There is no threshold level of public spending that is automatically consistent with attaining the 2015 target. However, historical experience and recent examples (see Chapter 4) suggest the following guidelines.

- At least 6 per cent of GDP should be spent on education.

- In countries where a substantial proportion of the population of primary-school age is out of school and drop-out rates are high, 60–70 per cent of the education budget should be allocated to primary education.

- There should be a greater emphasis on lower-secondary education, to improve transition rates from secondary school.

- Increased public investment in adult literacy is essential.

Changing public-spending priorities creates difficult political choices. It also creates winners and losers. Shifting the emphasis away from public investment in universities in favour of primary schools will hurt politically powerful urban middle-class constituencies, while benefiting a less powerful political constituency: namely, the poor. But choices in favour of improved equity can be made, if the political leadership is right. Ten years ago, Uganda dedicated the same share of its GDP to primary education as India did. Today, Uganda is spending almost 3 per cent of its GDP on primary education, compared with the Indian government's allocation of 1 per cent to primary schooling. Unlike its counterpart in India, the government of Uganda is making the right to a free and compulsory education a reality – and it is achieving rapid progress towards universal primary education.

As suggested in Chapter 4, governments have a variety of policy options for increasing public investment in basic education. These include switching expenditure from non-productive areas such as military spending into education, and reallocating resources from higher to lower levels of the education system.

Providing free education

No child should be denied the right to an education because of the poverty suffered by his or her parents. Yet for millions of the world's poorest people, education is not a human right, but an unaffordable luxury (Chapter 2). Inadequate public investment has progressively increased the cost of education to households, excluding many of the poorest.

Rising school fees, the costs of providing textbooks and buying uniforms, and – in most countries – a multitude of informal fees are all part of the problem. As part of their national education planning process, governments should adopt the following measures.

- Immediately abolish all formal school fees and legislate against informal charging practices.
- Reduce the pressure on households to provide teaching materials, by increasing public investment.
- Relieve poor households of the obligation to provide their children with school uniforms.

Cost sharing should be scrupulously avoided at the primary and lower-secondary levels, though it may have a role to play at higher levels of education.

Overcoming gender-linked inequalities

Education systems play a crucial role in shaping the life-chances of children, including poor children's chances to escape poverty. While education has the potential to act as a powerful force for human development, it often reinforces gender-determined disadvantage. Households may not value the education of girls as much as the education of boys; teachers often believe girls to be incapable of matching the achievements of boys; and school curricula and textbooks reinforce attitudes that ascribe a more dynamic role to boys. Some of the change has to come from within education systems. The recruitment of more female teachers, more gender-sensitive training for male teachers, the redesign of textbooks, and the provision of adequate sanitation facilities can all make a difference, as we saw in Chapter 4. So too can policies that reduce distances between home communities and schools, since this is far more negatively correlated with girls' attendance than it is with boys' attendance. Schools also need to be more responsive to local realities. When cultural practices preclude girls from starting school until their teenage years and involve early marriage, the fact of teenage pregnancy has to be accommodated within the school system and not be punished by exclusion. But in many respects the most important changes have to take place outside the school system. Social attitudes need to be changed, through public information and public campaigning. The following are among the priorities for the national education action plans:

- national political campaigning to develop more positive attitudes to girls' education;

- incentives for girls' education in the form of bursaries, free school meals, and accelerated withdrawal of fees for girl students;

- improved sanitation and security conditions;

- reducing the distance between communities and schools through the provision of village-level satellite schools;

- the elimination of gender bias in curricula and textbook design;

- an increased commitment to the recruitment of female teachers.

This is an area in which partnerships between governments and local communities are essential. The success of the Bangladesh Rural Advancement Committee (see Chapter 6) shows how local initiative can be scaled up into international action, achieving major advances in gender equity in the process.

Addressing the problems behind exclusion

Gender is only one source of inequity in education. Household poverty is also intimately related to educational disadvantage. The poor are less able to afford education; they often live in the most remote areas that are farthest from government service-providers; and they are more dependent upon child labour. Innovative approaches have been developed to overcome the problems associated with poverty. The Escuela Nueva programme in Colombia (see Chapter 6) succeeded because it geared the school term and classroom to fit the reality of local labour markets. In India, the Lok Jumbish programme developed school curricula that are perceived as relevant to the needs of poor households. The first step towards overcoming exclusion involves understanding why the poor do not send their children to school. Participative research has a crucial role to play, because the poor themselves are the best policy advisers when it comes to identifying the causes of exclusion. Community-based organisations and NGOs have a role to play in facilitating that research and in monitoring progress, because they are often in the most direct contact with the poor. But there is a danger of research being divorced from the policy-making environment. That is why research programmes must be placed at the heart of government programmes and carried out with active government involvement. Priorities for the national action plan should include the following:

- the development of participative research strategies aimed at identifying the structural causes of exclusion, bringing together local communities, civil society, and government;

- the integration of education policies and monitoring into national anti-poverty strategies;

The first step towards overcoming exclusion involves understanding why the poor do not send their children to school.

- more equitable public investment to improve the quality and accessibility of services provided in poor areas;
- the development of school curricula that meet the needs of poor communities;
- the adaptation of schools' annual calendars and daily schedules to fit local circumstances, such as the agricultural season.

Improving quality

Access to school is no guarantee of a good-quality education. Shortages of teaching materials are one problem. Another is an undue emphasis on rote-learning, which reduces children to playing a passive role in the classroom. In many countries the quality of education suffers further from the use of a second language as the initial teaching medium, and from inappropriate curricula design. Chapter 2 examined these quality-related problems in detail. There is no shortage of good examples of responses to these problems. BRAC schools in Bangladesh and the Escuela Nueva programme in Colombia have pioneered interactive learning methods, with positive outcomes in terms of educational attainment. In many developing regions, UNICEF and local NGOs have devised more appropriate approaches to teaching the children of ethnic minorities, with an emphasis on the use of their own first language. But progress in these areas depends critically upon a supply of well-motivated, well-trained, and well-supported teachers. This condition is lacking in most countries, and should be a central priority for reform.

International action

International co-operation has a critical role to play in accelerating progress towards the 2015 targets. As the Dakar Framework acknowledged, many of the poorest countries in the world lack the financing capacity to achieve education for all within an acceptable time-frame. For these countries, international resource mobilisation in support of strong national policies is vital. Various attempts have been made to estimate the costs of achieving universal primary education, none of them particularly satisfactory. The UN and the World Bank have produced a tentative cost estimate of $8bn per annum, over and above existing levels of spending on education. The problem with this figure is that it is derived from a simple multiplication of the number of children out of school by the average expenditure on each child currently in school. It does not take into account the need to raise per capita spending in order to improve the quality of schooling. Nor does it take account of the fact that the marginal costs of extending access to those not in school may be higher than average spending on those in school. For instance, the costs of integrating disabled children and communities in remote areas into mainstream education will inevitably exceed average costs. There are further anomalies associated with the UN–World Bank formula. Because it is based on average spending on children in school, it produces a result which suggests that the costs of achieving universal primary education are lower for Latin America and the Middle East (where average spending per student is relatively high) than for sub-Saharan Africa (where average spending is low).

In an effort to address some of these problems, Oxfam has developed separate cost estimates for sub-Saharan Africa. These are based on achieving universal primary-school enrolment in a context where at least $5 per student is spent on teaching materials (compared with $1 at present), and where the student–teacher ratio is reduced to 30:1. The estimates cover the costs of constructing over a ten-year period approximately one million classrooms to accommodate entrants to the school system, and budget provisions for doubling the secondary-school population over a ten-year period. The latter is important, for the obvious reason that sustained primary-school expansion is not feasible in the absence of higher transition rates to secondary school. The figure arrived at in our estimate is a total cost of **$3.6bn per annum over ten years**, which is around three times the UN–World Bank estimate for Africa. Aggregate assessments such as these inevitably obscure huge national variations. In countries where the unit costs of education provision are very high, there is often scope for efficiency savings (for instance, through improved deployment of teachers).

Universal primary education is affordable.

What emerges clearly from a range of cost estimates is that universal primary education is affordable. The average additional expenditure required in countries such as India and Pakistan amounts to around 1 per cent of GDP, rising to 1–2 per cent for sub-Saharan Africa. Of course, these figures translate into very large shifts in spending on education. India, to take one example, would need to double its primary-education budget to absorb another 1 per cent of GDP. And the budget requirements for Africa are clearly beyond the financing capacity of many countries. However, the absolute sums involved are modest. This is especially true when global spending requirements are set in the context of global wealth and spending patterns. The $8bn estimate provided by the UN and the World Bank is equivalent to the following measures:

- four days' worth of global military spending; or

- 0.02 per cent of global GDP; or
- one-third of the real cuts made to international aid budgets since 1992.

Measured in terms of the potential benefits for human welfare, poverty reduction, and global economic growth, these represent small investments with very high returns. The 0.02 per cent of global GDP required to achieve universal primary education represents less than 1 per cent of the share of national income mobilised by the USA to implement the Marshall Plan for reconstruction in Europe after the Second World War.

The global initiative should include the following elements:

Too much aid flows back to Northern countries in the form of contracts for consultants and construction programmes.

- an international commitment to mobilise $4bn per annum, or half of the costs of financing universal primary education, through increased aid as part of the global initiative for education;
- the development of a special initiative for sub-Saharan Africa, the region facing the largest gap between financing capacity and the resources required to achieve the 2015 targets.

Increased and improved aid

Broad quantitative targets should be set for mobilising additional aid. This could be achieved through more rapid progress towards the 0.7 per cent UN target and a more equitable pattern of aid allocation. It is indefensible that primary education receives less than 2 per cent of the OECD aid effort. Greater equity is needed also in the geographical distribution of aid. The low rate of disbursement to sub-Saharan Africa is a special concern, especially with regard to World Bank assistance (see Chapter 5). Finally, the effectiveness of aid is undermined by an undue emphasis on technical assistance and tied aid. Too much aid flows back to Northern countries in the form of contracts for consultants and construction programmes; too little flows into the education systems, where it is needed. Among the reforms that are needed are the following:

- at least 8 per cent of the aid budgets of each donor directed towards basic education;
- an increased emphasis on capacity building and support for the development of national education-sector strategies;
- less reliance on technical assistance, and the abolition of tied aid in governments' procurement programmes.

Earlier, deeper, and more effective debt relief

For many of the poorest countries, especially in sub-Saharan Africa, unsustainable debt constitutes a huge barrier to education for all.

The debts accumulated by previous generations are destroying the educational opportunities of the present generation. While the reformed Heavily Indebted Poor Countries (HIPC) Initiative marks a step in the right direction, it is still delivering too little, too late. Only eight countries have so far received debt relief under this scheme. While the headline figures for debt reduction are large, desperately poor countries such as Tanzania, Burkina Faso, and Mali will still be spending more on debt repayments after they have received HIPC Initiative debt relief than they are spending on primary education (see Chapter 5). This is not consistent with an international commitment to achieve universal primary education by 2015. Poor countries need broader approaches to debt sustainability that look beyond the financial capacity of governments to repay debts, to consider the human-development costs of debt repayment. Another problem with implementation of the HIPC Initiative is that the links between debt relief and poverty reduction remain weak. Far more needs to be done to ensure that debt relief is provided early – and that it delivers immediate and tangible benefits. Reforms are necessary in four areas.

No government in a low-income country should be spending more than 10 per cent of national revenue on servicing external debt.

- Earlier debt relief and lower debt-sustainability thresholds are needed, to ensure that governments develop the financing capacity to provide basic services.

- No government in a low-income country should be spending more than 10 per cent of national revenue on servicing external debt.

- Eligibility for debt relief should be determined by the development of concrete plans for using the savings for investment in poverty-reduction initiatives, with a mechanism capable of establishing a strong and immediate link between debt relief and poverty reduction.

- Eligible countries should be required to develop poverty-action funds through which to channel savings from debt relief into poverty-focused programmes that set clear and quantifiable targets for improving provision in education, health services, and other sectors. The funds should be subject to strict auditing and monitoring requirements.

Reforming IMF programmes

As the main shareholders in the International Monetary Fund, Northern governments bear primary responsibility for the content of its programmes. As shown in Chapter 5, these programmes have produced deep cuts in the education budgets of some of the world's poorest countries. Per capita spending has fallen in at least twelve countries undergoing adjustment under IMF auspices. In East Asia, the IMF's response to the financial crisis had the effect of prolonging and deepening the subsequent recession. Rising poverty and declining public investment in education caused serious setbacks in efforts to achieve education for all. Reforms are needed in several areas.

- The financing requirements for achieving the international develop-ment targets and the wider development goals defined in national poverty-reduction strategies must be reflected in IMF programmes.
- Less emphasis should be placed on achieving inflation targets through financial austerity, with governments allowed more flexibility in spending international aid (see Chapter 5).
- Priority social-sector budgets should be protected, and public-spending targets should reflect a commitment to free education.
- The IMF should not promote the opening of capital markets, because of the potentially adverse implications for government budgets and poverty.

Towards a global initiative

The global initiative envisaged under the Dakar *Framework for Action* provides the potential link between a strengthened national policy environment, created through national planning processes, and a renewed international aid effort. To succeed, it needs to establish a mechanism through which good policies get the international backing that they need to succeed. One of the weaknesses of the *Framework* is that it does not establish such a mechanism, partly because there are serious differences within the donor community over how it might operate. Some donors and international agencies – such as the United States and the World Bank – support the development of a global financing facility through which national plans can be supported. Others – such as the UK Department for International Development – place the emphasis on the development of national planning on a country-by-county basis through existing aid channels.

Although the issue has aroused much controversy, there is in fact a good deal of common ground. The World Bank has proposed a 'fast-track' mechanism, through which countries committed to the development of national plans aimed at ensuring universal access to good-quality basic education will receive additional support. Evidence of commitment would be provided through national sectoral plans for education and anti-poverty strategies, taking into account the level of budgetary provisions for basic education, efforts to reach excluded groups, and planned measures for improving gender equity. Around 20 countries have been identified as potentially eligible candidates, 13 of them in sub-Saharan Africa. Given that bilateral donors such as DFID will be supporting education-sector development through an increased aid budget in many of the same countries, some of the differences over the design of a global initiative may be more apparent than real.

For a global initiative to be meaningful, it needs to do two things. First, it has to mobilise a significant increase in resources by bringing together a wide range of actors. This has been achieved far more successfully in the health-care sector than in education. For instance, the Global Alliance for Vaccines and Immunisation (GAVI) has brought together UN agencies, the World Bank, private foundations, and the pharmaceutical industry to provide vaccines for six basic immunisations. Convened under the auspices of the World Health Organisation and UNICEF, the GAVI was launched with a $750m grant from a private foundation. Its aim is to address the widening gap in health status between rich and poor countries. It has now been integrated by the Group of Seven industrial countries into a wider global health initiative. This aims to meet targets for reducing child deaths, reducing the incidence of malaria and tuberculosis by 50 per cent, and cutting the number of young people infected with HIV/AIDS by 10 per cent by the year 2015. Notwithstanding some obvious differences between international co-operation in the fields of health services and education, it is difficult to see why a resource-backed global initiative that brings together governments, UN agencies, and private foundations could not identify targets and strategies for education. Investments to increase the supply of teaching materials, improve sanitation, and support classroom construction could bring tangible benefits in terms of achieving universal primary education.

The second requirement for a global initiative is that of establishing a clear and transparent eligibility mechanism. This happens under the HIPC Initiative, with countries qualifying on the basis of their debt profile, and by virtue of adhering to an IMF programme. One of the strengths of the Initiative, leaving aside the content of IMF programmes, is that it provides clear rules for automatic entitlement. Such rules need to be elaborated for the global initiative in education, without creating an unduly bureaucratic structure. An obvious starting point is the progress made by applicant countries towards developing and implementing a strong sectoral strategy in education.

Within the broad framework of the global initiative, there is a strong case for special treatment of sub-Saharan Africa. As shown in Chapter 2, the region is now far off track in relation to the 2015 targets. Moreover, while the average cost of financing universal primary education may be modest in relation to regional GDP, it is very large in relation to the financing capacity of the poorest countries with the biggest quantitative and qualitative deficits. Without an increased aid effort, the financing gap will not be closed. Oxfam's $3.6bn estimate of the cost of universal primary education translates into around 1.3 per cent of GDP, or a 20 per cent increase in recurrent budget spending on education. For some of the poorest countries, the financing gap is much larger. Public spending on the scale required is not a realistic option in the absence of a major international effort, probably to the extent of around $2bn per annum.

Conclusion

Ten years ago, the World Conference on Education for All raised hopes of an early breakthrough in international efforts to achieve the vision set out in the Universal Declaration of Human Rights. Those hopes were not realised. Since 1990, international summits have come and gone, producing few tangible results. Public apathy and cynicism have been the predictable outcomes. It does not have to be like this. The target of universal primary education by 2015 is eminently achievable – and the Dakar *Framework for Action* provides good principles for a workable strategy. Whether the strategy translates into progress on the scale required will ultimately depend not on the availability of resources, but on the political will of governments, North and South. What is clear is that another decade of failure on a par with that which followed the World Conference on Education for All will have devastating consequences for the millions of people around the world who endure poverty and inequality.

Appendix 1: The Education Performance Index (EPI)

The Education Performance Index (EPI) is a composite indicator that captures in a single measure three different aspects of education performance. Problems associated with the development of composite indicators are discussed in Chapter 3. The three indicators used are the net enrolment rate (NER), the completion rate (CR), and the ratio of female enrolment (F/NER) to male enrolment (M/NER). Table A1 summarises the data used.

Each of the indicators chosen captures an important dimension of education performance, though they are weak proxies for wider problems (such as education quality and gender equity in a broader sense). The EPI indicates the coverage of the formal education system, the success of that system in taking children from enrolment to completion, and the degree of gender bias in enrolment. The value of a composite indicator is apparent from even a superficial consideration of the relationship between net enrolment and gender equity. For instance, Sudan has approximately the same ratio of female to male enrolment as Venezuela, but less than half of its net enrolment rate.

One of the main problems in constructing a composite indicator is that of limiting substitution effects. This can be done by increasing the weights attached to shortfalls in performance in one or more areas. Normative judgement is an integral part of any weighting exercise. The EPI is based on a judgement that performance in each of the three areas should have an equal weight attached, and that shortfalls should be weighted to prevent good performance in one area compensating for bad performance in another. High rates of completion are not an indicator of good performance in a country with low enrolment and extreme gender inequity. The deficits measured by the EPI are departure from a perfect score (i.e. 100 per cent enrolment and completion, and complete gender equity). The female/male ratio figure is censored, so that when female enrolment is greater than male, the excess does not diminish the value of the index. The technical formula used is as follows.

$$EPI = \left\{ \frac{1}{3} \left[(100 - NER)^3 + \left(100 - \frac{NER for girls}{NER for boys} \right)^3 + (100 - CompletionRate)^3 \right] \right\}^{1/3}$$

Table A1: **Consolidated data for the Education Performance Index: net enrolment rates, completion rates, and gender equity at the primary-school level for 104 countries**

	Countries	Index value	NER	100-NER	CR	100-CR	M/NER	F/NER	F/M	100-cens f/m
1	Bahrain	0.55	100	0	99	1	100	100	100	0
2	Singapore	0.60	100	1	100	0	100	99	99	1
3	United Arab Emirates	0.94	100	1	99	1	100	99	99	1
4	Mauritius	1.04	99	2	100	0	98	99	101	0
5	Cuba	2.84	100	1	96	4	99	100	101	0
6	Jamaica	2.91	98	2	99	1	100	96	96	4
7	Sri Lanka	3.40	100	0	95	5	100	100	100	0
8	Tunisia	4.03	98	2	95	5	100	96	96	4
9	Indonesia	4.22	98	3	96	4	100	95	95	5
10	Uruguay	4.46	94	6	96	4	94	94	100	0
11	Rep. of Korea	4.51	94	7	100	0	93	94	101	0
12	St. Lucia	4.92	94	6	95	5	94	94	100	0
13	Cape Verde	5.40	98	3	92	8	98	97	99	1
14	China	5.73	96	4	92	8	97	95	98	2
15	Iran	6.20	97	4	93	7	100	93	93	7
16	Guyana	6.43	92	8	93	7	92	92	100	0
17	Algeria	6.53	95	6	95	5	99	91	92	8
18	Costa Rica	6.99	90	10	97	3	89	91	102	0
19	Brunei Darussalam	7.28	90	11	100	0	90	89	99	1
20	Syrian Arab Republic	7.30	94	7	95	5	98	89	91	9
21	Mexico	8.53	99	1	88	12	99	99	100	0
22	Botswana	8.65	97	3	88	12	96	98	102	0
23	Fiji	8.80	100	0	87	13	100	100	100	0
24	Chile	10.20	86	15	95	5	86	85	99	1
25	Namibia	10.56	92	9	86	14	88	95	108	0
26	Trinidad & Tobago	11.09	84	16	99	1	84	84	100	0
27	Bahamas	11.79	99	2	83	17	99	98	99	1
28	Jordan	12.13	83	18	98	2	82	83	101	0
29	Thailand	12.18	91	9	83	17	94	89	95	5
30	Iraq	12.27	90	10	85	15	95	85	89	11
31	Panama	12.43	98	2	82	18	99	96	98	2
32	Malaysia	12.80	89	11	93	8	97	81	83	17

33	Dominica	13.23	90	10	93	8	99	81	82	18
34	Egypt	13.52	81	20	99	1	81	80	99	1
35	Venezuela	14.42	91	9	84	16	98	83	84	16
36	Mongolia	15.17	79	22	92	8	76	81	107	0
37	Paraguay	15.27	90	11	79	21	89	90	101	0
38	Swaziland	16.07	81	20	83	17	82	79	96	4
39	Zimbabwe	16.23	84	16	79	21	84	84	100	0
40	South Africa	16.40	94	6	77	24	95	93	98	2
41	Argentina	16.85	94	6	77	24	99	89	89	11
42	Qatar	17.92	81	19	100	0	92	71	78	22
43	Philippines	17.98	96	4	74	26	97	95	98	2
44	Kenya	18.33	76	25	85	16	77	74	96	4
45	Barbados	18.87	77	23	80	20	79	75	95	5
46	Ecuador	18.91	94	7	73	27	98	89	91	9
47	Oman	19.08	73	28	99	1	74	71	96	4
48	Brazil	20.75	87	13	71	29	86	88	102	0
49	Belize	21.01	97	4	70	30	97	96	99	1
50	Peru	21.02	95	5	70	30	99	90	91	9
51	Cameroon	21.25	78	22	81	19	88	68	77	23
52	Zambia	21.61	69	31	92	8	70	68	97	3
53	Papua New Guinea	21.71	77	24	75	25	82	71	87	13
54	Bolivia	21.81	95	5	69	31	97	93	96	4
55	Vietnam	23.39	87	13	69	31	97	78	80	20
56	Kuwait	24.95	64	36	99	1	64	64	100	0
57	Morocco	25.42	69	31	85	15	79	59	75	25
58	Dominican Rep.	25.49	81	19	65	35	79	83	105	0
59	Nicaragua	25.85	80	21	65	35	78	81	104	0
60	Saudi Arabia	26.19	63	38	96	4	66	59	89	11
61	Ghana	27.91	61	39	84	16	65	57	88	12
62	Honduras	28.76	86	15	59	41	85	86	101	0
63	Gabon	28.98	97	3	58	42	98	95	97	3
64	Leosotho	29.24	66	35	68	32	60	71	118	0
65	India	29.36	75	25	67	34	67	48	72	28
66	Congo	29.42	69	31	64	36	70	68	97	3
67	Nigeria	29.63	60	41	92	8	67	52	78	22
68	Colombia	30.23	80	20	65	35	96	65	68	32

69	El Salvador	31.64	79	21	64	36	95	63	66	34
70	Bangladesh	32.17	84	17	55	45	89	78	88	12
71	Zaire	32.68	56	44	74	27	59	53	90	10
72	U. Rep of Tanzania	32.86	53	47	87	13	55	51	93	7
73	Comoros	32.97	60	40	84	17	72	48	66	34
74	Uganda	33.29	61	39	63	37	64	58	91	9
75	Gambia	33.75	55	45	87	13	64	46	72	28
76	Côte D'Ivoire	33.94	58	42	78	22	69	47	68	32
77	Laos	34.93	62	38	59	41	77	67	87	13
78	Togo	35.21	68	32	58	43	79	57	72	28
79	Burundi	36.17	54	46	75	26	64	44	69	31
80	Central African Rep.	36.55	65	35	74	26	83	47	56	44
81	Malawi	38.02	92	8	45	55	91	93	102	0
82	Senegal	38.97	46	54	91	10	52	39	74	26
83	Benin	41.03	55	46	63	37	68	41	60	40
84	Nepal	41.59	63	37	55	45	80	46	58	43
85	Sudan	41.84	40	60	94	6	43	37	85	15
86	Guinea-Bissau	42.92	50	50	53	47	55	45	82	18
87	Mauritania	43.82	50	50	77	23	67	34	51	49
88	Guatemala	44.35	68	32	52	48	91	46	50	50
89	Rwanda	46.06	36	64	69	32	35	37	106	0
90	Cambodia	46.89	60	40	59	42	84	37	44	56
91	Madagascar	47.00	60	41	37	63	56	63	113	0
92	Djibouti	47.68	32	68	96	4	36	28	78	22
93	Burkina Faso	47.89	34	66	87	13	40	27	67	33
94	Guinea	48.36	41	59	87	13	55	27	49	51
95	Eritrea	51.32	27	74	80	20	28	25	89	11
96	Mali	52.70	26	74	91	9	31	21	68	32
97	Mozambique	53.28	33	67	47	53	38	29	77	23
98	Chad	53.94	36	65	52	48	46	25	54	46
99	Pakistan	53.94	31	70	53	47	36	25	68	32
100	Angola	56.71	40	60	34	66	49	31	63	37
101	Haiti	59.43	36	64	47	53	52	21	39	61
102	Bhutan	60.56	37	63	88	12	60	15	25	75
103	Niger	61.63	24	76	88	12	48	17	36	64
104	Ethiopia	67.17	21	79	63	37	32	9	29	71

Appendix 2: List of background papers

All papers were commissioned by Oxfam International

Agence Saena: 'Investigation into Basic Education in Mali'

Darwood Al-Hidabi: 'Basic Education Baseline Research in Yemen'

Nancy Alexander: 'The Role of the World Bank and the IMF in Basic Education'

Fran Bennett: 'Education and Poverty in the UK'

Jaturong Boonyaratanasoontom: 'Education and the Economic Crisis in Thailand'

Oliver Brown and Katie Wiseman: 'Primary Education in Nepal: Unmet Needs and Inequality'

K. Daramaningtyas: 'Primary Education in Indonesia'

Kate Dyer: 'Primary Education in Tanzania'

Hanan Elhaj: 'Basic Education among Communities Affected by Conflict'

Sérgio Haddad: 'Elementary Education in Brazil: the Role of the State'

Sérgio Haddad: 'Academic Education in Brazil'

Taimur Hyat: 'Primary Education in Pakistan'

Taimur Hyat: 'Basic Education in India: the Unfinished Agenda'

Taimur Hyat: 'Primary Education in India: Another View'

M. Ibraimo and Patrick Watt: 'An Overview of the State of Primary Education in Mozambique'

Jessica Jitta: 'Access to Health and Education in Four Districts of Uganda'

Michael Kelly: 'Primary Education in a Highly Indebted Poor Country: the Case of Zambia'

Tilleke Kiewied: 'Educating Children in Bangladesh for a Better Future: the Challenges Ahead'

Masketi Masingila: 'Background Information on Basic Education in Kenya'

Alice Nankya Ndidde and Daniel Bahikwa: 'An Assessment of Universal Primary Education in Uganda'

Gerard Oonk: 'Elementary Education and Child Labour in India'

Oxfam GB in Angola: 'Survey of the Educational Sector (General Education in Angola)'

Oxfam GB: 'People's Access to Health and Education'

Oxfam GB: 'Education for Poor Children: Research Findings from Lao Cai Province, Vietnam'

Oxfam GB: 'Basic Education for the Poor: Constraints to Access in Three Communes of Huong Kile District, Ha Tinh'

Oxfam (India) Trust: 'Status of Education in Gujarat Primary Schools'

Oxfam (India) Trust: 'Primary Education in India: a National Study'

Oxfam International: 'Basic Education for All'

Mohga Smith: 'Health and Education'

Ines Smyth: 'Education and Conflict: Old Problems and New Agenda'

Nicola Swainson: 'Gender and Education'

Nittaya Thiraphouth: 'Basic Education in Cambodia'

Patrick Watt: 'Child Labour and Access to Education'

Notes

Introduction

1   Interview recorded in *Public Report on Basic Education in India*, Oxford University Press, 1998.

2   Kofi Annan: The UN Secretary General's Address to the World Education Forum, Dakar, 26 April 2000.

3   Quoted in D. Souter: 'The role of information and communication technologies in democratic development', *Info* 1.5, Camford Publishing, London, 1999.

4   International Monetary Fund: *The IMF and the Poor*, Fiscal Affairs Department, IMF, Washington, 1999.

5   UNESCO: *The Dakar Framework for Action*, Paris, 2000.

6   *Financial Times*: 'Empty words', Editorial, 1 May 2000.

Chapter 1

1   Aristotle: *Politics* III.9, Oxford University Press, Oxford, 1967.

2   Quoted in R. Selleck: *The New Education 1870–1914*, Isaac Pitman, London, 1968, p.13.

3   See, for example, T. Schultz : 'Returns to women's education', in E. King and A. Hill (eds.): *Women's Education in Developing Countries: Barriers, Benefits and Policies*, John Hopkins University Press, Baltimore, 1993.

4   On capabilities and freedom, see A. Sen: 'Capability and well-being' in M. Nussbaum and A. Sen (eds.): *The Quality of Life*, Clarendon Press, Oxford, 1993. *The Human Development Report* is published annually for the United Nations Development Programme by Oxford University Press, Oxford.

5   A. Sen: 'Radical needs. and moderate reforms', in J. Drèze and A. Sen (eds.): *Indian Development: Selected Regional Perspectives*, Clarendon Press, Oxford, 1997.

6   OECD Development Assistance Committee: *Shaping the 21st Century: the contribution of development cooperation*, OECD, Paris, 1996.

7   Based on UNICEF: *The State of the World's Children*, 1999, Table 8, p.127, Oxford University Press, Oxford, 1999,

8   Oxfam: 'Missing the Target', report prepared for the mid-term review of the World Social Summit, mimeo, Oxford, 2000.

9   Ibid.

10   UNICEF: *The State of the World's Children*, 1998, Table 1, p.96, Oxford University Press, Oxford, 1998.

11   D. Filmer et al.: 'Health Policy in Poor Countries: Weak Links in the Chain', World Bank, mimeo, October 1997, p34. There is evidence that poor households respond to health costs either by using facilities less, or by forgoing treatment. See A. Creese and J. Kutzin: 'Lessons from cost-recovery in health', in C. Colclough (ed.): *Marketing Education and Health in Developing Countries*, Clarendon Press, Oxford, 1996.

12 World Bank: *Poverty Trends and Voices of the Poor*, World Bank, Washington, 1999, p.23. On health inequalities in Brazil, see World Bank, *The Brazil Health System: Impact Evaluation Report*, World Bank, Operations Evaluation Department, Washington, 1998, p.9.

13 G. Bloom: *Health and Poverty in sub-Saharan Africa*, Institute for Development Studies Working Paper 103, University of Sussex, Brighton, p.10.

14 J. Sachs: 'Helping the poorest of the poor', *The Economist*, 14-20 August 1999, London.

15 The World Bank: *Global Economic Prospects and the Developing Countries*, World Bank, Washington, 2000, Table 1.8, p.29. The regional data are from the same source.

16 K. Watkins: *Economic Growth with Equity: Lessons from East Asia*, Oxfam, Oxford, 1998.

17 M. Ravaillon and S. Chen: 'What can new survey data tell us about recent changes in distribution and poverty?', *World Bank Economic Review* 11(2): 357-82.

18 K. Watkins, op. cit., 1998.

19 On the relationship between economic growth, inequality and poverty reduction, see H. White and E. Anderson: 'Growth versus Distribution: Does the Pattern of Growth Matter?', mimeo, Institute of Development Studies, University of Sussex, Brighton, 2000.

20 R. Kanbur and N. Lustig: 'Why Inequality is Back on the Agenda', paper presented at Annual Bank Conference on Development Economics, mimeo, World Bank, Washington, 1999. On inequality trends in the industrialised countries, see A. Atkinson: 'Is Rising Income Inequality Inevitable?', World Institute for Development Economics Research (WIDER) annual lecture, 1999, WIDER, Helsinki.

21 World Bank: *Global Economic Prospects and the Developing Countries*, op. cit., p29.

22 Ibid.

23 A. Cornia: 'Inequality and Poverty in the Era of Globalisation', paper presented at UN Millennium Conference, 'On the Threshold', mimeo, United Nations University, Tokyo, 2000.

24 Ibid., Table 1.10, p.33.

25 L. Hanmer and F. Naschold: 'Are the International Development Targets Attainable?', Overseas Development Institute, mimeo, 1999, London.

26 On the potential benefits of redistributive growth strategies, see F. Stewart: 'Income Distribution and Development', paper prepared for UNCTAD X high-level roundtable, February 2000, mimeo, UNCTAD, Geneva.

27 D.Dollar and A. Kraay: 'Growth is Good for the Poor', World Bank, Washington, 2000. For a critique of this paper, see Oxfam: 'Growth with Equity is Good for the Poor', mimeo, Oxford, 2000.

28 N. Birdsall and J. Londono: 'Asset Inequality Does Matter', mimeo, Inter-American Development Bank, Washington 1997, p.13.

29 United Nations Development Programme: *Human Development Report 1999*, Oxford, Oxford University Press, 1999.

30   A. Sen: *Freedom as Development*, Oxford University Press, Oxford, Chapter 8.

31   J. Caldwell: 'Routes to low mortality in poor countries', *Population and Development Review*, 12, 1986. For an overview of the literature on child mortality and maternal education, see J. Cleland and K. van Ginneken: 'Maternal education and child survival in developing countries: the search for pathways of influence', *Social Science Medicine* Vol. 27, 12, 1998; G. Bicego and J. Boerma: 'Maternal education and child survival: a comparative study of survey data from 17 countries', *Social Science Medicine* 36, 1993.

32   Government of Ghana: *Ghana Living Standards Survey: Report on Third Round*, Statistical Service, Accra, 1995.

33   Government of Pakistan: *Pakistan Integrated Household Survey Round 1: 1995–1996*, Federal Bureau of Statistics, Islamabad.

34   World Bank: *Better Health in Africa, Washington*, 1995; see also J. Cleland and K. van Ginneken: 'Maternal schooling and childhood mortality', *Journal of Biosocial Science Supplement* 10, 13, 1989.

35   K. Bourne and G. Walker: 'The differential effect of mothers' education on mortality of boys and girls in India', *Population Studies* 45, 1991, p.218.

36   See for example A. Barrett and A. Browne: 'Health, hygiene and maternal education: evidence from the Gambia', *Social Science Medicine*, Vol. 43, 11, 1996, p.588; E. Kalipeni: 'Determinants of infant mortality in Malawi: a spatial perspective', *Social Science Medicine*, 37, p.183, 1993; M. Nag: 'Political awareness as a factor in accessibility of health services: a case study of rural Kerala and West Bengal', *Economic and Political Weekly*, February 25, 1989, Bombay.

37   M. Kelly: 'Primary Education in a Highly Indebted Poor Country: the Case of Zambia', mimeo, Oxfam, Oxford, 1998.

38   A. Pinto et al.: 'Does health intervention ameliorate the effects of poverty-related diseases? The role of female literacy', *Journal of Tropical Paediatrics* 31, 1985.

39   M. Assiate and P. Watt: 'An Overview of the State of Education in Mozambique', mimeo, Oxfam, Oxford, 1998.

40   World Bank: *Primary Education in India*, Washington, 1997, p.45. See also R. Brugha and J. Kevany: 'Immunisation determinants in the eastern region of Ghana', *Health Policy and Planning*, 10(3), pp.312-18.

41   J. Caldwell and P. Caldwell: 'Education and literacy as factors in health', in S. Halstead (ed.): *Good Health at Low Cost*, New York, 1985; see also A. Bhuiya et al.: 'Factors affecting acceptance of immunisation among children in rural Bangladesh', *Health Policy and Planning* 10(3); 304-11.

42   J. Cleland and K. van Ginneken: 'Maternal education and child survival in developing countries', op. cit.

43   S. Cochrane and S. Farid: 'Fertility in sub-Saharan Africa: Levels and Their Explanation', World Bank, mimeo, Washington, 1984.

44   International Institute for Population Sciences: *National Family Health Survey 1992–93*, Government of India, Bombay, 1995.

45   See, for example, P. Dargent Molina: 'Association between maternal education and infant diarrhea in different households and community environments of Cebu, Philippines', *Social Science Medicine*, 38.2, pp.343-50; B. Reed et al.: 'The effect of maternal education on child nutritional status depends on socio-environmental conditions', *International Journal of Epidemiology*, 25, 3, 1996.

46   UNAIDS/World Health Organisation: *Report on the Global HIV/AIDS Epidemic*, Geneva, 1998.

47   J. Vandermoortele: *Absorbing Social Shocks, Protecting Children and Reducing Poverty: the Role of Basic Services*, UNICEF, New York, 2000, pp.15-16.

48   Ibid.

49   On the comparative performances of Kerala and Uttar Pradesh, see J. and H. Gazdar: 'Uttar Pradesh: the burden of inertia' in J. Drèze and A. Sen: *Indian Development: Selected Regional Perspectives*, Oxford University Press, Oxford, 1997, pp.33-108; T. Krishnan: 'The route to social development in Kerala: social intermediation and public action', in S. Mehrotra and R. Jolly (eds.): *Development with a Human Face: Experiences in Social Achievement and Economic Growth*, Clarendon Press, Oxford, 1997, Table 7.1, p.206.

50   Cited in A. Sen: *Development as Freedom*, op. cit., p.196.

51   The data for Pakistan and Vietnam are derived from Government of Pakistan: *Pakistan Integrated Household Survey*, op. cit.; Government of Vietnam, *Education in Vietnam: Trends and Differentials*, Statistical Publishing House, Hanoi, 1996, Chapter 4; UNDP, *Human Development Report*, 1998, op. cit., various tables.

52   L. Summers: *Investing in All the People*, World Bank, Washington, 1992.

53   S. Al-Samarrai and T. Peasgood: *Educational Attainments and Household Characteristics in Tanzania*, Institute for Development Studies, Working Paper 49, University of Sussex, Brighton, 1997, p.27.

54   D. Bundy and H. Guyatt: 'Focus on health, education and the school age child', *Parasitology Today*, 12, 8, 1996, pp.2-3.

55   UNICEF: *The State of the World's Children 1997*, Oxford University Press, Oxford, 1997.

56   Partnership for Child Development: 'The anthropometric status of school-children in five countries in the Partnership for Child Development', *Proceedings of the Nutrition Society*, 57, 1998, pp.149-58.

57   J. Ricci and S. Becker: 'Risk factors for wasting and stunting among children in Metro Cebu, Philippines', *American Journal of Clinical Nutrition*, 63, 1996, pp. 966-75.

58   D. Bundy and H. Guyatt: 'Focus on health', op. cit.

59   Child Health and Development Centre/Oxfam: 'Public Health and Education in Uganda: Evidence from Four Survey Sites', mimeo, Oxfam, Oxford and Kampala, 1999.

60   Ibid.

61   C. Dolan et al.: 'What's New in the Health and Nutrition of the School-age Child and in School Health and Nutrition Programmes?', Partnership for Child Development, mimeo, Oxford, 2000.

62　J. Del Rosso: 'School Feeding Programmes: Improving Effectiveness and Increasing the Benefit to Education', Partnership for Child Development, mimeo, Oxford, 1992.

63　C. Ruggeri-Laderchi: 'Food Transfers and Poverty: the Case of Peru', mimeo, Queen Elizabeth House, Oxford University, Oxford, 2000.

64　Data from Government of Vietnam: *Education in Vietnam: Trends and Differentials*, Hanoi, 1996; World Bank: *Zambia Poverty Assessment Volume 11*, Washington, 1994.

65　For the standard World Bank perspective on rates of return to education, see G. Psacharopoulous: 'Returns to investment in education: a global update', *World Development*, 22, 9, 1994. On the critique of rates of return analysis, see P. Bennell: 'Rates of return to education: does the conventional pattern prevail in sub-Saharan Africa?', *World Development* 24, 1, 1995; J. Knight and R. Sabot: 'Is the rate of return on primary schooling really 26 per cent?', *Journal of African Economies*, 1, 2, 1991.

66　G. Psacharopoulous: 'Returns to investment in education: a global update', op. cit.

67　P. Bennell: 'Rates of return to education: does the conventional pattern prevail in sub-Saharan Africa?', op. cit.

68　A. Foster and M. Rosenzweig: 'Learning by doing and learning from others: human capital and technological change in agriculture', *Journal of Political Economy*, 103(6), 1995.

69　On rural development as a driving force for poverty reduction, see H. Hill: *The Indonesian Economy since 1966*, Cambridge University Press, Cambridge, Chapter 7.

70　World Bank: *Primary Education in India*, Washington, 1997, pp.34-5.

71　P. Collier and J. Gunning: 'Explaining African economic performance', *Journal of Economic Literature*, March 1999, pp.64-111.

72　A. Appleton et al.: 'Education and agricultural productivity: evidence from Uganda', *Journal of International Development*, 8, 3, 1996.

73　Inter-American Development Bank: *Facing up to Inequality in Latin America*, IADB, Washington, 1999, p.39.

74　E. Funkhouser: 'The urban informal sector in Central America: household survey evidence', *World Development*, 24, 11, 1996.

75　B. Herz et al.: *Letting Girls Learn*, World Bank Discussion Paper 133, Washington, pp.13-14; Z. Tzannatos: *Women and Labour Market Changes in the Global Economy*, World Bank, Washington, 1998.

76　M. Ul Haq and K. Ul Haq: *Human Development in South Asia: The Education Challenge*, Oxford University Press, Oxford, 1998, p.24.

77　World Bank: *Bolivia: Poverty, Equity and Income*, Washington, 1996, p.7.

78　A. Marshall: *The Principles of Economics*, London, 1890.

79　R. Solow: 'A contribution to the theory of economic growth', *Quarterly Journal of Economics* 70 (1): 65-94.

80　G. Becker et al.: *Human Capital*, University of Chicago Press, Chicago, 1993.

81   World Bank: *The East Asian Miracle: Economic Growth and Public Policy*, Washington, pp.51-54.

82   M. Ul Haq and K. Ul Haq: *Human Development in South Asia: the Education Challenge*, op. cit.

83   N. Birdsall et al.: *Inequality as a Constraint on Growth in Latin America*, OECD, Paris, 1992.

84   World Bank: *Zimbabwe Country Economic Memorandum: achieving shared growth*, Washington, 1994.

85   Inter-American Development Bank: *Facing up to Inequality in Latin America*, op. cit., p.65.

86   On the effects of education on wage structures in Brazil and South Korea, see N. Birdsall et al., *Inequality as a Constraint on Growth in Latin America*, op. cit., pp.185-6.

87   Inter-American Development Bank: *Economic and Social Progress in Latin America*, IADB, Washington, p.278. Educational differences are estimated to have accounted for around one-third of income differences in Brazil between 1960 and 1970 – and the impact of education has almost certainly increased since then. See G. Psacharapoulous and M. Woodhall: *Education for Development: an Analysis of Investment Choices*, World Bank, Washington, 1985.

88   D. Filmer and L. Pritchett: *The Effect of Household Wealth on Educational Attainment around the World: Demographic and Health Survey Evidence*, World Bank Policy Research Working Paper, 1998.

89   Based on A. Gosling et al.: *The Dynamics of Low Pay and Unemployment in Early 1990s Britain*, Institute for Fiscal Studies, London, 1997.

90   Quoted in D. Souter: 'The role of information and communication technologies in democratic development', *Info* 1,5, 1995, Commonwealth Telecommunications Organisation, London.

91   On the growing importance of knowledge in production and firm behaviour, see A. Burton-Jones: *Knowledge Capitalism*, Oxford University Press, Oxford, 1999; L. Throw: *The Future of Capitalism*, Nicholas Brealey, London, 1997, Chapter 4; P. Drucker: *Post-capitalist Society*, Butterworth-Heinemann, Oxford, 1992, pp.17-43. For a broad overview of globalisation, see A. Giddens: *The Third Way*, Polity Press, Cambridge, 1998, pp.28-34.

92   M. Castels: 'Information technology and global capitalism', in W. Hutton and A. Giddens: *On the Edge*, London: Jonathan Cape, 2000.

93   D. Souter: 'The role of information and communication technologies in democratic development', op. cit.

94   W. Wriston: 'Bits, bytes and diplomacy', *Foreign Affairs*, 76, 5, 1997.

95   F. Cairncross: *The Death of Distance*, Orion, London, 1997, p.212.

96   Ibid.

97   M. Castels: 'Information technology and global capitalism', op. cit.

98   World Bank: *World Development Report, 1998: Knowledge for Development*, Washington, 1998, p.24.

99   On primary commodities, see K. Watkins: *Globalisation and Liberalisation: the Implications for Poverty Reduction*, UNDP, New York, 1998; and on terms of trade for labour-intensive manufactured goods, see A. Berry et al.: 'Globalisation, Adjustment, Inequality and Poverty', background paper prepared for 1997 UNDP *Human Development Report*, UNDP, mimeo, 1997.

100 N. Bowie: 'ICT and Access: the Haves and the Have Nots', paper presented at OECD Roundtable on Lifelong Learning and New Technologies, Philadelphia, 8-10 December 1997.

101 M.Castels: *End of Millennium*, Vol III, *The Information Age*, Blackwell, Oxford, 1998, p.92.

102 D. Souter: 'The role of information and communications technologies in democratic development', op. cit.

103 Ibid.

104 A. Burton-Jones: *Knowledge Capitalism*, op. cit., p.204.

105 P. Ryan: *Knowledge Diplomacy: Global Competition and the Politics of Intellectual Property*, Brookings Institute Press, Washington DC.

106 F. Cairncross: *The Death of Distance*, op. cit., p.223. On the relationship between income inequality and education, see J. Honkilla: *Investment in Education and Income Inequality*, WIDER, Research in Progress Paper 21, 1999. Some economists have argued that increased international trade has reduced return to unskilled labour in industrialised countries through competition between low-wage and high-wage economies. See, for example, A. Wood: *North–South Trade, Employment and Inequality*, Oxford, Oxford University Press, 1994.

107 Joseph Rowntree Foundation, *Inquiry into Income Distribution and Wealth*, Vol. 1, p.15, Joseph Rowntree Foundation, York, 1995.

108 Birdsall N: 'Life is unfair: inequality in the world', *Foreign Policy*, Summer 1998; J. Castaneda: 'Mexico's circle of misery', *Foreign Affairs*, July 1996.

109 C. Dugger: 'Technology widens chasm in India', *International Herald Tribune*, 23 March 2000.

110 A. Sen: 'Radical needs and moderate reforms', op. cit., p.21.

111 F. Leach: 'Gender, education and training: an international perspective', *Gender and Development* 6.2, Oxfam, Oxford, 1998.

112 J. Galbraith: *The Good Society: the Humane Agenda*, Houghton Mifflin Company,1996, p.59.

113 Aristotle: *Politics*, op. cit., pp.451-52.

114 T. Paine: *Rights of Man*, Oxford University Press, Oxford, 1995, p.297.

115 W. Carr and A. Hartnett: *Education and the Struggle for Democracy*, Open University Press, Milton Keynes, Chapter 3.

116 Emma Rothschild: 'Condorcet and Adam Smith on education' in A. Rorty (ed.): *Philosophers on Education*, London, 1998.

117 Adam Smith saw education as an antidote to the mental degradation caused by the division of labour. Although he did not suggest compulsory schooling, he put forward a plan to make schooling more accessible to the poor through a system of incentives, which in his view were needed to counter the disincentives for poor households to send their children to work. Hence the need for public authorities to 'facilitate, encourage, and even impose upon almost the whole body of the people the necessity of acquiring those most essential parts of education'. See *The Wealth of Nations*, Oxford University Press, Oxford, 1987, p.785.

118 J. S. Mill: *Utilitarianism, on Liberty, and Considerations of Representative Government*, Dent, London, 1972, pp.160-163.

119 Robert Lowe, cited in Carr and Hartnett: *Education and the Struggle for Democracy*, op. cit., p.85.

120 A. Green: *Education and State Formation*, Macmillan, Basingstoke, 1990, p.259.

121 W. Carr and A. Hartnett, *Education and the Struggle for Democracy*, op. cit.

122 One of the strongest indictments of colonial education systems remains Walter Rodney's *How Europe Underdeveloped Africa*, Bogle-L'ouverture, 1983, pp.261-87.

123 Africa Education Commission: *Education in East Africa: a Study of East, Central and South Africa*, Phelps-Stokes Fund, 1924. The Commission's report reads as a strikingly modern document that retains a powerful resonance for education planning. It condemns 'the wholesale transfer of the education conventions of Europe ... to the people of Africa,' and calls for school curricula to be adapted to local conditions. Among its central recommendations was the demand for schools to be adapted to the needs of local communities in rural production and trade: 'Arithmetic may give liberal portions of time to calculations related to the transactions of the village markets and the elements of agricultural exchange.'

124 W. Rodney: *How Europe Underdeveloped Africa*, op. cit., p.264.

125 G. Myrdal: *Asian Drama: an Enquiry into the Poverty of Nations*, Pelican, London, p.1635.

126 See, for example, Julius Nyerere's *Education for Self-reliance*, Government of Tanzania, Arusha, 1968.

127 R. Howard-Malverde and A. Canessa: 'The school in the Quechua and Aymara communities of Highland Bolivia', *International Journal of Educational Development* 15, 3, 1995; see also D. Hahn: *The Divided World of the Bolivian Andes: a Structural View of Domination and Resistance*, New York, 1992.

128 N. Mandela: *Long Walk to Freedom*, Penguin, Harmondsworth, 1997.

129 USAID: *An Analysis of the Impact of Literacy on Women's Empowerment in Nepal*, Advancing Basic Education and Literacy (ABEL) Project, Washington, 1997.

130 Ibid.

131 T. Hyat: 'Basic Education in India: the Unfinished Agenda', mimeo, Oxfam, Oxford, 1998.

132 Movimento sem Terra: 'Education and the Landless', mimeo, Recife, 2000.

Chapter 2

1   UNESCO: 'The Dakar Framework for Action', text adopted by the World Education Forum, Dakar, Senegal, 26-28 April 2000, UNESCO, Paris, 2000.

2   A. Coote (ed.): *The Welfare of Citizens: Developing New Social Rights*, Institute for Public Policy Research, London, 1991.

3   M. Pigozzi: *Implications of the Convention on the Rights of the Child for Education*, UNICEF, New York, 1997.

4   UNESCO: 'World Declaration on Education for All and Framework for Action to Meet Basic Learning Needs', World Conference on Education for All, Thailand, 1990.

5   Ibid.

6   A. Little: *Beyond Jomtien: Implementing Primary Education for All*, Macmillan, London, 1994, Chapter 1.

7   UNESCO: 'World Declaration on Education for All and Framework for Action to Meet Basic Learning Needs', op. cit.

8   On the core international development targets, see United Nations: 'World Summit for Social Development: Programme of Action', New York, 1995; United Nations: 'Beijing Declaration and Platform for Action: Fourth World Conference on Women', New York, 1995; OECD: *Shaping the 21st Century: the Contribution of Development Cooperation*, Development Assistance Committee, Paris, 1996.

9   OECD: *Shaping the 21st Century*, op. cit.

10 C. Colclough and S. Al-Samarri: *Achieving Schooling for All: Budgetary Expenditure on Education in sub-Saharan Africa and South Asia*, Working Paper 77, Institute for Development Studies, Sussex, 1998. The 6–14 age group represents 46 per cent of the 15–65 age group in sub-Saharan Africa, compared with 32 per cent for all developing countries. See *World Education Report 1995*, UNESCO, Paris, 1995.

11 The projection is based on net enrolment rate data. Figures for 1995 are derived from UNESCO, *Education for All: Achieving the Goal: Statistical Document*, UNESCO, Paris 1996, Part 11; UNICEF: *The State of the World's Children*, 1998, New York, Table 4. Data for 1990 are derived from the 1997 UNESCO *Statistical Yearbook*, Paris, 1997. Where net enrolment data are not available, they have been estimated on the basis of adjusted gross enrolment rates.

12 On the impact of HIV/AIDS on education in Africa, see UNAIDS: *Global Epidemic Update*, December, 1998; World Bank: *A Chance to Learn: Knowledge and Finance for Education in sub-Saharan Africa*, Africa Region, 2000, pp.32-3.

13 UNICEF: *The State of the World's Children*, 1998, op. cit., p.8.

14 P. Rose et al: *Gender and Primary Schooling in Ethiopia*, Research Report 31, Institute for Development Studies, University of Sussex, 1995, p.25.

15 World Bank: *Primary Education in India*, Washington, 1997.

16 T. Hyat: 'Primary Education in Pakistan: an overview', mimeo, Oxfam, Oxford, 1998.

17 O. Brown and K Wiseman: 'Primary Education in Nepal: Unmet Needs and Inequality', mimeo, Oxfam, Oxford, 1998.

18 E. Schiefelbein: *School Related Economic Incentives in Latin America: Reducing Drop-out and Repetition and Combating Child Labour*, Innocenti Occasional Papers, Child Rights series, 12, UNICEF, 1997.

19 UNESCO: *Wasted Opportunities: When Schools Fail*, Paris, 1998, p.21.

20 L. Wolff et al: *Improving the Quality of Primary Education in Latin America*, World Bank Discussion Paper 257, p.31.

21 Inter-American Development Bank: *Economic and Social Progress in Latin America*, Washington, 1996, p.278.

22 World Bank: *Peru: Poverty Assessment and Social Policies and Programs for the Poor*, Latin America and Caribbean Region, World Bank, Washington, 1993, p.29.

23 UNESCO: *Statistical Yearbook*, 1997, op. cit.

24 P. Rose et al.: *Gender and Primary Schooling in Ethiopia*, op. cit., pp.24-5.

25 C. Colclough: *Achieving Schooling for All in sub-Saharan Africa: Is Gender a Constraint or an Opportunity?*, Institute for Development Studies, Sussex, 1999.

26 UNESCO: *Adult Education in a Polarising World: Education for All, Status and Trends 1997*, Paris, 1998, p.26.

27 World Bank: *Bolivia: Poverty, Equity and Income*, Latin America and the Caribbean Region, World Bank, Washington, 1996.

28 OECD: *Education Policy Analysis*, Paris, 1997.

29 S. Carey et al.: *Adult Literacy in Britain*, HMSO, London, 1997, Chapter 6.

30 Trend data for Pakistan are derived from UNESCO: *Statistical Yearbook 1998*, op. cit.; for China from World Bank: *China 2020: Development Challenges in the New Century*, Washington, 1997, Figure 4.3, p.48.

31 On adult-literacy programmes, see UNESCO: *Adult Education in a Polarising World*, op. cit., part 3.

32 On problems in comparing educational attainment across countries, see V. Greaney and T. Kellaghan: *Monitoring the Learning Outcomes of Education Systems*, World Bank, Washington, 1996; R. Barro and J. Lee: 'International comparisons of educational attainment', *Journal of Monetary Economics*, 32, 1994.

33 UNESCO: 'The Dakar Framework for Action', op. cit.

34 E. Hunushek: 'The economics of schooling: production and efficiency in public schools', *Journal of Economic Literature* 24, 1986.

35 An example is W. Heneveld and H. Craig: *Schools Count: World Bank Project Design and the Quality of Primary Education in sub-Saharan Africa*, Technical Paper 303, Washington, 1996.

36 On an attempt to combine measurement of the non-academic and academic aspects of school performance, see P. Sammons et al.: *Key Characteristics of Effective Schools: a review of school effectiveness research*, Institute of Education, University of London, 1999.

37 M. Pigozzi: *Implications of the Convention on the Rights of the Child for Education*, op. cit.

38 V. Chinapah: 'Handbook on Monitoring Learning Achievement', UNICEF, New York, mimeo, 1997.

39 PROBE: *The Public Report on Basic Education in India*, Oxford, Oxford University Press, 1999.

40 United Nations: *Challenges and Opportunities: Basic Education for All in Pakistan, Report of a UN Inter-Agency Mission on Basic Education*, New York, 1995.

41 T. Saxena et al.: *School Effectiveness and Learners' Achievement at Primary Stage*, Department of Measurement, Evaluation, Survey and Data Processing, National Council of Educational Research and Training, New Delhi, 1995.

42 M. Kelly: 'Primary Education in a Highly Indebted Poor Country', mimeo, Oxfam, Oxford, 1998.

43 T. Peasgood et al.: *Gender and Primary Schooling in Tanzania*, Research Report 33, Institute for Development Studies, Sussex, p.36.

44 Campaign for Popular Education: *Hope Not Complacency: the State of Primary Education in Bangladesh*, 1999, Dhaka, 1999.

45 V. Greaney et al.: *Bangladesh: Assessing Basic Learning Skills*, World Bank, Dhaka, 1998.

46 K. Appiah: 'Ghana: Common Country Assessment', Government of Ghana, mimeo, Accra, 1999; UNDP: *Ghana Human Development Report*, Accra, 1997.

47 On learning outcomes in sub-Saharan Africa, see World Bank: *A Chance to Learn: Knowledge and Finance for Education in sub-Saharan Africa*, op. cit.

48 M. Carnoy and C. de Moura Castro: 'Improving Education in Latin America: where to now?', Inter-American Development Bank, mimeo, 1996.

49 L. Wolff et al.: *Improving the Quality of Private Education in Latin America and the Caribbean*, World Bank Discussion Paper 257, 1995, p.17.

50 Oxfam: 'People's Access to Health and Education', mimeo, Manila and Oxford, Oxfam GB, 1998.

51 Cited in UNICEF: *State of the World's Children 1999*, op. cit., p.24.

52 Campaign for Popular Education: *Hope Not Complacency*, op. cit., p.60.

53 UNESCO–UNICEF: *Schooling Conditions in the Least Developed Countries: syntheses of the pilot survey*, Paris, 1997.

54 United Nations: *Challenges and Opportunities: Basic Education for All in Pakistan*, Report of a UN Inter-Agency Mission on Basic Education, op. cit.

55 K. Dyer: 'Tanzania Country Study', mimeo, Oxfam, Oxford, 1998.

56 Al-Hidabi: 'Primary Education in Yemen', mimeo, Oxfam, Oxford, 1998.

57 Inter-American Development Bank: *Economic and Social Progress in Latin America: making social services work*, Washington, 1996, p 278.

58 On the importance of teaching materials for educational attainment, see M. Lockheed and A. Verspoor: *Improving Primary Education in Developing Countries*, World Bank, Washington, 1991, pp.47-57. Improved access to teaching materials generates very rapid improvements in educational attainment among poor communities previously denied access. See R. Harbison and E. Hunushek: *Educational Performance of the Poor: Lessons from North-east Brazil*, World Bank, Washington, 1992.

59 S. Roy et al.: *Achievement Level of Primary School Children at the End of Class 4*, Indian Statistical Institute, Calcutta, 1995.

60 M. Nkamba and J. Kanyika: *The Quality of Education: Some Policy Suggestions Based on a Survey of Schools*, Ministry of Education, Government of Zambia, Lusaka, 1998, p.51.

61 World Bank: *A Chance to Learn: Knowledge and Finance for Education in sub-Saharan Africa*, op. cit., p.16.

62 M. Ul Haq and K. Ul Haq: *Human Development in South Asia 1998*, Oxford, Oxford University Press, 1998.

63 On trends in teachers' salaries, see A. Adedji et al.: *Pay, Productivity and Public Service: Priorities for Recovery in sub-Saharan Africa*, UNICEF, New York, 1995; L. Wolff et al.: *Improving the Quality of Basic Education in Latin America: Toward the 21st Century*, World Bank Discussion Paper 257, 1995; UNESCO: *World Education Report: Teachers and Teaching in a Changing World*, UNESCO, 1998.

64 G. Lungwala: *Basic Education for Some: Factors Affecting Primary School Attendance in Zambia*, Ministry of Education, Government of Zambia, Lusaka, 1998, p.4.

65 N. Ho-Ming and C. Ping-Yan: 'School-based teacher development in Guangzhou, China', *International Studies in Educational Administration*, Vol.27, 2, 1999.

66 C. Wetta et al.: 'Cost-effectiveness of Basic Education in Burkina Faso', mimeo, UNICEF, Ouagadougou, 1996. See also Novib: 'Primary Education in Burkina Faso: a case study', mimeo, Amsterdam, 1998.

67 R. Loewensen and M. Chisvo: 'Rapid social transformation despite economic adjustment and slow growth: the experience of Zimbabwe', in S. Mehrotra and R. Jolly: *Development with a Human Face: Experiences in Social Achievement and Economic Growth*, Clarendon, Oxford, 1997, pp.192-94.

68 S. Mehrotra and P. Buckland: *Managing Teacher Costs for Access and Quality*, UNICEF Staff Working Paper, New York, 1998; on the status and conditions of teachers, see UNESCO: *World Education Report*, Paris, 1998.

69 M. Lockheed and A. Verspoor: *Improving Primary Education in Developing Countries*, World Bank, Washington, 1991, p.57.

70 G. Lungwala: *Basic Education for Some: Factors Affecting Primary School Attendance in Zambia*, op. cit., p.68.

71 O. Brown and K. Wiseman: 'Primary Education in Nepal', op. cit.

72 World Bank: *Uttar Pradesh Basic Education Programme*, South Asia Department, Washington, 1993.

73 World Bank: *Improving Basic Education: Community Participation, System Accountability, and Efficiency*, World Bank, South Asia Region, 1996, Washington, p.4.

74 PROBE: *The Public Report on Basic Education in India*, op. cit.

75 World Bank: *North West Frontier Province Primary Education Programme*, South Asia Department, Washington, 1995.

76 S. Bashir: 'Public versus Private in Primary Education', mimeo, Faculty of Economics, London School of Economics, 1994.

77   C. Ugaz: 'The State of Education in Peru', mimeo, World Institute for Development Economics Research, Helsinki, 1998.

78   T. Hyat: 'Primary Education in Pakistan' op. cit.

79   S. Haddad: 'Academic Education in Peru', mimeo, Oxfam, Oxford, 1998.

80   N. Thirapouth: 'Basic Education in Cambodia', mimeo, Oxfam, Oxford, 1998.

81   On the critical role of female teachers, see B. Herz et al.: *Letting Girls Learn: Promising Approaches in Primary and Secondary Education*, op. cit., pp.48-9.

82   M. Ul Haq and K. Haq: *Human Development in South Asia 1998*, op. cit.

83   P. Rose et al.: *Gender and Primary Schooling in Ethiopia*, op. cit., p.48.

84   M. Ul Haq and K. Haq: *Human Development in South Asia 1998*, op. cit., Chapter 8.

85   PROBE: *The Public Report on Basic Education in India*, op. cit.

86   On problems associated with school curricula, see M. Lockheed and A. Verspoor: *Improving Primary Education in Developing Countries*, op. cit.; p.45; World Bank: *A Chance to Learn: Knowledge and Finance for Education in sub-Saharan Africa*, op. cit., pp.40-43.

87   UNICEF: *The State of the World's Children*, 1998, op. cit.

88   Association for the Development of Education in Africa (ADEA): *Prospective Stocktaking Review of Education in Africa*, Paris, 1999.

89   R. Villanueva: 'Improving Education Quality with a Children's Perspective', mimeo, Save the Children Fund, London, 1997.

90   World Bank: *Bolivia Education Sector: a Proposed Strategy for Sector Development, Latin America and Caribbean Region*, Washington, 1993, p.14.

91   E. Furniss: 'Primary Education: the Development of Bilingual Materials for Ethnic Minorities in Viet Nam', UNICEF, Florence, mimeo, 1996.

92   The BRAC approach is described in C. Lovell and K. Fatema: *The BRAC Non-formal Primary Education Programme in Bangladesh*, UNICEF, New York, 1989.

93   UNICEF: *The State of the World's Children*, 1998, op. cit.

94   Oxfam: 'Improving Teaching Skills in Lao Cai', mimeo, Oxfam, Oxford, 1998; 'Education for Poor Children: Research Findings from Lao Cai Province, Viet Nam', mimeo, Oxfam, Hanoi, 1998.

95   Community Aid Abroad: 'Statement on the Australian Government's policy on Aboriginal education', memo, Sydney, 1998.

Chapter 3

1   Derived from UNESCO: *Statistical Yearbook*, 1997, Paris, 1998, Table 4.1.

2   C. Colclough: 'Achieving Schooling for All in sub-Saharan Africa – Is Gender a Constraint or an Opportunity?', Institute of Development Studies, University of Sussex, mimeo, 1999, p.11; UNESCO *Education for All: Achieving the Goal*, Paris, 1996, p.28.

3   The figures are for current expenditure in 1995, derived from UNESCO: *World Education Report: Teachers and Teaching in a Changing World*, Paris, 1998, Table 11, p.160.

4   E. Beaton et al.: 'Science Achievement in the Middle School Years', Boston College, mimeo, 1996, p. 95.

5   C. Colclough: *Educating All the Children*, Clarendon Press, Oxford, 1992, pp.20-22.

6   UNESCO: *World Education Report: Teachers and Teaching in a Changing World*, Paris, 1998, Table 11, p.160; Table4, p.134.

7   K. Lewin: 'Secondary Schooling in Developing Countries: a Preliminary Analysis of Issues', mimeo, UNESCO, Paris, 1999.

8   OECD: 'Education Policy Analysis 1997', Centre for Educational Research and Innovation, Paris, 1997, p.81.

9   Quoted in *Guardian*, 16 January 1998. See also T. Blair: 'Education: the story so far', *Prospect*, February 2000, London.

10   T. O'Shea and E. Scanlon: 'Virtual Learning Environments and the Role of the Teacher: Report of a UNESCO/Open University international colloquium', Paris, mimeo, 1997.

11   UNESCO: *World Education Report: Teachers and Teaching in a Changing World*, op. cit., p.87.

12   Several OECD countries have developed large-scale initiatives aimed at transferring new education technologies to developing countries in partnership with the private sector. See, for example, Tony Blair: 'We must not let the children down', *Guardian*, 4 April 2000.

13   For a discussion of issues in the development of composite indexes, see UNDP: *Human Development Report*, 1997, New York, pp.17-18.

14   There is often a wide discrepancy between average national income and human welfare indicators. By focusing on the non-income dimensions of human welfare, the annual UNDP *Human Development Report* and its accompanying Human Development Index have highlighted the fact that good policies can produce health and education outcomes far better than would be predicted on the basis of per capita income.

15   Inter-American Development Bank: *Economic and Social Progress in Latin America: Making Social Services Work*, Washington, 1996, p.242.

16   D. Filmer and L. Pritchett: 'Household wealth and educational attainment: evidence from 35 countries, *Population and Development Review* 25 (1), March 1998, pp.85-120.

17   Ibid., pp.95-96.

18   Ibid., p.106.

19   Government of Vietnam: *Education in Vietnam: Trends and Differentials*, Statistical Publishing House, Hanoi, 1996.

20   World Bank: *Peru: Poverty Assessment and Social Policies*, Human Resources Division, Washington, 1993, pp.27-8.

21   Government of Pakistan: *Pakistan Integrated Household Survey: Round 1 1995-1996*, Federal Bureau of Statistics, Islamabad, 1997, Table 2.4, p.16.

22 World Bank: *Niger Poverty Assessment: a Resilient People in a Harsh Environment*, Population and Human Resources Division, Washington, World Bank, 1996, p.64.

23 Agence Saena: 'Enquiry into Basic Education in Mali', Institute of National Statistics and Information, Government of Mali, mimeo, Bamako, December, 1996.

24 World Bank: *Zambia: Poverty Assessment, Vol. 11*, Human Resources Division, Washington, World Bank, 1994, Tables 1-2, Appendix 2.

25 T. Peasgood: *Gender and Primary Schooling in Tanzania*, Research Report 33, Institute for Development Studies, Sussex University, 1997, pp.37-8.

26 Figures derived from UNESCO: *Statistical Yearbook*, Paris, 1998; UNESCO: *Education for All: Achieving the Goal*, Paris, 1996.

27 T. Hyat: 'Basic Education in India: the Unfinished Agenda', background paper prepared for 'Education Now' report, Oxfam, Oxford, 1998.

28 D. Filmer and L. Pritchett: 'Educational Enrolment and Attainment in India: Household Wealth, Gender, Village, and State Effects', mimeo, Washington, World Bank, September 1998.

29 D. Filmer: 'The Structure of Social Disparities in Education: Gender and Wealth', World Bank Policy Research Report, mimeo, November 1999, World Bank, Washington.

30 UNICEF and National Planning Commission, *Children and Women of Nepal: a Situation Analysis, 1996*, UNICEF, Katmandu, 1996.

31 Government of Pakistan: *Pakistan Integrated Household Survey: Round 1 1995-1996*, Federal Bureau of Statistics, Islamabad, 1997, Table 2.4, p.16.

32 C. Colclough, P. Rose and M. Tembon: 'Gender inequalities in primary schooling: the roles of poverty and adverse cultural practice', *International Journal for Educational Development*, Volume 19, 1999.

33 D. Al-Hidabo: 'Basic Education Baseline Research in Yemen', background paper prepared for 'Education Now' report, Oxfam, Oxford, 1998.

34 On poverty in north-east Brazil, see World Bank: *Brazil: the Health System*, Operations Evaluation Department, 30 June 1998, pp.7-11; on education indicators for the north-east, see S. Haddad: 'Elementary Education in Brazil: the Role of the State', background paper prepared for 'Education Now' report, Oxfam, Oxford, 1998.

35 World Bank: *The Philippines: a Strategy to Fight Poverty*, East Asia and Pacific Regions, Washington, 1996, pp.33-4.

36 UNDP: *Philippines: Human Development Report*, UNDP, Manila, 1997.

37 D. Daramaningtyas: 'Primary Education in Indonesia', background paper prepared for 'Education Now' report, Oxfam, Oxford, 1998.

38 On the contrast between Kerala and Uttar Pradesh, see J. Drèze and A. Sen: *India Economic Development and Social Opportunity*, Oxford University Press, Oxford, 1995; V. Ramachandran: 'On Kerala's development achievements' in J. Drèze and A. Sen: *Indian Development: Selected Regional Perspectives*, Oxford University Press, Oxford, 1997.

39   D. Filmer and L. Pritchett: 'Educational Enrolment and Attainment in India: Household Wealth, Gender, Village, and State Effects', mimeo, World Bank, Washington, 22 September 1998.

40   Oxfam: 'People's Access to Health and Education', mimeo, Oxfam, Oxford, November 1998.

41   D. Donovan et al.: *Development trends in Vietnam's northern mountain region, Vol. 1*, Centre for Natural Resources and Environmental Studies, Vietnam National University, Hanoi, 1997.

42   Oxfam: 'Education for Poor Children: Research Findings from Lao Cai Province', mimeo, Oxfam, Hanoi, 1998.

43   G. Nambissan: 'The schooling of Dalit children in India', *Economic and Political Weekly*, 1011-24, 20-27 April 1996, Bombay.

44   Oxfam India: 'Status of Education in Gujarat Primary Schools: a Survey', background paper prepared for 'Education Now' report, 1998.

45   World Bank: *Peru: Poverty Assessment and Social Policies*, Human Resources Division, Washington, 1993, pp.27-8.

46   K. Deninger and A. Heinegg: 'Rural Poverty in Mexico', mimeo, World Bank, Washington, October 1995.

47   A. Panagides: 'Mexico', in G. Psacharopoulpous and H. Patrinos: *Indigenous People and Poverty in Latin America*, World Bank, Regional and Sectoral Studies, Washington, 1994; World Bank: *Mexico: Second Primary Education Project*, Staff Appraisal Report, March 1994, Human Resources Operations Division, Washington, 1994.

48   D. Steele: 'Guatemala' in G. Psacharopoulpous and H. Patronis: *Indigenous People and Poverty in Latin America*, op. cit.

49   World Bank: *Bolivia: Poverty, Equity and Income*, Latin America and the Caribbean Region, Washington, 1996.

50   D. Macisaac: 'Peru', in G. Psacharopoulpous and H. Patrinos: *Indigenous People and Poverty in Latin America*, op. cit.

51   D. Steele: 'Guatemala', op. cit.

52   Data for India derived from T. Krishnan: 'The route to social development in Kerala', in S. Mehrotra and R. Jolly: *Development with a Human Face: Experiences in Social Achievement and Economic Growth*, Table 7.1, p.206, Oxford: Oxford University Press, 1997; World Bank: *Primary Education in India*, Table 3.2, p.58, Washington, 1997.

53   Data for Pakistan derived from Government of Pakistan: *Pakistan Integrated Household Survey*, op. cit.

54   Data for Vietnam derived from Government of Vietnam: *Education in Vietnam: Trends and Differentials*, Statistical Publishing House, Hanoi, 1996; data on the district of Lao Cai derived from Oxfam: 'Education for Poor Children: Research Findings from Lao Cai Province', mimeo, Hanoi, 1998.

55   Data for Zambia derived from World Bank: *Zambia: Poverty Assessment, Vol 11*, Human Resources Division, Washington, World Bank, 1994.

56   Data from Mexico derived from K. Deninger and A. Heinegg: 'Rural Poverty in Mexico', op. cit.; World Bank: *Mexico: Second Primary Education Project*, Staff Appraisal Report, March 1994, Human Resources Operations Division, Washington, 1994; A. Panagides: 'Mexico', in G. Psacharopoulpous and H. Patrinos: *Indigenous People and Poverty in Latin America*, op.cit.

57   Data derived from M. Kelly: 'Primary Education in Zambia', background paper prepared for 'Education Now' report, Oxfam, Oxford, 1998; World Bank: *Zambia: Poverty Assessment, Vol 11*, Human Resources Division, Washington, World Bank, 1994, Tables 1-2 Appendix 2.

58   Data derived from World Bank: *Bolivia: Poverty, Equity and Income*, Latin America and the Caribbean Region, Washington, 1996, pp.10-11; World Bank: *Bolivia Education Sector*, Latin America and the Caribbean Region, Washington, 1993, pp.3-5, 14-15.

59   Data derived from R. Harbison and W. Hanushek: *Educational Performance of the Poor: Lessons from Rural Northeast Brazil*, World Bank, Washington, 1992, p.34; S. Haddad: 'Elementary Education in Brazil: the Role of the State', background paper prepared for 'Education Now' report, Oxfam, Oxford, 1998.

60   Data derived from *The Philippines Human Development Report*, UNDP, Manila, 1997; the figures for the settlement of Tuarmanding are based on an Oxfam field survey.

Chapter 4

1   United Nations: *Universal Declaration of Human Rights*, Geneva, 1948, Article 26.

2   UNICEF: *Implementation Handbook for the Convention on the Rights of the Child*, New York, 1998, p.391.

3   A. Sen: 'Radical needs and moderate reforms', in J. Drèze and A. Sen: *Indian Development: Selected Regional Persepctives*, Chapter 1, Oxford, Oxford University Press,1997.

4   UNESCO: 'Framework for Action', programme adopted at the World Education Forum, Dakar, Paris, April 2000.

5   M. Bray: *Counting the Full Cost: Parental and Community Financing of Education in East Asia*, World Bank, Directions in Development Series, Washington, 1998, p.2.

6   Government of Tanzania: *Public Expenditure Review, Vol 1*, Dar-es-Salaam, November 1999.

7   M. Bray: *Counting the Full Cost*, op. cit., pp.17-29.

8   L. Wolff et al.: *Improving the Quality of Primary Education in Latin America and the Caribbean: Towards the 21st Century*, World Bank Discussion Paper 257, Washington, 1994, p.71.

9   C. Colclough: 'Achieving Schooling for All in sub-Saharan Africa – Is Gender a Constraint?', mimeo, Institute for Development Studies, Sussex University, 1998, p.8.

10   F.Stewart: 'Education and Adjustment: Experience of the 1980s and Lessons for the 1990s', mimeo, Commonwealth Secretariat, London, 1991.

11   On the debate over cost-recovery, see K. Watkins: 'Cost-recovery and equity in the health sector: the case of Zimbabwe', in G. Mwabu, C. Ugaz, and H. White (eds.): *Patterns of Social Provision in Low Income Countries*, Oxford, Oxford University Press, 2000.

12   For example, C. Griffin: *User Charges for Health Care in Principle and Practice*, Economic Development Institute, Seminar Paper 37, 1987, World Bank, Washington. For an overview of the debate on cost-recovery in education, see C. Colclough: 'Education, health and the market: an introduction', in C. Colclough (ed.): *Marketising Education and Health in Developing Countries*, 1997, Oxford, Oxford University Press. See also K. Lewin and D. Berstecher: 'The costs of recovery: are user fees the answer?', *Institute for Development Studies Bulletin* Vol. 20 (1), 1989, pp.59-70.

13   M. Bray: *Counting the Full Cost*, op. cit., p.4.

14   S. Reddy and J. Vandermoortele: *User Financing of Basic Social Services*, UNICEF Working Paper, New York, 1996.

15   D. Booth: 'Coping with Cost-recovery: a Report for the Swedish International Development Agency', Stockhom University, mimeo, 1995.

16   D. Narayan and D. Nyamwaya: *Learning from the Poor: a Participatory Poverty Assessment in Kenya*, World Bank, Environment Department Papers, No. 34, 1996, p.39. On the importance of seasonal income flows to the affordability of basic services see S. Russel: 'Ability to pay: concepts and evidence', *Health Policy and Planning* 11(3), pp.219-17.

17   World Bank: *Tanzania: Social Sector Review*, Eastern Africa Department, Washington, 1995.

18   PROBE: *Public Report on Basic Education in India*, PROBE Team, Oxford, p.32.

19   World Bank/Government of Vietnam: *Vietnam: Financing of Social Services*, Vol. 1, Hanoi, 1997, p.22.

20   O. Brown and K. Wiseman: 'Primary Education in Nepal', mimeo, Oxfam, Oxford, 1998.

21   E. King: 'Does the Price of Schooling Matter? Fees, Opportunity Costs and Enrollment in Indonesia', World Bank, mimeo, Washington, 1995.

22   Derived from Government of Tanzania: *Poverty and Welfare Monitoring Indicators*, Vice President's Office, November 1999, Table 7, p.71; Government of Tanzania: *Public Expenditure Review*, op. cit., Vol 1, p.53.

23   Oxfam GB: 'Report on Financing and Delivery of Basic Services at the Commune Level in Ky Anh, Viet Nam', mimeo, Hanoi, 1996.

24   Government of Tanzania: *Public Expenditure Review*, Vol 1, op. cit., pp. 42-3, 53-4.

25   Ibid., 54.

26   Poverty indicators for Eastern Province are taken from World Bank: *Zambia Poverty Assessment*, Vol 11, 1994, various tables.

27   M. Chisvo and L. Munro: 'A Review of the Social Dimensions of Adjustment in Zimbabwe, 1990-1994', mimeo, UNICEF, Harare, 1994.

28   Oxfam GB: 'Education for Poor Children: Research Findings from Lao Cai Province', mimeo, Hanoi, June 1998.

29   World Bank: *The Poor and Cost Recovery in the Social Sectors of sub-Saharan Africa*, Human Resources and Poverty Division, Washington, September 1995.

30   World Bank: *Kenya Poverty Assessment*, 1995, Washington; D. Narayan and D. Nyamwaya: *Learning from the Poor: a Participatory Poverty Assessment in Kenya*, World Bank, Environment Department Papers, No. 34, 1996, p.39.

31   P. Gertler P and P. Glewwe: 'The willingness to pay for education in developing countries: evidence from rural Peru', *World Bank Economic Review* 6 (1): 171-88.

32   Participatory Assessment Group: 'Participatory Poverty Monitoring in Zambia', mimeo, Government of Zambia, Lusaka, p.67.

33   K. Dyer: 'Primary Education in Tanzania', background paper prepared for 'Education Now' report, mimeo, Oxfam, Oxford, 1998. The interviews in Shinyanga were carried out by Oxfam project staff.

34   K. Watkins: 'Cost recovery and equity in the health sector', op. cit.

35   On one of the best-known examples of community financing, see M. Hill: *The Harambee Movement in Kenya: Self-help, Development and Education among the Kamba of Kitui District*, London School of Economics, Monograph on Social Anthropology 64, London, 1976.

36   On national inequalities linked to community financing capacity, see M. Bray, *Decentralisation of Education*, World Bank, 1996, pp.16-19.

37   A. Seel: 'Can Sector-wide Approaches in Education Reach the Poor? Early Lessons from Uganda', mimeo, paper presented at the Oxford International Conference on Education and Development, 13 September 1999, Department for International Development, London. On Malawi, see World Bank: *Levelling the Playing Field: Giving Girls an Equal Chance for Basic Education*, Washington, 1996.

38   P. Rose: *Gender and Primary Education in Ethiopia*, Institute for Development Studies, Sussex University, Research Report 31, 1997, p.110.

39   On the case for financing basic social services through general taxation, see R. Burgess: 'Fiscal reform and the extension of basic health and education coverage', in C. Colclough (ed.): *Marketising Education and Health in Developing Countries*, op. cit. On alternative approaches to budget management, see UNDP: *Budgets as if People Mattered: Democratising Macroeconomic Policies*, New York, 2000.

40   K. Watkins: 'Cost recovery and equity in the health sector', op. cit.

41   M. Ibraimo and P. Watt: 'An Overview of the State of Primary Education in Mozambique', mimeo, Oxfam, Oxford, February 1999.

42   World Bank: *Peru Poverty Assessment,* Latin America and Caribbean Region, Washington, 1993.

43   Government of Gambia: *Community Education Survey Report*, Central Statistics Department, Banjul, 1995.

44   S. Chao and O. Alper: 'Accessing basic education in Ghana', *Studies in Human Development* 1, World Bank, Africa Region, Washington, 1998, pp.7-10; on the problems of using wage rates and labour-force participation to measure the costs of female labour, see B. Herz et al.: *Letting Girls Learn: Promising Approaches in Primary and Secondary Education*, World Bank Discussion Paper 133, Washington, 1991, p.11.

45   N. Stomquist: *School-related Determinants of Female Primary School Participation and Achievement in Developing Countries: an Annotated Bibliography*, World Bank Discussion Paper 83, Washington, 1987.

46   On differences in labour-time allocation within the household, see I. Palmer: *Gender and Population in the Adjustment of African Economies: Planning for Change*, International Labour Office, Women, Work and Development Series, Geneva, 1991; D. Elson: *Gender-aware Policy Making for Structural Adjustment, A Report to the Commonwealth Secretariat*, no date, Commonwealth Secretariat, London.

47   I. Palmer, ibid.

48   See, for example, D. Jamison and M. Lockheed: 'Participation in schooling: determinants and learning outcomes in Nepal', *Economic Development and Cultural Change*, pp.279-306, 1987; World Bank: *Gender and Poverty in India*, South Asia Division, Washington, 1991.

49   B. Herz et al.: *Letting Girls Learn: Promising Approaches in Primary and Secondary education*, op. cit., p.27.

50   PROBE: *The Public Report on Basic Education*, op. cit., p.29.

51   USAID: 'The Demand for Primary Schooling in Rural Ethiopia: a Research Study', mimeo, USAID, Addis Ababa, 1994, p.85.

52   S. Chao and O. Alper: 'Accessing basic education in Ghana', op. cit.; for a similar perspective on Tanzania, see A. Mason et al.: *Household Schooling Decisions in Tanzania*, Poverty and Social Policy Department, 1996, Washington.

53   On the negative impact of distance to school for girls' attendance, see C. Brock and N. Cammish: *Factors Affecting Female Participation in Education in Seven Developing Countries*, Department for International Development, Serial Number 9, p. 20, London, 1997.

54   B. Herz et al.: *Letting Girls Learn*, op. cit., p.29.

55   The following is derived from Government of Pakistan: *Pakistan Integrated Household Survey: Round 1 1995-1996*, p.10.

56   Ibid.

57   UNICEF: *Situation Analysis of Children and Women in Pakistan*, Government of Pakistan and UNICEF Country Programme of Cooperation, Islamabad, 1987.

58   World Bank: *Zambia Poverty Assessment*, Volume 1, Southern Africa Division, Washington, 1995.

59   M. Ibraimo and P. Watt: 'An Overview of the State of Primary Education in Mozambique', op. cit.; see also B. Walker: 'Addressing Gender Issues in Education in Mozambique', mimeo, paper presented to Oxfam Workshop on Education and Development, February 1999, Bangkok. On problems of harassment, see USAID: *Beyond Enrollment: a Handbook for Improving Girls' Experience in Primary Classroom*, USAID, 1996.

60   Agence SAENA: 'Investigation on the Implementation of Universal Basic Education in Mali', mimeo, Ouagadougou, June 1998.

61   Quoted in A. Sen: 'Development: which way now?', *The Economic Journal*, December 1983; pp.745-62.

62 Participatory Assessment Group: 'Participatory Poverty Monitoring in Zambia', mimeo, World Bank, Lusaka, May 1995, p.63; N. Stromquist: *Gender and Basic Education in International Development Cooperation*, UNICEF, New York, 1994.

63 P. Rose: *Gender and Primary Education in Ethiopia*, op. cit.

64 T. Peasgood: *Gender and Primary Schooling in Tanzania*, op. cit.

65 USAID: *Educating Girls: Strategies to Increase Access, Persistence and Achievement*, Advancing Basic Education and Literacy Project, Washington, 1991; Swainson et al.: *Promoting Girls' Education in Africa: the Design and Implementation of Policy Interventions*, Serial No. 25, Department for International Development, London, 1998; R. Gordon: 'Girls cannot think as boys do: socialising children through the Zimbabwean school system', in *Gender, Education and Training*, Oxfam, Oxford, 1998.

66 C. Brock and N. Cammish: *Factors Affecting Female Participation in Education in Seven Developing Countries*, op. cit.

67 P. Birckhill: *Textbooks as an Agent of Change: Gender Aspects of Primary School Textbooks in Mozambique, Zambia and Zimbabwe*, Swedish International Development Agency, Education Division, Documents 3, 1996.

68 USAID: *Educating Girls: Strategies to Increase Access, Persistence and Achievement*, op. cit.; Swainson et al.: *Promoting Girls' Education in Africa*, op. cit.

69 FAWE: *Women Making a Difference: Dynamic African Headmistresses*, FAWE, 1995, Nairobi; see also UNESCO: *In Our Own Hands: the Story of the Saptagram – a Women's Self-reliance and Education Movement in Bangladesh*, Paris, no date.

70 International Labour Office: *Child Labour: Targeting the Intolerable*, International Labour Conference, 86th Session, 1996, Geneva; P. Graitcer and L. Lerer: *Child Labour and Health: Quantifying the Global Health Impacts of Child Labour*, the World Bank, Washington, 1998. On the varied forms of child labour and the distinction between hazardous and non-hazardous forms of work, see A. Bequele and W. Myers: *First Things First in Child Labour: Eliminating Work Detrimental to Children*, UNICEF/ILO, Geneva, 1995.

71 P. Fallon and Z. Tzannatos: *Child Labour: Issues and Directions for the World Bank*, Social Protection and Human Development Network, Washington, 1998, p.2; F. Siddiqui and H. Patrinos: *Child Labour: Issues, Causes and Interventions*, Human Resources Development Working Paper 56, World Bank, Washington, 1995.

72 On the MVF, see G. Oonk: *Elementary Education and Child Labour in India*, India Committee of the Netherlands, Amsterdam, 1998. See also UNICEF: *State of the World's Children 1999: Education*, New York, 1999, pp.48-9.

73 Brazil Network on Multilateral Financial Institutions: 'The Debt Problem and Social Sectors in Brazil', mimeo, Recife, 1998.

74 C. Lequesne: *Reforming World Trade*, Oxfam Insight series, Oxford, 1997.

75 International Confederation of Free Trades Unions: *Fighting for Workers' Human Rights in the Global Economy*, ICFTU, Geneva, 1998, pp.17-30.

76 On the Harkin Bill, see C. Lequesne: *Reforming World Trade*, op. cit.

77 J. Bhagwati: 'Trade liberalisation and "fair trade" demands: addressing the environmental and labour issues', *The World Economy*, 18, 6,1995; on the debate on trade sanctions, see A. Melchior: 'Child labour and trade policy', in B. Grimsrund and A. Melchior (eds.): *Child Labour and International Trade Policy*, Institute for Applied Social Science, Oslo, 1996. The problems associated with the use of trade sanctions to address child-labour problems are described in K. Watkins: *Globalisation and Liberalisation: Implications for Poverty, Distribution and Inequality*, UNDP, Occasional Paper 32, Human Development Report Office, 1998.

78 On the international campaign to end exploitative child labour in the production of footballs for European markets, see Save the Children: *Stitching Footballs: Voices of Children*, Save the Children, London, 1997.

79 On the global campaign against child labour, see Global March: 'Worldwide Crusade against Child Labour', mimeo, New Delhi, 1998.

80 Global March: 'Steps to a New Convention on Child Labour', mimeo, New Delhi, 1998.

81 UNICEF: *The State of the World's Children 1996*, New York, p.13.

82 I. Smyth: 'Education and Conflict: Old Problems and New Agenda', background paper prepared for 'Education Now' report, Oxfam, Oxford, 1998.

83 Ibid.

84 UNICEF: *Peace Education in UNICEF*, Working Paper Series, New York, July 1999, Chapter 2.

85 J. Drèze and M. Saran: *Primary Education and Economic Development in China and India: Overview and Two Case Studies*, Working Paper 47, STICERD, London School of Economics, 1993.

86 N. Birdsall, D. Ross, and R. Sabot: 'Inequality as a constraint on growth in Latin America', in D. Turnham et al., *Social Tensions, Job Creation and Economic Policy in Latin America*, OECD, Paris, 1994, p.184.

87 World Bank: *Latin America and the Caribbean: a Decade after the Debt Crisis*, Latin America and the Caribbean Region, Washington, 1993.

88 Even low-income countries implementing strong economic reform programmes have often failed to increase revenue mobilisation. This has been identified as a major problem in IMF-World Bank adjustment programmes. See, for example, World Bank: *Tanzania: Preliminary Document on the Initiative for Heavily Indebted Poor Countries*, International Development Association, Washington, 1999, p8; Government of Uganda: *Background to the Budget 1997/98*, Ministry of Planning and Economic Development, June 1997, Kampala, 1997, p.38. Over a decade of adjustment, Uganda has increased government revenue by less than 2 per cent of GDP to the still relatively low level of 13 per cent of GDP.

89 Derived from data in World Bank: *World Development Report 1997, Knowledge for Development*, Washington, 1998, Table 14, p.216.

90 ISODEC: Taxation in Ghana, 'Integrated Social Development Centre', mimeo, Accra, December 1999, p.16.

91 S. Mehrotra: 'Social development in high-achieving countries: common elements and diversities' in R. Jolly and S. Mehrotra (eds.): *Development with a Human Face: Experiences in Social Achievement and Economic Growth,* Clarendon Press, Oxford, 1997, p.41.

92 On the financing requirements for universal primary education in sub-Saharan Africa, see C. Colclough: 'Achieving Schooling for All in sub-Saharan Africa: is Gender a Constraint or an Opportunity?', op. cit., Table 6; on South Asia, see M. ul Haq and K ul Haq: *Human Development in South Asia,* UNDP, Oxford, 1998, Table A, p.149.

93 For a description, see S. Yaqub: 'How Equitable is Public Spending on Health and Education?', mimeo, background paper to the *World Development Report 2000/1,* September 1999, World Bank.

94 UNICEF/World Bank: 'Universal Access to Basic Social Services: a Key Ingredient for Human Development', document prepared for the Hanoi meeting on the 20/20 initiative, UNICEF, New York, 1998.

95 The following is derived from national budget data and World Bank poverty-assessment documents.

96 World Bank: *The Poor and Cost Recovery in the Social Sectors of sub-Saharan Africa,* Human Resources and Poverty Division, Washington, September 1995.

97 M. ul Haq and K. ul Haq: *Human Development in South Asia,* op. cit., p.136. S. Mehrotra: *Social Development in High-achieving Countries: Common Elements and Diversities,* op. cit., chapter 2. On the Ugandan case, see Government of Uganda: *Education Sector Strategic Investment Plan 1997-2003,* Kampala, June 1998.

98 S. Yaqub: 'How Equitable is Public Spending on Health and Education?', op. cit., p.12.

99 World Bank: *The Philippines: a Strategy to Fight Poverty,* East Asia and Pacific Regions, Washington, 1996, p.36.

100 M. St Ana: 'A national perspective', in Oxfam: 'Basic Education in the Philippines', mimeo, Manila and Oxford, 1998.

101 World Bank/Government of Vietnam: *Vietnam: Financing of Social Services,* Vol 1, op. cit.

102 Oxfam: 'Education for Poor Children: Research Findings from Lao Cai Province', mimeo, Vietnam, June 1998.

103 UNDP: *Human Development Report 1997,* UNDP, New York, 1997, Table 19, p.227.

104 On military spending in Pakistan, see R. Sivard: *World Military and Social Expenditures,* Longman, London, 1996, p.45.

105 M. ul Haq and K. ul Haq: *Human Development in South Asia,* op. cit., Table A, p.149.

106 Figure cited in *International Security Digest,* London, May 1994.

107 *The Economist* 6-12 June 1998: 'India's bad budget', p.80; 'Asia's nuclear arms race', p.83.

108 T. Hyat: 'Primary Education in India', op. cit.

109 On the Light Combat Aircraft project, see Stockholm International Peace Research Institute: *SIPRI Yearbook 1998*, Oxford University Press, Stockholm, 1998, p.273. See also *Jane's International Defence Review*: 'The Light Combat Aircraft Project', July 1998.

110 Estimates based on unit costs in primary education, derived from World Bank: *Primary Education in India*, Washington, 1997, Chapter 10 and Appendix B, p.267.

111 Stockholm International Peace Research Institute: *SIPRI Yearbook 1998*, op. cit., Table 6.4.

112 E. Cairns: *A Safer Future: Reducing the Human Costs of War*, Oxfam Insight series, Oxford, 1997.

113 World Bank: *India: Achievements and Challenges in Reducing Poverty*, World Bank Country Study, Washington, 1997, pp.21-2. On the subsidisation of Zambia's copper mines, see T. Kenny: 'Deregulation, Privatisation and the Denial of Social Rights in Zambia', mimeo, Refugee Study Centre, Oxford University, 2000.

114 C. Ugaz: *Decentralisation and the Provision and Financing of Basic Services: Concepts and Issues*, World Institute for Development Economics Research, Working Paper 130, April 1997, Helsinki.

115 S. Haddad: 'Academic Education in Brazil', mimeo, Oxfam and Acao Educativa, 1998.

116 D. Yu: 'Decentralisation of the Finance System, Price Reform and Commune Disintegration: the Changes in China's Health Care System', mimeo, paper presented at World Institute for Development Economics Research Seminar, Helsinki, March 1997.

117 World Bank: *Vietnam: Fiscal Decentralisation and the Delivery of Rural Services*, East Asia and Pacific Region, Washington, 1996.

118 Ibid.

119 Government of Tanzania: *Public Expenditure Review*, op. cit., p.43, 54-6.

120 C. Ugaz: *Decentralisation and the Provision of Basic Services*, op. cit., p.5.

121 E. Ablo and R. Ritva: *Do Budgets Really Matter? Evidence from Public Spending on Education and Health in Uganda*, World Bank Policy Research Working Paper 1926, Africa Region, Washington, 1998, pp.12-13.

122 World Bank: *Primary Education in India*, op. cit., Table 9.3, p.224.

123 World Bank: *A Chance to Learn: Knowledge and Finance for Education in sub-Suharan Africa*, Africa Region, 1999, Washington, p.21.

124 G. Kingdon: *Private Schooling in India: Size, Nature and Equity Effects*, London School of Economics STICERD Working Paper 74, London, August 1996.

125 World Bank: *Pakistan: Improving Basic Education*, South Asia Region, 1996.

126 M. Kelly: 'Primary Education in a Highly Indebted Country: the Case of Zambia', op. cit.

127 C. Colclough: *Educating All the Children: Strategies for Primary Schooling in the South*, Oxford, Oxford University Press, 1993, pp.36-7.

128 C. Ugaz: 'The State of Education in Peru', mimeo, World Institute for Development Economics Research, Helsinki, 1998.

129 World Bank: *Bolivia: Poverty, Equity and Income,* Latin America and the Caribbean Region, 1996, p.16.

130 C. Graham: *Private Markets for Public Goods: Raising the Stakes in Economic Reform,* Washington, The Brookings Institute, September 1987.

131 J. Kim: *Can Private Schools Subsidies Increase Schooling for the Poor? The Quetta Urban Fellowship Programme,* World Bank, Development Research Group, Working Paper 11, 1998.

Chapter 5

1   UNESCO: *Framework for Action to Meet Basic Learning Needs,* UNESCO, Paris, 1990.

2   UNESCO: *World Declaration of Education for All,* UNESCO, Paris, 1990.

3   Ibid.

4   World Bank: *A Chance to Learn: Knowledge and Finance for Education in sub-Saharan Africa,* Washington, 2000.

5   R. Johanson: *Sector-wide Approaches for Education and Health in sub-Saharan Africa,* Human Resources Division, World Bank, Part 1, Washington, November 1999.

6   Ibid.

7   OECD: *Development Co-operation Efforts and Policies of the Members of the Development Assistance Committee: 1998 Report,* OECD, Paris, 1998.

8   World Bank: *Global Development Finance: Analysis and Summary Tables,* Washington, 1999, p.71. On recent cuts in the US aid budget, see K. Morrison and D. Weiner: *Declining Aid Spending Harms US Interests,* Overseas Development Council Paper, Washington, April 2000.

9   Ibid.

10 Data derived from OECD Development Assistance Committee for 1992 and 1997.

11 Eurostep: *The Reality of Aid 1998/1999,* Earthscan, London, 1998, p.8.

12 Derived from OECD Development Assistance Committee data.

13 Derived from OECD Development Assistance Committee reporting system, Paris, 1998.

14 OECD: *Development Co-operation: Efforts and Policies of the Members of the Development Assistance Committee,* op. cit.

15 In 1998 Britain reported to the Development Assistance Committee spending of $3m on basic education, or 1.4 per cent of total disbursements. This figure was an understatement, for a variety of reasons. Projects in which education is part of a wider programme may be coded under a non-education heading; projects in which basic education is part of a wider education programme may not be reported as 'basic'; and some of the grants to NGOs for education are not listed. Taking into account spending in these under-reported areas, total provisions for basic education were

estimated at $117m, or 5 per cent of total bilateral aid. (Source: UK Department for International Development, 'Note on UK Expenditure on Basic Education', mimeo, London, 2000.)

16   Government of Australia: *One Clear Objective: Poverty Reduction through Sustainable Development*, Report of the Committee of Review, Canberra, 1997; see also Community Aid Abroad (CAA): 'Response to the Simons Report', mimeo, CAA, Sydney, 1997. On the Australian education programme, see N. Bennet: 'Ausaid's Education and Training Assistance: Future Directions', mimeo, National Centre for Development Studies, Canberra, 1998.

17   World Bank: *Education Sector Strategy*, Human Development Group, Washington, 1999, Chapter 5.

18   World Bank: 'The World Bank: Education Sector Investment Lending', mimeo, Human Development Network, Washington, 1998.

19   World Bank: *A Chance to Learn: Knowledge and Finance for Education in sub-Saharan Africa*, op. cit.

20   D. Dollar et al.: *Assessing Aid*, World Bank Policy Research Report, Washington, 1999.

21   R. Lensink and H. White: 'Aid allocation, poverty reduction and the Assessing Aid report', *Journal of International Development*, Vol 12.3, April 2000.

22   Government of Uganda: *Education Strategic Investment Plan: 1997-2003*, Vol 1, Kampala, Ministry of Education, 1997.

23   On the Baluchistan Primary Education Programme, see C. Rawley: *Including Girls in Basic Education*, USAID, Washington, 1997; World Bank: *Levelling the Playing Field: Giving Girls an Equal Chance for Basic Education – Three Countries' Efforts*, Washington, 1996.

24   On the GABLE programme in Malawi, see K. Tietjen: *Educating Girls in sub-Saharan Africa: Towards Defining USAID's Approach and Emerging Lessons for Donors*, USAID, Washington, 1995; see also Oxfam: 'Aid and Education: the Squandered Opportunity', Oxford, 2000.

25   D. Dollar et al.: *Assessing Aid*, op. cit.

26   World Bank: *A Chance to Learn: Knowledge and Finance for Education in sub-Saharan Africa*, op. cit.

27   W. Heneveld and H. Craig: *Schools Count: World Bank Project Design and the Quality of Primary Education in sub-Saharan Africa*, World Bank Technical paper 303, Africa Technical Department, Washington, 1996, pp.41-2.

28   P. Bennell and D. Furlong: 'Has Jomtien made any difference? Trends in donor funding for education and basic education since the late 1980s', *World Development* Vol 26.1, 1998, pp.45-59. On the use of technical assistance to promote donor self-interest, see World Bank: *Lessons and Practices 7: Technical Assistance*, Operations Evaluations Department, 1996.

29   On the thinking behind sector-wide approaches, see UNICEF: 'An Information Note on Sectoral Investment Plans and Sector-wide Approaches', mimeo, New York, 1997; A. Cassells: 'Sector-wide Approaches to Health Development: Concepts, Issues and Working Arrangements', mimeo, Department for International Development, London, 1997.

30 D. Dollar et al.: *Assessing Aid*, op. cit.

31 S. Lister: *Implementing Sector Development Programmes in Ethiopia*, Mokoro, Oxford, 1998.

32 UNICEF: 'An Information Note on Sectoral Investment Plans and Sector-wide Approaches', op. cit.

33 R. Johanson: *Sector-wide Approaches for Education and Health in sub-Saharan Africa*, op. cit.

34 R. Kanbur and T. Sandler: *The Future of Development Assistance: Common Pools and International Public Goods*, Overseas Development Council, Washington, 1999, Chapter 3. On the case for donors pooling their resources under the national budget, see J. Vereker: 'Reducing Poverty: the Key to Stability and Progress', mimeo, Address to House of Representatives, Washington DC, 18 April 2000, Department for International Development, London, 2000.

35 H. White: 'Budget Support as an Emerging Aid Modality: the experience of the Zambian health sector investment programmes and its relevance for Japanese aid', mimeo, Institute of Development Studies, University of Sussex, July 1999.

36 UNICEF: *The State of the World's Children*, UNICEF, New York, 1998.

37 The initial HIPC Initiative is described in A. Boote: *Debt Relief for Low Income Countries*, IMF, 1998.

38 UNICEF-Oxfam: 'Debt relief and Poverty Reduction: Meeting the Challenge', paper presented at the Heavily Indebted Poor Countries Review Seminar, United Nations Commission for Africa, July 1999, Addis Ababa, UNICEF, mimeo, New York, 1999.

39 Ibid.

40 L. Hanmer et al.: 'Are the DAC targets achievable? Poverty and human development in the year 2015', *Journal of International Development* 11.4, June 1999.

41 The new HIPC Initiative is described in D. Andrews et al., *Debt Relief for Low Income Countries: the Enhanced HIPC Initiative*, IMF, Washington 1999.

42 T. Killick: *Solving the Multilateral Debt Problem: Reconciling Relief with Acceptability*, report prepared for the Commonwealth Secretariat, Commonwealth Secretariat, London, 1995. On the adverse implications of 'debt overhang' for economic growth, see G. Helleiner: *External Debt and External Finance for sub-Saharan Africa: the Continuing Problem*, UNICEF, New York, May 1994.

43 Oxfam: 'Multilateral Debt: the Human Costs', Oxfam Position Paper, Oxford, 1996.

44 W. Easterly: *How Did Highly Indebted Countries Become Highly Indebted? Reviewing Two Decades of Debt Relief*, World Bank, Policy Research Paper 2225, Washington, 1999.

45 J. Sachs: *Implementing Debt Relief for the HIPCs*, Centre for International Development, Harvard University, August 1999.

46   For a brief history of debt relief for low-income countries in the 1980s, see Overseas Development Institute: *Recent Initiatives on Developing Country Debt*, Briefing Paper, April 1990. On developments during the first half of the 1990s, see T. Killick and S. Stevens: 'Mechanisms for Dealing with the Debt Problems of Low Income Countries: an Efficiency Audit', paper presented at IMF-World Bank conference on External Financing for Low-income Countries, Washington, December 1996, mimeo, World Bank, Washington, 1997.

47   P. Mistry: 'The Multilateral Debt Problems of Indebted Low-income Countries', mimeo, UNCTAD, Geneva, 1993.

48   M. Martin: 'Official Bilateral Debt: New Directions for Action', mimeo, External Finance for Africa, London, 1993.

49   Oxfam: 'Making Debt Relief Work: a Test of Political Will', Oxfam Position Paper, Oxford, April 1998.

50   The reformed HIPC Initiative is described in International Monetary Fund and International Development Association: 'Modifications to the HIPC Initiative', mimeo, Washington, July 1999.

51   The debt-sustainability threshold was lowered from a net present value debt-to-export ratio range of 200-250 per cent, to a single figure of 150 per cent. The debt-to-government-revenue ratio was also lowered, from 280 per cent to 250 per cent, although governments have to meet other criteria to qualify for debt relief on this basis, including a GDP/export ratio of 30 per cent and a GDP/revenue ratio of 15 per cent.

52   International Monetary Fund: 'Debt Initiative for the Heavily Indebted Poor Countries', mimeo, April 2000.

53   International Monetary Fund and World Bank: 'Progress Report on Heavily Indebted Poor Countries', mimeo, Development Committee, Washington, 15 April 2000. The net present value of debt is a measure that takes into account the degree of concessionality in loans, or debt contracted at an interest rate below the prevailing market rate. It is the sum of all future debt-service obligations, discounted at the market interest rate.

54   International Monetary Fund and World Bank: 'Progress Report on Heavily Indebted Poor Countries', op. cit.

55   Oxfam: 'The Truth about Debt', mimeo, briefing paper prepared for the Group of Eight Summit in Okinawa, June 2000, Oxford.

56   IMF staff estimate, mimeo, Washington, June 2000. The figures for projected revenue collection are derived from Government of Tanzania: *Public Expenditure Review*, Vol 1, Dar-es-Salaam, 1999.

57   Cited in UNICEF: *Children in Jeopardy: The Challenge of Freeing Poor Nations from the Shackles of Debt*, New York, 1999.

58   Institute for Development Studies: *Poverty Reduction Strategies: a Part for the Poor?* Policy Briefing 13, University of Sussex, April 2000.

59   International Monetary Fund and World Bank: 'Progress Report on Poverty Reduction Strategy Papers', mimeo, paper prepared by the staffs of the World Bank and the International Monetary Fund, 13 April 2000, Washington.

60 Government of Tanzania: 'Note on Poverty Reduction Strategy Paper Process for HIPC Debt Relief', mimeo, Dar-es-Salaam, 2000.

61 This approach is described in UNICEF/Oxfam: 'Poverty Reduction and Debt Relief: Meeting the Challenge', mimeo, New York and Oxford, 1999.

62 Government of Uganda: 'Poverty Action Fund (PAF): Report on PAF', July 1998, mimeo, Kampala. Details of the PAF's operations are set out in Government of Uganda: 'Poverty Action Fund: Guidelines and Modalities', mimeo, Kampala, 1998.

63 R. Johanson: *Sector-wide Approaches for Education and Health in sub-Saharan Africa*, op. cit.

64 On the place of the IMF in the adjustment process, see Oxfam: 'The IMF: Wrong Diagnosis, Wrong Medicine', Oxford, 1999.

65 R. Johanson: *Sector-wide Approaches for Education and Health in sub-Saharan Africa*, op. cit.

66 International Monetary Fund: *The IMF and the Poor*, Fiscal Affairs Department, Pamphlet 52, 1999.

67 Ibid.

68 G. Abed: *Fiscal Reforms in Low Income Countries: Experience under IMF-supported Programmes*, IMF, Washington, March 1998.

69 International Monetary Fund: *ESAF: Is It Working?*, IMF, Washington, 1999.

70 T. Killick: *Adjustment, Income Distribution and Poverty in Africa: a Research Guide*, Overseas Development Institute, London, 1998.

71 A. Goetz and R. Jenkins: 'Uganda: Creating a Framework for Reducing Poverty', mimeo, Institute for Development Studies, University of Sussex, 1999.

72 The design and implementation of the IMF adjustment programme in design is described in IMF: *The External Review of the Enhanced Structural Adjustment Facility*, Washington, 1998. See also K. Watkins: *The Oxfam Poverty Report*, Oxfam, Oxford, 1996.

73 Government of Zimbabwe: *Zimbabwe: a Framework for Economic Reform (1991-95)*, Ministry of Finance, Harare, 1991.

74 R. Davies: 'Assessing the Causes and Sustainability of the Budget Deficit', mimeo, Department of Economics, University of Harare, 1996.

75 World Bank: 'The Public Sector and Poverty Reduction Options', Background Paper for Zimbabwe Country Economic Memorandum, 1995.

76 IMF: *The External Review of the Enhanced Structural Adjustment Facility*, op. cit.

77 World Bank: *Understanding Poverty in Zimbabwe: Changes in the 1990s and Directions for the Future*, Washington, 1996.

78 Government of Zimbabwe: *Results from Sentinel Surveillance*, Ministry of Public Services, Labour and Social Welfare, Harare, 1996.

79 Ibid.

80 IMF: *External Review of the Enhanced Structural Adjustment Facility*, op. cit.

81 On this issue, see T. Addison: *Underdevelopment, Transition and Reconstruction in sub-Saharan Africa*, World Institute for Development Economics Research, Research for Action 45, Helsinki, 1998.

82 Government of Tanzania: *Public Expenditure Review Consultative Meeting: Budget Sustainability and Management*, Dar-es-Salaam, 1999, p.13.

83 J. Stiglitz: *More Instruments and Broader Goals: Moving Towards the post-Washington Consensus*, World Institute for Development Economics Research, Annual Lecture 2, Helsinki, 1998.

84 On East Asia's success in reducing poverty, see K. Watkins: *Growth with Equity: Lessons from East Asia*, Oxfam Insight series, Oxford, 1998.

85 On the impact of the financial crisis on poverty in East Asia, see World Bank: *East Asia: the Road to Recovery*, Washington, 1998.

86 World Bank: *Indonesia: Education in Indonesia, from Crisis to Recovery*, Washington, 1997.

87 K. Daramaningtyas: 'Primary Education in Indonesia', mimeo, Oxfam, Oxford, 1998.

88 Ahujaj et al.: *Everyone's Miracle: Revisiting Poverty and Inequality in East Asia*, World Bank, Washington 1997. See also World Bank: *Thailand: Education, Achievements, Issues and Policies*, Washington, 1998.

89 J. Ablett and I. Slengesol: *Education in Crisis: the Impact and Lessons of the East Asia Financial Shock, 1997-99*, Human Development Network, Washington, February 2000.

90 Ibid.

91 S. Sumato, A. Wetterberg, and L. Pritchett: 'The Social Impact of the Crisis in Indonesia: Results from a Nationwide Kecamatan Survey', mimeo, World Bank, 1998, pp. 19-20.

92 Cited in J. Boonyaratanasoontom: 'Education and the Economic Crisis in Thailand', mimeo, Oxfam, Oxford, 1998.

93 J. Ablett and I. Slengesol: *Education in Crisis: the Impact and Lessons of the East Asia Financial Shock, 1997-99*, op. cit.

94 Department for International Development: *Health Targets Strategy Paper*, London, 1999.

95 On the background to the East Asia crisis, see K. Sharma: *Understanding the Dynamics behind Excess Capital Inflows and Excess Capital Outflows in East Asia*, United Nations, Department of Economic and Social Affairs, New York, 1998.

96 J. Grieve-Smith: *Closing the Casino*, Fabian Pamphlet, Fabian Society, London, 2000.

97 J. Sachs: 'The IMF and the Asian flu', *American Prospect*, March-April 1998; on the impact of short-term debt claims on financial systems, see M. Feldstein: 'Refocusing the IMF', *Foreign Affairs*, March/April 1998.

98 For a critique of the IMF's response to the East Asian crisis, see P. Krugman: *The Return of Depression Economics*, Penguin, London, 1999.

99 J. Sachs: 'The IMF and the Asian flu', op. cit.

100 Oxfam: 'The IMF: Wrong Diagnosis, Wrong Medicine', op. cit.

101 World Bank: 'Back-to-school, Indonesia 1998/99: What Worked Well, What Didn't? A Report on the Scholarships and Grants Programme', mimeo, Washington, 1999.

102 J. Ablett and I. Slengesol: *Education in Crisis: the Impact and Lessons of the East Asia Financial Shock*, op. cit.

103 J. Griffiths et al.: *Latin American Perspectives on Managing Capital Surges*, World Institute for Development Economics Research, Working Paper 12, 1997.

104 D. Rodrik: 'Who Needs Capital Account Convertibility?', Essays in International Finance 207, mimeo, Princetown University, 1998. On the IMF's support for capital market liberalisation, see S. Fischer: 'Reforming the International Monetary System', David Fisch lecture, November 1998, mimeo, IMF, Washington.

105 S. Griffiths-Jones: 'Towards a Better Financial Architecture', mimeo, Institute for Development Studies, University of Sussex, 1999.

106 J. Grieve-Smith: *Closing the Casino*, op. cit.

Chapter 6

1 S. Reddy and A. Pereira: *The Role and Reform of the State*, United Nations Development Programme, Office of Development Studies, Working Paper, 8, New York, 1998.

2 W. Carr and A. Hartnett: *Education and the Struggle for Democracy*, Open University Press, Buckingham, 1996, pp.77-81.

3 Government of Uganda: *Education Strategic Investment Plan 1997-2003: Strategic and Programme Framework*, Kampala, June 1998.

4 Government of Uganda: *Background to the Budget 1997/98*, Ministry of Planning, Kampala, June 1997, p.31.

5 Government of Uganda: *Education Strategic Investment Plan 1997-2003*, op. cit.

6 S. Mehrotra et al.: 'Social policies in a growing economy: the role of the State in the Republic of Korea', in S. Mehrotra and R. Jolly (eds.): *Development with a Human Face: Experiences in Social Achievement and Economic Growth*, Clarendon Press, Oxford, 1997, pp.283-6.

7 D. Tyrrell D et al.: 'Botswana: social development in a resource rich economy', in R. Jolly and Mehrotra S (eds.), *Development with a Human Face*, op. cit.

8 M. Carroy and J. Samoff: *Education and Social Transition in the Third World*, Princeton University Press, Princeton, 1989.

9 S. Mehrotra: 'Social development in high achieving countries: some lessons', in R. Jolly and S. Mehrotra (eds.), *Development with a Human Face*, op. cit.

10 Cited in J. Acharya: *Citizens Initiative on Primary Education in India*, Dora, New Delhi, 1997.

11 S. Haddad: 'Academic Education in Brazil', mimeo, Oxfam, Oxford, 1998.

12 J. Tilak: 'A fundamental right', *Seminar* 464, April 1998, Bombay, pp.36-42.

13 M. ul Haq and K. ul Haq: *Human Development in South Asia*, Oxford: Oxford University Press, p.54.

14 T. Hyat: 'Primary Education in India', mimeo, Oxfam, Oxford; Government of India; *Annual Report 1997-1998*, Department of Education, New Delhi, 1998; on the District Primary Education Programme, see World Bank, *Primary Education in India*, Washington, 1997.

15 PROBE: *Public Report on Basic Education*, Oxford, Oxford University Press, 1998, chapter 9.

16 M. Kelly: 'Education in a Highly Indebted Country: the Case of Zambia', mimeo, Oxfam, Oxford, 1998.

17 For an overview of the relationship between States and non-government organisations, see D. Archer: 'The Changing Roles of NGOs in the Field of Education', mimeo, paper presented to Oxford Conference on Education, September 1993; see also A. Jellema: *From Providing to Enabling*, ActionAid, London, 1997.

18 ActionAid: *Building Better Schools: a Review of Sixteen Years of ActionAid Support to Kenyan Education*, ActionAid, London, 1996.

19 On BRAC, see T. Kiewied: 'Educating Children in Bangladesh for a Better Future', mimeo, Novib/Oxfam, Amsterdam 1998.

20 S. Reddy and A. Pereira: *The Role and Reform of the State*, op. cit., pp.24-5.

21 PROBE: *Public Report on Basic Education in India*, op. cit.

22 J. Tendler and S. Freedheim: 'Trust in a rent-seeking world: health and government transformed in north-east Brazil', *World Development*, Vol 22, 12, pp.1771-91.

23 On the general background to these programmes, see R. Govinda: *Lok Jumbish: an Innovation in Grassroots Level Management*, UNICEF, New York, 1997; D. Archer: 'The changing roles of non-governmental organisations in the field of education', *International Journal of Educational Development*, 14 No3, pp.223-32, 1994.

24 Swedish International Development Agency, *Towards Education for All in Rajasthan: Lok Jumbish and Shiksha Karmi Projects*. Report of a monitoring mission January-February, 1996, Department for Democracy and Social Development, Stockholm, 1996.

25 Rajistan Shiksha Karmi Board (RSKB), *Rajkastan Shiksha Karmi project: a report*, RSKB, Jaipur, 1994.

26 Swedish International Development Agency, *Towards Education for All in Rajasthan: Lok Jumbish and Shiksha Karmi Projects*. op. cit.

27 R. Govinda: *Reaching the Unreached through Participatory Planning: a Study of School Mapping in Lok Jumbish*, National Institute of Educational Planning and Administration, New Delhi, 1996. Lok Jumbish: Project Document 1998: Phase III – 1998-2003, mimeo, Lok Jumbish, Rajasthan. Swedish International Development Agency, *Towards Education for All in Rajhastan: Lok Jumbish and Shiksha Karmi Projects*, op. cit.

28 On the BRAC approach to education, see T. Kiewied: 'Educating Children in Bangladesh for a Better Future', op. cit.

29 C. Colclough: *Educating All the Children*, Clarendon Press, Oxford, pp.164-5.

30 P. Jain: 'Programme and management of integrated primary education in developing countries', *World Development*, 25 No 3, 1997.

31 C. Lovell and K. Fatema: *The BRAC Non-formal and Primary Education Programme*, UNICEF, New York, 1989, pp.10-17. Academy for Educational Development (AED): *Primary Education for All: Learning from the BRAC Experience*, AED, Washington, 1993.

32 On the Community Schools Project, see UNICEF: *The Community Schools Movement in Egypt*, UNICEF, New York, 1997; UNICEF: *Prospects 1993*, New York, 1993; see also C. Colclough: *Educating All the Children*, op. cit., pp.135-8.

33 This section is based on R. Torres: *Alternatives in Formal Education: Colombia's Escuela Nueva Programme*, UNICEF, New York, 1997.

34 United Nations: *Challenges and Opportunities: Basic Education for All in Pakistan*,Report of a UN Inter-Agency Mission, April-May 1995, New York, 1995.

35 T. Hyat: 'Primary Education in Pakistan', mimeo, Oxfam, Oxford, 1998.

36 M. ul Haq and K. ul Haq: *Human Development in South Asia*, op. cit., pp.129-30.

Index